Callas Kissed Me...Lenny Too!

Books by John Gruen:

The Sixties: Young in the Hamptons (Charta, 2006)

Facing the Artist (Prestel, 1999)

Flowers & Fables (Creative Editions, 1996)

Keith Haring: The Authorized Biography (Simon & Schuster, 1991)

The Artist Observed: 28 Interviews with Contemporary Artists (A Capella Books, 1991)

People Who Dance: 22 Dancers Tell Their Own Stories (Princeton Book Company, 1989)

The World's Great Ballets (Harry N. Abrams, 1981)

Erik Bruhn: Danseur Noble (Viking Press, 1979)

Gian Carlo Menotti: A Biography (Collier MacMillan, 1978)

The Private World of Ballet (Viking Press, 1975)

The Party's Over Now (Viking Press, 1972)

The Private World of Leonard Bernstein (Viking Press, 1968)

Close-Up (Viking Press, 1968)

The New Bohemia (Grosset & Dunlap, 1967)

Callas Kissed Me...Lenny Too!
A Critic's Memoir

John Gruen

 powerHouse Books Brooklyn, NY

FOR MY JULIA

Chapter 1: 1926–1939 Europe

My birth certificate is a beautiful thing to behold. By now it's quite parched with age. After all, it was filled out in 1926. But this worn, yellowing piece of paper has an air of true nostalgia and old-world charm, particularly since it's in French, issued in the Republique Francaise, le département Seine-et-Oise, arrondissement Pontoise, in the small town of Enghien-les-Bains, some ten kilometers north of Paris. The certificate, signed by Pierre Patenotre-Desnoyers, the mayor of Enghien-les-Bains, states that on the 12th of September 1926, at 8:15 a.m., a son, Jonas, was born to Abraham (b. Cairo, Egypt, 1890) and Aranka (b. Radzivilov, Russia, 1890). This extrait du registre des actes de naissance was issued to my parents on the 16th of September. They folded it neatly, tucked it away safely, and brought it with their newborn son back to Paris, where my three brothers awaited us.

As my mother told it, I was not the baby my parents longed for. Indeed, I was not longed for at all. The family was quite complete as it was. There was Leo, 16, the crown prince; Martin, 14, the gifted introvert; and Carl, ten, the extroverted mischief-maker. My mother was very clear that what this family did not need—and at such a late date, she was 36—was another son. The whole thing was a huge mistake and disappointment because, as mother so innocently put it, if there was to be another baby, at least let it be a baby girl! But no such luck. Mother definitely had had her fill of boys. Still, there were a few things about me that made my parents smile. For one thing, I was quite adorable—very light blond and very blue-eyed, unlike my brothers. For another, I was born in France and forever a French citizen. My brothers were born in Berlin. And then, of course, there was the story of my actual birth.

Family history has it that my mother was a gambler. As a young married woman, she loved visiting the casinos of Europe and would stand at roulette tables for hours, losing my father's money. We were apparently quite well-off. My father was a successful diamond dealer. With their base in Paris, my parents were very familiar with the little gambling town of Enghien-les-Bains, a few miles north of Paris. Enghien was and still is terminally picturesque. It has a lovely lake and near it, a very grand, ornate casino. It seems that just when my mother should have taken to her bed in our Paris apartment to await my arrival, an overwhelming urge to stand at the roulette tables at Enghien assailed her.

My father tried to stop her but there was no stopping his hugely pregnant and headstrong wife. She called for a taxi and, bigger than life and twice as determined, marched into the casino. No sooner had she placed her first bet at the roulette table that her pains began. Valiantly, she continued to play. Within a short time, her water broke. Members of the management carried my mother into the casino's sumptuous empire foyer and laid her on a gorgeous chaise lounge. Seeing that a birth was about to take place, they made an emergency call to the local midwife. My mother was quickly transported to a private home at 17, rue Alphonse Haussaire and my father was summoned to Enghien at once. But I did not make my appearance as quickly as was anticipated. Indeed, it was not until the following morning at around 8 a.m. that the midwife performed her duties...and voila! There I was—the perfect little baby boy my mother did not want.

In 1929, when I was three years old, our family moved to Berlin, never to return to France. I could never get either my father or mother to explain why. My eldest brother, Leo, intimated that there were great financial difficulties incurred through some very shady business dealings. Besides, said my brother, the family had lived in Berlin long before I was born. It was where my brothers were born and where my father had begun to establish himself in the jewelry business. What is more, all of my mother's family— her parents, sisters, and brothers—were still living in Berlin, and I would now have grandparents, aunts, and uncles to spoil me.

In Germany, I became conscious of my surroundings. My mother's relatives seemed to be swarming all around us. Even my Aunt Linda's dog, a white schnauzer named Mäuschen, appeared in our Berlin apartment at all hours of the day and night. As for my parents, they were a fugitive presence. Sometimes they were there, but mostly, they were not. What is more, they were seldom affectionately demonstrative or even talkative.

My father had a wonderfully exotic background. He came from a Romanian-Jewish family that had immigrated to Cairo, where my father was born on July 17, 1890. I never knew what his family did except that there was dark talk of illegal horsetrading and that the family was exceedingly poor. As a boy my father was obliged to sell fans on the sweltering streets of Cairo. From the beginning he had to fend for himself, and whatever he earned had to be shared with parents, his brothers, and his sister. As for his formal education, it was extremely limited. But my father had an extraordinary gift for languages. In addition to Arabic, Turkish, and French, he spoke German, Italian, and, much later, English. He was a handsome man, tall, thin, red-haired, with a little mustache. Elegant despite his poverty, early photographs reveal a relentless energy emanating from his eyes and his body.

In Cairo, my father became an apprentice to a jeweler, where he learned to design and make little rings, brooches, and necklaces. Thus began my father's career as a talented jeweler and jewelry designer. His mother, the formidable Giselle, ruled the roost. She encouraged her oldest boy to make a better life for himself. At age 18, he left home.

I was intrigued by my father's birthplace–Egypt! I often pictured my father in full Arabian regalia, leading an Arab camel brigade in battle with jeweled saber drawn high or as a fiery-eyed sheik, like Valentino. No matter how often I pressed him in later years to tell me stories of his Egyptian life, he said simply, "I had a very hard time there," and went no further. Still, he did recall for me one highlight of Egyptian youth. At age 15, he appeared as a supernumerary in Verdi's *Aida*, the opera that originally premiered in Cairo in 1871, which inspired his great love of Italian opera. In 1908, he left Egypt, worked his way through Turkey and the Balkans, and finally settled in Paris, where he became an apprentice to Cartier. The famous jewelry firm provided encouragement and a livelihood.

My mother's background is likewise cloaked in vagueness. She was born in Radzivilov, which at the time was part of Russia and later became part of Poland. Her parents, Joseph and Deborah Dodeles, were as peripatetic as my father's family. Aunt Esther, my mother's youngest sister, once told me that her family was Greek (Dedalus was the original name), and not Jewish. Joseph, my maternal grandfather, ultimately established himself in Berlin with his wife, Deborah, three daughters, Aranka (my mother), Lina, and Esther, and his sons, Martin and Carl. There he founded the jewelry firm Dodeles & Company.

My father, ever restless, and by now much given to travel, chose to interrupt his apprenticeship at Cartier to visit Berlin. So taken was he by this exhilarating and bustling city of the 1920s that he resolved to find work as a jewelry designer in the German capital. As fate would have it, he obtained employment at Dodeles & Company. At 19, my father proved so industrious and clever that he became a frequent guest in the Dodeles household. There were, after all, three marriageable daughters. In time the predictable happened. Tall, comely Aranka, with her smooth black hair, kind eyes, and warm smile, touched the heart of young Abraham. When both turned 20, their wedding date was set. The following year, Leo was born, followed by Martin, and Carl. Ten years later, in Paris, I came daringly onto the scene! The burgeoning family moved into a large, sumptuously furnished apartment near the center of Berlin. All seemed to be happiness and prosperity.

I recall a tremendous bustling in our German household, where only German was spoken. There were my brothers, noisy and disruptive, and my parents, of whom I caught only glimpses. There were the frequent visits of my aunts, uncles, and grandmother (my grandfather Dodeles had died by the time I was born). And there were maids and a cook. Because I was so little, I was placed in the hands of our maids, who saw to it that I was nicely dressed and fed. My mother must, on occasion, have spent time with me, because I remember feeling a rush of warmth and happiness whenever I was near her. I remember loving her very much. Still, I felt removed from my immediate family, not because I wasn't cared for, but because I was never made to feel that I belonged to any of them. Certainly the span of ten years between my brother Carl and I had a great deal to do with this. My three brothers merely tolerated me. My parents led a rather full social life and my mother seemed to spend more time with her own family than with any of her sons.

In 1932–when I turned six–I attended my first school in Berlin. There is a tradition in Germany that on the very first day of school every little boy and girl receives a giant cardboard cornucopia, all glittery and color-fully decorated, filled with candies, cookies, and small gifts. Invariably a photograph is taken of the youngsters, all dressed up in their new school outfits, usually wearing a backpack containing their first schoolbooks. The photograph would show them holding their huge candy-filled gift in their arms and the legend beneath the photograph would read, "Mein Erster Schulgang" (My First School Day). I still have mine.

I was quite happy in my German school rooms surrounded by children my own age. I have another photograph of myself sitting in a classroom with my hands folded. This was me, "der kleine Jonny," as I was called, with my drawings pinned on the back wall, including one depicting a house, and another a church. Sitting in the back row was a little boy holding a small flag bearing the Nazi swastika. I knew nothing of the Nazis at the time, but I had heard the word Nazi at home and could sense that it was a word spoken in derision and fear.

What stands out most in my memories of my three years in Berlin were the times my school friends would invite me to play in their homes. I envied the loving attention they received from their mothers—the ready smiles and loving hugs. To be in these homes, seeing so much affection gave me my first awareness of what can only be described as self-pity—something I barely understood. But I realized with a certain deep sadness that I was definitely not loved in this spontaneous way by my own mother, father, or brothers.

My father's strictness continually played havoc with my brothers' upbringing. Father was short-tempered, fond of threats, quick to berate, insult, and to deliver blows. He was despotic, tyrannical, a shouter, a slapper. He would find so much to criticize in each of my three brothers that they finally stopped defending themselves and let the shouting, the criticisms, and the slaps come flying. He instilled fear in all of us, but we all knew he was proud to be the father of four sons. It gave him pleasure to walk down the street with three strapping teenagers and me, his youngest, trotting behind. But he had very little understanding of his children.

My mother mostly stood by and said nothing. She had become the good German hausfrau obeying her husband. She seldom defended her sons and never interfered with the shouting and the slapping—never saying "stop," or "enough," or "let him go." At such times I felt a sense of betrayal and humiliation. It was all so unfair. I could never understand how a mother could be so insensitive to the needs of her children. I equated the word "mother" with the words "goodness" and "love," "kindness" and "protectiveness," but clearly she was as terrified of my father as the rest of us. It was because our mother seemed to be on the side of my father that none of us could ever really put our trust in her, never really confide in her, never bring our problems or our troubles to her. And yet, when I was little, I loved my mother very much. I did not know what to do about the great love I felt for her. If I showed how much I loved her, she might well tell my father, who would inevitably think it a bad thing. I did not ever want to incur my father's wrath, and so my feelings were kept inside, making for a childhood of untold frustration, anger, sadness, and shame.

To compound everyone's misery, the Nazi era was upon us. Talk at home, from the little I understood of it, centered on how difficult things were becoming for Jews in Germany. My father had at first continued in his jewelry business, but as time went on he quite suddenly transformed himself into, of all things, a travel writer! Since he spoke several languages and was very personable and ambitious, he found rapid success in Germany's tourist trade, traveling to the most famous resorts, spas, and tourist attractions while writing for a distinguished German travel book publisher. His articles were a great success. Where his knowledge of writing had sprung from was anybody's guess, but he plied his trade for many years. Having become a travel writer, he had changed his life completely.

This was my father's profession when the Nazi persecution of the Jews began. None of us could believe that a man named Adolf Hitler could ruin our lives forever. No Jew in Germany really believed that Hitler wanted to annihilate the entire Jewish race. Many German Jews utterly denied this, because their entire lives were spent in Germany and they were Germans through and through. That Hitler had such an agenda seemed so unbelievable and so absurd that many people, including my mother's family, just decided that they would pay no attention to any of this. "It will all blow over," they kept saying.

In 1933 my father clearly saw the writing on the wall. Being amazingly prescient, and highly protective of his family, he convinced his German publisher to allow him to travel to Italy to drum up some business in the Italian tourist market. Since Germans had always adored vacationing in Italy, why not do a German book on the most fabulous Italian resorts? My father was soon on his way to Italy to establish contacts with major Italian tourist destinations. Upon his arrival in Milan, the hub of Italian publishing, my father soon learned of things that were neither aired nor published in Berlin. He learned that the Nazis were preparing to round up every Jew they could find and place them in concentration camps. He learned that Hitler and the Nazi party were about to launch the most devastating persecutions imaginable, that Jewish property was to be destroyed, that Jewish men, women, and children would be routed from their homes in the dead of night, herded into trains, and taken to death camps. Learning all this, my father instantly phoned my mother and told her to pack up all our valuables, take the children, leave the furniture, and as quickly as possible quit Berlin for Milan. He told her to ask no questions—time was of the essence. He also told my mother to call her own family and tell them to leave Germany at once and come to Italy.

Small as I was, I recall my mother's frantic state of mind. She was beside herself with confusion, anxiety, and fear. Still, ever obedient to her husband's wishes, she first called her mother and sisters and told them what my father had learned. Her words fell on deaf ears. My grandmother thought my mother had gone quite mad. There was no way that they were going to leave their homes or their beloved city. Only the youngest of my aunts, Esther, saw some wisdom in my father's precaution.

Several anxious days passed. My mother packed her suitcases. She packed her jewels, her other valuables, the passports and other important papers. She told us not to breathe a word to anyone about our trip, especially not to our maids. She told them we were going to Milan to visit my father for a few days. On a gray and windy day, the five of us left our apartment, waved goodbye to the maids, and took a taxi to Berlin's Hauptbahnof.

Numb with apprehension, our mother walked to the ticket counter and, following my father's instructions, purchased five round-trip tickets to Milan. My father felt that five one-way tickets would arouse suspicion. We waited on the platform for what seemed like an eternity. Finally, the Milan-bound train pulled in. We quickly boarded, found our compartment, and settled in. From that day forward I always had a passion for trains. They represented both safety and daring adventure. They also represented a certain state of anxiety. To me, boarding a train is never without some apprehension, something unknown that might or might not happen.

The journey to Milan took most of the day and the night. On the following morning, when the train pulled into the Milan railroad station, I vividly remember seeing my father standing on the platform, waiting for us, clutching an enormous bouquet of red roses for my mother. Smiling, he placed the roses into my mother's arms and embraced her, then embraced each of his sons. He led us out to a great big touring car. My father drove a long distance to a modern, pale-brick apartment building at Viale Boezio, 6. It was very spacious and comfortable. My mother burst into tears, because by bringing us to Italy, my father had saved us all. Her tears were for her own family–her mother, brothers, and sisters. What would become of them in Germany?

"Here in Italy, we will be safe," said my father. "The Italians are very good people. Nothing bad will happen to us here." It was 1933. I was six years old, going on seven.

Chapter 2

My three brothers were coming of age. Leo had turned 23, Martin was 20, and Carlo was 16. Being ten years younger, I never fully understood their lives. My brothers never confided in me or spent much time with me. None of them continued their formal education. Their wish was to enter into some type of business career and have lots of fun. For all intents and purposes I was an only child. I was well fed, well dressed, and often patted on the head. Because I was only six, my father was not yet hitting me, but cruelty would continue toward my brothers. My father found all sorts of opportunities to lay hands upon my brothers over some inconsequential lie, a wrong word, a wrong look, a denial, a demand, an assertion. He would raise his voice in a terrifying way. I knew I was supposed to love my father, but I just didn't know how to love a man, who on the one hand did everything to protect his family, but on the other, did everything to alienate it. The rages always seemed to center on issues of gratitude. My mother, when he screamed at her, was never sufficiently grateful for the "good life" he was providing for her. My brothers were never grateful enough that they owed their lives to him.

My life in Italy gave me a pleasurable sense of identity that I had never felt before. When I was enrolled in school, La Scuola Gattamelata, in Milan, I suddenly transformed into an Italian boy. By 1935 when I was eight, I felt incredibly alive, especially as the Italian language really became my own. There was something so harsh about German, the language in which my father shouted. Italian was pure music by comparison. Italy made me conscious of so many things! It became the land of endless revelation, especially because of the music. There was so much music around me! I heard it issuing from windows, from shops, from restaurants, from street corners, and from the throats of the people. Italy seemed to be made of music.

I don't mean to over-romanticize it, but as a little boy I was surrounded by the sounds of people singing, which made me very happy. There were the popular songs coming out of the radio, and there were the achingly beautiful male and female voices singing opera. Those long songs with orchestral accompaniment were glorious, and, oh, those duets, trios, and quartets! All that music entered my whole being, and I was besotted with joy. Indeed, in Italy all of my senses came alive. My first opera was held in the open air at Milan's Castello Sforzesco. The opera was *Aida*, in which my father had held a spear as a boy in Cairo. What I witnessed was utterly amazing and spectacular. I couldn't believe what I saw. There were real elephants, camels, horses, dogs, and what seemed to be thousands of people on the vast stage. I was mesmerized. It was the beginning of my love affair with Italian opera and with classical music. In time I would see *La Bohème, Tosca, Madame Butterfly, La Traviata,* and *Otello,* among others. In the summer I'd see them at Castello Sforzesco, in the winter at La Scala.

Italy held so many other delights—food, for example. It was where I had my first plate of spaghetti—spaghetti con salsa di pomodori, generously sprinkled with grated Parmesan cheese. How I loved spaghetti. Eating made me feel positively patriotic. Not only did I love every form of pasta—ziti, rigatoni, fusilli, linguine, tagliatelle—but the antipasti—the salami, the pepperoncini, the formaggi—all the good meats, the fish and the sweets, including torrone nougat, which I especially loved. In Italy I first found gustatory heaven.

Then there was art. The paintings, the sculptures, the frescoes! My parents were not museum- or church-going people; indeed they had very little visual sense. There was no art on the walls of our apartment in Milan. I do remember walking into lots and lots of churches with our maid or on my own or with friends and looking at many holy paintings—the Christ, the Madonna and Child, the endless saints and heavenly angels.

In the 1930s, I may have contributed to the further deterioration of Leonardo da Vinci's severely peeling "The Last Supper," as I too picked and peeled little slivers of paint off the famous fresco at the refectory of Santa Maria delle Grazie. Our school made many museum visits. We were herded into the museums of the Castello Sforzesco or the Palazzo Brera, or the various municipal art palaces of Milan. I was struck by the old masters and was continually amazed at the way paint could be transformed into realistic landscapes and figures and animals, or huge, fantastic battle scenes. I loved to read the beautiful musical names of the Italian old masters: Piero della Francesca, Giovanni Pico della Mirandola, Jacopo della Quercia, Antonello da Messina, not to mention Tiziano, Il Bronzino, Mantegna, Tintoretto, Michelangelo, and Carpaccio. Little by little I became aware that I was living in a city and a country not made only of music but also made of art. Almost all my aesthetic responses were formed in Italy, and to this day, I can directly attribute my love of music, art, theater, cinema, poetry, and literature to my

Italian experience. Throughout my Italian childhood I was developing a great big Italian soul, because, unlike my brothers or my parents, I was developing into a genuine Italian boy with Italian friends, Italian schooling, Italian music, Italian art, and Italian food, in a great big Italian city, under a great big beautiful Italian sky. I believed that Italy would be my country, the place where I would live for the rest of my life.

When my father was off traveling to his various resorts for weeks at a time, our household was happy. My mother seemed as happy about my father's absences as were my brothers. And so, life was orderly, especially with the presence in our home of two wonderful maids. The younger maid, Giuseppina, was in charge of me. I was ten years old and Giuseppina, who must have been no more than 17 or 18, was unforgettable. I remember her as very smart, very lively, and very pretty. She had long, lustrous black hair that she kept braided atop her head and occasionally let down. She had a lovely eager face, fierce black eyes, and a smooth rosy complexion that smelled of fresh country air. Giuseppina had a very tender smile, and she worked very hard and loved me very much. She was ardently Catholic and loved going to church and attending mass. I was often taken along, accompanying her in and out of myriad churches, listening to priests saying endless masses in Latin. Slowly but surely, I was receiving a fairly complete, if superficial, Catholic education. I too came to love the rituals of the church, loved being amongst the worshippers, loved looking at the large paintings and frescoes of the saints, the Madonna and Child. The smell of incense, so mysteriously pungent, represented a kind of holiness to me. It was the odor of sanctity and when breathing in its smoky mists, I felt blessed and purified.

The sound of the organ, so reedy and piercing, yet soothing, offered ever greater access into a state of blessed spirituality. During Easter or Christmas or other Catholic holidays, of which there are so many in Italy, there were always the invisible choirs in the church lofts. I was utterly transported by what I was certain were the voices of angels. On Sundays, Giuseppina and I would get up very early and go to a nearby church to hear early mass. Afterward, Giuseppina and I would take a circuitous little walk to the nearby hospital. We would stand at one of its rear entrances where, at a certain hour, the newly dead were carried on stretchers to waiting hearses. It was a grim scene because relatives would also gather at this rear entrance for a last glimpse of their loved ones. We could see the white, emaciated faces of the dead, and each time a stretcher was brought out, a heart-rending wail was heard from a relative. These moans and groans and sobs were cues for Giuseppina to draw me close to her body and squeeze the life out of me. It was a physical act that scared me because Giuseppina would let out a gurgle of ecstasy as she drank in the vision of the cadavers and the weeping, wailing people around us. She would knead my body into hers, up close to her breasts, and the whole thing felt erotic and a little scary. These visits to the newly dead with Giuseppina would be a weekly Sunday ritual that I endured as best I could. Thinking back on it, Giuseppina, whom I loved more and more, initiated me into the mysteries of the sorrowful and the desperate.

At home, there was never any talk of religion and as far as I knew, no one in my family attended a synagogue, held to the Jewish rituals, or celebrated any of the Jewish holidays. It seemed I was the only member of my family who practiced any religion at all—and it was firmly the Catholic religion. Giuseppina was passionate about attending mass. Each time we went, she would tell me to pay close attention to the sermons, all of which were centered on all sorts of horrible sins. I thought that acts like these would hurl us all straight into the fires of hell if we dared to practice them. I barely understood what all the fulminating was about, but I sensed that sex, of which I really knew nothing, had a lot to do with it. What was it about sex that drove the priests to such lengthy and threatening discourses? Was sex bad? Was it dangerous? Was it forbidden? What exactly was it? And just how did you do it?

The fact is, Giuseppina was really my mother, my father, my keeper, my mentor, and last but not least, my lover. For one thing, Giuseppina still insisted on bathing me, which I resisted more and more, because I would soon turn 11. It was also her habit of slipping into my bed when it was time to go to sleep. She would come into my room after the lights were turned off and in a long white nightgown with her thick black hair loosened, she would lie down next to me. I felt the strong heat of her body next to mine and the incredibly strange softness of her breasts beneath her nightgown. Soon the nightgown would come off and at her urging, so did my pajamas. Giuseppina would hold my very thin and bony body tightly next to hers. I did not know what to make of this. She would touch my penis and what hung below it. I was utterly confused about what was going on. Giuseppina was very gentle. She kissed me and stroked me and called me "Giovannino-mio." I mostly remember her warmth and her smell, the slight scent of a lilac perfume, which was sweet and mysterious to me. What I felt were sensations unlike any others. For me to have Giuseppina in my bed was like having a great big pet next to me, a great big wonderful animal that emanated a strong, loving, and soothing heat. I remember trying to look at Giuseppina but there was no turning on of the lights; she would not allow it. Still I could see her shape and her black, black hair, black eyes, the contour of her breasts and feel her soft skin next to mine.

One of the strangest things about sex at age 11 is that if you are sweetly handled by someone you know, and it is in no way violent or aggressive or hurtful, it really feels very, very nice. It is a wonderful introduction to being loved physically. I never felt as though I was being violated or abused or that something was being done to me against my will. The truth is, I quite enjoyed these bedtime visits from Giuseppina. At the same time, I also knew that what she was doing wasn't quite right. It must have been all the guilt I accumulated throughout our church-going experiences, all that sinning the priests were talking about that would hurl us straight into hell. I was much confused, but as far as I was concerned, Giuseppina, with her strange impulsive ways, had me completely in her spell. Of course I was totally ignorant about lovemaking or reproduction. All I knew was that a woman conceived, got big, and out came a baby. I had a vague notion about penises being inserted into vaginas but knew nothing of conception nor the intense gratification of it all. Following Giuseppina's various excursions to my bed, it occurred to me that these visits might make me a father. This was a terrifying thought. What would I tell my parents? Would I have to marry Giuseppina? I was only 11 years old!

I don't know exactly how, but I suspect that one of my brothers, I believe it was Carlo, saw what was going on. He must have realized that Giuseppina, who took such good care of me, also hopped into bed with me, and he told my parents. Giuseppina was dismissed from our household. My parents told Giuseppina that what she was doing was a crime. I felt so terrible and guilty, especially since I did not speak up or defend her. I remember Giuseppina packing her things. I remember her terrible sobs. And I remember her looking at me for a long, long time before turning away and leaving our house. She left without saying a word to me. After several years together, after all that intimacy, there were no goodbyes, no hugs and no kisses. It was wrenching for us both, and I did not say a word in her defense. I did not know what words to use and for that I felt very ashamed. Giuseppina still lives in me. And it is to her–her boldness, her tenderness, her passion–that I owe whatever so-called sexual normalcy I may possess.

Chapter 3

Our life in Italy proceeded more or less peaceably. My father traveled extensively and became very successful as a travel writer. Italians began to address him as "Signor Dottore" or "Commendatore." He felt very happy in Italy. He was respected, made "una bella figura." As they grew older, my brothers were able to move out of the apartment we all shared on the Viale Boezio. One by one, they either found jobs or girlfriends. As the youngest, I continued to live with my parents. For an 11-year-old boy, to live with nearly 50-year-old parents seemed strange. We simply weren't suited to each other. I was too young. They were too old.

I continued going to school and began discovering more about myself, both psychologically and physically. By the age of 12-going-on-13, I had grown considerably taller, gotten bigger and gawkier, and upon looking in the mirror, found how thoroughly unattractive I had become. Gone was the adorable little Giovannino. In his place stood an awkward boy at the cusp of young manhood, his face pudgy and unfocused, his body out of proportion, with legs too long and torso too short. No one thought I looked ugly, but I thought I looked grotesque. It would take at least four more years before I would become relatively satisfied with my appearance.

It was now 1938. My father, upon returning home from his business trips, would show signs of restlessness and concern, which I had not seen before. The fact was, Italy was under the domination of Il Duce, Benito Mussolini, who had become a central figure in Italian politics. His portly figure and buffoonish ways filled us with amusement and bemusement. Italian boys were instilled with the knowledge that our Duce was always right—"Il Duce ha sempre ragione!" My father would say, "Il Duce will never do to us what Hitler did." It seemed to us that our life in Italy would continue despite the horrors that befell the Jews in Germany, that our lives would continue to be filled with the music and sunshine and beauty that was Italy. We lived our lives there as though we were Italian citizens.

There was still a king and queen in Italy during the 1930s, Vittorio Emanuele III and his wife Margherita. I was always thrilled at the thought that we were living among royals. When Mussolini came on the scene, it seemed to be a real step down from the pomp and regality of monarchs and briefly we were under the dual protection of both a monarchy and a fascist regime. As a schoolboy living under the fascists, I was obliged to learn patriotic songs and to follow the edicts of Il Duce, which were all aimed at promoting the glories of Italy. We were made to feel that to live under Mussolini was one of the greatest privileges. School children were allowed to participate in certain political activities. For example, I wore a uniform which transformed me into "un figlio della lupa"–the son of a she-wolf, suckler of the twins Romulus and Remus, symbols of ancient Rome. This association with the greatness of Italy's past made us unbelievably proud. The uniform consisted of knee socks, short dark green pants, and a black shirt over which two white sashes were crossed from the shoulders forming an "X" across our chests. There was a beautiful blue satin kerchief draped around our necks and held together by a buckle. We wore a black fez-like hat with a hanging tassel. Last was a beautiful silver monogram, the letter "M," to be pinned where the white sashes crossed against the black shirt. I naturally assumed that the letter "M" must stand for the word mama. Instead, I was quickly corrected, it stood for Mussolini. We would march in those uniforms, and sing patriotic songs along the streets of Milan led by a young fascista also in full regalia. As we got a little older, we were no longer called the figli della lupa, but Balilla, named after the teenage Genoese hero who led the Italians in a crucial battle against the Austrians in 1746.

My knowledge of Italian politics was naïve and confused. Yes, there were the patriotic feelings instilled in us at school about the greatness of Italy, the greatness of the hero, Garibaldi, the greatness of Mussolini and all that he stood for. My schooling had indeed turned quite political. I now had Il Duce to reckon with. He was my leader, my dictator. At home, there awaited a dictator of another sort. But my home life did not change as dramatically as my school life. One of the few joys of my home life was that we always had a piano. My father may have been despotic but he loved music, and it was he who urged my brothers to learn to play the piano. How and when they learned to play it was quite mysterious to me. I had never seen them practice nor seen a teacher work with them. Perhaps they had gone outside the home for lessons, but hearing them play was certainly a terrific treat. Tino, my middle brother, was particularly musical, and it was from him that I learned of the classics: the Chopin nocturnes and waltzes, the Beethoven sonatas, the Brahms Hungarian dances, and lots and lots of Bach, which he especially loved to play. Brothers Leo and Carlo could also play, but they possessed another gift: they could sit at the piano without sheet music and play all the popular songs of the day. How did they do it? I tried hard but could never, ever do this! I desperately wanted to play by ear, but even more so, I wanted to play the classics like my brother Tino. I asked my mother if she would let me have piano lessons. She said that my brothers would teach me, but they had neither the desire nor the patience for it. Finally it was decided that a piano teacher would come to the house to give me lessons.

The teacher turned out to be a tall and quite handsome young man named Signorino Tullio. I was 11 and incredibly eager to emulate not only my brothers, but also the pianists I had heard on the radio and in the movies–those romantic figures, usually dressed in white tie and tails, their hair worn long and curly or heavily pomaded and seductively slicked back. Their hands would ever so suavely glide over the keyboard or, their arms raised high, decoratively fall upon the keys for that final cascade of thrillingly executed runs and arpeggios.

From the first, I could tell that Signorino Tullio found my eagerness most appealing. And from the first, he guided my faulty attempts at note reading with endless patience. Tullio could not have been more than 20, and I recall that he had very light blue, deep-set eyes, pale skin, silken blond hair, and a prominent and beautifully sculpted nose. To me, he was the image of a glamorous, highly romantic-looking young pianist. My lessons proceeded smoothly and after some weeks, I overheard Tullio telling my parents how very musical I was. Indeed, each time I did things well, Tullio would reward me with certain prolonged pats. "Bravo Gianni!" he would exclaim. At times his hand would gently squeeze my thigh, or my hair would be affectionately tousled. And so it was that in time, these piano lessons would turn into lessons in which caresses and even kisses would play a part.

Inevitably, when we were alone, sitting on the piano bench together, Tullio would grasp my genitals and one memorable time, even touch himself. It was music-making fraught with sex and sensuality, and it held a certain furtive delight. I was neither frightened nor disgusted, although I was certainly perturbed and flustered. Then again, my experiences with Giuseppina had somehow prepared me for the fact that so-called grown-ups had these sexual urges, and I was somehow chosen to elicit them. I submitted to Tullio's kisses, caresses, and gropings, and good boy that I was, practiced my scales and learned my sharps and flats. Slowly I began to fall desperately in love, if not totally with Tullio, then certainly with keyboard music. Curiously, I did not feel guilty. I did not associate what I experienced with Giuseppina, with Tullio, or increasingly, with myself, as having anything to do with sinning. Despite my Catholic upbringing, I never felt I would be hurled into the flames of hell and made to suffer the agonies of perdition. I firmly believed that something which felt so good, which involved hugs and kisses and caresses, couldn't possibly be punishable by the wrath of God. Surely God, the saints and all the angels, would only smile upon a boy who seemed so dearly loved and who engendered so much passion. Italy utterly liberated me: psychologically, spiritually, intellectually, and sexually. I know this, because each time I return to Italy I am a person transformed. I am returned to the country of my boyhood. Layer upon layer of complex anxieties acquired in America fall from me, and upon speaking the Italian language—which has miraculously remained with me—and upon breathing the Italian air, I am thrust back to a time when life was decidedly simpler, more vivid, more exhilarating, and more emotionally satisfying.

My parents loved Venice, and we went there almost every summer for the six years we lived in Italy. As the youngest, I was brought along while my brothers either stayed in Milan or found other escapes during the summer months. It was a joy for me to be near the sea, but it was hard being left to my own devices so much of the time. My parents enjoyed going off by themselves to restaurants, to cafes, or on shopping trips. I was taken along from time to time, looking quite adorable in my Dutch-boy haircut and sailor suit, walking smartly next to my well-dressed, aging parents. However, I was often left in the charge of waiters and waitresses, maitre d's, cooks, or hotel managers, all of whom my father asked to keep an eye on me, for which they received a sizeable tip. They would feed me if my parents were not back in time for lunch or dinner or went out on the town. They saw to it that I got back to my room, and told me when it was time to go to bed.

These summertime experiences in Venice in the company of these helpful, kind-hearted strangers gave me a taste for life lived in hotels. It was a life lived with people who enjoyed serving you. A life with people who often seemed to care more for you than your own mother and father.

Looking back on it, it was mostly the waiters who took care of me–old ones, middle-aged ones, young ones. I think they enjoyed having me around. I would sit in their kitchens, often at long tables where food was being prepared. Or I would be invited to sit where the waiters, waitresses, or cooks had their meals.

Looking at photographs of myself taken at that time, I seemed to have been quite a sweet looking boy with a quick, responsive smile. I was fussed over, which pleased me no end. I was petted and hugged. At meal times, with my parents absent, I would sometimes be seated in the large, elegant hotel dining rooms. There I was, a little boy, all alone at a great big table, being served by attentive waiters. I think I enjoyed being eyed adoringly by the other guests who threw me warm smiles each time I looked up from my soup or pasta.

My favorite waiter at the Hotel Excelsior, where we often stayed, was Ugolino Aldebrando. I still remember his name because he wrote it down for me on a beautiful big postcard of Piazza San Marco. Across the other side of the card he printed his name, Ugolino Aldebrando. I kept the card, along with other treasures, in a special locked box in Milan. This waiter– probably in his mid 20s–walked with a rather pronounced limp. I was always immensely impressed by the fact that despite his limp, he carried his trays or dishes or bottles of wine with the greatest aplomb and dexterity. Ugolino seemed very brave to me because, although afflicted, he was incredibly sweet-tempered and actually quite funny. He would make funny faces at me or wink at me behind my parents' back.

I loved my stays in Venice, whether left alone or not. Venice looked like no other city I had ever seen–it was magical and truly dazzling. I was allowed to play on the Lido beach near our hotel, but I was always told not to stray too far. One time I wandered away and became completely lost. I did not know where I was, and my heart started pounding in fear. The more I walked the more lost I was. At one point I sat down on the sand and looked at all the people around me as I tried to see if my parents might be looking for me, but they were not. It must have been at least an hour before I finally began to cry. Soon I was distracted from my weeping by the sight of all the other children playing games, building castles, or splashing in the water. They all knew where they were, and everything seemed so normal and so safe. Life was going on as usual except that I was utterly forsaken, and there was a knot in my stomach. After quite a while I looked up and there was my father bending over me, looking very angry. It was the first time I received a big slap in the face. He said: "I told you not to go far, but you did. You disobeyed me." He slapped me again, then took me gruffly by the hand and we walked back to where my mother was sitting on a towel under a sun umbrella. There were no hugs, no kisses, no delight in seeing me. All she could say was, "Why did you disobey your father?"

If Venice gave me anything, it was a great and lasting love and affection for waiters. I felt safe and loved in their company. Many years later, my own family would try to stop me from engaging in long conversations with Italian waiters, especially if they were young and attractive and could speak a beautiful Italian. With them, I would invariably flirt shamelessly, feeling the warmest glow as I looked up into their smiling faces.

Chapter 4

By the age of 12, content with the life I was leading in Italy despite difficulties at home, I had become a child who found his happiness within himself. When my father got into one of his rages, I would just stop my ears, or busy myself with something–anything. When he shouted, I would move away and pray he wouldn't find me and hit me, which he sometimes did. Why did he do this? Did I do something wrong? But I don't remember doing anything that was terribly wrong. Perhaps I had dropped a plate and it broke, or said something in the wrong way. I never really knew what precipitated his rages.

Even though these outbursts made our lives miserable, we all just kept on going. My mother, for her part, continued to be depressed over what might be happening to her family in Germany. Then, in 1938, signs began appearing in the windows of my father's favorite Milanese coffee houses: "Dogs and Jews not allowed" read the signs in Biffi or Motta in the Galleria at the Piazza del Duomo. One would read in the papers how Mussolini and Hitler were beginning to visit one another, and how an alliance was being forged. My father was devastated by it all, but I was more or less oblivious until one day at school the teacher informed me that all children of the Jewish faith would be transferred to another school. I didn't know what to make of this. Frankly, I wasn't even sure if I was Jewish. As a family we were certainly not keeping to any of the Jewish rituals or traditions.

The teacher now called out the names of those children who would be entering this new school which, we were told, would be exclusively for Jewish children. My name was among those he read. I went home and told this to my parents. They were terrified. There must have been about a dozen or so Italian Jewish children in my class, and when I returned to our school the next day, a small bus was waiting for us. We drove quite a distance to this new Jewish school, and when we got there, we were issued yellow armbands that bore the Star of David. We were told to put these on our left arms and that we had to wear them at school. We were also told that we could no longer wear our Fascist uniforms or march in the streets of Milan singing patriotic songs.

When I got home that day, I told my parents what had happened. They were angry and frightened. Little by little things began to deteriorate for the Jewish people of Italy. One day, my parents learned that Jewish families could no longer employ household help. Our maid, Maria, who had been with us since the beginning of our time in Italy, would have to be let go. When my parents gave her this news she burst into tears and asked, "What have I done?" My mother told her she had done nothing and that the new Italian law was forcing us to release her. She told Maria that she must leave or risk getting us all into terrible trouble. She asked, "Ma perche? Perche? Why? What do Jewish people look like? Why can't they have maids?" My parents had no answer.

My father decided that I was not to return to the new Jewish school. He kept me at home as he watched the political tides shift against Italian and non-Italian Jews. The moment Mussolini shook hands with Hitler, my father realized he must again do the impossible. This time he contacted one of his brothers, Alexander, who was in the jewelry business, and who had migrated from Egypt to France to Argentina. He married a French woman, produced three children, and moved to Buenos Aires, where he lived during the time that my own family lived in Italy. Alexander decided to leave Argentina after he realized that he and his family could have a better life in the United States, specifically New York City. My father and he had kept up a correspondence, informing each other of events in their respective lives, throughout those years.

Thus it was that my father contacted Uncle Alexander in New York, asking him to secure visas for us so that we too might immigrate to America. Toward the end of 1938, word reached us that visas were being provided for us and that my uncle had done everything he could to bring us over. There was only one problem: visas were available only for my father, my mother, and for myself. There would be no visas for my three older brothers. My parents could not believe this. Why would the Americans want to break up a family? It seemed impossibly cruel to my parents that this could be the case. But the fact was that all three of my brothers were denied entry into the United States because they were born in Germany. The German quota for entry into the United States was closed. My parents and I were given visas because the quota for Egypt, Russia, and France, where my father, mother, and I were born, were open. We could gain entry into the United States, but my three brothers would have to be left behind, something my parents would never consider.

My parents were desperate. Here were their three sons, each just in his twenties, none with a profession or career, and none with any prospects for a secure future. My father said: "I cannot leave without my family. I don't want to leave Italy without all my boys." He tried everything. Despite living in Italy for nearly seven years and making many important contacts over time, he was unable to do anything to alter the situation. The German quota was closed—and that was the end of it.

It was an absolute tragedy for my parents to have to make the decision to leave my three brothers with the impending terror that might be in store for them. But the day came when my father decided that we simply had to leave before the climate became even more hostile. And so, on a very tearful day, we packed our suitcases. I remember my brothers remaining behind in the Milan apartment on Viale Boezio where we had once all lived together.

My father had obtained one of the last passages to America on the Italian steamer, the SS Vulcania leaving from Trieste, one of Italy's great seaport cities. We boarded a train from Milan to Trieste, and between the intermittent sobs of my mother and the look of desperation on my father's face, I too felt a sense of dread and loss. But the real reason for my unhappiness was not that we were leaving on a boat for America or over what terrible things might befall my three brothers. My unhappiness stemmed from the fact that I did not wish to leave Italy. I did not wish to leave Milan or my friends. I thought that I could find a way to continue to live in Milan. I devised a scheme with my closest friend Dino, who was decidedly not Jewish, but very Catholic. I said to him, "Listen, Dino, do you think your parents would let me live with your family while my parents are in America? I would live with you and be raised by your family. I'm practically a Catholic already! I don't even know what it means to be Jewish. That way I won't have to leave…wouldn't have to be with my parents alone, without my brothers." Dino said he would ask his parents. He came back and said they were willing to take me in. He said, "My father will call your father and they will make the arrangements." I was overjoyed.

As promised, Dino's father called my father and said that he understood the situation and that he would be happy to take me in as one of his family. He said I could stay with them as long as I wanted, and perhaps, when I got a little older, could join my parents in America. When my father heard this, he told Dino's father that he must be completely, utterly, and totally out of his mind. "Thank you very much," said my father, "but there is no way my son will remain in Italy." When he hung up, he turned to me and said, "Do you realize that if you stay here, we won't have any of our children with us. You are only 12 years old and don't have any idea what will happen to you or your brothers." All this replayed itself in my mind as we stood at the Milan railway station waiting for the train that would take us to Trieste.

The train pulled in. The tears flowed as my parents bade farewell—perhaps for the last time—to Leo, Tino, and Carlo. Finally, we boarded the train and traveled in sad silence for hours and hours until we came into Trieste. We arrived around noon and went to the great piazza facing the sea, and there we could see anchored the SS Vulcania. It was not a huge ship, but it looked quite majestic under a slate gray sky. I believe we stopped for something to eat at a restaurant near the pier. My father double-checked all the papers and the visas that my uncle had procured for us. I had my first glimpse of American money, which my father furtively showed me. It looked so strange because all the bills were of the same small size and the same greenish color. The Italian bills, on the other hand, were very large and flamboyant, of varying sizes and colors and design embellishments with images of royalty, military heroes, or artists.

Soon came the moment when we boarded the SS Vulcania. We were shown to our cabins after a long boarding process during which our documents were scrupulously examined. My mother said she was not feeling well and immediately went to her cabin to lie down. My father and I went to an outside deck to watch as the boat slowly departed the shores of Trieste. The moment was utterly sad. Would I ever see Italy again? Would I ever see my friends again? What would life be like for me in America? I looked at the churning, swirling waters below. The ship's horn was blasting. White smoke emanated from its chimneys. The shore grew ever more distant as gusts of a February wind began to chill our faces. My eyes began to tear (or was I crying?) and I thought, "I don't speak any English! No one will understand a word I'm saying!"

But then I remembered all the American movies I had seen in Milan. They were all dubbed in Italian, of course. In Italy, every American movie star spoke fluent Italian. But now I would see American movies in America—and all the movie stars would be speaking English! And I would learn my English from them...from Gary Cooper, Spencer Tracy, Clark Gable, Cary Grant, Errol Flynn, Bette Davis, Barbara Stanwyck, Joan Crawford, Lana Turner, Ginger Rogers, Loretta Young, and yes, even little Shirley Temple, whom I had loved since I was seven years old.

Quite suddenly I felt excited. I was, after all, going to America! To AMERICA! And I was going to speak English! And I was going to live in New York! It was all going to be stupendous and fabulous, and I was going to do stupendous and fabulous things, even though I knew in my heart that I would be facing a great big stupendous and fabulous unknown! As the SS Vulcania gave one last blast of its mighty horn, Trieste and all of Italy seemed mysteriously to disappear.

Chapter 5

Having resolved to put a much happier face on leaving Italy, I began exploring the ship on my own. My parents seemed buried in their grief, and, as usual, paid little attention to me or my wanderings. I met other refugee kids on board and there were ping-pong tables in the recreation area. Amazingly, I became a whiz at ping pong. I was happy to be on an Italian ship, with Italian personnel, especially at mealtimes, when I could chat with the Italian waiters, who were serving and hovering in the dining rooms. There we all were, everyone speaking Italian, eating Italian food, and ostensibly still living in Italy—though floating toward a brand new world.

The trip took ten days. On our arrival in New York harbor on February 23, 1939, it was bitterly cold. I don't think I had ever experienced such cold weather. It was early morning, with mist in the air, and we were told that if we wanted to see the famous New York skyline and the Statue of Liberty, we were all to gather on the ship's upper deck at around 6 a.m. This we did, including my mother, who pulled herself out of her sick bed for the occasion. We climbed the stairs to the open deck on the first-class level. Hundreds of people had gathered in the freezing cold. A steady, insistent wind chilled our bones. The boat was moving very slowly, and suddenly, out of the mist, like a mirage, the entire city rose before us. There stood the skyscrapers with their thousands upon thousands of windows glowing in the dim sunlight. The colors of the sunrise were changing from mauve and pink to gray. Finally, the morning was the color of steel. And we, on the slowly moving ship, were in the grip of an awed and stunned silence. Even more extraordinary was our first sight of the Statue of Liberty. We could not believe how big she was. There she stood, Miss Liberty, clad all in green with one arm raised holding her torch. And there were those impassive eyes, that enormous face. She was a beckoning, maternal figure, welcoming us all to the land of the free. She was like a majestic tragedienne, a symbol of nobility and generosity—a great and awkward goddess possessed of enigmatic yet positive powers.

Ellis Island refugees were mustered in or out. My father and I were on tenterhooks about my mother because we had learned that if you were sick, you were sent back and not allowed into the country. We were terrified that this would happen to my mother. My father told her that she must really pull herself together. He told her to stand up straight, smile, and not complain or cry. "Make it look as though you are the picture of health and happy to have arrived in this wonderful country," he told her sternly.

It was a scary moment when we approached the doctors who examined us all, but we were given clean bills of health and passes to board a ferry to take us to the isle of Manhattan. On the pier stood my uncle Alexander. I had never seen him before, and he did not resemble my father at all. He was a tall man with a charming smile and happy, welcoming eyes. After long and effusive embraces, he took us by taxi to his apartment at 310 West 72nd Street, where we lived for a brief time.

The apartment was on the 16th floor, a dizzying height for me. Back in Milan, no apartment building ever reached those stratospheric heights. We entered the large apartment and met Manya, my uncle's wife, and their three children, my cousins Anita, aged 16, Suzy, aged 14, and their little brother Jackie, aged five. They were all smiles, but as they spoke no Italian, we could only hug and smile some more—giggle, really, because we were all hugely awkward and embarrassed.

Soon we were all settled in, but my mother's stomach condition worsened, and as her pains increased, it was decided that she should be taken to the hospital, where the doctors discovered a major gallbladder problem. She needed to have surgery immediately—a dreary beginning to her American life. As for my father, he had absolutely no prospects. He spoke no English. Soon, he plunged into a terrible depression over my mother's illness and his three sons whose fate in Europe he dreaded and with whom he had not been in contact since leaving Italy. I was no comfort to my parents. I was unable to show them any affection nor was I able to talk to comfort them. I had grown into an awkward 13-year-old, self-engrossed, confused by our suspended state of existence in the home of my uncle, and unhappy over the state of my own fate in this exciting and bewildering country.

My mother's gallbladder operation was successful, but she had to remain in the hospital for several weeks. In the meantime, my father felt he could not impose on his brother much longer and started looking around for an apartment. I had no idea about my father's finances, but one day he announced that he and I would be moving to an apartment at 567 Fort Washington Avenue in a neighborhood called Washington Heights. This proved to be way uptown in Manhattan—around 182nd Street—far from the excitement of midtown and Times Square. As it turned out, during and after World War II, Washington Heights was the neighborhood where many German-Jewish refugees started a new life.

While my parents were non-observant of the Jewish faith while we lived in Italy, the moment we reached America my father suddenly redis- covered his dormant sense of religion. Living in Washington Heights, and being among German Jews, he found it a comfort to be able to communicate with his fellow refugees. He could speak seven languages including Arabic, and his German was excellent—all he needed to do was learn some English and Yiddish, which he eventually did. There was a synagogue nearby and he began to attend services, and the rabbi introduced him to various other rabbis, cantors, and Jewish officials in the neighborhood. It was through them that my father found his way into his first American profession, as a tie-and-shirt salesman, who traveled to the various Jewish communities in New York State, New Jersey, Connecticut, and Pennsylvania. Through a network of synagogues, my father was able to find Jews in need of ties and shirts. As an awkward, miserable, and belligerent teenager, I remember taking the subway with my father all the way downtown to Orchard and Delancey Streets, then strongly Jewish neighborhoods, where my father shopped for his stock of shirts and ties to take on the road. The shirts came six to a box, six boxes of which I had to help carry back home every time my father needed to restock.

There was something so dismal about all this—so heartbreaking too— that the only emotion I felt was shame. I remembered my father being called "Signor Dottore" and other so-called titles of respect in Italy, and remembered his pride at being a published author of travel books and of his leading a life of a certain distinction. In America, knowing so little English, he was reduced to peddling shirts and ties—taking buses and much later traveling by car in search of a living. Oddly enough, he didn't seem to mind it as much as I did.

As for my own life in America, one of the biggest problems was not speaking any English. This made life a misery. I tried as hard as I could to pick up the words and when we moved to Washington Heights, it was decided that I should be enrolled in a junior high school in the neighborhood. There, I was a boy truly out of the ordinary. My clothes were peculiar and totally European. I wore knickerbockers and a beret, and of course all the other kids looked at me and just laughed and laughed.

They called me a "damn refugee" and I was regularly beaten up by some bullies who felt that, because I was foreign, I didn't deserve to live. I had bloody noses and mean fights. In America, I quickly learned, it is very hard to be different. You could be different, but you had to know how to be different, and at the tender age of 13, you do not yet know how to do this. My first year was really awful. But I got used to the bullying, the blows, the insults. I wasn't very strong and didn't defend myself too well, except for one memorable time, when I suddenly found the strength and the fury to beat the meanest of the bullies to a point of near death. I may have fractured his skull—he did not return to school for many weeks. He never came near me again.

As I knew I would, I learned English by going to the movies. In my neighborhood there was a movie house called the Empress. Admission was ten cents in 1939. I saw some marvelous films. I listened very intently, and made it a point to sit very close to the screen, which made it hard to see but easier to hear. I also listened to the radio a lot, and I was fairly quick to pick things up. I said many things incorrectly. I would often say, when introduced to someone new, "Oh hello, I am so charming to meet you"—things of that sort. I had a heavy middle-European accent made up of German and Italian inflections. Anyway, I did enjoy school, even with my heinous classmates. Some teachers were intrigued by my background, and encouraged my efforts to become American. I was striving for something…anything.

I didn't know what was going on inside me most of the time. I didn't know what to like or what to dislike. I didn't know what to wear. I copied everyone, as young people will do. Because I was often left on my own, I had to invent my whole person by myself, and there were many difficult, insecure moments. Little by little I began to get involved with schoolwork and other things I loved. I loved classical music and began listening to it more and more. Because I had little money and was dependent on a very small weekly allowance, I decided that I was going to need something to do after school to earn some more money. I went to the local grocery store and asked the owner if I might be a delivery boy. He was a nice man and said, "Fine, it's hard work, but you'll make tips."

I began to deliver groceries and found I absolutely hated it. I hated carrying the bags. I didn't like going to other people's apartments. I didn't even like taking the little tips I was given. It wasn't that I didn't want the money, it was just that I felt demeaned by the whole process. After a week or so, I told this very nice grocer that my mother wasn't feeling well and that I must stay home to look after her, which was a great big lie. He understood, and my delivery-boy days came mercifully to an end.

In the meantime, I was doing everything possible to Americanize myself. It was a terrible struggle. On top of it all, I had begun to sprout pimples, the bane of my existence. Those wretched pimples lasted for several long years. I would purchase medicines and cover-ups and my mother made me drink tomato juice with yeast in it, which ended my relationship with tomato juice forever.

But there were a few compensations, especially the movies. *Gone with the Wind* was released in 1939, the year we arrived. I absolutely had to see it. As it was playing at the Astor Theater at Times Square, a first-run movie house, admission would be quite expensive. I practically forced my mother to take us both to the Astor Theater. I was desperate to see Vivien Leigh and Clark Gable in this four-hour epic film, with music by Max Steiner and a cast of thousands; never mind that I barely understood the language, or that I knew nothing of the American Civil War, or that my mother would not be able to understand a single word of what was being said.

It was winter. The weather was awful. My mother didn't want to go. I insisted on going. Finally, off we went all bundled up. It was the coldest day of the year. We took the subway to Times Square. It had begun to snow and to sleet. My mother, always shaky on her feet, trudged along behind me. To get there on time, I took my mother's arm to cross the wide, wide, street. Suddenly, she slipped and fell. I was mortified. People came running to help her and luckily she wasn't hurt. Despite her obvious distress, I made her run to the box office. She got out her billfold, paid five dollars for us both—and we walked in just as the lights were going down.

The newsreel came on, showing scenes of war-torn Europe—Nazi troops marching into Poland, Jews being persecuted on the streets of Berlin. I could hear my mother beginning to sob. She still did not know the fate of my three brothers. She missed her sons terribly. "Where are my boys?" she said. "Where are my boys?" I looked around me in embarrassment. I told her to stop crying. At last, the newsreel ended. Then came the cartoons–Bugs Bunny, Looney Tunes. Finally, *Gone with the Wind* began. The music surged. The story unfolded. I had never seen a more beautiful woman than Vivien Leigh–so radiant, so piquant, so full of life, so seductive, so "Fiddle dee dee!" I was lost. For a brief moment I wished the actors were all speaking in Italian again, so I could understand them better. But their English, mostly spoken with a soft drawl, began to sound more and more familiar to me. I concentrated as hard as I could on the words they were saying.

There was an intermission after two hours during which we sat and listened to more of Max Steiner's lush music. I was enthralled. My mother had more or less composed herself. She asked me when this was gong to be over. I told her, "You have to sit there another two hours." She said, "Ach, mein Gott!!" I didn't care if it lasted another six hours! I was totally mesmerized. When the movie ended, I decided *Gone with the Wind* was the greatest movie I had ever seen. Not only because of its great length, which I thought was so fabulous, but because the story was so quintessentially American, and thus incredibly exotic to me. Everything about it was new to me, including the strong emotional pulls of each of the principal characters–the yearning of Scarlett O'Hara for Ashley Wilkes, the manly, brutal passion of Rhett Butler for Scarlett, the overwhelming goodness of Olivia de Havilland's Melanie, Hattie McDaniel's poignant loyalty, and Butterfly McQueen's goofy, addled confusions. It was all too marvelous!

Oh, how I wanted to be part of American life! And, oh, how I wanted to be a part of American show business.

To that end, I began memorizing a number of the day's popular songs. In the 1940s, you could buy sheets with the lyrics of the songs sung by Patti Page, Frank Sinatra, Perry Como, Margaret Whiting–singers I loved to listen to on the radio and on recordings. I had a very good ear and had no problem memorizing the tunes. Memorizing the lyrics was more difficult, but memorize them I did, and sang them to myself in a tenor-going-to-baritone voice. In fact, I fancied myself a rather good, rather "interesting" singer, and even dreamed of a career as a crooner.

One day, one of our neighbors–a certain Mrs. Twersky–heard me singing some of my favorite pop tunes. She said, "You know, John, over at the Audubon movie theater they're holding amateur nights. You should go and audition." I got excited. I thought, "Why not?" Maybe I'll attract the attention of a movie scout and be this very alluring, very young discovery. I was 16 now, tall for my age, blond, blue-eyed, and really not bad looking at all. When the morning came I covered all my pimples, put on my good blue suit, and walked to 161st Street and Audubon Avenue where this big theater was located. I went in, was ushered onto the stage and auditioned. I passed the audition and was told I would be part of their weekly amateur night. I would appear on the following Wednesday night after the six o'clock movie.

My vocal selection was a song entitled "Deep Purple." I had chosen this song because it was the No. 1 song for many weeks on a radio program called *Your Hit Parade,* to which I listened religiously. It was sung by Bea Wain, whose voice I thought was gorgeously beautiful. The song was very melodic, very romantic, very sophisticated. And so, on that particular Wednesday night, I asked my mother to accompany me to the Audubon Theater for my debut as a pop singer.

After seeing my mother to her seat, I went backstage and found quite a few contestants gathered in a waiting room. They all seemed much older than I was, and I began to feel very nervous. Nevertheless, I had practiced my song until I was blue in the face and felt I would do a good job. Finally, the MC went out on the stage and announced that the night's winner would be selected by the amount of applause he or she would receive when he placed his hand over their heads at the conclusion of the contest. The winner would receive $100.

The first contestant was a woman whistler. She wore a long blue taffeta evening gown and around her shoulders was a silver fox boa. She whistled "Tales from the Vienna Woods" in a very complex and long-winded arrangement of her own. Her whistling was loud and unpleasant. Next came a young guy who played a tango on the accordion. After him came a female tap dancer, who nearly tripped and fell on her face. Still, she recovered and got a lot of sympathetic applause from the audience. I was called next.

I walked out on the enormous stage. A pink spotlight followed me to center stage where a microphone was situated. The pianist behind me started to play. I launched into "Deep Purple." I could feel my voice trembling and my knees shaking. The song was not going well. I could hear the audience shuffling in their seats. I tried to sing with more feeling. "When the DEEP-purple FALLS!" But I knew it didn't help. At last, the song was done—it was over—I took a very quick bow as the audience just sat there. My number was followed by a violinist, a guitarist, another singer, a drummer, and a ventriloquist. I heard none of them. I only knew I had done very, very badly.

At the end of it, all the contestants filed on stage. The MC began walking behind each one of us, placing his hand above our heads. When I felt him standing behind me, there were perhaps two or three clapping hands. The winner that evening was the lady who whistled "Tales from the Vienna Woods." The audience just clapped and clapped for her. I was desolate—heartbroken. I rushed to where my mother was sitting and dragged her out of the Audubon Theater as quickly as possible. My career as America's youngest, most unusual crooner was over.

In New York I continued to find it very hard to fit in. Nevertheless, I made some interesting friends. Through one of my more intellectual classmates, I remember once meeting a handsome couple in their thirties, who sort of adopted me. One day, they took me home with them and we all listened to string quartets by Bartók. She was quite beautiful and he was quite handsome. I thought they were the most sophisticated people in the world because they lived in a beautiful midtown apartment, surrounded by many paintings, lots of books, and comfortable couches and chairs. There was something very potent about this couple—something very seductive and sexy.

I was invited to their home for dinner. I had now known them for about a month. I was still 16, almost 17. The music was going, more string quartets. At one point, before the meal began, the husband asked if I would like to take a shower with them. I was quite startled, but they were so charming about it that I agreed. We all went into their bedroom and took our clothes off. As he undressed, I saw the husband slowly stroking himself until he was hard. I was both shocked and mesmerized, and began to become excited as well. His wife, in the meantime, stood naked in front of a long mirror, touching her beautiful breasts and admiring herself. Soon, she approached us both and, as her husband and I both stood very near each other, she lowered herself to her knees and alternatively took each of us in her mouth. Finally, as I watched, she brought her husband to a resounding climax.

We now stood in their bathtub under a cascade of warm water. We embraced and soaped each other, and my friends began kissing, then kissing and holding me as well. We soon found ourselves on their very large bed. My friends made love—but they included me with their loving embraces. I told myself I was experiencing life-in-the-raw. It was oh so heady, so sophisticated, so New York! And it felt so very good and it was oh so utterly thrilling, so grown-up, so gorgeously bizarre!

Chapter 6

Our home life focused on our need to know what was happening to my three brothers, Leo, Tino, and Carlo. We had not yet heard from any of them—not since very early on while they were still able to remain in Italy. They wrote to my uncle's West 72nd Street address and I think there was even a phone call. But then there was silence. My father and mother were absolutely desperate and of course they thought the worst. Months passed when word finally came from the two youngest, Carlo and Tino. They were headed for China from Italy. My parents were stunned by this information, but it turned out that there was a possibility for Jews to go to China—to Shanghai—where there was a Jewish encampment, a ghetto really, where Jews could live in relative safety and could even work.

My parents suddenly realized that two of their sons were out of immediate mortal danger. To their astonishment, news came that my mother's youngest sister, Esther, had also immigrated to China to live in the same ghetto, and was in touch with Carlo and Tino. Aunt Esther informed us that my grandmother Dodeles and my aunt Lina had been awakened in the middle of the night, taken from their apartment in Berlin, put on a train, and sent to the Dachau concentration camp. There they perished in the Nazi ovens. There was more grieving in our household. My mother took to her bed, and my father disappeared into a dark, dark silence.

As for my brother Leo, there was no word at all. The eldest, the crown prince, had literally vanished. Leo, the most adored, was still in Italy when Carlo and Tino left for China. He chose not to go to Shanghai, and Carlo and Tino had no idea what had happened to him. All the while the war continued, and I remember that most of my father's energies were directed toward trying to bring my brothers to America. How he could accomplish this, he did not know.

Through some Jewish contacts, my father learned of a place in downtown Manhattan called Hebrew Immigrant Aid Society (HIAS) that helped Jewish refugee families in New York locate relatives in war-torn Europe and elsewhere. This organization arranged for care packages to be sent abroad, and helped pave the way for relatives, once found, to make their way into the U.S. My father haunted their offices, and, from time to time, I grudgingly went along to fill out forms and translate for my father. As it turned out, the HIAS did make some headway in helping my two Shanghai-based brothers obtain visas for entry into the U.S. and even located someone in Milan who knew my brother Leo and who reported that Leo had left Milan for Brussels.

And so the hunt for Leo began in Brussels. One day, the phone rang in our apartment. It was Leo himself! He had contacted Carlo and Tino in Shanghai and gotten our telephone number. Leo told my father on the phone that he went to Brussels to visit a friend, who promised to help him find a job and hide him from the Nazis. But both he and this friend—a young man—were apprehended by Belgian Nazi sympathizers and placed in a concentration camp called Breendonk. After several weeks Leo took his life in his hands and made a daring escape from the camp. There were no details, but Leo was now living in hiding somewhere in Belgium and he gave my father the address. My father lost no time in alerting HIAS and soon more care packages were sent off to Belgium. In time, Leo too received his visa to enter the U.S. And then, the wonderful day came when all three of my brothers were able to fly to New York to be reunited with us. It had been almost five years since we saw them on that railroad platform in Milan. It seems that the U.S. government, because of the devastation to the Jews in Germany and elsewhere, finally relaxed its quota allowance for Jews born in Germany and throughout Europe.

How ironic that the HIAS building, located at 425 Lafayette Street, would years later house the Public Theater and the offices of Shakespeare in the Park, and that the man responsible for it all, Joseph Papp, would change the face of the American Theater. And how even more amazing that in the year 2003, long after Joe Papp's death, let alone my parents' death, this self-same building, where my father and I came to seek help for my brothers in the early 1940s, should house the musical—*Radiant Baby*—based on my biography of the young artist Keith Haring, directed by the Public Theater's General Director, George C. Wolfe.

Over 60 years later, I attended rehearsals of this musical in my capacity as artistic consultant, and every day, upon entering the Public Theater, I would glance at the plaque near the Public Theater's entrance commemorating the fact that the HIAS had been situated in this very building!

When all my brothers landed in New York, I was finishing my studies at the High School of Commerce, an all-boys school, dedicated, as its
name implies, to commerce. It was the word "commerce" which appealed
to my father when it came to choosing a high school for his fey and artistic
16-year-old son. The school was located in one of the drabbest sections of
New York—on West 66th Street between Broadway and Amsterdam Avenue.
It was 1942, and it would take more than 20 years for Lincoln Center to
be built in that location to beautify and gentrify the neighborhood. When
the High School of Commerce, where I suffered a multitude of teenage
woes, was finally razed, a beautiful tower was built to take its place—The
Rose Building—which now houses the School of American Ballet, the school
associated with the New York City Ballet, which would eventually play a
major role in my life.

Although I was miserably unhappy attending the High School of
Commerce, taking business courses I hated, science courses I didn't or
wouldn't understand, and generally detesting most of my teachers, whom
I found uninspired and culturally uninformed, I did have one inner island
of happiness: I met a girl I really liked, Valencia. She was about my age
and attended a high school in Washington Heights. I found her very, very
beautiful except that she was rather bow-legged. Still, she had a way of
standing that quite disguised this fact and she wore longish dresses or
slacks to further hide this unfortunate, small flaw of nature. Valencia had a
lovely smile, with perfect teeth. She had high cheekbones and the greenest
eyes! Her hair was shoulder-length and golden blonde, parted in the middle
and worn upswept or down to her shoulders.

Valencia's family, I soon learned, was among the very few Catholic
families living in this predominantly Jewish neighborhood. The Yanceys
had lived there way before the German-Jewish refugee invasion had taken
place, but were very welcoming to a young refugee boy with a rather thick
and peculiar accent, who liked their daughter. It was all quite innocent, of
course. I barely knew what to do with girls, and because Valencia was quite
witty and intelligent, I was happy just to be her friend. It's true I eyed her
small yet nicely shaped breasts through her dresses, blouses and sweaters,
and imagined stroking them and kissing them…which, after much begging,
I was eventually allowed to do.

Because I had a very small weekly allowance, I could hardly afford to
take Valencia on dates. Still, I found ways of making the most of what I
could afford. I remember one date vividly. My movie-mania being in full

flower, I learned that my all-time favorite movie star, Bette Davis, would be opening in a movie at my all-time favorite New York movie theater—Radio City Music Hall. The movie was *The Little Foxes* and it also starred Herbert Marshall and Teresa Wright. The film was based on a hit play by Lillian Hellman, which on Broadway had starred Tallulah Bankhead as the tempestuous Regina Giddens, the fiery, treacherous member of a corrupt Southern family. I knew Bette Davis, in the Bankhead role, would be twice as tempestuous, fiery, treacherous, and corrupt—and I couldn't wait to see her.

I invited Valencia to see *The Little Foxes* with me on the very day it opened at Radio City Music Hall. "Great!" she said. "At what time will you pick me up?" I said, "At 7:30." She said, "Fine. Maybe you can come by and have some dinner before the movie." I said, "No. I mean 7:30 in the morning." She said, "What?" I said, "We'll have breakfast then get to the movie by 9 a.m., which is when the stage show begins."

The immense (seating capacity 6,000!) and glamorous attraction of Radio City Music Hall during those early years was the sumptuous, elaborate stage shows, which alternated with the feature presentation and which changed with each new movie. These shows included the fabled Rockettes (usually seen in the grand finales of each show) and a majestic organ, which rose up out of the orchestra pit at the beginning of each show, a symphony orchestra, solo singers, comedians, variety acts of every sort, and a bona-fide classical ballet company—perhaps the first legitimate ballet troupe in America—featuring some very talented and beautifully trained dancers in tutus and on pointe, dancing classical ballet. (I was often strangely overcome by the mysterious beauty of this ballet part of the stage show.) But the biggest advantage for me was that if you went to Radio City Music Hall when it opened at nine o'clock in the morning, the admission was only 50 cents! This was a true bargain for over four hours of entertainment. After breakfast, Valencia and I had the best time seeing *The Little Foxes*, with Ms. Davis at her meanest and most acerbic.

During the course of the next two years, I didn't know who I was or where I was or how I was. As with every teenager, confusion reigned. As for my sex life, I was definitely drawn to girls, but didn't really know what to do with them. I felt clumsy, not mindful of their needs—only of mine. I was also drawn to men. Being like me, men were so much easier. After Valencia, who eventually moved out of the city, there were a string of girls I really liked. There was Gloria Alexander, who worked in the garment center on Seventh Avenue. I found her elegant, sophisticated, and fun.

There was Ita Grintuch (my parents' favorite), who worked as a nurse in a Yonkers mental facility. She was tall, regal looking, ample-bosomed, with a heart-shaped face of considerable beauty. Her ambition was to be a deeply committed and loyal Jewish housewife. What proved insurmountable for me was her living and working in Yonkers, which was miles and miles away from Manhattan. While we were dating, she was willing to meet me downtown—at a movie, a restaurant, or even at my house. But after each of our Manhattan dates, she insisted on being taken back to Yonkers, where she shared an apartment with two other nurses. I hated the endless subway ride to Yonkers with a passion, hated the trip back to Manhattan, hated the thought of having to do this again and again. I finally told Ita that Yonkers stood in our way—that I was going bonkers taking her back to Yonkers. She was stunned, and considered this a very flimsy excuse for our breaking up. My parents were even more upset—they thought I made the mistake of my life. But break it off I did and it was a huge relief.

Other girlfriends—all Europeans, all Jewish—included Hannah Loewenstein, Eva Schoenberger, and Hilde May. Hilde May, who lived in Washington Heights, wanted to become an opera singer. She had a very loud, though musical, soprano voice and the look of a diva. I really loved Hilde, but not in any romantic way. She was quite a bit older than I and, while quite lovely and feminine, never made my heart beat faster...still, we remained good friends for many years.

As for my interest in men, it developed more gradually. To me, men always seemed far less complicated than women. Especially American men. There was an essential innocence about them that always appealed to me. And an awkwardness acquired through that stifling America impera-tive of having to be a "man" or else, and having to prove themselves as the "stronger" or the "provider" or the "doer" or the "instigator" or the "aggres-sor." Somehow, American men bore these cumbersome attributes with a certain compelling poignancy—a kind of tentative pride that often filled me with compassion and adoration. And, of course, a man's sexual anatomy wasn't as complicated or mysterious as a woman's. He had a penis, it was up front, and that was that. Women had vulvas and labia and clitorises and breasts and nipples and special erotic spots, and they liked things slow, all of which confounded me and made my love-making, such as it was, anx-ious and clumsy. Strangely enough, I always felt that too much knowledge of the female anatomy would deaden my desire. I liked the mystery of it all, even as it confused me and rendered me fairly incompetent.

My sexual exploration notwithstanding, my teenage turmoil centered far more on what I was going to do with my brand new life in America. Would I finally master the English language? Would I ever lose my peculiar accent? Would I ever get away from my parents? Turning 17 on September 12 of 1943 in Manhattan in New York City in the United States of America was to experience a whirlwind of emotions, all of them conflicted: depression, hope, confusion, fear, elation and excitement. I was a boy/man in a new land still fully engaged in a war with my past homelands, in a country I hardly knew or understood, a country that nevertheless took me in but seemed to demand, "Well, then…now that you're here, what are you going to do about it?"

Chapter 7

When I graduated from the High School of Commerce in 1943, no "business" bells went off in either my mind or heart. My father naturally thought I would now find a well-paying job and become a serious young businessman. What kind of business, neither of us knew. Once again, I let my father down. Instead of finding a job, I decided to apply for entry into The City College of New York (CCNY). I knew that going to college would liberate me from the tyranny of business courses and finally put me in touch with things I longed to pursue: music, drama, literature, art, languages. My high school grades were just good enough to get me accepted, and I rushed to CCNY on Convent Avenue to enroll. On hearing what I had done, my father had one of his famous fits of fury. He was utterly opposed to my going to college, considering further education a complete waste of time. I told him I'd get an even better job if I went to college. That's how it was in America. But he yelled and carried on and finally told me I would regret my decision, because in America you had to earn money. You had to go out and get a job and support yourself. He said that it was time for me to become independent. What he meant was that he no longer intended to support me.

Although my mother sided with my father on almost everything, this time she persuaded him to let me be. I was the only son still at home, and she wanted me around, especially since he was away so much of the time, selling his shirts and ties. This was something of a relief. I could continue living at home. I would continue to get a small allowance and I could attend college—a dream come true.

Several months passed, then my father announced that he was through being a traveling salesman. He had made the decision to find his way back into the jewelry business. He had met some jewelers who worked in New York's jewelry district on West 47th Street, and they helped him to get started in one of the jewelry exchanges that dotted the block. In a matter of weeks, my father was back in the world he had known as a youngster, back in Cairo, Paris, and Berlin. It wasn't the world of Cartier, but it was a world that my father, enterprising as ever, would succeed in for the rest of his days. It all began on a very small scale—soldering and repairing rings or selling watchbands, or inexpensive chains, necklaces, bracelets, and earrings. Eventually these would be replaced by more and more expensive items until finally, my father could boast whole showcases of diamond rings and diamond watches in platinum settings that were dazzling but alas, quite often in rather poor taste.

Once again, my father had come to a foreign land to make battle with a new and daunting set of circumstances. It would take him just over five years to establish a comfortable home in New York, to speak adequate English, to bring his three sons over from war-torn Europe and Shanghai, and to forge a successful jewelry business that would see him and my mother financially solvent for many years to come.

As for me, being a college student was an exciting new adventure. I loved the Gothic-style buildings of the CCNY campus and I loved my courses—English and French literature, music history, German, and poetry, among others. I began to meet other students and began to make friends. I even joined the glee club and made a small name for myself by founding the City College Music Club, which would meet to listen to recordings of all the great composers. I programmed discussions of piano music, of vocal music, of chamber music. I asked our music history teacher to come lecture, and our glee club conductor to talk about choral music. It was all very fulfilling and fun.

At this time, a major event would touch my life and the life of my parents. We became American citizens. It was 1944. We had now lived in America for five years. My parents somewhat half-heartedly applied themselves to the study of American history. Because I was still a minor, I would receive my citizenship through my parents. And on the appointed day, we all went to a courthouse in lower Manhattan to be asked questions about the Constitution, the American system of government, and the names of various presidents. Then the solemn moment arrived. We were asked to pledge allegiance to the American flag and on that day, August 29, we were duly sworn in as citizens of the United States. It was one of the very few times my father seemed to beam all day long.

It never occurred to me that having become an American citizen, and about to turn 18, I might now be eligible to be drafted into the

United States Army. The United States was, after all, still at war. I frankly thought that the U.S. Army would certainly not be interested in a pimply-faced teenage refugee boy, who still had trouble with the English language, and whose head was decidedly in the clouds. I was wrong. A few weeks after my 18th birthday, Uncle Sam advised me by letter that he desperately needed me to report to my local draft board, where I would be given a thorough physical, asked a few questions ("Do you like girls?"), and promptly shipped off to a place called Fort Dix, New Jersey, where I would be inducted and begin my basic training. It all happened so quickly that I had no time to even think that after my basic training, I might very well be shipped off to war and get killed. My only comfort was that for the first time in my life, I would be on my own—would no longer have to live with my parents in depressing Washington Heights, would be out of the dreaded clutches of my father, and would, at long last, be a free agent without responsibilities, except of course the responsibility of becoming that totally alien and unexpected new being—an American GI.

A certified American, khaki-clad GI I became, but not overnight, not even after months of training. But once inducted at Fort Dix, I was shipped off to Camp Blanding, near Jacksonville, Florida, for final combat training where I slowly encountered the person I had no idea dwelled within me. He was a quite rigorously disciplined young man, fully attentive to the drills of his sergeants and the commands of his officers. What is more, so focused was he on the workings of his rifle and on his firing exercises that the novice GI soon received a medal for sharpshooting from his company commander, and garnered the puzzled admiration of his army buddies. To top it all off, this young soldier became absurdly healthy, stood as straight as a rod, sporting a Florida suntan of very manly elegance.

Still, my time at Camp Blanding, in the American South, exposed my absolute ignorance of certain aspects of American history—the Civil War, for example. I had no idea why fellow soldiers kept addressing me as a "damned Yankee" or generally cursing me for being from the North. It all had to be explained to me. Then I remembered *Gone with the Wind*, and it all came back to me. But surely, that war was over ages ago. Not at Camp Blanding it wasn't. At Camp Blanding, most of my fellow GIs still seemed to be fighting the Civil War, and during combat training you needed to watch your back if you were from New York or any points due north. "Friendly fire" was a frightening reality at Camp Blanding.

Another vivid reality for me was the abundant presence of black soldiers in our camp. In those days they were called Negroes and I must confess to being quite intimidated by them. When I was growing up in Italy, there were no black people to speak of. Indeed the first time I ever saw a black person in Italy was in the newsreels during the 1930s, when Italy was at war with Africa. They were fighting Abyssinia and Eritrea, as Il Duce sought to overthrow the African emperor Haile Selassie. There were also some fabulously talented Negroes in Shirley Temple films, which I adored as a child in Italy. Then of course, I noticed many black people in New York when we first landed in America. But at Camp Blanding, blacks seemed to dominate the number of soldiers in every unit.

I may have gone through the right soldierly paces at Camp Blanding, and I might have won a sharpshooting medal, and I tried desperately to fit in, but the fact of the matter was that as a soldier, I was almost instantly labeled an outsider, or to put it more colorfully, was deemed a "faggot frog," a "queer French ass-licker," a "Yankee cocksucker," and the like. It was amazing to me that the military environment, at least as I experienced it, seemed obsessed with the language of homosexuality. The references to queer men were continuous and all-pervasive, and to my further astonishment, queer hanky panky was decidedly present and perpetrated. It was done on the sly, to be sure, but with astonishing regularity and by a large number of soldiers and officers. It was in the army that I was most often propositioned, and from some very surprising quarters.

And so my life at Camp Blanding was, to say the least, eye-opening. It was fraught with hard work, confusion, exhilaration, self-doubt, and a newfound self-awareness. Still, along with considerable stress, army life afforded me a certain genuine sense of happiness. I felt the pride of self-reliance, the joys of accomplishment, and my English, though still heavily accented, was improving! Months passed. Most of us were certain to be shipped overseas, either to Japan or to Europe. And quite a number of us were, in fact, sent abroad for active duty.

In the meantime we were all aware that Camp Blanding was also receiving trainloads of POWs, prisoners of war, from Europe. They came mainly from Germany and Italy, and they were housed in barracks some distance from where we were quartered. We could watch them doing morning calisthenics and other army exercises. It was strange observing these refugees–captives really–now living in America. I felt oddly at one with them–felt like visiting them, talking to them, hearing them speak their German and Italian. But we soldiers were admonished to have nothing to do with the POWs.

One morning, the commander of our unit called me into his office. He informed me that because my record indicated I had been raised in Europe and could speak French, German, and Italian, he wanted to enlist my services as both an interpreter and a censor for the POWs at the camp. I would in fact be doing "intelligence" work, and would be in charge of reading every letter sent by the prisoners to their families abroad. My job would be to cross out all reference to where we were stationed, what they observed at the camp or anything to do with U.S. troupe movements, etc. If there were any letters of a dangerously sub-versive nature, I was to inform my superiors. Needless to say, I was both overwhelmed and proud to be given this hugely responsible job. While I was still obliged to participate in basic training, some of it would be curtailed to allow me to work in the camp's military offices.

I was provided with a desk, a telephone, many black markers, and much scrap paper. In time, I was brought to the POW encamp-ment where I was introduced as a "liaison" soldier. I exchanged a few words in German or Italian with a dozen or so of the prisoners. It felt oddly familiar, and the men seemed positively elated to meet someone who could speak their language. Almost all of them seemed thrilled to be in America–away from the terrors of combat and hostility. Here they were among the sheltering palms and colorful skies of Florida, where every day was another warm, sunshine-filled day of safety. No one complained. As for their letters, they were far from incendiary or subversive. The Italian men wrote mostly to their "Mammas," telling them about the strange new foods they were consuming–particularly some weird things called "hamburgers" and some awful stuff called "grits." They wrote that they were safe and sound and treated well. In some letters there were some inadvertent references to location, which I promptly blacked out, and a few allusions to American army train-ing methods, which I also blacked out. But for the most part, the let-ters were utterly harmless and were promptly sent off to their various European destinations.

By 1945, many in my unit had been shipped overseas. There were fewer and fewer of us in my barrack. I assumed that because of my work with the POWs, I was spared being sent abroad. Still, I was amazed that given my language skills, I was not sent to Germany or Italy. And then it happened. All units still remaining at Camp Blanding were ordered to "fall in" in the large clearing near our barracks. When the sergeant called "At ease!" an announcement came over the loudspeakers. "Hostilities have ceased in Europe. The war in Europe is over." At first there was silence. Then all hell broke loose as the men cheered and shouted and hugged one another.

Upon being honorably discharged from the U.S. Army, my heart sank. The thought of returning to live with my parents in Washington Heights filled me with dismay and despair. But having no money to speak of (the army had mustered me out with about $100), I was obliged to return to my dreary, small room where I would have to put up with my increasingly cantankerous father and depressingly passive mother. The chief reason for my father's cantankerousness was that after all the trouble and pains he had taken to bring my three brothers to America and to New York, not one of them had the will or the desire to deal with his bad temper or aggressive ways. My father made some attempts to bring all of my brothers into his jewelry business, but only my brother Leo, the eldest, had any real interest in it. Indeed, Leo made some progress in setting himself up as an independent jeweler—also on 47th Street—until the day it was discovered that certain crooked business dealings would force him to quit the profession under an alarmingly dark cloud.

Finally, brothers Leo, Tino, and Carlo all moved out of the city, far, far away from my parents. My father felt hugely angry and mortified at this turn of events, feeling both abandoned and betrayed. His three grown sons, the boys he had prayed day and night might come to America and work side by side with him, the sons he wanted reunited as a family, chose instead to fend for themselves. They refused my father's help and advice, removed themselves from his presence—a presence they decided was intolerable after all they had been through.

Clearly I, too, needed to get away from my father, from my misery and from New York. Still, I loved New York City madly and I came to love it as no other city in the world. Walking down Fifth Avenue was one of the biggest thrills of my life. Looking up and seeing the Empire

State Building, or the Chrysler Building, or Rockefeller Center–it was all so Gershwin, so jazzy, so showbiz, so piano-runs, so xylophone, so low-down trumpets. And I loved the glamour of the city. The gorgeousness of the store windows, the swank people and Central Park! So glorious! I loved the city so much that I wanted to devour it. I hated the thought of leaving it. But leave it I had to. Luckily I had an out, the GI Bill of Rights, which enabled anyone who had been drafted and honorably discharged to attend the college or university of his choice. One applied and if accepted, the government would pay your tuition and, where applicable, send you a small stipend to live on. Your GI Bill would stay in effect for as long as you had served in the armed forces. I had not even served a full year before being discharged, but even several months of the GI Bill was better than nothing. Of course I could have continued to go to City College but that would have meant staying in New York and living with my parents. I really didn't want to do that. I desperately needed to get away.

I consulted Peter, an American friend, who understood my dilemma. "Look," he said, "you need to see the real America. New York is not the real America." I said, "Where is the real America?" He removed a large atlas from a bookcase, laid it on a table and said, "Close your eyes." I heard him turning the pages. "Don't look," Peter said. "Now give me your index finger." This I did. He placed it on a spot on the page. "OK, now open your eyes." I looked down. "This is America," he said. He had placed my finger on the state that, to me, looked like it was pronounced "EE-O-VA." "It's pronounced, IOWA, not EEOVA!" said Peter. "And it's located in the Middle West. In the middle of America. Now that's America!" "But are there universities in the Middle West?" I asked. "Of course there are, you idiot!" said Peter.

I lost no time in applying to the University of Iowa in Iowa City, and in a matter of weeks, and to my absolute joy and delight, I was accepted as a freshman for study under the GI Bill. It has to be understood that my choice of the University of Iowa was predicated solely on the advice of my friend Peter and because I was desperate to get away from my parents. It was only many months later that I realized I could have applied to far more illustrious colleges or universities. Mind you, there was nothing wrong with going to Iowa, but I was utterly ignorant of the cachet of Ivy League colleges and universities. I had no idea I could just as easily have applied to Harvard, Yale, Princeton, Stanford, Brown, or even New York's Columbia University. It just never occurred to me that these places were very distinguished temples of education and that by attending them I could have gotten myself some very fancy pedigrees, let alone college degrees of real clout. But in the five or six years I had lived in America, no one had ever said a word to me about Ivy League schools. And, ignorant fool that I was, I never asked.

Chapter 8

And so it was, that on a terribly cold day in February 1945, I announced to my father that I was leaving New York to attend the University of Iowa. Once again, he was furious and picked up one of the three books in our apartment and flung it violently at me. His tirade centered on how I owed my life to him, what an ungrateful wretch of a son I was, and how my place was with him at the Jewelry Exchange. It was a tirade I would not soon forget. When it was over, I told my mother that I was taking the Greyhound bus to Iowa City in the morning. She of course sided with my father, and said that I was the only son left to help him in his business, and that for everyone's sake I should not leave.

On the next morning, with a single suitcase in hand, I took the subway to the Greyhound bus terminal on 42nd Street, and bought a one-way ticket to Iowa City, Iowa. Before leaving the apartment, I kissed my mother goodbye but did not say goodbye to my father. Indeed, he and I would not speak for the next two years. The bus would be leaving mid-afternoon and would arrive in Iowa City the following morning.

I don't believe I have ever experienced the kind of cold weather that greeted me when the bus pulled into Iowa City. It was a February morning and to be sure, it must have been 15 below zero. It had also been in February that we first landed in the United States. It was cold then too, but nothing like this! I stood there with my suitcase, bewildered. Finally I found a luncheonette, had some coffee to warm me up, and asked where the administration building might be. It sounded like a very long walk, but I found it and, half-frozen, made an inquiry about a place to live. I knew I didn't want to live in a campus dormitory–too impersonal. And so, I was given the addresses of several rooming houses and was told that I would have to present myself in person.

My very first encounter with Midwestern hospitality was a shock. The landlady heard my pronounced European accent and said that they did not take in foreign students, just Americans. I told her that I was an American citizen and had served in the U.S. Army. "Don't matter," she said, and quickly closed the door. The second landlady was friendlier, but after a brief chat said the room had already been taken. Then I met the third landlady and she seemed positively charmed by my accent. "Where are you from, dear?" she asked smiling. "Italy by way of New York," I replied. "Come aright in! I'm Rosa Bellocchio! My folks came over from Sicily!"

So I found my first lodgings at the University of Iowa, a large, sunny room with, as it turned out, a built-in roommate—one Frank Casa. He was a short, black-haired, bright-eyed young man of Italian extraction, who also attended the university. I learned that Frank was an art major studying to become a painter. I would be sharing the rent with him, and he would become my first university chum.

I then met the university counselor, and we laid out my course of study. Although prior to the army I had taken courses at CCNY for nearly one year, I felt that I should start out fresh. I was very anxious to start speaking English without the accent, which had been a constant source of embarrassment to me. But the university did not offer any lose-your-accent courses. The counselor suggested classes in English literature. He also thought that some acting classes might help with my accent, and said that the university had a particularly fine drama department located across the river that was headed by Professor Edward Maybe. I instantly loved his questioning name. I was also urged to try out for the recently established Writer's Workshop, which was then headed by the American poet Paul Engle. The workshop is today renowned for nurturing and producing some of the best young writers in the country. There were hundreds of other courses I could take—my head was spinning.

The University of Iowa was huge, boasting some 10,000 students, including many exchange students from all parts of the world. The campus, with solid old buildings and tree-lined walks, was bisected by the Iowa River, a sizeable waterway that lent a certain romantic aura to university life. There was a huge Student Union where one could go for study periods or get-togethers, lectures, and concerts. Comfortable and handsomely decorated, the Union also contained a music room where one could listen to classical recordings for hours on end. A very fine concert-grand piano stood near one of the Union's stately French windows.

As a liberal arts student, I naturally veered toward all the "artistic" courses available. I lost little time enrolling in English and American Literature and eventually, after submitting some poems and a story, was admitted into the prestigious Writer's Workshop. In addition, I crossed the

Iowa River Bridge to explore the very handsome University Theater where the drama department was situated and where courses were taught in acting, playwriting, stage design, lighting, costume design, and all subjects relating to the professional stage.

When I was given an appointment at the theater to talk with Professor Maybe, I began spouting off about my great love of acting and how I wanted to take lots and lots of acting courses and hopefully become a great star of the American stage. He heard my rather absurd accent. He was most amused and in a very kindly way asked what I was going to do about it. He felt my accent might prove an impediment to my acting ambitions. I told him that I would do everything in my power to get rid of it. I also pointed out that if I were not successful at getting rid of it, I would nevertheless pursue an acting career—perhaps in the movies. After all, Paul Henreid (who costarred with Bette Davis in *Now, Voyager* and with Ingrid Bergman in *Casablanca* and whom I slightly resembled) had quite a pronounced accent. He was, accent and all, quite successful. I also cited Greta Garbo, Marlene Dietrich, and Hedy Lamarr as having accents and yet succeeding in films. And of course there was Peter Lorre.

Professor Maybe, a rotund man and a chain smoker, chuckled à la Sidney Greenstreet in *The Maltese Falcon* and said, "You're in luck! It so happens that we've just brought over from England the very distinguished stage director, B. Iden Payne. He will be giving courses in Shakespeare and will be staging several Shakespeare plays. I think it would be good for you to work with him."

Not only did I work with B. Iden Payne on Shakespeare's great dramatic works in the classroom—one of the most moving and thrilling experiences of my life—but Payne cast me, accent and all, and at age 19, in two of Shakespeare's greatest plays: *Julius Caesar* and *Twelfth Night.* In *Julius Caesar* I played Cinna the poet, a small but seminal part. In *Twelfth Night,* I was cast as Malvolio, one of the leading roles. When I suggested to Mr. Payne that his production of *Julius Caesar* could stand some background music, he readily appointed me "musical consultant" to the production. For the play, I chose some atmospheric passages from Shostakovich's *Symphony No. 1,* which Payne thought worked just beautifully.

As for my acting potential, it clearly needed time to develop. I performed my two Shakespearean roles with considerable skill and bravado—and I loved being on stage. The accent did not disappear, although speaking Shakespeare's words as spoken and pronounced by the British B. Iden

Payne helped immeasurably. My speech was slowly veering toward a more British inflection and in the following months, I tried to view as many films as possible starring my favorite mentor of the screen, Laurence Olivier. His speaking voice struck me as being the epitome of British purity and sophistication. It took quite a bit of time, but eventually I positively oozed elocutionary refinement. My English was now so over-the-top British that even I thought every word out of my mouth sounded utterly phony. But this affectation was still very much in the future. For the moment I continued to speak like a German/Italian refugee.

When B. Iden Payne moved to a new post in Austin, Texas (where he died in 1976), the University of Iowa lost a wonderful teacher and an inspired advocate of drama. Somehow I do not wish to recall the name of the woman who replaced him, for she made my life in the drama department a total misery. She simply did not take to me, thought I had no acting talent whatever and to prove it, cast me, accent and all, in a totally inappropriate role–GI Joe in Booth Tarkington's play *Seventeen*. Even as I protested that the role would prove an embarrassment to us all, she insisted that I play the part and said with a sneer, "If you want to be an actor, you've got to be able to play any role that's handed to you."

When the play opened, I fell right on my face. Though I tried hard, I was practically laughed off the stage. I recalled my singing debut at age 15 during the amateur contest at the Audubon Theater in Washington Heights. I remember giving my tremulous, high-pitched rendition of "Deep Purple," and hearing three people in the audience, including my mother, clapping. Suffice it to say that my acting career began and ended with my three performances at the University Theater in Iowa City. Two of them were quite good, the last a disaster. Perhaps I shouldn't have given it up. Perhaps I should have stuck with it, perhaps it might even have worked out had I landed in Hollywood. I just knew in my heart of hearts that if Paul Henreid could do it, so could I!

I did not look back, but enthusiastically threw myself into the Writer's Workshop and wrote all manner of stories and poems, which, while pretty weird, seemed incredibly original to me. However, when Professor Paul Engle took me aside and said, "John, your stuff feels as though it were written underwater with an underwater pen. Are you sure you want to do this?" my heart sank. Paul Engle felt that most of my work was too heavily larded with surrealistic overtones that transformed the imagery of my poems into pretentious drivel. As I did not yet have a firm grip on the English language,

I overcompensated by turning everything I wrote into aqueous fantasies as self-conscious as they were ludicrous. Of course at age 19, failure and defeat are not easily accepted. I quit the Writer's Workshop certain in the knowledge that one day, when I achieved great fame as a writer, my name would haunt Paul Engle.

I next plunged into nineteenth- and twentieth-century English and American literature. I read endless books. Reading had always been a passion of mine. When I discovered Henry James I was enthralled. This author's way with the English language was so phenomenal that I thought I would never have to read another work of fiction, so magnificently wrought were his novels and stories. Not only were James' sentences endless and convoluted, but they contained the essence of emotional drama and psychological insight. The more I read James, the more enamored I became of English as a language. I decided I would make it my business to read all of James; at least all the novels and stories. And so I did, including *The Princess Casamassima, The Wings of the Dove*, and *The Golden Bowl*, my three favorites.

I read and read. Once I got to Hemingway and F. Scott Fitzgerald, let alone Henry Miller and Gertrude Stein, I felt I was getting a really first-rate education in literature. I thought that becoming a writer was still an option. I told my supervisor that I would do my BA in English. He said that would be fine as long as I kept up my other grades.

During the time I was a drama student, I would have to cross the bridge over the Iowa River to reach the drama department. On frequent occasions I would make this trek with my roommate Frank Casa, on his way to the art department. As it happened, an extremely striking young woman often crossed the bridge walking towards us on her way back to town. I noticed her right away and as she nodded to Frank Casa in greeting, I asked him who this was. "Oh that's Jane Wilson," he said. "She's a student in my drawing class." When I saw Jane Wilson crossing the bridge several more times, I asked Frank if he would introduce us. "What would be the point?" he said. "She's going out with the head of the art department."

"Well I could at least meet her," I returned.

"Look, if you're thinking of dating her, forget it," said Frank. "She's definitely taken."

I could not get Jane Wilson out of my mind. Every time I saw her, the more she resembled my two favorite film stars: Gene Tierney and Dolores del Rio, with their high cheekbones and elegant figures. There was an air about Jane that intrigued me. She looked so European...so quietly glamorous! I absolutely had to meet her! But in the 1940s you didn't just walk up to a girl and ask her out on a date. That's not the way it worked.

One day Frank Casa and I decided to attend a screening of a French film held in the chemistry auditorium. The film was Marcel Pagnol's *La Femme du Boulanger*, starring the great French actor Raimu. Frank and I found seats and before the lights went down, I suddenly saw Jane Wilson enter the auditorium. I nudged Frank. "Look, there's Jane Wilson! She's by herself! Please Frank, introduce us!" He refused. Without a moment's hesitation I jumped out of my seat and before Jane could get seated I rushed up to her and said, "My name is John Gruen. Will you have dinner with me tomorrow night?" Jane Wilson was so startled that she blurted out, "Yes, alright." I took her address and said I'd pick her up at seven the next evening. I floated back to my seat next to Frank: "Jane Wilson agreed to have dinner with me tomorrow night," I whispered as the lights went down. "Well, what do you know!" said Frank.

Jane Wilson and I dined at the Huddle, one of Iowa City's most popular restaurants. Of course I did most of the talking, but I did ask a lot of questions. I needed to learn everything about this ravishing girl. Rather than being European as I had imagined, I learned that she was Iowan through and through. She had been born on a farm in Seymour, Iowa. Her father, Wayne, had started out by running a farm, then went to college to become a civil engineer. Her mother Cleone Marquis was a published poet and novelist. Jane had a younger sister named Ann. The family moved frequently, from Seymour to Pella to Leighton to University Park to Oskaloosa, and finally to Iowa City. Her parents had recently divorced and she was now living with her mother and sister in an apartment in Iowa City. All three Wilson women were attending the university, Jane having received her BA in painting and now working toward a master's, her mother working toward a master's degree in political science, and Ann, two years Jane's junior, majoring in French.

As she quietly and often wittily answered my questions, I looked at Jane. She was a girl not given to dramatizing herself. There was a directness and warmth about her that positively enchanted me. Of course I needed desperately to know about her relationship with the formidable Dr. Lester D. Longman, head of the art department. "What relationship?" asked Jane. I told her that Frank Casa claimed she was dating him. "Absolutely not! What gave him that idea?" "Frank said you were 'taken,'" I told her. "That's complete and utter nonsense," she said. "I like Dr. Longman. We get along. But there's no romance, I assure you. The man is married. He has children." And there again was that wonderful Jane Wilson smile.

Of course I never shied away from dramatizing myself and so, upon hearing that Jane was not, as Frank put it, "taken," I proceeded to enthusiastically describe my European background, my years in France, Germany, Italy, and New York. I made it all sound quite sophisticated, debonair, and "grown-up." Although I was careful to omit one fact: that I was Jewish. I felt that so beautiful a girl as Jane Wilson, so profoundly Midwestern, born on a farm, and the product of a deeply Anglo-Saxon culture, might harbor some anti-Semitic feelings. I did not wish to squelch our romantic relationship before it even began. My strategy was to first win her heart, then drop the bomb about being Jewish.

Our first date ended with Jane announcing that Dr. Longman, my recent rival, had offered her a teaching assistantship for the coming semester. She would be teaching four courses in the Art History Department: A General Survey of Art History, Italian Renaissance Art, Ancient Art, and Oriental Art. Because of this heavy workload, Jane hinted that there would not be much time for dating. My heart sank.

I took the hint but paid no attention. I went to my supervisor and told him that I had decided to take my master's degree in art history. I was about to receive my bachelor of arts in English (it would soon be 1947), and I was ready to embark on a brand new course of study. The real truth of the matter was that I wanted to enroll in all of Jane Wilson's courses and see as much of her as I possibly could. As I told Frank again and again, "This woman shall be mine!"

Not only did I enroll in Jane's classes, but to my total surprise, I actually fell in love with art history—most likely because I had also fallen in love with Jane Wilson. Sitting in darkened rooms, looking at endless slides, listening to the myriad stories of art and artists filled me with astonishing happiness. The more I learned, the more I wanted to know. I often recalled my young life in Milan and Venice when I actually stood before the very masterpieces Jane and the other teachers were flashing on the screen. And after all, was I not also responsible for the partial destruction of Leonardo da Vinci's "The Last Supper"? Clearly, art history was in my blood.

My courses with Jane Wilson went swimmingly. I even garnered straight A's on my tests and papers. As for dating, we did manage the occasional dinner and, to my great joy, Jane finally invited me home to meet her mother and sister. As I saw them together I realized that each one had clearly cornered the market on beauty. When I was shown a photograph of Dad–Wayne Wilson himself–I further understood where Jane's exotic appearance came from. Wayne was the proverbial 1920s dreamboat, especially in his World War I uniform. For her part, Cleone had beautiful, deep-set blue eyes, a wonderfully shaped nose and chin–a poignant turn-of-the-century face. Ann, the 18-year-old, was the physical opposite of Jane. She was very blond, very blue-eyed, very pink-cheeked, and possessed of great humor and the most giggly laugh in the world.

Of course a small cloud would appear just as my romance started. It was pointed out to me by the ever more envious Frank that the university had a rule forbidding students to be romantically involved with teachers. This, it seemed, was a definite no-no, which might get Jane fired and me expelled. My response to this dire possibility was Scarlett O'Hara's favorite retort: "Fiddle dee dee!" In fact, I told Jane how romantic it would be to meet in secret–at the local graveyard, at out-of-town restaurants, or in bars, or for late night trysts in my room.

Jane said, "We'd better cool it for a while."

I said, "No, my darling. I want the world to know I'm dating you!"

At first we were cautious, but little by little we brazenly appeared everywhere together. We were seen dancing at the local clubs, dining at the local restaurants, and appearing at concerts and lectures at the Student Union. No one complained and no one stopped us. It would seem that because Jane was also a student, and was still taking classes in painting and art history, the student-teacher rule did not really apply to us. But it was fun to play the "secret romance" game while it lasted.

In the mid 1940s, the University of Iowa art department boasted some extraordinary teachers in both its studio and art history courses. Jane's primary painting teacher was James Lechay, a distinguished New York artist noted for his semi-abstract still lifes, figures, and landscapes. She also worked with Mauricio Lasansky, the eminent Argentinean printmaker, and took classes with Umberto Albrizio. Art history classes were given by, among others, Dr. William Heckscher, Lester D. Longman, and, most notably, Mary Holmes–whose brilliant lectures and dynamic personality could literally turn one's life around.

Just past middle age, volatile and glamorous, Mary Holmes offered a vision of art history steeped in life and humanity. Jane and I were riveted by her lectures on the Italian and Northern Renaissance painters, and on the Dutch and Flemish masters. In particular I recall her stunning slide lectures on Rembrandt's self-portraits, painted from youth to old age. These lectures alone proved unforgettable lessons in psychological insight and were deeply moving.

My supervisor in art history was Dr. William Heckscher, a protégé of the great art historian, Irwin Panofsky, whose courses in Renaissance and Medieval art were steeped in iconography and symbolism. I was struck by the more lurid masterworks I encountered, particularly the horror-filled paintings by Hieronymus Bosch. Most of all, however, I was deeply moved by the work of Matthias Grünewald, and thought his Isenheim Altarpiece was probably the greatest work of art I had yet encountered. I was so affected by his rendering of the Crucifixion and its accompanying panels that I thought of making Grünewald the subject of my master's thesis. When many months later I presented this idea to Dr. Heckscher, he instantly nixed it.

"No, no," he said, "not Grünewald. You're a Rubens man. You belong in the Baroque. Grünewald has been done to death."

"The Baroque? Rubens? But I'm not interested in the Baroque. I'm not interested in Rubens and his monstrous women."

"You won't have to write about his work," Dr. Heckscher said. "I have an idea for you that no one has tackled before. You'll write your thesis on Rubens' own collection of Greek and Roman sculpture–his antiquities, for which he built his own museum right on his property in Antwerp! All his work was inspired by antiquity–it's a great subject."

I hated every minute of it, but my master's degree did indeed center on Rubens and his collection of Greek and Roman sculpture. Its title was *Peter Paul Rubens: Collector and Antiquarian*, and it proved so thoroughly researched, illustrated, and well written that Dr. Heckscher arranged for me to receive a scholarship to New York University's Institute of Fine Arts for PhD study. I simply couldn't believe it!

But all that happened much later. What happened much sooner–on March 28, 1948, to be exact–was the major event of my young life at the University of Iowa, namely, my marriage to Jane Wilson.

Chapter 9

On our wedding day, slated to be the happiest day of my life, Jane fainted dead away as she walked with me down the aisle of the Congregational Church in Oskaloosa, Iowa.

It was Easter Sunday, March 28, 1948. My bride-to-be, looking radiant in her white wedding suit trimmed with silver fox around the bell sleeves, suddenly passed out and dropped to the floor as we approached the altar. The organist stopped her selection from Humperdinck's *Hänsel and Gretel.* The preacher, standing ready to marry us, knelt down by Jane's side. Jane's mother instantly rushed over. We all tried to revive Jane. In a moment, Jane opened her eyes.

"What happened, darling?" I said.

"I don't know," she answered.

"Don't you want to marry me?"

"I don't know. I don't know."

We all helped Jane up. She insisted she was okay. The preacher now thought it might be a good idea for Jane and I to have a talk in his private office—just the two of us.

"Don't you want to marry me, Jane?" I repeated.

"Yes, I do want to marry you. But maybe we should wait a while."

"Wait for what, Jane?"

"I don't know. Just wait, I guess…"

"Either we marry or we don't marry," I said.

I do want to marry you, John."

"Well then, let's get married. Let's get married now."

Jane fell silent. Minutes passed. She looked at me. "Alright, John… Alright."

At around noon on that Easter Sunday in March, with the church redolent of Easter lilies, and the organist resuming her selection from *Hänsel and Gretel,* with Jane's mother, sister, and our college friend Eva Schlein all present, Jane and I stood at the altar, as the preacher bade us exchange vows, exchange rings, and, at last, pronounced us man and wife. "You may now kiss the bride," said the preacher. Jane, with her beautiful smile, turned and looked at me. I kissed her most tenderly.

My brand-new mother-in-law had arranged a very fine luncheon at Oskaloosa's best hotel. A good time was had by all. But in truth, my wedding day left me enormously shaken. The dramatic incident in the aisle, the wedding ceremony, the luncheon, and the return trip to Iowa City finally became something of a blurred and distressing memory. In fact there were excellent reasons for Jane's sudden blackout. And there were very good reasons for my own distress.

When you meet the woman of your dreams at 19, as I did, you are at once the dreamer and the dream. Reality is at best your daily existence—your classes, your studies, your grades, your teachers, your appearance, your lack of cash—in short, your daily chores and problems. Dreamland consists of the heady days of being in love—of being in a state of "otherness," swept along by feelings so strangely private, so personal, so uniquely your own, that their onslaught leaves you giddy with exhilaration and apprehension. Being with Jane, seeing Jane, thinking about Jane, fantasizing about Jane drove me a little crazy. Nearly two years of wooing her turned me into an obsessive young man, whose need to sway and influence her in all sorts of ways came close to being compulsive.

To begin with, there was Jane's quite extraordinary physical beauty. It just never failed to fill me with pride. With my long established penchant for movie-star gorgeousness, it seemed incredible to me that I should "possess" so ravishing a creature as Jane. She quite simply had that unmistakable look of American drop-dead glamour, and I responded to it with a passion that went way over the top.

Of course, I needed to embellish that glamour. Jane's tolerance of my shenanigans vis-a-vis her looks was remarkable, as she allowed me to alter everything from her clothes to her makeup to her hairstyle (at the time, I favored "buns" over the ears à la Anna May Wong or hair parted in the middle à la Hedy Lamarr or piled-on-top à la Gene Tierney). Long earrings were de rigueur at all times. I was always quick to suggest what she should wear when we went out (Jane had a limited wardrobe, but she did wonders with the little she had). One memorable evening I suggested she wear not one, but two dresses, one on top of the other, because the combination seemed to me both unusual and elegant. At other times, I insisted on wide black chokers to gird her lovely neck. Being partial to hats with dark veils, Jane obliged me by very occasionally wearing hats with veils that mysteriously shrouded her face.

In the great 1930s film, *Shanghai Express*, Marlene Dietrich uttered the immortal words, "It took many men before they called me Shanghai Lily!" In our case, it took many weird outfits, on both our parts (I loved wearing ties over turtlenecks) before the university called us "that screwball couple." Making an impression, even an outlandish one, never bothered me. Besides, what Jane and I wore wasn't really all that freakish or bizarre, just couture-ishly extravagant. So part of my love for Jane was trying to change her exterior–that is, to conform, to some vague Hollywood dream of mine, a dream that would one day lead us both to heavenly stardom of one kind or another. But this dressing up and showing off and trying to be outré was in reality a very small part of my involvement with Jane.

Because Jane, in her wise and charming way (she was, after all, an older woman of 21 going on 22) was, in fact, quietly instructing me on how to become a more thoughtful, less frantic person–from within, that is. Outwardly, I was still very much all over the place. I mean, I had pretty much roller-coasted my way through my university studies from wanting to be an actor, a film star, a writer, a literature major, and, finally, an art historian. As it turned out, I wasn't yet done with seeking a lifelong profession, and Jane was at the very center of this new and very ardent desire.

I had always and forever loved music. I had, of course, taken piano lessons in Milan and New York, had attended many concerts in New York, and been as mad for the opera as I was for the popular songs of the day. When I began my studies at the University of Iowa, I never missed a concert and was an avid visitor, often with Jane, to the music room in the Student Union. The moment I could afford one, I purchased a record player and as many classical recordings as possible. But what propelled me most urgently into my new "profession" was Jane Wilson herself–Jane Wilson and her compelling mezzo-soprano singing voice!

It was Jane who introduced me to the musical genre known as the "art song" and it was for the "art song" or, in German, for the "lied," or in French, for "melodies" or "chansons," that I developed a lifelong passion. It was now my heartfelt wish, much propelled by my love for Jane and her singing, that I wanted to become a European-born American composer. This wish, which manifested itself even as I was deep in my studies of English literature and art history, flowered steadily as I acquainted myself with more and more art songs and read more and more biographies of Franz Schubert, Robert Schumann, Johannes Brahms, Hugo Wolf, Gustav Mahler, and Claude Debussy, all of whom were master composers of the art song.

Mostly, however, my love of songs took lasting root just sitting at the piano in Jane's Iowa City apartment and haltingly accompanying her in the beautiful songs of the classical masters, but also of the ones Jane first introduced me to, by Francis Poulenc, Edvard Grieg, Jean Sibelius, Sergei Rachmaninoff, and Charles Ives, and the songs of the early Italian masters such as Scarlatti and Pergolesi. It was, of course, wonderful that Jane had earlier studied singing at the University. And, during the course of our courtship, I had attended church where all three Wilsons, Cleone, Jane, and Ann, sang in the choir. But I was totally surprised and completely bowled over by Jane's knowledge of vocal music in general and the classical repertoire in particular.

And so, with the encouragement of Jane, I resolved to become a composer, and specifically, a composer of art songs. It all began tentatively enough, with my enrolling in a composition class in the music department in order to learn the basics of harmony and counterpoint. It was not easy, and I struggled mightily with putting notes to paper, but little by little and with my knowledge of piano, I began to improvise, and with difficulty, notated some very primitive first compositions. These were little tunes of no consequence, which bore a decent lyric shape and contour. Several months later, I found some early Romantic German poetry and in emulation of Robert Schumann, my special favorite, began improvising melodies set to the words I had chosen.

Sitting at the piano and composing gave me terrific pleasure. And this pleasure was doubled, tripled, and quadrupled when I showed the songs to Jane and she began to sing them. It was positively thrilling to hear someone singing *my* songs! The feeling of joy was incomparable. Never before had I experienced the sensation of having actually created something– something I had composed and that someone else could interpret and make their own.

As I proceeded in my quest to be a composer, it was clear that I really could not yet again change my major. My work on my master's degree in art history had already begun, but I continued composing on my own, sometimes taking more music courses, but mostly composing at the piano in the Student Union or at Jane's house. When my songs became too complicated for me to notate, Jane, once again, came to the rescue, and with her keen knowledge of music, helped set down quite a number of my early compositions. Needless to say, this help of Jane's and her wonderfully felt interpretations of my earliest songs increased my need to be with her more and more. Jane and I made love frequently and it was both very beautiful and very difficult. I simply could not get enough of Jane. She was patient yet often anxious because of my eagerness and need. We both needed to learn. Still, being with Jane brought me the sort of happiness that I wanted to last forever.

First, however, I had to settle the Jewish question. There was nothing Jewish about the University of Iowa, and if there was, I did not know about it nor did I seek it out. If I was a Jew—and I never really felt like one—I was a very bad one. My more or less Catholic upbringing in Italy and my parents' lack of religious guidance resulted in my being confused about, and to a large degree, disinterested in any religious belief. To add to my confusion was my aunt Esther's long-ago remark that my mother's family was really Greek and not Jewish. Still, I was decidedly aware and conscious of the suffering of the Jews under the Nazi and Fascist regimes, and I knew, firsthand, of the Holocaust. But none of it transformed me into a believing or practicing Jew. Even when we first arrived in America, and when my father suddenly became a Jew par excellence, and even after I reluctantly studied Hebrew in preparation for my poverty-stricken bar mitzvah when I turned 13, I considered myself an atheist. No gods for me, thank you. Religion caused far too much trouble. Religion caused wars and strife and guilt. I wanted no part of it.

What I did know, and absolutely believed in, was that it was difficult being a Jew. That being a Jew could produce simple animosity in some, and unspeakable treachery in others. Having been ousted from two seemingly safe worlds—Germany and Italy—for being Jewish, gave me great and grave pause, because I understood that to reveal one's religion could prove dangerous and frightening and destructive.

It took many months, and throughout those months I never once heard Jane say anything that sounded remotely anti-Semitic. When I finally broke the news to her, saying, "Darling, I have something terrible to confess to you. I'm Jewish," she simply looked at me and said, "Yes? And...?" I said, "Does it matter to you that I'm Jewish?" "No, why should it matter to me?" she replied. End of conversation.

But when Jane accepted my proposal of marriage toward the end of 1947, when I was still 20 and Jane was 22, many pressures began to build. For one thing, Jane's mother did not take kindly to the news. Jane was, without question, the apple of her eye—Cleone absolutely adored her Jane—and to lose her to someone who had no prospects, no money, who was a foreigner and a Jew to boot, and who would take her away to, of all wicked places, New York City, was almost too much to bear. How were we going to live? Cleone, who was often given to irrational fears, was certain her darling Jane would be thrust into the dungeons of white slavery and would come to a horrible, unspeakable end.

When Jane spoke to her father, then living in Ames, Iowa, after his divorce in 1945 (he was persona non grata in Cleone's household in Iowa City), he gave her his blessings, but no doubt also registered his own reservations. As far as I know, Jane's sister, Ann, seemed to think our getting married was just fine.

When I telephoned my parents in New York with the news, the first question out of my father's mouth was, "Is she Jewish?" When I told him she was not Jewish, he instantly thought my getting married was a terrible idea. I was too young, I had no prospects. What good was my college education? I had no job, I had no money. I was crazy. I should never have left New York, and "You're a Jew. You shouldn't be marrying a shiksa!" When I asked my parents if they would come to Iowa for the wedding, they said no, they would not come. "After you graduate, you'll come home and get a job. Later, you'll look around. You'll find a nice Jewish girl, and you'll get married."

Of course, I knew very well we were too young to get married. At least, I knew I was too young to get married. But despite the insecurity of our futures, I also knew that getting married, at least as far as I was concerned, was the best thing I could possibly be doing. As for Jane, I knew she had trepidations. I knew she was shaky about it. It would be a very big step for her. She had only just received her master's degree in painting—it was the spring of 1947—and the prospect of marriage, possibly quick-to-arrive babies, must have seemed entirely too precipitous—especially for someone with hopes of making a career as a painter. But I assured Jane there would be no quick-to-arrive babies, that we would be very careful, that I very much wanted her to make a career as a painter, that one of the main reasons we would be going to New York was to be where art was burgeoning everywhere and where she might indeed make a career as a painter. And so she agreed.

While Cleone kept warning Jane of the perils of marriage, sex, and other disasters, she did finally manage to put a good face on it. She seemed, at last, to realize that keeping Jane from doing what she wanted to do would be counterproductive, and so, when a date was set, she even managed to look forward to it. There was, however, one thing she would not tolerate. Wayne Wilson, Jane's father, would be barred from the wedding. "I never want to see that man again," she announced. Jane would thus not walk down the aisle with her father–would not be given away by him–and it pained her very much.

One bright family note sounded when my brother Tino, who had inspired my piano playing and intellectual pursuits, called to say he would come to my wedding. Indeed, when my parents refused to attend, I called all my brothers inviting them to come, but only Tino accepted. I was so overjoyed that I asked Tino to be my best man, and he readily agreed.

As it turned out, on our famous wedding day, March 28, 1948, who failed to show up but brother Tino. We waited for him at the church until we could not wait any longer, and proceeded without him. This was yet another blot on our wedding day. (It would be months before I learned that Tino decided not to come to our wedding when his dentist could not repair a front tooth in time. Tino explained he was too embarrassed to call us about it.)

No wonder, then, that our wedding was fraught with apprehension and anxiety. Indeed, it was a wedding that almost didn't happen, and I often wondered if I didn't coerce Jane into marrying me…if I didn't practically force her into it…was marrying me what she really wanted?

Chapter 10

Our first weeks of marriage were total bliss. We had found a small, very pretty apartment in Iowa City, and, quite literally, began to play house. We arranged and rearranged the furniture, we shopped for groceries together, and Jane made her first forays into cooking breakfast and dinner. When we returned home during the late afternoon or early evening, it was love, love, love and much, much happiness. I was working on my master's thesis on Peter Paul Rubens, going to my art history courses, music courses, and, of course, socializing as much as possible to show off my beautiful bride.

Because my small GI Bill stipend was running out, it now occurred to me that, with Jane earning most of our keep, I too should be adding to our income. After asking around and talking with friends, the most profitable part-time job around was being an attendant at the local mental hospital. The pay was good at five dollars per hour and the hours decent. The work, it turned out, was quite intriguing. I was assigned to the male wing of the facility—a large, somber, gray slate building on the outskirts of Iowa City. My job was to assist the doctors and nurses whenever they needed help, but mainly, I was to observe the thirty-some patients on my ward, taking notes if anything untoward happened, and generally being available to them. There was an office in a corner of the ward, which was always kept locked. This was where I would sit, looking out through large, windows, observing the activities of the patients in the central day room. On either side of the day room were the bedrooms. I worked three days a week, from 7 a.m. to 10 a.m. and from midnight to 3 a.m. It was a disruptive schedule, but there was plenty of time for study and paper-writing while on duty.

Most of the patients at the facility were either schizophrenic or manic-depressive. Almost all of them were farmers of all ages. There were also a surprising number of university students, highly disturbed young men unable to cope. All were in various states of sedation, but when their medication wore off, we, the attendants, were put to the test. Some of the men came up to us, demanding to be released, others fought amongst themselves (we had to break them up), and still others began picking fights with us, hollering and cursing. It wasn't bedlam or the snake pit, but when patients became agitated, which they frequently did, we were instructed to call the doctors or male nurses, who swiftly arrived with hypodermic needles.

Working in a mental institution placed me in touch with the frailty of one's psyche. It was daunting to be at such close proximity to the workings of a disturbed and troubled mind, to hear the irrational ravings of men hallucinating, to observe strange, obsessive behavior, to encounter the numb silences of people unable or unwilling to speak. All of this concentrated misery began to work on my own mind, and, all too often, certain bad tremors of anxiety assailed me. When, one morning, I discovered one of the patients hanging from a ceiling fixture, strangled by his bathrobe belt, I thought it was time to move on. I needed to get back to my own reality. After six months, I quit.

Jane and I saw quite a lot of people during our last year at Iowa University. There were Miriam Schapiro and Paul Brach, both very talented students in the art department, who became close friends. There were the exchange students from India, Rukmini, Noshir, and Sushila, who would introduce us to the joys of Indian cooking and the beauty of Indian jewelry and garb. There were the Becks, Charles and Marjorie, the ultra-sophisticated, martini-swilling couple with whom we dined at our respective apartments, wearing black ties and evening gowns. There were the brilliant Bill and Jack, our homosexual friends, who made us laugh and gave us a glimpse into the gay life. And there were all the others, students and faculty members, such as Professor Austin Warren, in whose house we heard beautiful vocal duets and poetry readings, and Mary Holmes, who regaled us with tales of her adventurous, notorious early years.

Christmas of 1949 was fast approaching. Our nearly one-year marriage seemed to be working out nicely. There were people we knew who gave it six months. Even Dr. Lester Longman, the head of the art department, had grave doubts about it. Indeed, some weeks before we married, he called Jane into his office and suggested she not marry me. Instead, he offered her a full-time assistant professorship in the art department and a university down payment on a house in Iowa City. "You'll have a great career at the university," he told her.

Jane thought otherwise.

As for me, being married felt very comfortable.

Of course, living with a person is quite different from dating that person. And living with Jane during those first months together was to live with a girl not given to instantly opening herself up to me. She was very quiet, very introverted. There were long, long silences during which Jane would read or study or occupy herself with various chores. Jane was simply not a talker, and she was not given to asking many questions. This also manifested itself when we were out in company. More often than not, Jane was the silent one.

Without question, she may have been the silent one because I was invariably the noisy one. Throughout our life I was the talker, the arranger, the raconteur, the all-around bearer of gossip and irrepressible yakker, seemingly possessed of no "off button." This is not to say that Jane just sat there like a bump on a log. She certainly knew how to hold a conversation and certainly participated in exchanging ideas. It was just that she did not seem to have a gift for the quick repartee or the lengthy story or the witty aside or the swift comeback or indeed, empty chatter of any kind.

What never ceased to amaze me about Jane was that, for all her silences, she had the capacity of being totally clear, interesting, and communicative when delivering her classroom lectures. I mean, she talked non-stop for hours at a time on highly complex art history subjects. And, of course, Jane and I could talk intimately together, and we had quite a bit of private fun, because Jane also loved to laugh, and I could make her laugh with my silliness and outrageousness and "foreign-ness" and my eagerness to get responses from her. I would get a big response from her when I talked to her in Italian, a language that she didn't understand, but loved the sound of. This was particularly effective during our lovemaking.

Nine months passed after our wedding–no, there was no baby, I promised Jane to be very, very careful–and Christmas 1949 was upon us. Two college chums, Bob and his Mexican boyfriend, Miguel, came to us and suggested we drive Miguel's well-worn, pastel green Dodge to Mexico City. Mexico City!! Jane and I looked at each other.

"It could be our honeymoon," said Jane.

"Let's do it!" I said.

"Let's!" said Jane.

It was a mad and marvelous idea. Christmas in Mexico City! How utterly fabulous! Bob and Miguel–everyone called him Miguelito–had been roommates and lovers for several years. Bob was receiving his master's in English literature; Miguelito, still a sophomore, was a science major in biology. It was arranged that Miguelito's mother would put us up while Bob and Miguelito travelled throughout Mexico to get to know the country. It would be a two-week trip. We packed all of our winter finery, and on a sunny Monday morning set off in the direction of Texas. We were in high spirits, shouting many "Ole's!" anticipating fun and more fun south of the border. Jane and I quickly realized the old Dodge was not precisely in tip-top condition. But Miguelito, who was driving, said not to worry. "This car is indestructible," he said with a laugh. And on we drove all the way to the Mexican border city of Brownsville, Texas, which would lead the way into Mexico, and up, up across the Sierra Madre and finally, down into Mexico City. And so we drove and we drove; and halfway up the mountain all the pistons fell out of the Dodge.

The situation was dire. The Dodge would not budge. Miguelito was devastated. He got out, hailed a passing car, and explained what had happened. The driver very kindly took us and our luggage to the next little town, where Miguelito attempted to purchase pistons at a Mexican garage. He was told Mexican pistons would not fit American cars. What to do? We were hundreds of miles from Mexico City. The garage owner suggested that the local taxicab driver might get us there. Contact was made. A huge taxi drove up. The cab driver had decorated his taxi with rows of small religious icons, many pictures of saints, and little vases filled with flowers. He had asked his whole family to come see him off. As we all sat in the taxi, we saw our driver being hugged and kissed by his mother, wife, many children, and cousins. There were even some tears. It was a farewell scene that filled us with apprehension. Had Pablo, our taxi driver, ever attempted such a long and arduous trip? No one ever told us.

It was mid-morning when we left. It was nighttime when, to our amazement, the glittering lights of Mexico City came into view. The old Dodge had been left in the middle of the road, somewhere in the Sierra Madre. Miguelito and Bob said we would all have to get back to Iowa City on our own steam. When we reached the city, Pablo drove us to our respective doors—Bob and Miguelito to their hotel, Jane and me to the outskirts of the city and Miguelito's mother, whose house looked to us not quite finished and smelled of freshly poured concrete. We paid Pablo a hefty sum, severely cutting into our Mexican budget. Still, we had arrived. Our Mexican honeymoon had begun.

After a restless night, we awoke to find Miguelito's mother, Rosalia, standing at our bedroom door. She was all smiles. "This house is not yet finished," she announced. "The bathroom has no windows and no doors–but, come along, children, I have prepared a wonderful breakfast for you!" Rosalia was unbelievably kind, unbelievably sweet-natured. We stayed in her unfinished house for two or three nights. Finally we explained to Rosalia that we needed to be in the city itself and she understood. We moved to the Hotel Geneva, a well-known tourist spot for American visitors to Mexico City.

Now comfortably ensconced, we visited as many Mexico City sites as possible, and one memorable night, visited a club where the famous Mexican cabaret star, Tongolele, was making an appearance. When Tongolele sang, "Un Poquito de tu amor, nada mas," wearing an outrageously sexy costume of a skirt of dagger-like protuberances suggesting phalluses and a glittery, daringly low-cut top, we were utterly mesmerized.

One day, as we shopped for some pottery in a well-known ceramics shop, we were approached by an elegantly dressed gentleman. He addressed us in English.

"Are you new to Mexico City?" he asked.

"Yes, we are," we responded. "We're on our honeymoon."

"How charming!" said the gentleman. "I'm Andre Hegel and I wonder if I could invite you to a Christmas party given by some very good friends of mine this very evening. I think you'd enjoy it."

We hesitated. But Andre Hegel was so persuasive and so charming that we finally accepted his invitation. It was Christmas Eve and a Mexican-style Christmas Eve party would be fun to experience. Hegel gave us the address and told us that our hosts were a distinguished European couple and that we'd meet some interesting people. If this did not sound like a typical Mexican Christmas party, we nevertheless thought it would be fun to go.

Dressed in our glamour togs–Jane looking stunning in a long, deep, brown silk sheath, me wearing a black velvet suit–we arrived at the given address in a taxi, and were ushered into an elegant, multi-terraced apartment, decorated with colorful Japanese lanterns as well as an array of Christmas decorations. There was a Christmas tree and there were bartenders and tables with plentiful platters of food.

When Andre Hegel saw us, he greeted us effusively and brought us to where our hosts were standing. This was a tall, handsome couple in their sixties, who greeted us warmly and, in turn, introduced us to some of their other guests. We gathered our hosts were either German or Dutch by their accented English. Indeed, this seemed to be a gathering of Europeans. The only Mexicans in sight were the help.

Champagne was served, and the music was heard emanating from a corner record player. At one point, Jane and I got separated.

Then I saw her.

There, surrounded by admirers, dressed in an exquisitely tailored aquamarine suit, her blond, blond hair upswept, her blue, blue eyes and delicate face aglow, stood the movie actress I had seen only some short weeks ago on the cover of *Life* magazine: This was Miroslava! Today forgotten, but then a fast rising young film star, Miroslava had appeared in the Hollywood film *The Brave Bulls* opposite Mel Ferrer and proved to possess smoldering talent and glamour. Already one of Mexico's most popular film stars, the single-named Miroslava owed much of her success to her atypical blond looks. Because there was nothing Mexican-looking about her, she was the enticing blond Venus of the Mexican cinema.

I was thrilled just looking at Miroslava. She was indeed ravishing. And her being a film star made my head spin. Soon we were introduced. She was flattered that I had seen her on the cover of *Life*, and enchanted that I seemed to know all about her. She invited me to sit with her on a chaise. Who was I? What was I doing? What brought me to Mexico? Miroslava wanted to know all about me, but didn't seem to hear my answers, because she next asked if I'd care to dance with her. But of course, said I! And as we danced, I could see Jane looking at us.

When Miroslava spoke her excellent English, I detected a slight European accent. "Are you really Mexican?" I ventured. "No, my dear, I am Czechoslovakian. But in my movies, I am as Mexican as guacamole," she replied. She next wondered if I would be interested in seeing her being filmed at the Churubusco Studios, just outside the city. She was making a new movie, and shooting would start the following week. I told her we'd be delighted. "Oh, could you come just by yourself?" she asked. "I have already invited too many people–the director gets so upset!" I told her I would be thrilled to come.

Jane, in the meantime, looked rather neglected. I knew I should have gone to her, but thought it rude to leave the lovely Miroslava, who had taken such a keen interest in me and had once again led me to the chaise. When she asked if I had ever thought of acting in films, I prolonged my visit with her. "Of course," I told her. "I always dreamed of a career in films." "Perhaps I can help you," she said, looking deep into my eyes.

When I told Jane I had been invited to watch Miroslava being filmed at the Churubusco Studios, she asked, "And will you go?" I told her I thought I would. And I explained that Miroslava had invited too many people, and I was asked to come by myself. "I see," said Jane.

Before leaving the party, Andre Hegel asked us to meet him on the following day at the Passy Café, one of Mexico City's most elegant coffee houses. We agreed, and when we arrived we saw Hegel standing by the open fireplace of the café. He motioned me over to him as Jane was being seated at a table.

"Did you enjoy the party?" asked Hegel.

"Very much! Thank you for asking us!"

"You seem to have hit it off with Miroslava. Did you know her name is Miroslava Stern?"

"No, I didn't know. So, she's a Jewish girl."

"Yes! So, you and your wife enjoyed the party?"

"We really did! Thank you so much!" I repeated.

"Well, that will be 600 pesos, my friend," Hegel announced.

"What? You are charging us for coming to the party?"

"Yes, I am. And it's 600 pesos for each of you."

Andre Hegel had duped us into thinking the party was just a friendly gesture. In fact it was his business. It's how he made his living. In short, the man was a crook.

"You better pay up or I can make trouble for you in this country," said Hegel in a threatening tone of voice.

Wanting no trouble, I took 1,200 pesos from my wallet and handed it to him. I then walked over to Jane and asked her not to ask any questions, but to instantly get up and walk out with me. This she did, and, on the way back to the Hotel Geneva, I explained what had happened.

"I'm not surprised," said Jane.

On the following week, I had my date with Miroslava.

"So, you're going?" asked Jane.

"Yes," I answered. "I promised I would."

Churubusco was several miles out of Mexico City. I told the guard at the entrance gate my business and was asked to wait. An open mobile cart came for me and took me to where Miroslava was being filmed. When she saw me on the set, she waved enthusiastically. In the sequence being shot, Miroslava was being lifted onto a bed by her leading man. The script called for her to act quite drunk, resist her man, and punch his shoulders, talking fast (in Spanish, of course), but slurring her words. Finally, the leading man threw her on the bed, stood over her and began laughing raucously, at which point the director called, "Cut!"

There were other guests on the set, and when the scene was over, Miroslava walked over to greet them, some more effusively than others. When she came up to me, she greeted me with a light but lingering kiss on the lips.

"Can you stay for lunch?" she whispered, seductively.

As I had already been on the set for at least two hours, I declined. It suddenly dawned on me that Miroslava might have some sexual designs on me. In fact, I was certain of it and I felt quite ridiculous and stupid. Besides, Jane seemed awfully quiet just before I left for Churubusco that morning. And so, despite being quite attracted to the sensuous Miroslava, and despite my hopes for a career in films in exotic Mexico, I thought I had better leave and head back to my Jane.

The note that awaited me in our hotel room was simple and to the point. "I've flown back to Iowa City." It was signed, "Jane."

Chapter 11

It took several weeks before Jane would be her old self again toward me. How stupid—how totally insensitive of me to have pursued another woman on my honeymoon—what was I thinking? Like a fool, I was thinking that the beauteous Miroslava would get me into the movies, and I'd make lots of money, and Jane and I would live happily ever after. I was such an idiot! And I had hurt Jane with my ridiculous, thoughtless behavior. It was inexcusable. I kept humming the song, "Blame It on My Youth!" just to make Jane laugh. But laugh she did not. One thing was clear. The name Miroslava would never cross my lips again.

Now it was back to my studies, my thesis, my degree. Then, at last, came my graduation day! In September 1949, I received my master's degree in Art History, and with it, the confirmation from New York University's Institute of Fine Arts that I would begin my scholarship study for a PhD within a matter of weeks. I was also informed that I would receive a small monthly stipend to see me along. I must admit that I was not entirely convinced that another four years in the classroom was what I needed or wanted. Still, attending the Institute in New York would, of course, be a very great honor. Hugely prestigious, the Institute had for years produced major art historians, and who was I to question, even for a moment, my extreme good luck?

It was totally incredible to me that I had spent nearly five years at the University of Iowa, had received both my bachelor's and master's degrees and, to top it all off, had gotten married. If I had wanted to discover the "real" America, there was no question that in the Middle West I found both the "salt-of-the-earth" America as well as its arch-conservatism. The liberal-minded and the closed-minded coexisted in a part of the country that was as flat and fertile as it was unpredictable and surprising. It was now time to bid farewell to it all, to the Midwest, to college, to hard work and all kinds of foolishness and innocent, carefree bliss. Real life was awaiting us, and it was as scary as it was somehow thrilling.

As with our Mexican adventure, we once again obtained a ride with two school chums, Miriam Schapiro and Paul Brach, who were also graduating, and like us, heading straight for New York City. Paul had a large, solid, jeep-like car, maroon in color, in which we could pack all of our belongings. For some reason, Jane sat next to Paul, who was driving. Mimi sat with me in the back. We were approximately 50 miles outside of Iowa City, when Paul, almost as much of a nonstop talker as I was, began extolling the quickness of his reflexes, how, if need be, he could stop on a dime, negotiate an unexpected turn, tackle a sudden curve. No sooner had he completed his self-congratulations than the car hit a rather large rain puddle. Paul and his reflexes stepped on the brake, and the car behind rammed into us. There was a severe jolt. I was thrown out of the car, but luckily, was merely shaken up. Jane, on the other hand, sitting in front, had hit her head on the windshield. When I looked at her minutes later, her face was covered in blood. I nearly fainted at the thought that Jane's face might forever be damaged. Jane had also twisted her ankle, and when she tried to walk, could do so only with difficulty. The Brachs suffered no injuries to speak of. The driver behind us was also unhurt. Paul Brach insisted we sue him as he had accident insurance. When we did, it would be many months before we received the grand sum of 50 dollars.

I don't know how we did it, but immediately after the accident Jane and I managed to return to Iowa City in more or less one piece. After washing off her bloodied face, we found that Jane's injuries were not as severe as we had thought and, luckily, her face remained unblemished. As for her ankle, it continued to hurt, and she had to walk supported by a red ruffled umbrella which we had brought along. When we got back to our old apartment in Iowa City, hoping to recuperate, our former landlady announced we could stay for only one night. She had rented the place, and the new tenants were about to move in. On the following morning, we purchased two plane tickets for New York, and in a matter of hours landed at LaGuardia Airport.

I had already decided that we would spend our very first night in New York at the fabled Hotel Algonquin, where, during the twenties, the famous "Round Table" had reigned, and where the likes of Alexander Woollcott, Dorothy Parker, Marc Connelly, Robert Benchley, George S. Kaufman, and other literary pundits spun their bon mots and witticisms. I told Jane I wanted us to feel the aura and frisson of that period.

Immediately upon checking out of the Algonquin the following day, we headed for the only neighborhood in which we were willing to live: Greenwich Village. After talking the Algonquin's front-desk man into looking after our luggage for a few hours, we contacted a Village real estate office. The woman in charge of Mason Real Estate took one look at us and said, "I have the perfect place for you–319 West 12th Street, right off Hudson! You'll love it. Lots of artists live there!"

She was absolutely right. We did love it. The rent was 48 dollars a month, and far more importantly, it was the front room of the parlor floor in a pretty brownstone house. There were French windows facing the street, bearing beautiful, lacy grillwork and, in the living room, parquet floors and a wood-burning fireplace. How perfect! How fabulous!

But where was the kitchen? And where was the bathroom?

"Well, there is no kitchen," said the agent, with a smile. "You'll buy yourselves a hotplate. As for the bathroom, it's on the floor above. Actually, it's a very nice bathroom, but it's a 'share.' You'll get used to it."

The lure of the lovely parlor, its fireplace, its long, long windows, and the sun streaming into the room just then, proved irresistible. We took the place at once. Never mind about no kitchen or bathroom. These were minor problems. All would be resolved in time. What was important was that we had a New York address, soon we'd have a phone, and, oh joy!, we would be living in Greenwich Village!

Greenwich Village, with its endless, picturesque streets, its history, its atmosphere, its aura of creativity and daring adventure, was where we belonged. And now here we were! We had joined the fabled army of artists, writers, poets, musicians, actors, and dancers, who had all made great names for themselves–Henry James, Willa Cather, Edna St. Vincent Millay, Eugene O'Neill, and endless others…it was all positively head-spinning. The first thing we did was buy some white paint. Jane went to work on the walls. I unpacked our record player, our 78s, and put on Lotte Lehmann singing Schumann. We bought a hotplate and a folding card table. We bought dishes, glasses, knives, forks, and spoons. We bought pots and pans. We put the hot plate on the card table, we made room for the dishes, and voilà, our kitchen! Water was transported down from the bathroom upstairs. As the lady said, we got used to it.

The house was indeed filled with artists. On the top floor lived Ben Garber, a dancer with the Martha Graham Dance Company. On the floor below lived an actress studying with Stella Adler. On the floor below her, a gay couple–a writer and printmaker. The couple immediately next door to us in what would have been the rear end of the floor-through, who were not artists at all, made the greatest impression on us. We met all the neighbors, and they couldn't have been more interesting, sweet, or neighborly. But it was the Maiales who truly touched our hearts. She was a young wife, large with child. He was a delivery truck driver for the Duvernoy Bakery Company. Their name was Maiale, Theresa and Joe, and they were as kind and as good as gold.

After living on 12th Street for about two or three weeks, the Maiales invited us to their place. We talked. They were Italian-American, struggling to make a living, but wildly excited about the impending birth of their first child. His job delivering bread, rolls, and cakes was keeping body and soul together, which was certainly more than we could say.

I had begun attending classes at the Institute of Fine Arts, but my stipend would not be forthcoming for at least another four weeks. Jane was looking for a job to no avail. We were by now dangerously low on cash. My parents were not helping us, which was fine with me. The money Jane's father had given us was coming to an end. When we told our tale of woe to the Maiales, they were sympathetic and understanding. We could certainly empathize with one another. They too were constantly strapped for money and the baby was on its way. That night they invited us to a spaghetti dinner and some Chianti.

The next morning, when Jane again went out looking for a job, she opened the apartment door and there, outside, leaning against it, was a big bag filled to the brim with bread, rolls, bagels, and other fresh baked goods. Joe Maiale had left the bag for us before making his early-morning rounds of deliveries for the bakery. He did this week after week.

When we thanked them again and again, they said they were simply tired of hearing our stomachs growl through the thin wall that separated us. It was the sort of generous gesture we would never forget.

Aunt Manya, Uncle Alexander, Aunt Esther, my father Abraham, mother Aranka, grandfather Joseph; brothers Leo, Martin, and little Carlo in the front row, Berlin, mid 1920s

Kindergarten, Berlin, 1931 (John Gruen third row from bottom, right of aisle)

John Gruen, "Figlio della Lupa," Milano, 1937

John Gruen, age 6, with parents, Lido, Venice, Italy, June 27, 1933

John Gruen, age 6, in grandmother's apartment on the first school day with the traditional gift cone, Berlin, 1932

John Gruen, age 13, with parents, New York City, 1939

Private John Gruen, Camp Blanding, Florida, May 1945

John Gruen, University of Iowa, 1947

"Writer's Workshop," Paul Engle's house, Stone City, IA, late 1940s (Jane Wilson in light sweater sitting in front row, John Gruen next to her in white shirt and dark tie and sweater.

Jane Wilson and John Gruen's wedding portrait, Iowa City, IA, 1948

Honeymoon, Mexico City, 1948

John Gruen, New York City, 1950s; photograph by Marion Morehouse (Mrs. E.E. Cummings)

Close-up of Jane Wilson, the Foy Model Agency, New York City, 1957

ΣLΣKTRA

e. e. cummings
rainer maria rilke
franz kafka
friederich hölderlin

New Songs

by
john gruen

georgiana bannister ★
soprano
john gruen
piano

JANE WILSON

Leonore Fabisch, John Gruen's psychoanalyst, New York City, 1950s

Album cover, Elektra 1, *New Songs by John Gruen*, 1951

Loly Eckert and Barney Rosset just married, with John Gruen and Jane Wilson,
New York City, August 1953 (Grove Press window in the back left)

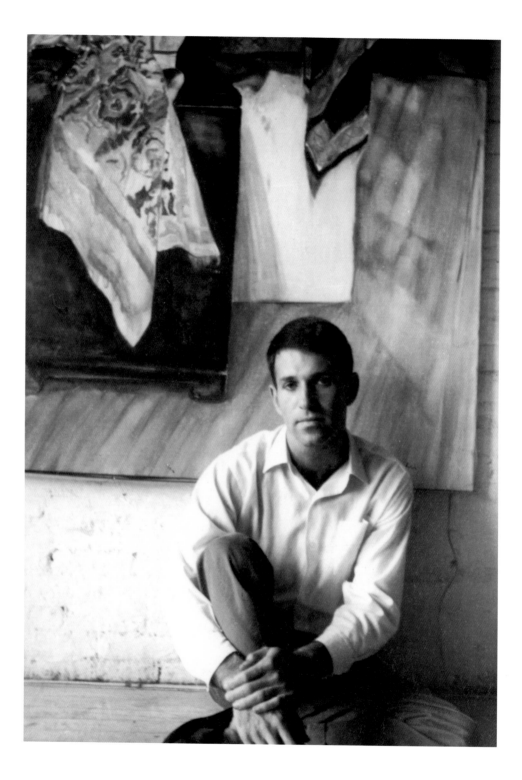

Alvin Novak, Hoboken, NJ, 1957

Alexander and Hella Hammid, Catskills, NY, 1956
Larry Rivers and Maxine Groffsky, New York City, 1957

John Gruen and Patricia Neway, singing John Gruen's songs "To the Harbor Master" and " River," poems by Frank O'Hara, New York City, 1960; photograph by Hella Hammid

Press clips, Patricia Neway at Carnegie Recital Hall with songs by John Gruen, New York City, 1960

John Gruen and Eleanor Steber in her apartment, New York City, late 1950s

Chapter 12

New York University's Institute of Fine Arts was very grand indeed, situated on East 78th near Fifth Avenue in an ornate beaux arts building of great beauty; classes were held in elegantly appointed rooms. The first professor I encountered was a certain Dr. Schoenberger, whose specialty was medieval art. I will confess that I nearly fell asleep when yet another ground plan of Chartres was flashed on the screen. My heavy lids became even heavier as Dr. Schoenberger droned on and on in a heavy German accent. As I sat there half-dozing, I wondered if I could really go through with this. Was I really ready to kill myself over more and more art history? Did I really want to be an art historian? Did I really like academe? What about my music? My songs? My composing?

Clearly, I was resisting the scholarship and ultimately my PhD. I felt that a new chapter in my life had begun and it did not include four more years of study. Not when Jane and I were living down the street from artists like Willem de Kooning, Franz Kline, Mark Rothko, and Jackson Pollock. These people were creating a brand new living and breathing art that critics called abstract expressionism, and it was all happening just a few blocks from us. Of course I was riddled with guilt because it seemed as though I was letting the University of Iowa down, letting Jane down and, no doubt, letting myself down. I didn't know what to do.

Some time elapsed. I trudged on with my studies unenthusiastically. Finally, early one morning as Jane and I were lying in our single bed, I turned and faced her.

"I can't go on with my PhD," I said.

"Really? What's wrong?" said Jane.

"I can't do it anymore. I can't concentrate. I'm unhappy. I hate it! I don't want to study anymore. I want to live!" I said.

"You mean you want to live as in Susan Hayward?" said Jane.

"Yes! I'll get a job," I said.

"Well, you'd better find one quickly," said Jane, who mercifully did not try to dissuade me and didn't seem all that upset.

"I'll go find a job right away," I promised.

That very morning, I skipped the Institute of Fine Arts and went looking.

I had often passed Brentano's bookstore on Fifth Avenue and 47th Street, and thought, wouldn't it be grand to work there? I could work in the art book department. I felt I knew all about art books. After all, I had a master's in art history. Besides, I had always heard that Brentano's attracted the most glamorous clientele. Even Greta Garbo bought her books there. I decided to give Brentano's a try.

I walked into the sedately elegant atmosphere of the wood-paneled store and quickly found the art book section. A tall, middle-aged gentleman seemed to be in charge. After nonchalantly browsing through some art books I asked him if by any chance there was an opening in his department. I then proceeded to fill him in on my "fabulous" art background. When the gentleman answered, he spoke with a heavy Russian accent. "We might have something. When can you start?" I told him I could start immediately–even that very afternoon. He said, "Come back tomorrow morning at nine o'clock. I will speak to the manager about you."

I appeared punctually at nine o'clock the next morning, obtained the job, and for the next four years worked more or less happily at Brentano's. The four years it would have taken me to get a PhD at the Institute of Fine Arts were spent at Brentano's, first as a book salesman, then, two years later, as an assistant book buyer. I know I forfeited a good job at some university or museum as Dr. Gruen. God knows, I would have been making a much higher salary. But, for the moment, Brentano's suited me just fine. Besides, working there, I could also make time for my music, because I still harbored the great wish to be a composer.

Jane in the meantime also found herself a job, landing in the bookstore of the then very fashionable Hotel Marguery on Park Avenue. But the job was over almost as soon as it began. The two women who ran the shop were lesbians. So lovely a girl as Jane drove both these women quite mad, and matters became entirely too complicated for Jane. The atmosphere was entirely too contentious. She quit after only a few weeks.

Of course, Jane had, from the very first, always known she wanted to be a painter. Indeed, from the moment we had settled ourselves on West 12th Street, Jane improvised an easel, purchased some inexpensive canvas and some stretchers, unpacked her paints and brushes, stretched her canvases, and began to paint small still lifes and figures in landscapes.

No matter what we were doing, Jane would always return to her easel. Jane loved her independence. She had always wanted to earn some money in order to sustain it, but selling her paintings was not yet in the offing.

One day, one of our gay neighbors suggested that Jane try fashion modeling. "You have the look." He said. "You've got the face and the figure. Honey, you're just plain gorgeous." He said he had a friend who might be able to help. This friend told Jane that in order to begin a modeling career, she would need to put together a portfolio of photographs. Without it, nothing would happen. This friend very kindly sent Jane to a number of fashion photographers who were willing to do some free "test" shots. She got the prints, but the photographer kept the negatives.

Slowly, Jane accumulated enough of a portfolio to start making rounds to the studios of fashion photographers, fashion magazines, and advertising agencies. Because of her striking looks Jane was told she was too exotic looking. It was the 1950s, a time of the all-American, peaches-and-cream girl–like the Rheingold beer girl, the Breck shampoo girl, and Tippi Hedren. The 50s were not about exoticism in America. While hardly the Latin type, Jane nevertheless struck many potential modeling agencies as being a bit too foreign-looking. Though one agency thought she was ravishing–no, not the famous Ford Agency, but its close rival (at least in name)–the tiny Foy Agency.

The Foy arranged for a composite of Jane's best photographs as well as a single headshot and sent these out to potential clients. A few photographic modeling jobs began to trickle in, but it was very tough going. She was either too tall, too short, too skinny, too sophisticated, or not sophisticated enough. Jane was not a complainer, but I could tell that the constant rejections were getting her down. Modeling, it turned out, could be humiliating and depressing.

Of course, we were assuming that modeling meant photographic modeling–that Jane would appear in the pages of *Vogue*, *Harper's Bazaar*, and *Glamour*. (Ironically, this would indeed happen, but mostly after Jane stopped modeling and was photographed as an artist).

If she did not entirely succeed as a photographic model, Jane nevertheless found success and a steady salary as a showroom model in the Garment District on New York's Seventh Avenue. Among the several designers Jane worked for during the 50s was Lyena Dodge, a Russian-born, Paris-trained designer. Her line of clothing was as elegant as it was beautifully structured. Lyena and her American-born husband, Roger Dodge, became close friends.

So it was that Jane and I both found jobs in New York, but the burning question now remained: What about our careers as artists? How did one become a professional painter or composer in New York City? How could one hold down a full-time job to pay the rent, put food on the table, and also make it as a serious artist? Our favorite answer to such troubling questions was, "Let's move!"

And so began our years of New York City wanderlust, moving for one reason or another from 319 West 12th Street to 123 Waverly Place to 51 West 11th Street to 324 Bleecker Street to 128 East 72nd Street to 241 East 18th Street to 317 East Tenth Street and finally to our present address on the Upper West Side.

All that moving may have seemed sheer foolishness or restlessness, but for us moving meant a new beginning, a new start, upward mobility, and the thrill of the unknown.

Chapter 13

Waverly Place in Greenwich Village is short and picturesque. It shoots off Washington Square North, and its houses are uniformly charming. When we read the ad in *The New York Times*, the apartment seemed too good to be true: a parlor floor, a garden, French windows, a bath, a full kitchen, and a beautifully furnished interior. The rent was outrageously reasonable. We telephoned and a woman, cultured of voice, answered. "Do come by and take a look. I think you'll like it."

Like it? We absolutely adored it. And we were much taken with the owner, Mrs. Girard, a woman in her sixties, beautifully coiffed and, sadly, confined to a wheel chair. She was there to show us the premises, and she couldn't have been more solicitous. The place was absolutely perfect.

"When can we move in?" I asked.

"Why, immediately," said Mrs. Girard. I could tell that Jane was thrilled. She had not seen a real kitchen or a bathroom since Iowa!

It was after we agreed to move in, after we made small talk, and after I had written out a check for one month's deposit and one month's rent that Mrs. Girard announced that she too would be living in the same apartment.

"You won't even know I'm here!" she exclaimed. "I stick pretty close to my own room and my son comes to take me out for some fresh air three or four times a week."

"But the ad said nothing about your living here too," I ventured.

"Oh, now, now," she said, sweetly, "Don't you like this place? Isn't it beautiful? I promise I'll be as quiet as a church mouse."

Jane and I looked at each other. We stood up and once more surveyed the apartment. "What do you think?" I said. "What do you think?" Jane answered. "I think we should take it. Mrs. Girard seems awfully nice."

And so we moved into 123 Waverly Place. Mrs. Girard's son helped us to settle in, while Mrs. Girard, in her wheelchair, looked on smiling and nodding benevolently. As it turned out, our landlady's room was situated in a way that did not interfere with our own comings or goings. It is true that she made use of her kitchen, but she saw to it that our mealtime schedules would not conflict. Soon, however, we felt obliged to invite her into the living room, simply because it was the decent thing to do. We soon learned that Mrs. Girard was a trained beautician and manicurist. On occasion we would glimpse a man or a woman sitting in Mrs. Girard's room facing her wheelchair, a little worktable between them, being given manicures. We too were now and then treated to lengthy and elaborate manicures, which Mrs. Girard called her "little ritual of bliss and beauty," and it was certainly a refreshing way to spend some time together. "It's the least I can do for all the kindness you children have shown me!"

There is nothing like living with a person in a wheelchair to bring out one's guilt. Of course, Jane and I felt obliged to do some of Mrs. Girard's shopping for her. And, of course, we would make it a point to keep her company and include her in some of our social gatherings. As it turned out, her son did not come as often as she had said, and so on occasion, I took it upon myself to wheel her up and down Waverly Place or into Washington Square.

However, when Mrs. Girard began to thump on our bedroom door with her cane at four o'clock in the morning in a complete panic, yelling, "Children! Children! Do you smell smoke? I think the house is on fire! I can't move. Please, please help me!"—we felt that it was time to bid farewell to 123 Waverly Place.

Mrs. Girard was terribly disappointed when we announced our plans to move. She said, "Oh, please don't move! I so love having you here. I've grown quite attached to you. You've become like a son and a daughter to me!" Within a day or so we packed our belongings and moved. We had lived on Waverly place for less than two months.

The apartment we moved into at 51 West 11th Street was one of the last surviving tenements on that elegant block. Indeed, the house was decidedly untouched by maintenance. But it was between Fifth and Sixth Avenues, and, of course, we just loved that. We lived on the second floor rear, with north light.

Partly furnished, it boasted a sagging bed matched by a sagging armchair. In an alcove near the entrance door was a little gas stove, and next to it, a little gas refrigerator that sounded as though a flock of canaries had taken up residence in it. But there was a handsome marble fireplace. As she had done previously, Jane set up her portable easel, her paints and small canvases. But first she painted all the walls white. Finally, the place looked pretty and comfortable. The upright piano we had on 12th Street was taken out of storage (there was no room for it at Mrs. Girard's) and brought to 11th Street.

My parents were still living way uptown in Washington Heights, and we both finally felt obliged to see them at least once in a while. But I really dreaded those visits. What was worse, my father's place of business was practically across the street from where I worked at Brentano's. We were both located on West 47th Street. This circumstance caused me to develop more guilt about constantly avoiding my father. I could have easily walked across the street during my lunch hour and spent time with him. But being so near to him filled me with anxiety and gloom. On the rare occasions I did go and see him, I saw a man, quite alone, clearly disappointed with his life, all too ready to blame his unhappiness and dissatisfaction on his four sons. I wanted no part of that. Besides, my parents were not remotely interested in my life, in my marriage, in Jane, in her work or mine. They did not help us when we first arrived in New York and, my pet peeve, my father would call Jane "lady," as in, "Pass the salt, lady."

Working at Brentano's placed me in a milieu of urbanity and culture. I felt very much at home there. Beautifully dressed men and women entered the store, lingered, purchased books, and departed. Some I recognized instantly. When Greta Garbo walked in, I froze. She picked up a book and slowly examined its contents. Wearing a tight-fitting beret and broad-shouldered suit, she stood quite close to me and I was able to gaze at her face. While unthinkably beautiful on the screen, and ravishing in photographs, to see Garbo in person was to know the immediacy of vibrant and inspired perfection. She must have been in her late forties, but her features and the mesmerizing aura of her persona were so compelling that my heart pounded and pounded with excitement.

There was a circumference of silence around her, and I did not know whether to intrude upon it or not. Finally, I could not resist. "May I help you, Miss Garbo?" I said. She lifted her eyes and silently stared at me. I was at once riveted and transported. Her answer was simple: "No," she replied, and put down the book and left the store.

One later afternoon, at nearly closing time, an unusual-looking, well-dressed gentleman approached the art books section. I recognized him at once. The upturned mustachios gave him away. This was the famous Spanish-born, Paris-based Surrealist, Salvador Dalí.

"Do you have my book, *The Secret Life of Salvador Dalí*?" he said in a heavy French accent.

"Mais bien-sur, maitre!" I replied in flawless French. Dalí looked both startled and delighted.

"Comme vous êtes charmant," he said, and added, "What a pleasure to meet such a sophisticated young man who speaks such beautiful French!" I quickly brought him the book and told him how thrilled I was to meet him. "That is all very well my boy, but have you read it?" "I'm afraid not," I replied. "I see," said Dalí. "Please gift wrap this, and put a beautiful ribbon around it." I did as he bade and after a few minutes, handed him the beautifully wrapped book. He took it and with an extravagant gesture, handed it right back to me. "Pour vous, jeune homme," he said. "It is my gift to you."

"Mr. Dalí," I said, "this is really most generous of you!"

"Aren't you going to open it? Go on, tear it open," he said. This I did. Dalí now retrieved a fountain pen from an inside pocket, opened the book to the title page and wrote, "Pour John Gruen. Bonjour! Salvador Dalí. 1950." With that, he closed the book, and said, "Read and at last you will know Dalí!" And off he went, out of the store.

Still in the glow of Dalí's generosity, it took me several minutes to realize that he had failed to pay for the book. It didn't matter. The book was Dalí's gift to me. I put it in a Brentano bag, and at closing time, proudly brought it home and said to Jane, "Look what Salvador Dalí gave me!"

At the University of Iowa, one of our poetry texts in English lit was a small but thick anthology entitled *A Little Treasury of Modern Poetry* by Oscar Williams. My well-worn copy was among the few textbooks I chose to bring to New York. One of the pleasures of the little volume were the several pages of small oval portraits of the poets in the book—Shakespeare, Goethe, Wordsworth, Byron, Keats, T.S. Eliot, W.H. Auden and, last but not least, Oscar Williams!

Williams' portrait showed an eager, sharp-featured man in round glasses, looking like a startled owl.

Like Garbo and Dalí, I recognized him at once as I watched him wandering into Brentano's, heading straight for the poetry section. Leaving my post, I rushed over to him to ask if I could help him. "Do you have Oscar Williams' *A Little Treasury of Modern Poetry*?" he asked tartly.

"Yes, indeed we do, Mr. Williams."

"Oh, you know my name?" he said, smiling broadly.

"Certainly, Mr. Williams. Why, your anthologies were the mainstay of my poetry classes at the University of Iowa!"

"I'm very glad to hear it. What is your name, young man?"

And thus began our rather shaky friendship with Oscar Williams, his wife, the poet and painter Gene Derwood, and, through them both, many of his wide circle of literary friends. Indeed, it was through Williams that Jane and I entered the highly prestigious, tightly-knit, competitive and back-biting world of the so-called "little magazines."

We met some of the *Partisan Review* crowd, the *Poetry Magazine* crowd, and the *Hudson Review* crowd, and glimpsed all the other poets and writers who would gather at the small Williams/Derwood penthouse on New York's seamy and dangerous Water Street in the desolate downtown Manhattan of the 1950s. Visiting them was traumatic since we had to wait for several long minutes before Gene Derwood made her way down in the very slow, manually operated elevator to unlock the front door of the darkened factory building in which she and Oscar lived. It seemed to take forever, as we found ourselves surrounded by weaving drunks and sinister, threatening types of every sort.

Gene Derwood was given to wearing long capes and big berets. Her voice was raspy and filled with gloom. I found her witch-like. Whenever she spoke, there seemed to be some dreaded foreboding message behind even her most pleasant words. She ushered us into her living room, around which sat some of New York's best known literati: John Crowe Ransom, William Jay Smith, Philip Rahv, Louis Simpson, Anthony Hecht, among others. To us they seemed the most sophisticated bunch.

The talk centered around outré literary matters–style, poetics, symbolism, as well as such "of the moment" subjects as psychoanalysis, alcoholism, or high anxiety–all this as liquor flowed and words became more and more elliptical. For his part, Oscar Williams spoke very little but was the agile dispenser of drinks and food. Gene Derwood sat erect on a stool and added the occasional portentous and cryptic pronouncement. To me, all that literary talk, all those profundities sounded ponderous and leaden and self-important.

The intellectual atmosphere struck me as being airless and impenetrable. What struck me as most amusing about our literary evenings at Oscar and Gene's was the food, which invariably consisted of only one dish, mashed potatoes–lukewarm mashed potatoes that were dispensed onto a paper plate by Oscar Williams. Twenty minutes later, Oscar would come around again to ask, "More mashed potatoes, anyone?"

The most memorable evening we spent at Gene and Oscar's was when they threw a party for the Welsh poet Dylan Thomas. Jane and I had heard about Dylan Thomas before we even met Oscar, and had gone to hear him read his work at the Y Poetry Center on 92nd Street. It was an unforgettable experience. The poetry was like a gust of fresh wind, certainly compared to the mostly grim poetry readings we had attended in the past. Here, by contrast, were works touched by life, touched by music, etched in fire. The water birds and herons of Thomas' poems really took wing. One could hear the whoosh of their flight as they hovered over landscapes and shorelines that shimmered through summer trees and autumn winds. To hear Thomas read with his beautifully inflected Welsh accent was to be engulfed in these exhilarating climates. How refreshing to hear such inspired reading! What a contrast from the somnambulistic drone of most of the other poets we had heard!

Dylan Thomas had been invited to visit the United States and Oscar Williams took it upon himself to be one of his guides and protectors while in New York City. What Williams could not protect Thomas from was the poet's intense sense of insecurity and discomfort while in the States, which is why he became more and more dependent on alcohol. Thomas could be found at any number of New York City bars, mostly the White Horse in the Village, surrounded by friends, fellow poets, admirers, and hangers-on, drinking the night away as if tomorrow might never come. Thomas just drank and drank and drank. And it was drink that ultimately killed him. Perhaps the most profoundly gifted poet of the twentieth century could not control his addiction.

On the evening of the party for Thomas, Gene and Oscar asked us to come early so that we might be able to talk with him before the other guests arrived. When Gene opened the door she started shushing us profusely, pointing to a prone, snoring Thomas. He was, as she put it, "resting." We tiptoed into the room and sat in total silence for about ten minutes, beholding Thomas in his red woolly shirt and unruly curly hair. Finally Thomas stirred, rubbed his eyes and sat up. On the floor at his feet stood four full quarts of beer.

When Thomas started talking, his conversation was as crisp and lucid as his poetry. If he was suffering from a hangover, he did not show it. I asked him to describe the Welsh town in which he lived, and the house that he shared with his wife Caitlin and his two small children.

With the same cadences that marked his readings, Thomas described his home to us. Every tree, every flower, every bird, assumed a vivid, tremulous life of its own. The images were so clear and so magical, that in contrast the room we sat in appeared gray and ghostly. It was poignantly clear he desperately missed his home, his wife and children.

As his description progressed, however, he progressed further into the beer at his feet. He had spoken for about an hour and now his speech became slurred and finally incomprehensible. It was at this moment that guests began arriving. They were the usual entourage of poets, writers, editors, critics, and painters. Gene had set up a small portable easel in the center of the living room. For years, she had been painting small portraits of her friends, an adjunct to her life as a poet. Gene now placed a small blank canvas board on her easel and began busily arranging her oils and brushes. Her plan was to capture Thomas in a portrait that she had been planning for weeks.

Because of Thomas' condition–he was sort of reeling around among the guests–it seemed hardly the occasion to embark on such a project. But we could tell by her darting, flashing eyes that she was inspired and deter-mined. So concentrated was her activity at the easel that she paid not the slightest attention to her guests (by now some two dozen). Oscar Williams, however, scurried around the room taking care of the amenities and the drinks. Thomas now stood practically invisible in one corner of the room, hidden by a crowd of admirers.

People were sitting on the floor, on chairs, on couches, on small side tables or crouching in every available spot. We kept wondering how Gene was going to manage her masterpiece. She had just turned off every light, save a small lamp covered by a red silk shade on a low coffee table near her easel. It was the only source of light for her painting. Thomas had now plopped himself down on a couch and Gene desperately applied paint to her small canvas, her eyes darting madly from Thomas to the emerging portrait.

We noticed one guest, the beautiful poet Helen Coggeshall, there with her husband, the painter Calvin Coggeshall, imploring Thomas to read some of his poems. She had brought along one of his poetry collections and had pre-selected several poems that she wanted him to read aloud. Never unmindful of a beautiful woman, Thomas listened to her beseeching and seemed ready to comply. As Mrs. Coggeshall handed him the volume, he fell to his knees, lifted her dress and plunged his head beneath it. Stunned, the elegant and well-bred Mrs. Coggeshall allowed the poet to nestle only momentarily. She then gently pushed him away, pressed the open volume of poetry into his hands and commanded, "Please, Mr. Thomas, do read to us!"

Thomas lurched to a standing position, tore the book from her, ostenta-tiously turned it upside down, and proceeded to give a mock reading con-sisting solely of loud, moose-like bellows, nonsense syllables–a ten-minute blast of cacophonous sounds that made no sense whatsoever, all the while gesturing madly like a Roman Emperor in the throes of a seizure. It was during this "oration" that Gene reached the peak of her inspiration, feverishly applying stroke after stroke upon her minuscule canvas. It was also during Thomas' wild and woolly reading that Oscar elected to serve dinner. "We are having mashed potatoes!" he announced, cheerfully. He wove zanily in and out between his guests, balancing paper plates, serving the mashed potatoes as best he could to the large crowd.

Thomas had now finished his ranting and collapsed into a mumbling heap on an empty chair. Polite conversation ensued but the atmosphere became oppressive and uncomfortable. The mashed potatoes were barely consumed. Drinks were being gulped down and finished. It became apparent that the party was over. The only person totally unperturbed by the bizarre proceedings was Gene Derwood at her easel, and we saw that she had indeed done a portrait of Dylan Thomas—a portrait of a red-haired man in a red shirt captured in a red light. Amazingly, she had caught much of the frenzy exhibited by Thomas during his drunken performance. By now the poet lay on the couch, fast asleep, snoring loudly. Glancing at him I saw an unreachable, exhausted man in the grip of yet another long alcoholic siege.

The evening in honor of Dylan Thomas had come to its end.

Chapter 14

Working in the fiction department at Brentano's bookstore was an extremely pretty and vivacious young woman by the name of Georgiana Bannister. She was so friendly, so full of life that I simply had to meet her. As it turned out, Georgiana was a young soprano, a scholarship student at New York's prestigious Mannes School of Music. Her goal was to become an opera and concert singer. She certainly had all the characteristics of a potential diva. It took no more than a few minutes of our acquaintance for me to regale Georgiana with my intense love of opera and, in particular, of the art song.

"Oh, how wonderful! You're a composer!" said Georgiana.

"Yes, I am. And I want you to sing all of my songs!"

We both laughed and indeed, decided to get together so that each could hear the other's "fabulous" talent. We made a date for her to come to our apartment so that she could meet Jane and also look at my songs. But before we did, Georgiana brought us a sample recording that she had made of some songs by Schubert and Debussy and several Italian operatic arias. It turned out that the lovely Georgiana Bannister had the clearest, most bell-like soprano voice! It was an instrument full of feeling, nuance, and character. Her German, French, and Italian diction was flawless, and she had admirable command of her vocal technique.

When the record ended, I sat at the piano and began to sing the songs I thought would be appropriate for Georgiana's limpid voice. Very quickly she read the music over my shoulder: she then sang song after song, exclaiming over their charm or originality or loveliness or strangeness. She quite overwhelmed me with praise! It was her way. When, on that evening, Georgiana announced she was in the process of putting together a song recital and wanted to include two or three of my songs, I knew I had found the first professional champion of my music.

Georgiana was born in Charlotte, North Carolina. She had already given various recitals around New York City and had performed with a number of chamber groups. In time, we became good friends. During coffee breaks at Brentano's we talked about our dreams and about our lives.

I soon learned that Georgiana was being wooed by a German gentle-man quite a few years older than herself. His name was Benno Bechhold, and he was in the hotel business. Benno, it turned out, was quite wealthy. "He owns the Savoy Plaza Hotel on Fifth Avenue," Georgiana confided. "And he wants to marry me."

"What are you waiting for?" I said. "He sounds ideal!"

"Well, I want a career, you know. I'm not sure I'm ready for marriage just now. But Benno is the sweetest man in the world. I want you and Jane to meet him."

The Savoy Plaza Hotel, one of the grandest and most luxurious hotels in New York, stood next to the Hotel Pierre on Fifth Avenue. (It would be razed years later to make way for the General Motors Building, which today is yet another Trump tower). To have a friend who was going out with the owner of the Savoy Plaza was, to my mind, a many-splendored thing. We looked forward to meeting Benno Bechhold, and when I announced to Georgiana that in a week or so, I'd be celebrating my 23rd birthday, she said, "Why don't we all celebrate it at the Savoy Plaza? I'll talk to Benno." And so she did. Benno turned out to be a distinguished-looking man in his sixties, tall and imposing, with sparkling blue eyes, graying temples, and that special European sense of generosity and *joie de vivre.*

On the evening of my birthday, we were seated in the grand ball-room of the hotel; we had a sumptuous meal and then danced for hours. The excellent orchestra kept playing the wonderful pop songs of the day and the champagne kept flowing. I felt incredibly happy, and I thought, Jane and I are in the most glamorous surroundings in the most glamor-ous city in the world. It conformed so perfectly to my dreams of leading a life of beguilement. The evening ended with all of us quite tipsy and affectionate. It was certainly one of the best birthdays of my life, and the event cemented our friendship with Georgiana and Benno. A year later Georgiana finally said "yes" to Benno, and the two remained happily married for many years.

In the weeks to come, Georgiana and I rehearsed my songs–those she would be singing at her upcoming New York song recital. These were set-tings of some Japanese haiku translated into French, as well as some songs based on the poetry of James Joyce. It was a joy to hear Georgiana sing my songs during her recital. But it was nothing compared to the recital she and I would be giving several months later.

As it turned out, a dear friend of ours, the poet John Logan, whom we had known at the University of Iowa, telephoned to say he was coming to New York to visit us. John, who at the time was teaching at St. John's University in Annapolis, Maryland, asked whether Jane would be interested in having an exhibition of her paintings at St. John's, and if I would like to give a recital of my songs there. Needless to say, we couldn't be more thrilled!

John Logan was a very gifted poet whose work was beginning to appear in the "little" magazines, and whose story was as remarkable as it was sad. At the University of Iowa he was one of the most promising students in the English Department and had participated in the Writer's Workshop. John, who was born in Iowa, was a tall, thin, gaunt fellow with an unusually beautiful face. It was Christ-like; deep-set eyes, high cheekbones, aquiline nose, and tapered chin. I remember playing some Chopin in the Student Union Lounge. He just stopped by and listened, and when I finished my "Nocturne," he told me how beautiful he thought my playing was. He then introduced himself.

John was amazingly well-read and knew a great deal about music, art, poetry and literature, and even more about theology. Indeed he seemed obsessed with the theology courses he was taking at the University and was, when I met him, in the process of converting to Catholicism, a religion he felt combined his great interest in the arts with a theology that offered forgiveness and a promise of redemption. So excruciatingly sensitive was John Logan, that I felt certain he was a young man besieged by demons of every kind. Some months after we met, John confessed to me that he needed to get married, and that he had met a young Catholic girl named Guenevere with whom he had fallen in love. At the same time John revealed to me his love of men. It was a conflict that would stay with him for the rest of his life. My conversations with John were steeped in the tribulations and confusion of young adulthood.

I told John about my own fears, my own attraction to men, and how conflicted I was about these feelings, particularly since I had this big, big love for Jane Wilson. He told me about his strong fear and hatred of his homosexual urges, and how they had to be exorcised. He wanted normalcy–marriage, children. He felt that every sinful thought he had would be eradicated if he embraced the Catholic Church. He urged me to go to mass with him, which I declined to do. I told John I had had my fill of masses when I was a child in Italy and that my mass-going days were over.

John was a wonderful friend–kind, thoughtful, and intelligent–really, something of a saint. In Iowa City, he had met Guenevere, plain of looks but deep of character, and very soon the two were married. Within weeks, Guenevere announced that she was pregnant, and nine months later little John was born. We were asked to be the baby's godparents. As a married man, John Logan seemed content. In time he graduated from the university and obtained a teaching position at St. John's College in Annapolis.

John truly loved teaching at St. John's. The curriculum was based on their Great Books program and he thrived in the atmosphere of learning. He became friends with the art and music departments, which is how he managed to give both Jane and I our first important solo show and recital. A definite date was set for both Jane's opening and for my recital. When I told Georgiana Bannister that she and I had been invited to perform at St. John's, she was overjoyed. We selected the songs we would perform and set up a rehearsal schedule. The songs would consist of some of my earliest efforts, settings of Friedrich Hölderlin, Franz Kafka, Rainer Maria Rilke, James Joyce, and E.E. Cummings, and would also include the haiku poems in French. For her part, Jane put together an exhibition of some 20 works consisting of still lifes, figures and landscapes. The year was 1951.

At St. John's, Jane's show was held in a spacious room in the art department. Her paintings were beautifully hung and well-lit, and the exhibition area soon filled with people. Jane looked radiant amidst her work. Seen all together, in this, her very first exhibition, her paintings offered genuine pleasure. Particularly notable was her sense of color, and a kind of instinctive and unerring sense of composition. Jane's work had not as yet coalesced into masterful finished works, but at every turn one sensed the genuinely felt impulses that informed each of her canvases. There was much praise for Jane's exhibition in the Annapolis press, and we were all terrifically proud of her.

As for my recital with Georgiana, it was held in the music department, in a small, handsomely appointed auditorium. Georgiana and I were well prepared, having practiced my songs ad nauseam in New York. My lovely soprano was in splendid voice and looked lovely in a simple black gown. I acquitted myself with considerable panache, accompanying Georgiana at the piano with youthful aplomb. After each group the audience responded warmly. When it was all over, there were some cheers and whistles. We felt as though we had arrived as young artists of the concert stage. The college gave us a wonderful reception, during which a young man came up to me and complimented my songs.

"My name is Jac Holzman, and I'm starting a record company," he said. "I'd like you to be my first recording artists." I looked at Georgiana. Georgiana looked at me.

"We'd be delighted! Absolutely delighted!" we said, practically in unison.

"Do you have a name for your record company?" I asked.

"Yes, I do," said Jac Holzman. "It's Elektra Records. You'll be Elektra 1."

The wonderful Jac Holzman, who had just offered us a recording contract, and a recording date in New York City, informed us that he had just graduated from St. John's and planned to make a career in music. He said he wanted to launch a record company in which the living composers themselves would be a part of the recording. He had all sorts of grand plans of enlisting well known contemporary composers like Milhaud, Poulenc, Hindemith, Copland, and Thomson, among others. He would feature their chamber music and vocal music, favorite forms of his.

In New York, Jac called us with our recording date and announced that the LP disc would be titled *New Songs by John Gruen.* I could not believe my good luck, nor could Georgiana believe hers. We had just started our careers and already had recording contracts! It seemed inconceivable and altogether fabulous. Elektra 1 appeared several months later and although it received very fine reviews from several distinguished critics it did not set the house afire in terms of sales. Indeed, poor Jac Holzman made no money at all on Elektra 1, and the record soon went out of print. Still he did not give up and almost immediately, switched from classical music to folk music and then on to a wide variety of genres, finally emerging as one of the top recording labels in the country. History, however, will note that Elektra 1 will always and forever be *New Songs by John Gruen.*

John Logan was responsible for it all. It was he who launched Jane's career as an artist. It was he who gave me my very first taste of what musical fame might be like. And it was John who, as the years passed, became the father of nine children. Eventually, he became an alcoholic and died much too early. As he grew older, John abandoned his Catholic faith and could not control his passion for fatherhood, men, or liquor. Indeed his drinking caused the ultimate rift between him and Guenevere. John died in a hospital in San Francisco in 1987. Jane and I kept in touch with

Guenevere, this loyal, much emotionally burdened woman, whom we met as a young bride in Iowa, and who brought up her many children with strength and courage. Indeed, to have known both John and Guenevere Logan in those long-ago days in Iowa City was to have experienced true and memorable friendship.

Chapter 15

The poet E.E. Cummings and his wife, Marion Morehouse, came to dinner one wonderful evening. It was just the four of us and the moment he stepped into our West 11th Street apartment, Cummings pretended we were all characters in a Chekhov play. With his poetic imagination clearly aflame, he spoke in a plaintive, Russian-tinged accent:

"Ah, Ivan Ivanovitch!" he called out, addressing me. "You are pouring our vodkas as though your heart were breaking! Come! Tell us about it–don't keep it all in. Speak freely!"

"And you, Lizavetha!" he said, embracing Jane. "How beautiful yet mournful you look! I tell you, this evening will not be a tragedy. It will be a comedy. We will talk of Moscow and Petersburg. We will talk of the summer and of the winter...and of the spring too. But not of the fall...the fall was the season Masha left me and I wept for seven whole years."

"Look who is with me!" pointing to Marion. "The Countess Vishnevskaya. We are first cousins, but love each other shamelessly. She has brought you lovely things to soothe your aching hearts–she had brought you bon bons and marzipan and gateaux ordered straight from Paris–all for you! This will be a glorious evening, believe me!"

All this I am paraphrasing, but so it went for much of the evening. As we dined, the dinner turned into a sumptuous Russian meal (it was just Jane's delicious roast chicken) and, as the wine flowed, Cummings amazed us by his extraordinary feats of memory, reciting whole passages from Tolstoy's *War and Peace* and Turgenev's *Fathers and Sons.*

A sour note was struck during dinner when our telephone kept interrupting Cummings' fabulous recitations. After the third interruption, Marion put a stop to it. She got up, went to the phone, unscrewed the "speaker" part, and stuffed some Kleenex tissue into it. The phone stopped ringing. (And it stopped ringing for three long days!)

I had read the poetry of Cummings in college, and was intrigued and enchanted by it. I loved the lower case of his name, the witty play of punctuation and the always allusive and brilliant shimmer of words offering poems that were both a feast for the eye and a joy to the ear. Mostly, of course, the poems touched the mind and the heart–especially the heart when it came to Cummings' love poems, many of which were as erotically exuberant as they were achingly beautiful.

We had met Cummings and his wife at a literary party, and I instantly wanted to speak with Marion, because, years earlier, I had quite fallen in love with her image as one of America's most ravishing fashion models. Marion was Edward Steichen's favorite model while he was a fashion photographer for *Vogue* and other publications during the 1930s. These photographs have become classics and are collected in many anthologies. Marion's face and figure epitomized American flair. Her look wasn't dreamy. It was down-to-earth, yet possessed of a radiant sophistication. Steichen's photographic genius–the way he posed Marion, the lighting, the atmosphere–produced images of compelling depth and artistry.

Marion Morehouse recalled her modeling years with a certain nostalgia. "Well, it was very hard work and not at all glamorous, but it had its rewards. I happen to have been the very first American fashion model to be sent abroad for a photo shoot. In those years there was no location shooting. You did most everything in the studio. But *Vogue* sent me to Egypt to be photographed. It was a fabulous experience and I was thrilled!"

Marion was Cummings' third wife, and when we met she was still a startling beauty who had now become a photographer of note. Indeed, her book, *Adventures in Value,* with text by Cummings, offered photographic images as forthright and plainspoken as Marion herself. They encompassed subjects from "effigies" to still life to nature to people, all imbued with compositional strength, clarity and feeling. I was immensely flattered when Marion invited me to 4 Patchin Place, where she and Cummings lived in the Village, to pose for a portrait. I sported a crew cut in those days. Marion's photograph of me made me look suave and somehow jaunty.

Cummings was a Harvard graduate and a rebel, an avid intellectual and a creature of politics. He traveled to Russia and throughout Europe. Beside writing poetry, which brought him fame, he wrote political tracts, novels and plays, which brought him notoriety. He didn't much like discussing his poetry; he preferred to write it, and sometimes to read it–for a fee. Mostly he liked to talk about his painting. Cummings was a trained artist who had exhibited his work while living in Paris and continued to paint and exhibit throughout his life. Cezanne was his god, but his work was less Cezanne than Pascin or Kuniyoshi. He loved doing portraits, and he made endless images of Marion—clearly, his muse, model, and love of his life. Cummings was, for the most part, something of a conservative—a sometime cantankerous man and a vitriolic complainer. He could be belligerent and yet he could also be so hugely endearing, entertaining, and charming that one just couldn't help wanting to be close to him, wanting to love him.

When I broached the subject of setting some of his poems to music, he told me instantly, "Be my guest, but don't expect me to like the result. I have no ear for music, and I know nothing about art songs." I would eventually write *Seven by Cummings*, a setting of seven of his love poems, which I consider one of my best song cycles. Cummings never heard it; he had died by the time I completed it.

Even as Jane and I began to meet more and more people both socially and professionally, we also kept our noses to the grindstone. Jane worked long hours as a model on Seventh Avenue. When she came home, it was time for dinner, and after dinner it was time to paint. When my day ended at Brentano's, I'd come home, fix myself a Scotch, get to the piano to work on my songs. Of course, this was a routine that could be easily interrupted. If Jane was too tired to cook or to paint, and if I didn't feel like working on my songs, we'd go out and grab a bite to eat, then wander over to the nearby Cedar Bar on Ninth Street and University Place.

We had heard about the Cedar Street Tavern, as it was officially called from the young poet and playwright, Arnold Weinstein and his wife, the soprano Naomi Newman, whom we had befriended. These were two of our talented New York friends, also trying to make names for themselves in the big city. Arnold and Naomi told us the Cedar Bar was where all the painters, sculptors, art dealers, art critics, poets and musicians got together. "You'll see and meet artists, like Jackson Pollock, Willem de Kooning, Franz Kline, Mark Rothko, Philip Guston, Robert Motherwell, and others—all of them revered giants of the still relatively small New York art scene."

And indeed, there they all were, at the Cedar Bar, sitting in the drab naugahyde booths of this nondescript, ill-lit, more than slightly depressing place, drinking endless beers or boilermakers and talking up a storm, arguing, and occasionally coming to blows.

These vociferous masters, who had already created the seminal full-fledged American style called abstract expressionism, were usually surrounded by a younger generation of ambitious artists, such as Larry Rivers, Howard Kanovitz, Mike Goldberg, John Grillo, Joan Mitchell, Giorgio Spaventa, Alfred Leslie, Marisol, and Grace Hartigan, among others.

These, in turn, would bring their friends, the poets Frank O'Hara, John Ashbery, Kenneth Koch, and the composers Morton Feldman and John Cage. And the day's art critics came to the Cedar Bar: Tom Hess and Clem Greenberg and, long before his dealer-to-the-art-stars days, Leo Castelli. Indeed the Cedar was not so much the scene of grand artistic pronouncements as a meeting place for solitary, thirsty artists looking for companionship, sex—even love.

The Ward twins—Joan and Nancy—pretty young Cedar Bar habitués, eventually paired up with Willem de Kooning and Franz Kline. De Kooning would soon be separated from his wife, Elaine, a charismatic painter and critic, who would make her own appearances at the Cedar, often with the equally charismatic Frank O'Hara. Some years later, Joan Ward and Bill de Kooning would become the parents of a very pretty blonde baby they named Lisa. She was de Kooning's only child, whom we watched grow into a wonderful-looking young woman whose life became as complex as it was charged with a certain charismatic luster. But they would eventually separate, and a voluptuous, beautiful young woman (also a twin) named Ruth Kligman would enter Bill de Kooning's life.

If all this sounds like a maelstrom of mad barroom melodrama, it was. Many of these events and encounters had indeed commenced or played themselves out at the Cedar Bar. Within a period of some five years—from 1951 until 1956 (the year of Pollock's death in a car accident, of which Ruth Kligman was a survivor)—the Cedar was among the major stomping grounds of New York's preeminent art world.

At times, the Cedar Bar would be supplanted as a gathering place by The Artists' Club, known simply as The Club, started in 1949. This space on Eighth Street near the Hans Hofmann School, became a far more official gathering place for artists, who banded together to hold meetings and discussions and, more often than not, throw terrific dancing and drinking parties. The late critic Harold Rosenberg, a huge bear of a man, told me that The Club was an adjunct of the Cedar Bar.

"It was formed so that artists could be with each other," he said. "The founding members consisted of Bill de Kooning, Franz Kline, Phillip Pavia, Ibram Lassaw, Lud Sanders, Landes Lewitin, Adolph Gottlieb, Mark Rothko, and Emmanuel Navaretta. The atmosphere of The Club was one of enthusiasm. They used to have hilarious board meetings. The main issue seemed always to be, "Who's going to sweep the floor?" or "Who's going to take care of making the coffee?" Then they decided to have dues, except nobody paid them. It was a riot, but we managed to make it work.

"There were some good discussions at The Club," Rosenberg continued. "I remember one that centered on the relationship between art
and poetry. The members sat around a table, got a couple of bottles of
booze, and talked about Baudelaire and Cezanne and the relation between
Cezanne and Mallarmé, which fascinated Bill de Kooning. By the way,
Jackson Pollock never came to those meetings—he preferred the Cedar Bar.
He didn't like doing stuff with coffee. But we had a lot of fun and a lot of
parties at The Club. All those characters brought records and all the artists
were terrific dancers. The Club turned into Roseland."

Jane and I were very much on the periphery of this swirling art world,
but somehow we made our presence felt, if seldom at The Club, then
certainly quite often at the Cedar Bar. Jane, always elegant, was eyed
and ogled by both the older and the younger male artists. Some would
not believe that she was a serious painter and we were both very careful
not to mention that she was working as a fashion model. Fashion models
would certainly not to be tolerated by such tough art-scene cookies as Joan
Mitchell or Grace Hartigan, both of whom would invariably come to the
Cedar dressed in well-worn jeans and paint-splattered sweatshirts, spew-
ing four-letter words, trying desperately to be "one of the boys." Grace
Hartigan even called herself George Hartigan for a while.

It was at the Cedar Bar, in the early part of 1952, where Jane was
approached by the young painters Wolf Kahn and Felix Pasilis. They asked
if she might be interested in joining a group of artists who wanted to form
a cooperative art gallery. Jane was an artist without a gallery and anxious
to exhibit. She readily accepted Wolf and Felix's invitation to become a
charter member of what became known as the Hansa Gallery.

Chapter 16

The cooperative galley was a New York phenomenon of the 50s. In addition to the Hansa Gallery, there already existed the Jane Street Gallery, organized by the painter Nell Blaine, and the Tanager Gallery, active on East Tenth Street.

The Hansa made its official debut in the fall of 1952 in a walkup tenement building on East 12th Street. It would later move to 120 Central Park South, near 57th Street. Its first director was a most endearing and dedicated young woman named Anita Coleman. She was totally selfless (if not masochistic) in her love of the gallery and its wildly diversified roster of artists. The name Hansa was the brainchild of painter Jan Muller, a German-born artist, who thought the old Hanseatic League, founded in the middle of the twelfth century by German and Scandinavian seafaring merchants to protect men, women, children, trade, and commerce from harm and banditry, would reflect the ideals of the gallery. Along with Muller, the roster of artists included Wolf Kahn, Felix Pasilis, Richard Stankiewicz, Jean Follett, Arnold Singer, Jacques Beckwith, Allan Kaprow, Miles and Barbara Forst, and Jane Wilson. Some years later George Segal, Lily Brody, Paul Georges, Myron Stout and Gandy Brodie would join this improbable mix of artists.

The point, of course, was to have artists take matters into their own hands. In the 1950s the New York art scene was far, far smaller than it is today. As Bill de Kooning put it, "We were all in our small corner." There were far fewer galleries, most of them clustered on 57th Street, almost none in downtown Manhattan. The chances of a new young artist being given a solo show was as remote as it was hopeless. Indeed, becoming a professional artist in New York was an uphill battle–hugely difficult for men, endlessly harder for women. And the cooperative galleries, where each artist paid his or her share of the rent, paid for general upkeep, for announcements, and mailings in return for a month's exhibition, seemed a viable and very exciting solution. Jane was thrilled to be a part of it.

Of course, I too was dying to be part of all the excitement. I offered my services to the Hansa Gallery, telling the group that I would act as their program director. I would bring lecturers and performers into the gallery, who, in turn, would attract an audience, a captive audience, who, in turn, would view the works on the gallery walls, might even purchase something, and tell the outside world what marvels were being introduced at the Hansa. I told them I would also introduce each of the exhibiting artists, and would speak glowingly of their work. Furthermore, I would charge admission; said admission helped to pay a twenty-five dollar honorarium for each invited guest, and the rest filled the Hansa coffers. All I needed in return was the monthly rental of about 50 folding chairs.

Amazingly, this all came about, despite the fact that meetings at the Hansa could be chaotic, filled with violent personal clashes and hysterical outbursts. There was always someone totally against one policy or another. Strangely enough, my suggestion sailed through without a hitch. I was officially made program director of the Hansa Gallery.

My first guest was James Johnson Sweeney, then the distinguished director of the Guggenheim Museum. His topic: "The Sculpture of Gaudi." We had a packed house. The second lecturer was the eminent Proust scholar, Wallace Fowlie. His topic: "Proust and Painting." Again, a great success. Then, wanting to switch gears dramatically, I engaged the tall, willowy folk singer, Cynthia Gooding, who, at the time, was something of a rage in New York. She came, she sang, she totally enchanted everyone. As arranged, each of these artists was paid 25 dollars. Mr. Sweeney said we could keep his fee and use it for another guest.

But there would be no other guest. I had a serious altercation with one of the gallery members, who felt I did not sufficiently praise his work during my introduction to Cynthia Gooding's evening. So angry and incensed was this painter, a hothead if ever there was one, and an enthusiastic user of hard drugs, that he threatened right then and there to bash my head in with a hammer. When I saw him actually reach for a hammer, I fled the gallery and resigned my post as program director the next day.

Jane, however, exhibited at the Hansa Gallery in 1953, 1955, and 1957. Each show was favorably reviewed in *The New York Times*, the *Herald Tribune* and in the various art magazines. Her abstract expressionist landscapes, figures, and still lifes, some influenced by the Abstract Expressionist painters, who all came around to the Hansa, were deemed out of the ordinary. But, in time, some members of the Hansa began to have reservations about Jane's approach to her subject matter, feeling it might be out of step with the more overtly abstract or semi-abstract direction the gallery wanted to cultivate.

During Jane's time with the Hansa, two more directors followed the patient, saintly Anita Coleman. These were Dick Bellamy, a scruffy, wraith-like, silent young man, who, during the 60s and 70s, went on to become an important dealer for emerging American artists, and the dynamic and energetic Ivan Karp, who would later be a force in the Leo Castelli Gallery, and later still open his own O.K. Harris gallery in SoHo.

Jane resigned from the Hansa Gallery in 1958. Her five years there were productive and illuminating; productive, because having a gallery meant having to produce works for her shows; illuminating, because Jane learned first-hand about the ins and outs of running a gallery, and also about the chaos and backstabbing that seemed to be part and parcel of the New York art world.

She herself was the object of controversy, because she was both a painter and a fashion model. (The secret finally got out!) The idea of a painter being a fashion model in the 50s was very unusual indeed, and the art world found it utterly preposterous if not infuriating. They thought it was downright embarrassing for a serious painter to embark on such a frivolous profession. Still, people found it quite intriguing that a young woman of astonishing good looks could paint with such highly motivated flair and personal conviction.

Jane also discovered that she very much liked earning her share of our keep, which her modeling provided. The alternative in the art world was securing a job as an art teacher, house painter, window dresser, non-licensed electrician and/or plumber, and other such proletarian, low-income, freelance jobs. Jane's being a fashion model and an artist suited us both quite well.

What is more, the media found Jane's double profession of serious New York painter and glamorous New York fashion model perfect "copy." Indeed, during Jane's five-year association with the Hansa Gallery, she was the subject of various stories and photographic spreads in *Time, Glamour, Coronet,* and most importantly, *Life,* which, in a double-page color spread, showed Jane reclining on one of our secondhand divans, in a story dedicated to up-and-coming American women artists.

The Hansa was not amused, especially since none of their other artists were thus celebrated. Matters came to a head in 1958, when Jane, with her newfound celebrity, was invited to be one of the contestants on the then wildly popular TV quiz show, *The $64,000 Challenge.* Her topic was art history, and she reached the $32,000 plateau when, alas, she was thrown a curve by the show's producers and lost the big prize. (She received a consolation prize of $1,000, some Revlon products, and all the Kent cigarettes we both could smoke.)

Our good friend, on the other hand, Larry Rivers, had also been tapped as a contestant on *The $64,000 Challenge* some time earlier. To everyone's amazement, the erratically schooled Rivers proved unbelievably smart and well-informed, and walked away with $32,000. (We all celebrated his victory at the Cedar Bar). What no one knew then was that Larry was shown the answers, and, as was soon revealed, the quiz show scandal broke out in headlines everywhere, ruining the reputation of various lives (Charles Van Doren, notorious guest of *Twenty-One,* for one).

Jane was not fed answers (as she told the district attorney during trials of the quiz shows), but her seven-week exposure on TV proved a boon. Her paintings began to sell, and her name was beginning to be known.

Indeed, during the early 50s, much was happening to us both.

Chapter 17

One of the problems was that my own life moved far more slowly than Jane's. Though I was ambitious and raring to be a success–any kind of success–I did not have the good fortune of having a single goal. Jane had a single goal: to be a painter. I just didn't. Yes, I wanted to be a composer, but only a composer of art songs, which, of course, limited me considerably. I knew that if I were a "real" composer, I would have to embark on a very thorough course of study in composition, preferably with a master composer or teacher, I would need to have the burning desire to write symphonies, concertos, operas, oratorios, and every kind of chamber music.

This, for my sins, I did not have. What I was prepared to do was go as deeply as I could into composing my songs. I also became enamored of improvising. I would sit for hours at the piano and work out endless ideas. I also developed a passion for an instrument I found in a secondhand store in Iowa City and had brought with me to New York: the zither! I just loved that zither! I'd improvise on it endlessly. I'd hold it on my lap and pluck away, either with my fingers or with a pick, or I'd strike the strings with a mallet. The sounds that emerged were quite magical and haunted–very *The Third Man*, but, in my hands, more beautiful! So much could be expressed on the zither, especially when amplified. I thought one day I might make productive use of this heavenly harp-like instrument.

And so, I continued to compose my art songs–for piano and voice–creating new song cycles or individual songs set to poems by T.S. Eliot, Wallace Stevens, Edwin Muir, and others. And, day in, day out, continued with my job at Brentano's bookstore. After two years as a book salesman, I felt I definitely had to advance in rank. During those years, I had met almost everyone on the staff including the head book buyer, a certain Miss Lillian Friedman, who was as smart, tough, and funny as she was canny about the book-buying business.

I loved Miss Friedman's wit and New York humor. She could really dish it out when book salesmen, all of them men, started salivating over some book or other. "OK, you can cut the crap now!" Miss Friedman would exclaim. "I'll take two copies!"

I talked to Miss Friedman about becoming her assistant. The problem was she already had one: Trudy Laub, who did a perfectly good job in her own rather quiet, unflappable way. But Miss Friedman thought she could use a lively and "quick" new person in her department—and I landed the job. I couldn't be more pleased. I earned more money and I learned a tremendous amount about the buying of books for a large and distinguished bookstore. Under Lillian Friedman's tough-love tutelage (she gave me a really hard time at the start), I got very good at what I was doing—and I did it for two years.

All the while, another of Brentano's employees entered our lives, Loly Eckert, who worked in the children's book department. She was German-born with the aura of a wan and weary Marlene Dietrich, and her life in war-torn Germany had been very difficult. Because of our European backgrounds, we would share each other's stories, usually in German, over coffee or lunch. Loly, despite her quite luminous appearance—she had those Dietrich cheekbones, pale skin and beautiful clear-blue eyes—seemed quite run down. I learned she had a terrible time during the war in Germany, had been married and had a child—a boy—who, while still an infant, died of malnutrition.

Loly divorced her husband and began moving in highly Bohemian circles, mingling with artists, poets, writers, actors, filmmakers, and leading, as she put it, a rather dissolute life. Through relatives, she was able to come to New York and make a new life for herself. Loly found a place to live in Greenwich House down in the Village, which made it quite easy for us to see each other socially. Jane and I took Loly on our rounds of various art events and parties. We knew that what she hoped for was to meet a man who could give her a stable life and, hopefully, more children. We became quite fond and protective of Loly, and our friendship would take some quite interesting and unexpected turns.

Meanwhile, Jane and I made friends with some of the artists we met at the Cedar Bar, most notably Joan Mitchell. We had seen Joan again and again at the Cedar, being "one of the boys," expressing strong opinions about art and life and the current state of American politics. A thoroughly seasoned devotee of words such as "fuck," "shit," "prick," and "cocksucker," Joan, quite sexy of figure, but rather plain of face, seemed irrevocably opposed to the uses of makeup, skirts, heels, or any other female accoutrement.

When we met Joan, she was married to a wiry, terrifically smart, somewhat myopic-looking fellow by the name of Barney Rosset. Both came from well-off Chicago families, and both were driven by a strong need to succeed. Joan's goal was to become a force in American art. Barney's was to become a major American filmmaker. Some years before we met her, Joan had been a realist painter—and she harbored ambitions of doing social-realist paintings à la Rivera and Orozco. However, this did not pan out—she either couldn't do it or got bored with the idea. She then went on to do highly charged landscape-inspired abstractions, which ultimately brought her lasting fame.

For his part, Barney made one feature-length film, a documentary entitled *Strange Victory*, dealing with racism. But the film didn't please him and in 1951, he turned his life around and purchased a small publishing house named Grove Press, which, under Barney's visionary aegis, would become one of the most controversial publishing firms in the country.

Joan Mitchell and Barney Rosset were a volatile married couple, but we quite liked each other and saw each other on many occasions. While Joan never really committed herself vis-à-vis Jane's work, she did attend Jane's openings and put a polite, if sour, face on Jane's increasing popularity. Joan and Jane were such opposites in temperament and appearance that this seemed to act as an odd bond between them.

I thought Barney was fascinating and I liked him immediately, even if he did have a wild and compulsive laugh and giggle and manifested a certain nasty sense of suspicion. He was terrifically well informed about politics, movies, literature, and art. But what especially appealed to me about Barney was the fact that he was half Catholic and half Jewish. Given my own half-Catholic, half-Jewish background, I could relate to this duality despite the fact that neither of us were practicing Catholics or Jews.

Unfortunately, we met the Rossets just as their marriage was coming apart, and the two were not always pleasant company. One night at dinner in our apartment Barney mentioned something about Joan having gained weight. At this, Joan picked up a ripe tangerine from a bowl on our table and forcibly aimed it at Barney. He ducked, and the tangerine splattered onto our freshly painted white wall behind him. This she did twice more, with accompanying invectives at the top of her voice. Finally, they left, and Jane set about wiping the tangerine muck off the wall. Indeed, Joan and Barney seemed to enjoy goading each other on—and there were other episodes we witnessed which were decidedly not pretty.

At last divorced, Joan began an affair with the painter Mike Goldberg. It was a brief encounter. They broke up, and, in time, Joan met the painter Jean Riopelle, who lived and worked in Paris. They fell in love. Joan joined him in Paris. Although Joan Mitchell and Jean Riopelle were together for many years, they too ultimately separated. For whatever reason, Joan elected to spend the rest of her life in a suburb of Paris in the house that once belonged to Claude Monet. She would return only briefly to New York for the openings of her shows, which grew increasingly more powerful with each successive exhibition. We did not attend her openings, and never saw Joan Mitchell again.

Joan died in Paris in 1992. She achieved what she set out to achieve. Her abstractions, rising out of the great innovations of de Kooning, Pollock and Clifford still contained all the fire, color and exuberance of her own quixotic personality. She was difficult, obtuse and cantankerous, but, like her art, she was the genuine article.

When, in 1952, out of the blue, Barney Rosset invited me to join his newly acquired Grove Press, I was stunned and delighted. He wanted me to be its first director of publicity. He thought my work at Brentano's and my somewhat flamboyant personality would provide Grove with a much-needed sense of identity. I accepted Barney's offer forthwith and promptly gave Brentano's my notice.

I was embarking on a brand new life in publishing. I would now be thrust into the world of publicity and public relations. I myself would have a new identity. And I would be part of a brand new, terrifically exciting publishing venture with a boss who was also my good, good friend. It was pure joy! When I told Jane all about it, we celebrated by deciding that the first thing we must do is MOVE! A new chapter was beginning, and it would play itself out at our brand new address: 324 Bleecker Street—still, most happily, in the heart of Greenwich Village!

Chapter 18

Our new apartment on Bleecker Street was on the second floor, over a shoe repair store. It was a floor-through, sunny and pleasant, looking out on a series of concrete backyards. There were no gardens, but we did look down on a lovingly cared-for fig tree, the pride and joy of the landlord.

We loved our new place, and as always, Jane made space for her easel, paints, brushes, and canvases in a corner of our bedroom. She continued to paint. She continued to model. Her cooking improved. (We cut way back on kidneys and rice). We saw lots and lots of people, drank lots and lots of beer and lots and lots of Scotch. We smoked up a storm. We attended lots of art openings, went to too many boring poetry readings, were present at all avant-garde music events, and saw lots and lots of quite terrible under-ground theater and dance which, only during the 1960s, with the advent of Caffe Cino, Café La Mama, The Judson Dance Theater, Circle in the Square, The Theatre de Lys, and The Phoenix Theatre, would begin to move into vigorous, adventurous, and startling new directions.

And, best of all, I had a brand new job!

The day Barney Rosset hired me to work at Grove Press, he and I both rushed up to West 23rd Street to buy me a secondhand desk, a secondhand swivel chair, a secondhand typewriter, and a secondhand filing cabinet. I insisted that everything be delivered to the office that very day. The office, it turned out, was Barney's apartment on West Ninth Street. I wanted to sit at my desk and start writing press releases immediately.

At the time, the Grove Press staff consisted of just Barney Rosset as publisher/editor, Donald Allen as editor, and Marilyn Meeker as book-keeper. I was the newcomer. I could tell by just looking at him that Donald Allen would not be my friend. He was one of those ultra-fey, watery-eyed, pale-skinned, queeny young men, who spoke in whispers, and would not look you in the eye or say "good morning" when you came to the office. We instantly loathed each other.

Marilyn Meeker was another story altogether. Warm, friendly, quick to smile and a very hard worker, she made sitting close to Donald Allen almost bearable. Of course, Barney was all over the place, often quite hysterical, an obsessive negotiator on the phone, ridiculously tight-fisted with his money, overly generous when it suited him, whiny and surly when something displeased him, and generally quite nasty over even the smallest mistakes. In addition, he had that really annoyingly compulsive nervous laugh and giggle that all of us had to put up with.

On the other hand, Barney was a truly admirable defender of the written word. At first, the earlier, inherited Grove Press backlist remained quaintly sedate, even arcane: *The Verse in English of Richard Crashaw*, Melville's *The Confidence Man*, *Selected Writings of the Ingenius Mrs. Aphra Behn*, all small classics in their own right.

However, it was when Barney added such titles as D.H. Lawrence's *Lady Chatterley's Lover* and Henry Miller's *The Tropic of Capricorn* to his list, and when he began to publish the works of the Marquis de Sade and the first-ever writings of Jean Genet, Samuel Beckett, William Burroughs, Hugh Selby, and Jack Kerouac, that the specter of American censorship raised its ugly head.

Barney was hounded by the censors, the post office, and the government itself, all of whom deemed his foreign imports pure filth and morally offensive. When it was discovered Barney also had Communist affiliations as a young student in Chicago, matters got even worse.

So incensed was Barney at the censoring of great literature that he went all the way up to the Supreme Court, sued the government and litigated on behalf of his authors for years on end. For his troubles, both the CIA and the FBI placed him under surveillance. Barney Rosset had become a menace to society, and, concurrently, became the most controversial and notorious publisher in America.

Barney's many censorship battles were eventually won, and the name Grove Press stood for upholding the First Amendment in all its glory. His fearlessness was heralded far and wide and to this day he remains a figure of great daring and vision.

When I knew him, Barney Rosset may have been a man of daring and vision, but privately, he was just a fellow who was miserably lonely. He had acquired Grove Press, his new, exciting toy, but he had also just divorced Joan Mitchell and he felt alone and unhappy. One night after work he invited me to have a drink with him at the Cedar Bar.

"You wouldn't know of some nice girl who'd like to go out with me, would you?" he asked. "I'm going kind of crazy."

"Well, let me just think," I said. "You know, I just might know of someone! There's a lovely German girl I used to work with at Brentano's. Her name is Loly Eckert. Maybe she'd be willing to go out with you."

"Great!" said Barney. "Can you arrange it?"

I told Barney I would talk to Loly. And talk to her I did. I warned Loly that Barney was difficult, but brilliant, that he was rich, but hysterical, that he was an up-and-coming publisher with real imagination, and finally, that he was my boss and my good friend. Loly agreed to meet him. A tentative courtship ensued. I frankly thought the two were not exactly made for each other—their backgrounds were dramatically different and there was something not quite right and awkward about their togetherness. Still, within a few months, Barney Rosset and Loly Eckert were married. The ceremony was at Grace Church, at Tenth Street and Broadway, directly across from Grove Press' new headquarters.

I was best man, Jane was matron of honor. I had done my good deed for Barney, finding him a lovely girl to be his wife, allaying his loneliness, filling him with what I hoped was great, great happiness. We saw them off on their European honeymoon. When they returned, Loly, her health and appearance much improved, was installed at Grove Press as, of all things, the firm's sales representative.

By this time, the staff had increased by the addition of Howard Turner, a totally engaging and wonderfully witty young editor, Susheila Lall, the young wife of the Consul General of India, who wanted to do something "useful" with her time, and, a year or so later, a handsome and very dynamic young American editor and translator named Richard Seaver, whom Barney had met in Paris and who knew all the important French writers of the period.

I loved my job as publicity director for Grove Press. I loved meeting the writers and loved squiring them around town and setting up interviews, loved writing press releases and writing the flap copy on the book jackets and loved dreaming up new ideas to publicize this or that new Grove Press title, loved being in the exciting milieu of the New York publishing world. We were all working very hard for very little money, all of us kind of playing it by ear, except, of course, for Donald Allen—so prissy and prim and professional, so know-it-all and smug.

I even had the chance to test my wings as a fledgling zither virtuoso. When, in time, Barney Rosset began bringing out his literary magazine, *The Evergreen Review*, he publicized it by taping a series of radio programs based on some of the magazine's content. I was invited to supply the background music for a number of these broadcasts, including "The Eye of Mexico," and "The Ferlinghetti Story." I strummed my zither for all it was worth, improvising the kinds of sounds I felt were appropriate to the various texts and subjects.

Of course, Jane and I continued to see Barney and Loly socially. We were very close friends. We would meet for drinks or dinner or at parties—at their house or at our house—and we were immensely delighted when they announced that Loly was pregnant with their first child. It was such joy when Loly later gave birth to a beautiful blond baby boy they named Peter.

Then, one Monday morning I got to the office, greeted everybody, and was delighted when Barney and Loly stopped by my desk to say they'd like to take me out to lunch that day. I thought perhaps a new Grove Press publicity project was in the offing.

We went to the Cedar Bar for lunch, and over drinks Barney suddenly announced that he was letting me go—that Grove Press could no longer afford me. Loly said that this did not for a moment mean the end of our great friendship. Barney, with his awful giggle, said Grove Press just wasn't earning enough money to sustain a publicity person. Loly said that they would miss me terribly. Barney raised his glass to me and said, "Don't feel bad, John. You'll find a new job in no time!" And he giggled some more.

I was totally crushed, bewildered and sick to my stomach. I felt betrayed by my friends. I could not believe I was being let go—fired! I thought I was doing a good job, and truly earned my piddling 25 dollars per week salary; that I was a vital part of the organization, that we'd be working together for years and years to come. I was devastated. I was particularly angry with Loly, whose life was so drastically altered by having met Barney through me. I could not finish lunch. I abruptly got up, returned to the office, cleared out my desk, and walked out the door without speaking to anyone.

Jane and I tried to see Barney and Loly socially after I had been fired. We attempted to re-cement our relationship. When Barney bought a house in East Hampton that had belonged to Robert Motherwell—the famous Quonset hut designed by Pierre Chareau—we visited them. Barney even invited me to help stage a music festival on his property, which I did, and the project definitely intrigued me.

I invited Elaine Lorillard to bring some of her Newport Jazz Festival artists, like Max Roach and Abbe Lincoln, to East Hampton, and I invited the Juilliard String Quartet and other classical artists to participate. The Festival went on, and it was a success. But it didn't help. Every time I looked at Barney or at Loly, I felt a sense of betrayal, and my stomach just turned. Finally, Jane and I stopped seeing them altogether. The friendship just went away. In fact, I decided never to speak to either one of them again.

It came as no surprise to me when I later heard that Barney and Loly separated and were divorced. Years later, I learned that Barney lost Grove Press during a hostile takeover. And I heard he married and divorced several more times and had several more children. It was all too bad, but frankly, on hearing all this news, I felt absolutely nothing…I just didn't give a damn.

Chapter 19

When I was still working at Grove Press, Jane and I met a young art dealer by the name of John Myers. Johnny, as everyone called him, was the director of the Tibor de Nagy Gallery, then located on East 53rd Street. The gallery was named after a charming Hungarian who actually founded it—he was the gallery's financial backer. De Nagy, an elegant, highly cultivated man, was a banker, and liked staying in the background. For his part, Johnny Myers was the very vociferous, effusive, gossipy, and quite brilliant director and front man. The Gallery's roster of painters included Larry Rivers, Helen Frankenthaler, Grace Hartigan, Jane Freilicher, Robert Goodnough, Alfred Leslie, Fairfield Porter, Mike Goldberg, Nell Blaine, and Elaine de Kooning, among others.

These were all young artists just starting out, and most of them proved to be as formidably talented as they were supremely ambitious. Johnny nurtured all of his artists, but there were some he positively worshipped. Among these, Larry Rivers was the cock of the walk. Not only did Johnny Myers champion Rivers' work, banging down museum doors, collectors' doors, critics' doors, anybody's doors to get Larry's paintings purchased, exhibited, talked about and written about, but he also fell madly and hopelessly in love with him. Indeed, the two had an affair, which Larry himself considered totally crazed.

As Larry told me, "John Myers really fell for me in a very big way. He was on the phone with me every two hours. He searched for me all over town if I wasn't home. He wouldn't stop phoning. And he helped me a lot. He would call people up and ask them to give me money. When I met him, he seemed fantastically knowledgeable and he dropped these French words. Myers brought something else into the whole thing of homosexuality for me. For one thing he was slightly older than the rest of us. Also, he was involved in other things besides art—he was a puppeteer, and was involved in the theater. He seemed to have some kind of relationship with the surrealists, which seemed like being in touch with history. We were all name droppers, but he really was the king. At any rate, he had looked at my work and I think he had already decided he was in love with me—or rather, that he wanted to make it with me."

Johnny Myers' obsessive pursuit of Larry Rivers was both poignant and comical, given that Larry, who died at age 78 in the summer of 2002, was not given to lasting commitments either to hetero or homosexual relationships. Indeed, Larry, who told his story with revealing and manic bravado in his autobiography, *What Did I Do?*, (written with Arnold Weinstein), loved both men and women, though not equally. Finally, it was the many women in his life who won out, offering Larry not only the best years of their lives, but in three instances, several children—a total of five little Riverses. There was his first wife, Augusta. Larry adopted her son, Joseph, and the two had another son, Stevie, together. There was the beautiful Welsh girl, Clarice Price, who became wife number two. They had two daughters, Gwynne and Emma. Then there was the painter Daria Deshuk, whom Larry did not marry. They had a son, Sam. Before and after, and in between and betwixt was a galaxy of men and women all of whom were in some way transformed by the exuberant, slovenly, erotic, gifted and impossibly chaotic personality of Larry Rivers, né Aloys Grossberg.

Certainly the painter Jane Freilicher, the poet Frank O'Hara, and the literary agent Maxine Groffsky, to mention but three, played major roles, sexual and otherwise, in Larry's life. But Larry was a friend and a success story to all the young painters, poets, jazz musicians and creative celebrities of this time. He was a magnet to us all in his seductive, down-and-dirty way.

I too was drawn to Larry, especially in the later 1950s, when we were all so young and beautiful and energetic and sexy. I felt I could easily throw myself into the gutter with Larry—and sometimes I did. We got drunk together, we fooled around together, we danced together…and what have you. And Larry was very fond of me and very kind to me. When I needed money, he lent me some. When I began to write professionally, and he got to be famous, he never denied me access to his person or his art. What is more, he did two marvelous portraits of me, one, a most flattering charcoal pencil drawing, another, a three-dimensional portrait "collage," all silver and pink, and mounted on a box. Larry also made a most imaginative collage for the cover of my very first book, *The New Bohemia.*

But, sad to say, Larry's lifestyle and mine didn't really mesh. We were different types altogether. As seductive as he was, Larry's life seemed in constant flux; mine was much quieter, more stable—at least on the surface. Larry's life was loud and raucous and in constant motion—mine just wasn't that hyped-up. Still, we remained lifelong friends. Even when he reached old age, he retained the quality of youthfulness—that electric, dynamic "something" which never ceased to ignite everyone around him. He was curious, opinionated, always ready for a good argument. He lived hard, loved hard, and, god knows, worked hard. He was, as they say, a force of nature—quite unforgettable, quite extraordinary, and I loved him a lot.

But back to Johnny Myers and the Tibor de Nagy Gallery. What was odd was that even as Johnny Myers was in hot pursuit of Larry Rivers and feverishly running the gallery, he had long been involved with a stage director named Herbert Machiz, who continued to be very much a part of his life.

Machiz was the first recipient of the U.S. State Department Fulbright Fellowship for Theater Research in Paris in 1949. He became an assistant to Orson Welles and, in New York, directed such notable revivals as *Cabin in the Sky* by John Latouche and Vernon Duke. But, for all that, to have known Herbert Machiz was to have known a nervous wreck of a man who was possessed of a certain innate vulgarity. He was one of those loud and overbearing theatrical types, who made even the most strident Tallulah Bankhead or Bette Davis impersonator seem demure. I personally found Herbert Machiz irritatingly offensive. This feeling was tripled when I actually found myself working with him.

As it turned out, Johnny Myers, even as he ran the Tibor de Nagy Gallery, had spearheaded a venture called The Artists Theater, dedicated to staging plays by fine arts writers and poets. This young, first-of-its-kind theatrical company operated between 1953 and 1969, staging some 16 original plays by such up-and-coming young poet/writers as John Ashbery, Frank O'Hara, Jimmy Merrill, Kenneth Koch, V.R. (Bunny) Lang, and Lionel Abel, among others. These works were mounted with stage settings and costumes created by the artists represented by the Tibor de Nagy Gallery—thus the name, The Artists Theater.

While Herbert Machiz seemed to have had a minor flair for quick-paced comedies in the Noel Coward vein, he seemed totally out of his depth directing plays of outré poetic sensibility. But Johnny Myers, in his perverse and ill-advised way, considered Machiz the ideal director for The Artists Theater and thus it was that poetic play after poetic play received the leaden directorial treatment by a man incapable of knowing the difference between tongue-in-cheek and foot-in-mouth or discerning the humor, charm, or intellectual delights contained in most of The Artists Theater's presentations.

It seems utterly ungrateful of me to complain about Herbert Machiz's lack of talent, his boorishness and vulgarity, when, at Johnny Myers' behest, Machiz repeatedly hired me to provide the musical backgrounds for several of The Artists Theater's plays. Of course, it was my haunting zither that both Myers and Machiz coveted. To strum my zither was to lend poetic mood and atmosphere to their productions, and I was more than happy to offer my magic to plays that Herbert Machiz seemed determined to ruin.

I lent my improvisational genius to Bunny Lang's *Fire Exit*, Norman Vein's *The Crime of Innocence* and Lionel Abel's *Absolom*, plays that did not, alas, survive in the annals of theatrical immortality. Still, it was the beginning of my professional life, short-lived as it was, as a theater and film composer. I went on to be hired by the actress and director, Julie Bovasso, to create zither intrigue for her productions of Jean Genet's *The Maids* and Michel de Ghelderode's *Escurial*. For the underground filmmaker, Willard Maas, I strummed the zither for his film, *The Mechanics of Love*, and did the same for Ian Hugo's (one of Anais Nin's husbands) quite beautiful short film, *The Gondola Eye*.

My most extravagant zither score was commissioned by the avant-garde German artist and filmmaker Hans Richter, who had made a name for himself in American with his surrealist film, *Dreams That Money Can Buy* (1947). Jane and I had met Richter through his cinematographer, Arnold Eagle, who told us Richter was about to embark on his second full-length surrealist movie, called *8 x 8*, an homage to Lewis Carroll's chess episode in *Through the Looking Glass*. Arnold Eagle had heard my score for Ian Hugo's film, which he had also photographed, and thought the sound of my zither would be perfect for Richter's *8 x 8*.

Richter adored the idea. Not only did he agree to my being the film's composer, but he invited Jane and me to be actors in the film as well. Jane was cast as the White Bishop and I as the Black King. A film star at last! I couldn't be more thrilled. But what was genuinely thrilling was our learning the names of our co-stars. As in *Dreams That Money Can Buy*, Richter enlisted all his artist friends to participate in the making of the movie, and the artist friends appearing in *8 x 8* included a veritable who's who of Dada and Surrealism: Marcel Duchamp, Jean Cocteau, Jean Arp, Jose Sert, Yves Tanguy, Alexander Calder, Max Ernst, Dorothea Tanning and Frederick Kiesler. Also in the cast were composer/writer, Paul Bowles, art dealer, Julien Levy, Jacqueline Matisse, and the architect Paul Weiner.

This fabulous conflagration of talent, had, like Jane and me, no film acting experience whatsoever. And yet, *8 x 8*, released in 1957, and shot on
the grounds of Richter's home in Connecticut and elsewhere, got made in
record time, thanks to the filmmaker's quite chaotic, improvisatory, and
hectic filmmaking style.

As for my *8 x 8* zither score, over which I labored for weeks on end, it
was to be the ultimate glory of my zither-playing career. So inventive yet
cohesive was my improvisation, so eloquent my melodies, so atmospheric
their harmonic fabric, that I was certain Hans Richter, upon hearing it,
would take me in his arms, look deep into my eyes and cry, "John, it's pure
genius!" Instead, Richter accepted my completed score, carefully captured
on tape, with a smile, but without a word of thanks. I did not hear from
Richter again, until weeks later, when he invited Jane and me to a private
screening of the film. The credits rolled. There were dim zither sounds in
the background...very dim sounds. Then, at last, came the music credit,
which I had envisioned as reading: "Music by John Gruen, performed on
the zither by the composer."

Instead what I read was "Sound Direction by Hans Richter with Robert
Abramson, Bebe and Louis Barron, John Gruen, Douglas Townsend. Lyrics
by John Latouche. Sung by Oscar Brand."

What Richter had done behind my back was to take my lovingly
composed zither score, lasting well over an hour, and combine it with
the music or "sounds" composed by others. What is more, whenever the
zither was heard by itself, the sound was sped up as in a cartoon cat-and-
mouse chase.

Needless to say, I was devastated by Richter's thoughtless treatment
of my effort. When I confronted him with dismay and anger, all he
could say was, "I think the score as it now stands is very beautiful—just
what I wanted!"

My last zither score was for The Artists Theater's production of Lionel
Abel's play, *Absalom*. This long-winded Biblical drama in three acts, once
again directed by the hysterical and dim-minded Herbert Machiz, was musically in need of more than just a lone zither. To that end, I enlisted the services
of a highly talented young Japanese composer name Teiji Ito. I had heard
Teiji perform on all manner of exotic percussive instruments and his mercu-
rial deftness on drums, marimba, wood blocks, bells, and many others, was
astonishing. He readily agreed to collaborate with me on what would be quite
a lengthy score, requiring many hours and weeks of rehearsals and taping.

As it turned out, Teiji Ito was the young lover of the underground film-maker, Maya Deren, a woman of unhinging energy and considered a goddess of avant-garde cinema Deren is best known for her collaboration with her former husband, filmmaker Alexander Hammid, of such 16 millimeter studies in ennui as *Meshes of the Afternoon* and *At Land* and such heavy-handed and self-conscious dance films as *Rituals in Transfigured Time* and *A Study in Choreography for Camera.*

It was my misfortune that rehearsals with Teiji Ito would have to take place in the apartment he and Deren shared in the Village. It took only one rehearsal for me to realize that she would also be part of the collaboration—that she would insinuate herself into every facet of our working time. When she wasn't giving us advice as to how the music should really go, she would leap across the room in frantic Jules Feiffer "dance ritual" fashion, or sing along with our improvisations in a high-pitched mewl.

The woman was unstoppable. Poor Teiji, years younger than Deren, and usually in a drug-riddled dream of his own, never said a word. He just played his drums and bells, gazing adoringly at his beloved. Finally, I put a stop to Deren's interference, telling her she was a dangerously disruptive element and that if she didn't stop prancing around or talking or singing while we were working, Teiji and I would part company.

Deren, hating my guts, removed herself from our workroom. When the score was completed, she went to Johnny Myers, Herbert Machiz, Lionel Abel, and anyone else who would listen, and told them that Teiji alone was responsible for the score of *Absalom,* that I merely plucked a few chords on my zither, but that Teiji was the real composer of the music. She insisted that my name be removed from the program. Deren also wrote me a ten-page letter, informing me that I had no soul, that my behavior indicated a very unhappy marriage, and that I needed to seek help for my many sad and pitiful neuroses.

Ironically, Maya Deren's former husband, Alexander Hammid, known as Sasha, and Deren's friend and cinematographer, Hella Heyman, who would later marry Sasha Hammid, became two of our closest friends. When I told Sasha and Hella my Teiji Ito-Maya Deren story, Sasha smiled, shook his head and said, "It could have been far worse, John. Maya was a handful from the very beginning."

Chapter 20

All that strumming on the zither for little underground plays and little underground films earned me very little money. Indeed, the pay for my composing and improvising efforts was basically zilch—25 dollars here, 30 dollars there, and once in a blue moon, 50 or 100 dollars. As for earning a living writing art songs, that was an even greater pathetic situation. The one and only time I made a few hundred dollars on my songs was when Jac Holzman of Elektra Records paid me something like 600 dollars for recording *New Songs by John Gruen*. Other than that, my songs did not earn one cent. Yet Jane was happy for me to be a composer, and she never once complained about my great lack of earning power. She made fairly good money, and for many, many months, she supported us both. And so, I continued to write song after song after song, and tried as hard as I could to get them performed and published.

At around this time—it was the mid-to-late 50s—I met several American composers, most notably the rotund and much revered Virgil Thomson and the young and exceedingly handsome Ned Rorem. Thomson, gay, gifted, and very grand, was exceedingly famous at the time we met, not only because of his operas, *Four Saints in Three Acts* and *The Mother of Us All*, written in collaboration with Gertrude Stein, but because he had become the most powerful music critic in America, writing for the *New York Herald Tribune*, one of the country's leading newspapers.

The American music world may have revered Virgil Thomson, but it also feared him. He was a critic of alarming outspokenness, one who could make or break a career and whose sharp and pointed reviews were lessons in clarity and musical acumen. Indeed, Thomson's writings on music are today considered journalistic accomplishments of the highest order, being at once meticulously informed and unnervingly direct.

I was brought to meet Thomson at his apartment in the Chelsea Hotel by William Flanagan, a young composer and music critic. Of course, I presented Thomson with my Elektra 1 recording of *New Songs*, which I had hoped he would play for the gathered guests. This did not happen, but I saw Thomson place the LP propped up near his record player so people could see it. This was a cocktail party consisting mostly of beautiful young men, although a few women were also present.

The painter Maurice Grosser, Thomson's longtime friend and companion, acted as charming cohost. I noticed immediately that Thomson was in his cups, and just now was being quite vociferous about "the Jewish musical mafia," consisting principally of Aaron Copland and Leonard Bernstein, whom he felt were not sufficiently interested in or smitten by his own work as a composer. He was particularly hard on Bernstein, who was then the hugely successful and popular young conductor of the New York Philharmonic.

I looked at Thomson as he stood in the middle of his beautifully appointed Victorian living room berating his fellow composers and found him full of envy, his eyes cold, mean, accusing. But then, he would stop, be all smiles and act the perfect host.

Months later, after we knew each other well, I asked Thomson why he had it in for Copland and Bernstein.

"Oh, I don't have it in for them," said Thomson, smiling broadly. "Not at all! I mean, Aaron Copland was an associate since the early twenties. That friendship went on in a general collegial relationship. As for Leonard Bernstein, he and I have always been terribly friendly. But we didn't seek each other out. We kind of operated on two sides of the fence. I didn't throw enough balls to him, and he didn't throw enough balls to me. If I had made a lot of plugs for him, and he had played my work constantly, that would have been another kind of a deal."

The fact is, as chief music critic for the *Tribune,* Thomson praised Bernstein very little, while other conductors received unstinting and lavish praise. It was because these conductors played Thomson's music, and played it often.

When Thomson resigned his *Tribune* post as music critic in the late 50s, almost all the conductors who performed Thomson on a regular basis dropped him from their repertory. Virgil Thomson and I had a friendship of sorts. He told me I was a handsome fellow. He said he was charmed because I was French-born, spoke several languages, and was, as he once put it, "a very savvy and sensitive connoisseur of music." After finally listening to my songs on the recording I had brought him, he announced that I had a "very special lyric gift," and encouraged me to proceed as a composer of art songs. He did feel I could stand some more study, particularly in matters of counterpoint and harmonic "coloration." This was my cue to inquire whether he would consent to becoming my teacher of composition and orchestration. He told me he had not taught in many years, but that yes, he would take me on as his pupil but only for a brief period of time. I told him I was poor and couldn't afford to pay him very much. He said not to worry about it, that we'd "figure out something."

Thus it was that Virgil Thomson became my most celebrated teacher, from whom I learned to keep my music simple, transparent, yet at all times personal and expressive. We worked together for less than a year, at which point he said he was too old and impatient to continue, and that I was too young and "quite a slow learner." Still, I got a tremendous amount out of my work with Thomson. He was something of a slave driver, but it was good for me. As for my paying him, he never charged me a cent. He just insisted on the occasional rather too-long-lasting hug.

It lay heavily on my mind and soul that Jane was supporting us both, while I was being the "genius" composer of the American art song. I felt it could not go on in this way. I needed to find a job.

Jane and I had by now become close friends of Lyena, her husband Roger Dodge, and their young son, Pryor. Indeed, we saw a good deal of them, and I was particularly struck by Roger's wide-ranging knowledge of the arts and the various collections and archives he had built in celebration of classical male dancing, jazz, and Cuban and South American popular music. Roger's collection of Vaslav Nijinsky photographs, for example, are today a valuable mainstay of the Dance Collection at the New York Public Library for the Performing Arts in Lincoln Center.

We'd spend hours at their apartment in the East 80s listening to endless recordings of all the American jazz greats Roger had collected, from Meade Lux Lewis to Pete Johnson to Charlie Parker. And we were equally mesmerized when Roger introduced us to the artistry of the great Carlos Gardel, the fabulous Argentine tango singer. It was Roger who taught Jane and I to execute the tango properly—all to the tangos of Gardel!

One evening, the Dodges invited Charles Rado, Jane, and me to dinner. Also present was Ylla, one of the Dodges' dearest friends and a celebrated animal photographer, who was represented by the Rapho-Guillumette agency. The dinner went extremely well, what with Ylla recounting wonderful tales about her exploits with wild animals in jungles all over the world, and Charles Rado discussing various psychological aspects of Shakespeare's *Hamlet*, the play that had obsessed him for years. By the end of the evening, I felt we had all become friends. Lyena Dodge, the designer for whom Jane worked on Seventh Avenue, recommended me to Charles Rado, a diminutive Hungarian who founded Rapho-Guillumette, a prestigious photographic agency. (The Guillumette part was a dour Frenchman, Rado's silent partner). After Magnum Photos, Rapho was the city's leading photo agency, with a branch in Paris. Lyena told me Charles Rado was just then looking for a young energetic person, conversant in the arts, who also loved photography, to help him run his agency as salesman and general factotum. A few days later, after an interview with Charles Rado at his office on 54th Street near Park Avenue, I was hired as the agency's new assistant and salesman.

Being an agent for photographers was a profession I had to learn on the job, and it would be hard work. It involved spending hours on the phone, soliciting work for Rapho-Guillumette photographers, and toting a large and heavy portfolio of photographic work to New York's leading advertising agencies and magazines. The idea was to persuade art directors at ad agencies and picture editors at magazines such as *Life, Look, Ladies' Home Journal,* and *The Saturday Evening Post* to use Rapho-Guillumete's gifted French and American photographers. These included Brassaï, Robert Doisneau, Sabine Weiss, Bill Brandt, Man Ray, Sanford Roth, Fred Lyon, Tana Hoban, and Ormond Gigli, among others.

What was extraordinary was that from the first, I was handling images on a daily basis by European photographers who would years later emerge as masters and whose works would sell for thousands of dollars. In the 50s, however, photography was not yet considered a legitimate art form, and selling photographs, particularly by Europeans, proved difficult indeed. But Charles Rado was a most persuasive agent and the editors at *Life* and *Look* and all the other magazines really respected this feisty little man who championed his photographers day in, day out. Indeed, Charles, with his Hungarian accent and slight lisp, was almost single-handedly responsible for bringing contemporary French photography to the attention of the American public via various brilliant photo-essays or single photographs that he placed in American magazines.

At Rapho-Guillumette my love of photography took root. I would drag out all the boxes filled with black and white photographs–our "stock pictures," as they are called–and pore over them for hours. I especially loved those very shiny, crisp European vintage prints of Brassaï–the pictures of Paris by night, with its demimonde of prostitutes, homosexuals, and languorous figures in seedy bars or under street lamps illuminating crooked

Paris streets. These pictures were full of the scent of decadence and allure—and I marveled at their cinematic immediacy and shadowy beauty.

I loved meeting Brassaï and Doisneau and all the rest when they visited New York. As I spoke French, it was easy to communicate with these artists, whom I engaged in long conversations about their lives and their craft. The fact is, I wanted to learn all I could about taking pictures—especially portraits—and Brassaï was especially helpful in giving me all manner of encouragement and tips on how to take the "perfect" portrait; tips that included ways of putting the sitter at ease ("Endless flattery is a must!"), to frequently moving the subject into various sources of light within an interior space or simply using "natural" light as often as possible ("For portraits, soft daylight is terrific!").

I toiled at Rapho-Guillumette for nearly six years. The pay was good. The work was interesting. And my boss, Charles Rado, while very demanding and quite neurotic, turned out to be a decent fellow. When he suffered a serious heart attack, which put him out of commission and out of the office for six months, I ran the office together with a lovely young woman named Anita (whom Rado kept wooing but did not win), and Sally Goodman, the most endearing wife of the poet and writer Paul Goodman. When Rado returned, I received a sizeable bonus for seeing to it that Rapho-Guillumette did not, under my aegis, go under or up in flames.

But much began happening in my life that made me wonder just how much longer I could continue being an agent for photographers. Some of what was happening to me was positively thrilling. Some other things were perfectly frightening. When I joined Rapho-Guillumette I had turned 27—and it was at 27 that I learned the meaning of the words "anxiety attacks."

It was not amusing!

Chapter 21

Where did they come from?

Why was my life suddenly made a misery by these awful, frightening anxiety or panic attacks, as they're now called? What was I doing that brought them on? Or what wasn't I doing?

While at work at Rapho's, I'd get ready for an appointment, walk out the door, and walk up Madison Avenue. Suddenly, out of nowhere, my head would feel light, my heart would start pounding, everything would begin to seem altered—the avenue, the buildings, the stores, the people. I'd start to feel faint and my heart would pound faster, more loudly, but mostly I'd feel very, very frightened. My whole being was in turmoil. I felt I might fall to the ground and die right there on the spot. At these times, I would stop walking and stand in a store's doorway hoping it would all pass. I'd stand there absolutely frozen and rooted in fear. I'd break out in a sweat. And at these times, I tried talking to myself: "It will pass. It will pass. Stand still. Calm down. Don't move. It will pass. Calm down."

Sometimes it did pass. And when that happened, I'd just pull myself together and go to the appointment, hoping no one would detect what I'd just been through. When the attack would not pass, I'd find a drugstore or a Chock full o'Nuts, sit at the counter, ask for a glass of water, order coffee, hoping it would all subside. Eventually, it did subside, and I'd leave, praying the attacks wouldn't return.

What I couldn't understand was *why*? Why was I having these horrible, horrible bouts of anxiety? Was there something physically wrong with me? Was it my heart? I honestly didn't think so. Then why was this happening to me? When the attacks wouldn't go away, when, in fact, they lasted longer and became more frequent, I told Jane about them. She was concerned, of course, but said what she always says when something goes wrong with me: "Go see a doctor, John. Go see a doctor."

I didn't want to go see a doctor. I hated going to doctors. I wanted to figure it out for myself.

Even though my heart was pounding hard and I knew I would die on the spot, and I broke out in sweats, I always recovered, and I continued to feel OK…until the next time. Of course, I knew in my heart of hearts that it had to be something psychological. But what could it be? If I could just pinpoint the thing that was causing these anxieties, they would probably go away.

So I thought about everything that was going on inside me—especially the things that were really bothering me. I thought about the fact that I wasn't performing very well in bed these days. And Jane wasn't having an easy time of it either. This was very troubling. I thought about all the queer fantasizing I was doing. I thought about my really strong physical attraction to Sasha Hammid, the ex of the scary Maya Deren. I thought about all those things, and more—all the guilt-provoking things that might be producing my attacks.

I was also feeling terrible about my career as a composer, how, despite my so-called talent, I was going exactly nowhere with it. And Charles Rado, my boss, was really getting me down with his badgering about being more productive as a photo agent: work harder, solicit more clients, bring in more money. I felt I was not succeeding on any front—not in bed, not at the piano, not composing, not at work…nowhere at all.

All this hard thinking, all this acknowledgment of my failings and of my guilts did not stop the anxiety attacks. In fact, as the months dragged on, they were getting more acute. Finally, after much hesitation, I talked to Sasha and Hella Hammid about my problem. Hella, in her no-nonsense way, said it loud and clear: "Get thee to an analyst, John—and do it *now*! And I've got one for you! Mrs. Leonore Fabisch. She's terrific. I'll call her for you."

Now, I knew all about psychoanalysis. That is to say, I knew all about it from the outside. At Iowa University, I took a psychology course—read a lot of Freud and Jung and Adler. And I continued reading Freud in New York—I thought the stuff was great. Also at Iowa, when I worked at a mental hospital briefly, I met and talked to real live analysts as they plied their dark and sullen craft. Jane and I had friends who were being analyzed or coming out of analysis or about to go into analysis. Being in analysis was the intellectual sport of the 40s and 50s.

But the thought of being psychoanalyzed myself really stopped me cold. I didn't feel it was for me—not because I thought I was such a normal, well adjusted fellow—but because I felt it would sap my talent, my energy, would make me less interesting or interested. I didn't want to know all that much about myself, didn't want to probe the depths of my feelings. I wanted there to be some mystery about one's inner life. Most of all, I didn't want to talk about my sex life or my secret desires or my private yearnings. I didn't want a stranger intruding on any of that. Basically, I just wanted to have a bit of success, and I wanted to be happy with my life and my accomplishments.

And yet...and yet. The anxieties just wouldn't go away. Finally, I called Mrs. Leonore Fabisch. Hella was right, she was entirely wonderful, this German-born woman, with her large, luminous eyes, quiet voice, soft German accent, had studied with Dr. Carl Jung in Switzerland and was herself analyzed by Jung.

I had an anxiety attack on the way to my first session. I had visions of myself lying on a couch, paralyzed and unable to say a word. When I got there, I was welcomed by Mrs. Fabisch herself, and ushered into her office—a very peaceful room. There was no sign of a couch. Mrs. Fabisch motioned me to a comfortable chair facing her desk. "Jung didn't use a couch," she said. "We face each other. We look at each other. We are with each other."

Unsurprisingly, I very quickly found my tongue, and instead of falling into a deep silence, as I had feared, a torrent of words spewed forth as I began telling Mrs. Fabisch how I really didn't believe in psychoanalysis, that it would interfere with my creative life, that it would rob me of my identity and on and on and on.

She listened with eyes intently fixed on mine, just the slightest hint of a smile playing on her face. When I was done, she let a few long moments elapse, then she quietly said, "Mr. Gruen, why don't you tell me something about your father?"

Thus began three years of analysis with Mrs. Fabisch. These were twice-weekly visits at 25 dollars per session, which Mrs. Fabisch kindly allowed me to pay whenever I could. Within two weeks, my anxiety attacks abated. Within a month they almost disappeared, although they occasionally made return visits.

Resistant at first, I slowly came to depend on my 50-minute sessions, doing Mrs. Fabisch's bidding in terms of writing down my dreams (I have reams of dreams in notebook after notebook!), of discussing the events of my life as they were occurring right then and there, day by day, night by night (with Jung, you talk about now more than then—more about the present than the past), and I came to understand that being in a good analysis was like going to school about yourself, learning about the dynamics of your personality and how these dynamics, these conscious and unconscious forces within you, interact with the world around you—your family, friends, acquaintances.

Actually, you don't become another person, and you certainly don't lose your creative abilities or your talents or your inner person or any of that. What happens is that you come to know yourself better and learn to be calmer about the things that trouble you. You learn to deal with your shortcomings and the shortcomings of others, and to make peace with the demons that make your heart go bump in the night and thump in the day.

Working with Mrs. Fabisch had its good days and its bad days. There were no solutions, no defining answers, no resolved chords. But as you delved into your dreams and into your thoughts and into your actions, what emerged was a better capacity for living with yourself and with others. It didn't come all at once, but come it did…slowly and without announcing itself. There you suddenly were, no longer so anxious, no longer so torn— and all your secret desires remained intact, but not biting your head off.

Of course, I was lucky. I had support and I had care. As they say in the parlance of romance: I had the love of a good woman! Jane was always there, even when I wasn't.

Chapter 22

As it turned out, while still at Rapho, and throughout my years in analysis, my songwriting career suddenly took a turn for the better. No, I did not, alas, succeed in getting any of my songs published, but I got them sung–and this time by some very stylish singers. Even as I was toiling rather unhappily at Rapho-Guillumette, many of my weekends and nights at home were spent composing more and more songs and song cycles. One of the highlights of this period was meeting the poet Wallace Stevens, whose haunting poem, "Thirteen Ways of Looking at a Blackbird," I had recently set to music.

As was my wont, I often wrote letters to the poets whose work I was setting, asking their permission to use their poetry and, of course, inviting them to come hear what I had done with it. I knew Stevens worked as an insurance executive in Hartford, Connecticut, and I addressed my letter to him at the Hartford Insurance Company. To my great surprise and pleasure, he answered to say he'd be in New York in a week's time, and would be pleased to come by the apartment to hear my cycle. He did warn me, however, that he had no ear for music, a surprising admission from a poet whose work was, to my ears, made of music.

Stevens arrived at Bleecker Street one late afternoon, and we found this tall, burly, somewhat gruff-looking gentleman to be as cordial as he was unassuming and unpretentious. Unfortunately, he hadn't counted on the presence of our two black kittens, Tristan and Isolde. "I'm quite allergic to cats," he announced. We placed the cats behind closed doors and offered Stevens some wine. Stevens began to relax. Upon seeing some of Jane's paintings on the walls, he remarked on their strength and sensitivity.

In my rather shaky tenor voice, I sang Stevens my setting of "Thirteen Ways", 13 very brief stanzas that musically and vocally (I hoped) illustrated the compelling aspects of Stevens' blackbird. When it was over, Stevens said all the appropriate things; how it seemed to him I had captured the poem with originality and élan. But, again, he reiterated the fact that music in general and vocal music in particular was not his strong suit. Still, we spent the rest of the afternoon discussing how hard it was to be an artist and the perils of being practitioners of the so-called "smaller" forms, such as poetry and song. "You can't really do it, unless you've got a job on the side," he said.

Soon after Wallace Stevens returned to Connecticut, I received a short but warm letter from him on Hartford Insurance stationery thanking us for our hospitality and "the fine music." This would be the first of a brief correspondence of some seven or eight letters Stevens and I exchanged. Some of this correspondence centered on my songs and on his poems. After Stevens' death, this brief but very meaningful correspondence later found itself in *The Letters of Wallace Stevens*, edited by the poet's daughter, Holly Stevens, and published in 1966.

And so I was writing my songs, was studying with Virgil Thomson, was going to analysis with Mrs. Fabisch, and was working at the Rapho-Guillumette photo agency. Of course, Jane and I continued our socializing, going out with friends, seeing lots of art shows, but making particular time for song recitals and the opera, which we attended with some regularity at the invitation of richer friends.

One memorable recital we heard was given by the soprano Patricia Neway, who had achieved fame as the deeply affecting Magda Sorel in Gian Carlo Menotti's opera *The Consul*, which premiered on Broadway in 1950. Neway's voice was of the highly charged operatic variety, strong and almost contralto-like in timbre, yet able to climb seamlessly toward the higher reaches of the soprano range. I was much taken with Pat Neway's ability to interpret song as if it were the most meaningful of utterances. Every word was audible, every inflection of every phrase was expressive. As I listened to her, I longed for this unusual artist to sing my songs. Some time later, I heard that Neway would be offering another recital, this one dedicated entirely to songs based on the poetry of James Joyce, and sponsored by The James Joyce Society.

I lost little time in contacting the Society to announce that I too had written a song cycle based on Joyce's poetry, namely *Pomes Penyeach*, and how could I get the cycle to Ms. Neway? They very kindly obliged by sending my songs to the soprano, and a few days later, Neway herself called to say she loved them very much, and would include a number of them on her recital.

We made a date to meet and go over my songs, and, as expected, I found Pat a most thrilling interpreter of my music. As it turned out, she had long been a champion of contemporary music and had, in fact, given three all-Joyce recitals in New York City. Then, one day, much to my Joy, Pat called to say that Lyrichord Records would be recording an all-Joyce album and that three of my *Pomes Penyeach* would be included. The LP record was titled *Songs to Texts by James Joyce* with Patricia Neway, Soprano, and Robert Colston, Piano. There were also Joyce songs by Thomas de Hartmann, Samuel Barber, Seymour Barab, and Israel Citkowitz.

My professional relationship with Patricia Neway, whom Jane and I came to love and admire greatly, culminated some years later with an all-Gruen recital at New York's Carnegie Recital Hall. This came in the year 1960, and it promised entrée into the music publishing world that had yet to pay the slightest attention to me. But the recital was well attended and quite a success.

The two most important papers, *The New York Times* and the *New York Herald Tribune*, sent their music critics, Ross Parmenter from the *Times* and William Flanagan from the *Trib*, and both wrote glowingly about the songs. As for the music publishers, they came and they went home again. Although they had sat for weeks and months on the manuscripts I had earlier sent them, none of them responded. I may have been disappointed, but this did not prevent me from seeking out more fabulous singers to sing my consistently unpublished songs.

The most spectacular of my singers was the Metropolitan Opera diva, Eleanor Steber, she of the silvery voice and thrilling interpreter of Mozart, Verdi, Puccini, and Wagner. I met Miss Steber toward the close of her great operatic career, which flourished during the 40s and 50s. Now her voice was no longer as lustrous as it once was. And, alas, the soprano was also battling a drinking problem. Indeed, it was a moment in Steber's life where an "anything goes" and "je m'en fou" attitude seemed to engulf her, even propelling her into singing pop songs, wrapped in a towel, at the Continental Baths, one of New York's most popular gay establishments, a place made famous by the equally notorious appearance there by the totally adorable, very much younger and sassier Bette Midler.

But Eleanor Steber was a dream. I absolutely adored her. When I met her in the late 50s at a reception given for her by Samuel Barber (in 1948, she had commissioned and premiered in his ravishing

Knoxville: Summer of 1915 and in 1958 would premiere the title role of his opera *Vanessa* at the Metropolitan Opera), I approached Steber about looking at some of my songs. She agreed and upon my sending her several cycles, she telephoned inviting me to her apartment on West 55th Street.

Steber and I went over all the material, and she fixed her attention on a cycle I had just completed, *The Adele Songs*, set to three poems by the young American poet and lyricist Kenward Elmslie. A kind of lowdown, bluesy cycle about a down-and-out vaudeville performer, the songs amused and charmed Miss Steber. Singing the cycle in her living room that day, Steber sounded as glorious as ever. She agreed to include them in one of her forthcoming recitals.

As luck would have it, I was just then invited to give a recital of some of my songs at radio station WNYC. It suddenly occurred to me that perhaps Steber might like to premiere *The Adele Songs* on the air. What could I lose? I called her and she instantly agreed. This time I thought a pianist other than myself should accompany Steber, and I enlisted the services of my very gifted young, unthinkably handsome friend, Alvin Novak. When they met, the two got along famously, and I was present at WNYC as Eleanor Steber sang the world premiere of *The Adele Songs*, along with several other works of mine, over the air. It was utterly sublime to have my music sung by one of the great voices of the century.

But Steber was not my only diva. Ever since I heard a recording of the *Alexander Nevsky Suite* by Prokofiev with soprano soloist Jennie Tourel, I coveted this marvelous singer as another ideal interpreter of my music. The darkly luscious sound of her voice, so uniquely insinuating and vividly personal, brought a new dimension to any performance, whether on the operatic stage or in recital. Unlike Steber, however, Tourel was not an easy catch. I truly had to pursue her. Not even an introduction by Leonard Bernstein, whose songs I heard Tourel sing at Town Hall, with Bernstein at the piano, softened her to my pleas. I particularly wanted Jennie Tourel to sing a French song cycle I had written called "Paroles," based on the poetry of Jacques Prévert. The songs would suit her admirably, what with their slight cabaret aura and Tourel's sensual, seductive style.

Finally, after further arduous attempts, Miss Tourel gave me her telephone number, and asked me to call her in two or three weeks. This I did, only to be told by her secretary that Tourel was either busy or on tour or unable to speak to me. One day, I saw her walking along 57th Street. I marched right up to her and, like a rejected lover, said: "Why are you avoiding me? Why won't you return my phone calls? Why won't you look at my music? Don't you know that I love you? Your voice? Your artistry?"

In a very melodious and markedly Russian accent, Tourel, said, "You really are a terrible pest, Mr. Gruen. But alright, come and see me tomorrow at teatime and show me those songs of yours."

She gave me her address, on West 58th Street, and on the next day, I made my way to her apartment, which was spacious and elegant in the Louis XVI mode. She was gracious and listened intently as I sang and played the six songs of my Prévert cycle–"Paroles". When it was over, she said, "I like them. I will sing them in Saigon. I am going on a tour of the Orient. I will sing your songs in Saigon."

"What about New York?" I ventured. "Won't you sing them in New York too?"

"Well, let's see how they go over in Saigon," replied Tourel.

As tea was served and as I regaled her with flattery and praise, Tourel nodded and nodded and just never stopped smiling. But hidden in those many nods and many smiles was a wicked kernel of mockery, which quite unexpectedly hurt my feelings.

Tourel soon departed on her tour of the Orient. She was gone for weeks. When she returned I telephoned her.

"How did my songs go over in Saigon?" I asked.

"You won't believe what happened," said Tourel. "They put me in a movie house for my Saigon recital. The stage, it was very raked. Everything went well until after intermission. Yours was the cycle right after intermission. When I came out, the people, they clapped. Then the lights went down. My accompanist started to play, I started to sing the first of your songs, 'Je suis allé au marché aux oiseaux.'

"All of a sudden, I heard the audience gasp. Then I felt a big push from behind. It was the piano! The piano was rolling down the stage–it was on top of me. I screamed. My pianist was trying to hold on to the piano, but it was too heavy. Men came running from backstage to catch the piano before it rolled over me and into the orchestra pit. I was run over by a piano! It was terrible–the men, they took me backstage–they saved my life. It was terrible. I could not go on with the concert–I was in pain from the big push. So, your songs did not go over in Saigon–I could not sing them. Maybe later...another time. The songs are very pretty, but I must hang up now. Goodbye!"

Thus it was that Jennie Tourel never sang my French song cycle or indeed any of my songs–and I decided never to pester this great singer again.

Chapter 23

There were few opportunities in America for a composer who specialized solely in art songs. What music publishers hammered home to me was that art songs simply didn't sell, that they would lose money publishing them. If I were to write operas, oratorios, religious choral works, or chamber music, then they might consider publication.

It was discouraging, but I plowed on. It had long occurred to me that poetry readings could be enormously enhanced if the poet, instead of droning on by himself, had some musical accompaniment, if the reading were more like a jazz combo, with the spoken text and other instruments forming a unique whole.

To that end, I enlisted all our poet friends to come to the apartment on Bleecker Street so that I might improvise a musical score for piano, zither, and drums as they read their poems into a tape recorder. The project turned out to be a real hoot. Frank O'Hara came and read about ten of his best poems as I sat at the piano, with my zither in my lap and a small drum at my side. I was a one-man band. Of course, I was given the poems beforehand so that I could study them and so that my improvisations would not be a helter-skelter affair, but appropriate to each poem.

John Ashbery, Kenneth Koch, Arnold Weinstein, and others came to the house, taping their poems as I pianoed and zithered and drummed away. The idea, of course, was that we would take these little shows on the road, to the various downtown coffee houses that featured poetry readings. But almost no coffee house had a piano or indeed a cabaret license or enough space or what-have-you for this little dream of mine to pan out. Still, I have some of the tapes we made, and they sound amazingly fresh, especially the Frank O'Hara collaboration, which New York's The Poetry Project, Ltd. released as a commercial CD in 2007.

My life as a composer culminated and finally came to an end with two commissions. The first came from my friend Alexander (Sasha) Hammid, the filmmaker, who had himself been commissioned to make a documentary about the United Nations. It would be the first major film depicting the inner workings of the U.N., which had recently opened its doors in New York City and begun to go into full operation. The film would depict the towering building, its workforce and its ideals. To my total astonishment, Sasha invited me to compose the score for this important undertaking, which would be titled *Workshop for Peace*. "But please, no zither!" said Sasha. "Our budget allows for a small orchestra."

As my orchestration skills were limited, I looked around for a talented young composer to orchestrate my piano score. I found him in the person of Mitch Leigh, who would soon find fame and fortune with his score for the Broadway hit, *Man of La Mancha*. Mitch's orchestration for *Workshop for Peace* proved adequate, though hardly inspired, and the same may be said for my music. I wanted to please Sasha so much that I ended up getting myself musically tied in knots, and I felt I disappointed everyone concerned. Still, the film was deemed unique enough to have been included in the collection of the Film Department of the Museum of Modern Art.

The second commission was far more meaningful to me, and it put an end to my songwriting career. The commission came from the soprano Alice Esty, whom Jane and I had met through the duo pianists, Robert Fizdale and Arthur Gold. Bobby and Arthur, or "The Boys," as they were called, were enormously gifted pianists who met at Juilliard, became lovers, then, though no longer romantically involved, continued to live together and share their international careers and lives in a wonderfully appointed, beautifully decorated apartment on Central Park West and a lovely summer house in Water Mill, Long Island. Quite apart from their terrific talent as pianists, they also had a special talent for collecting the very rich. Nothing pleased Bobby and Arthur more than hob-nobbing with figures of American and international society, the European titled, and all the major artists of the day.

Alice Esty was one of their richest conquests. The enormously wealthy widow of William Esty, who had founded the exclusive William Esty advertising company (they handled Rolls Royce for one and Chesterfield cigarettes for another), was of hearty Swedish stock. Regal, beautiful Alice Swenson, a graduate of Bates College, began her career as an actress in the late 1920s, performing in the avant-garde plays of E.E. Cummings and Edna St. Vincent Millay at the Provincetown Playhouse in Greenwich Village.

Alice also studied singing, and, after her marriage to William Esty, commissioned such well-known composers as Francis Poulenc, Darius Milhaud, Paul Bowles, Virgil Thomson, and many others, to write song cycles for her, which she would then premiere and perform in concerts at New York's Carnegie Recital Hall. While a most diligent and disciplined singer, Alice Esty was not, unfortunately, blessed with a compelling or beautiful voice. Her soprano was somewhat harsh and unsteady. More often than not, there were lapses in pitch and intonation. Of course, she had embarked on a singing career quite late in life and this hardly helped. Still, when she began giving recitals at Carnegie Recital Hall, the entire New York music intelligentsia attended, not because of Alice's vocal allure but because she was introducing new music—new songs by important composers—that would eventually find their way into the canons of contemporary vocal music.

Indeed, many of Esty's commissions were later published and, like Poulenc's ravishing song cycle *Le Travail du Peintre* to poems of Paul Éluard, would achieve international and lasting popularity among the world's major recitalists.

Our first vision of Alice Esty was as she descended a short flight of stairs into the lobby of Carnegie Hall, following a recital given by the great German soprano Elisabeth Schwartzkopf. Alice was flanked by Robert Fizdale and Arthur Gold, both of whom seemed to be propping her up. She was dressed to the nines, especially in the glittering diamonds department. She wore a delicate diamond tiara, a diamond choker, diamond bracelets, diamond earrings, and several diamond brooches. In her long sable coat, she literally lit up the lobby.

She was also lit up in a less glittering way, as she stumbled, in a genteel manner, toward the exit and onto the street, with "The Boys" propelling her safely into her waiting limo. Though utterly dedicated to her singing and her music, Alice Esty had a serious drinking problem, which, at the time we met her, was in high gear. Amazingly, as the time approached for her various song recitals, Alice would sober up and plunge into the study of her new commissions, aided by her coach, advisor, and piano accompanist, David Stimer, a short, tubby, balding man of a certain devious demeanor and personality.

Alice had by now become a very close friend of ours and she felt particularly close to Jane, buying several of her paintings and eventually studying painting with her. Years later, when Alice had stopped drinking as well as singing, and had become a rather overly dignified elderly woman, Jane and Alice developed an even closer friendship, based on their mutual love of art.

Indeed, while consistently hearing and praising my songs, she was not forthcoming with a commission. Of course, I wasn't Poulenc and I wasn't Milhaud. I wasn't even Paul Bowles. Still, I thought I was pretty good. And other people thought so too. Consequently, I did not retreat from my quest quietly or politely. I mean, we were really close friends, and I felt I could speak my mind. As I so often put it to Alice, "What is your problem?"

Well, David Stimer was her problem. Alice finally confessed to me that it was David Stimer, her mentor and accompanist, who insisted I not be given a commission. Stimer had heard my songs and apparently hated them. He also hated me. Why, I'll never know. Probably because he thought I was too pushy–and I guess I was.

I sulked whenever Alice came to visit or we went to her house or we went out together. Alice just laughed. I sulked and let her know how unfair she was being to a young composer who was dedicating his entire life to the art song, and how could she, the queen commissioner of art songs, not include me as one of her composers?

At last, Alice relented. I seemed to have shamed her into it. Over the strong objection of David Stimer, she handed me a check for $600, and told me to write her a song cycle. She even knew the poet she wanted me to set: the up-and-coming young James Schuyler.

My song cycle would be performed at her next recital. It was a bitter-sweet victory. When I completed the cycle of five James Schuyler poems, entitled *Greetings from the Chateau*, Stimer looked at it, hated it, and, as Alice reported, told her he would play it in public only once–during her recital– and never again. *Greetings from the Chateau* was one of my very best efforts, and it was the hit of Alice's recital. What is more, Stimer accompanied it bril-liantly, as though it were the most beautiful song cycle in the world. But true to his word, he never performed it again, either with Alice nor anyone else.

Somehow this episode, along with my long-acknowledged decision that my composing days were coming to an end and that my talent, whatever it was, was not potent enough to justify struggling on with it, I called a halt to the notion of becoming America's most gifted art song composer. I just didn't want to die poor–or utterly disappointed. It was definitely time to turn my life around, maybe start earning some real money, maybe even start living like people who made real money.

Perhaps it was time to move again–to go live where the rich live and see if some of it rubbed off. I mean, I was young, fairly good-looking, had a gorgeous wife, spoke several languages, was even in analysis, and had put in years as an agent for photographers. Why couldn't I do some agenting on my own? Why not quit Rapho-Guillumette and start my own agency? And not just for photographers, but also for singers, filmmakers, and actors, an agency that would encompass many arts and disciplines. It would start small and grow into–who knows–the William Morris Agency or some such talent giant.

I discussed it with Jane. She listened. I told her we must move uptown– out of the Village–to Park Avenue! I said I wanted to start something on my own. She listened some more. I told her I'd start looking in *The New York Times* for a new apartment. She perked up a little bit. (Bleecker Street was getting a bit claustrophobic. I needed more breathing room. Jane needed more space to paint.) Finally, I did it. I looked at the apartment ads and there it was! 128 East 72nd Street! Between Park and Lexington! Where the rich live! We went to see it. Of course, as always with us, it was the seediest, most rundown brownstone on a beautiful block. Still, the rent was fairly reasonable, it was a parlor floor-through, it had a fireplace, a wood-paneled dining room, and parquet floors. As far as I was concerned, it was pure luxury. And that address! So swank! So chic! I wanted. I couldn't wait to get in there. When we finally stood, just the two of us, in the living room of our new apartment on East 72nd Street, I looked at my corn-fed farm girl and said, "Oh baby, we've really come a long way!"

Chapter 24

The stationery was elegant, the business cards were embossed, and the address was fabulous, yet the prospects for John Gruen Enterprises were dim. Whatever gave me the idea that I could single-handedly become an agent for people in differing creative disciplines? For one thing, I didn't really have the contacts. Yes, I knew the photography world. It was really small. But the film world? The music world? The pop music world? I was clearly delusional. Or my ego was definitely out of control.

Poor Alexander Hammid, Cynthia Gooding, William Van der Veer–my first clients–they had supplied me with endless biographical material and samples of their work–films, clippings, folk song recordings, and photographs. I made the phone calls, I walked the streets. I tried. And tried! For one whole year, I tried. And it was a bust. I got nowhere. And it was a misery. So I gave up. I had to. My attempt at multi-agenting was driving both me and Jane crazy. Finally, I put an end to it, and gave it all up. My three clients understood–and we remained friends. But what a disaster!

After that, I took a nosedive both spiritually and psychologically. I was especially miserable over Jane's having to support us. Still modeling, she made good money, but I was young–just 28–and energetic, and it just about killed me that I lacked the talent for earning a proper living. So what did I do? I threw myself into the gutter.

Well…it wasn't total debauchery, but I stayed out nights–I drank quite a bit and I did things I wasn't proud of…messy things. I saw people I didn't really care for. And I did it all on my own–without Jane. I went to straight bars. I went to gay bars. There, I went into back rooms and let people grope me and fondle me, and I groped and fondled them in return, and I went home with some of them–out of lust and unhappiness. And the more I wanted to stop, the more I continued doing it. And when I returned home to our so-called glamorous digs on East 72nd Street, and took a walk around the block to clear my head, I came to realize what a cold and impersonal neighborhood it really was. All those doormen walking poodles. All those pinched, well-dressed men and women walking stiffly in an aura of well-groomed apprehension.

Suddenly, the fabulous East Side seemed fabulously dead to me. There was no bustle, no excitement, no liveliness. It was superficial, phony, affected—"Just like me!" I thought. And I shuddered.

One day I got to the apartment and found Jane at home. She had not gone to work that day. I sensed something was up. For an entire year, Jane had not said a word about the failure of John Gruen Enterprises; had, in fact, handed me her checks to be deposited in our joint bank account. She saw I was making a big effort. She also saw how unhappy I was—and how badly I was behaving when idleness and depression and anger got hold of me. And she never said a word.

But on this day Jane had something to say:

"I've quit my job. I'm through modeling. I've given them notice. I'm just going to paint full-time now."

"But, but...but, you can't do that," I sputtered. "Who's going to pay the rent?"

"We're moving back to the Village. You're going to find a job. You're going to pay the rent," said Jane.

We had lived on East 72nd Street for exactly one year. There is no question but that Jane's decision to call a halt to the life we were living saved me and saved our marriage.

In those years, the late 50s, we had no difficulty finding a new and nicely appointed apartment. This time around we landed not exactly back in the Village, but fairly close to it—on East 18th Street, near Gramercy Park. It was another parlor floor-through and it was sunny, bright, and fairly spacious. Not only did I regain my footing there, but much, much more!

Having abandoned agenting and composing, I wondered what I would do next. This time it would have to be something really substantial and steady as well as personally meaningful. And, most importantly, I would really need to make some decent money. I thought hard about this, and finally decided that the one aspect of my background that I had never fully tapped was my writing ability. I had no illusions about suddenly becoming a brilliant writer of fiction—that would just have been another exposure to the foul fumes of failure. But I did feel that I probably had a real talent for journalism—and, in particular, in the field of art and music criticism—the newspaper and magazine variety. No day passed that I didn't devour the entertainment pages of *The New York Times* and the *New York Herald Tribune* and most of the art and literary magazines. It was my morning ritual to read in the *Trib* what Walter Kerr had to say about the newest play or what Virgil

Thomson had to say about the latest genius of the podium or what Walter
Terry had to say about the latest god of the dance.

Although I had never written a word of art or music or dance criticism
in my life, I somehow felt confident enough to make becoming a newspaper
critic my goal. It felt right and it felt good and it filled me with renewed ambition. Since I had a fairly close friendship with America's greatest living music
critic–namely, Virgil Thomson–I lost little time in asking him if there might
be a place for me in the music department of the *Herald Tribune*. His answer
was quick and to the point: "No, baby, there isn't." And he helpfully added,
"Someone has to drop dead before a job becomes available at the *Trib*." But
I persisted, practically begging him to at least make some inquiry.

Virgil must have said something to somebody, because, a few days
later, I received a call from someone named Jay Harrison, who said he was
the music editor at the *New York Herald Tribune*, asking me if I'd be free to
do some "stringing" for them. To be a "stringer" for a newspaper meant
you were a freelance writer, not on the staff, who handled surplus assignments, covering events that regular staff members could not, or would not
write about. Thus a musical stringer would review concerts or other musical events that would appear without the writer's name or byline at the top
of the published review. Only his initials would appear–and only at the
bottom of the review.

I instantly agreed to be a *Trib* music stringer. The pay was minimal–
something like five dollars per review–but it was a major foot in the door. I
called Virgil to thank him profusely for his recommendation, and he said that
if I followed his dictum of simply reporting what happened and how it happened and, at times, why it happened, then what emerged would be a critical
piece that would reveal what I personally thought about any given event.

It was a rather too subtle way of letting people know what I felt about
a recitalist or conductor or composer, but after immersing myself in Virgil's
music criticism, I came to understand that the manner in which you
describe a concert made clear how you felt about it. It was up to you to
find the right words to describe what you saw and heard and felt, but those
words had to have the ring of truth and reveal a clarity and a resonance
that would bring the event to life.

It took me quite a while to put Virgil's dictums into effect, and even
longer to bring my own, personal voice into music reviewing. What I finally
came to realize was that a newspaper must impart clearly written and
accurately described information to the public, whether reporting on the

terrors of war or the artistry of a Carnegie Hall song recital–that indulging in hyperbole or hyperventilated prose would be counterproductive to the precepts of good journalism.

Of course I was an utter novice. Everything I learned about criticism or journalism was "on the job." Everything I learned about a newspaper was "on the job." Having never attended a single journalism course, I felt like a fish out of water about my first reviewing assignment. It was horrific and the artist in question was the renowned classical Spanish guitarist, Carlos Montoya, who was giving a recital at Town Hall.

Although the guitar was hugely popular at the time, classical guitar concerts were infrequent. Apart from that, the guitar was never one of my favorite instruments, nor did I know the finer points of how it's supposed to be played. I dreaded having to write about Montoya and his damned guitar. But, of course, off I went to the concert and then rushed back to the *Herald Tribune* building on West 41st Street (mercifully, not far from Town Hall) to write my first music review.

What must be understood is that 40 years ago, all newspaper critics wrote on deadlines on a typewriter. There were no computers. This meant that a review had to be typed up and handed in to the editor within the span of, say, 20 to 30 minutes. In those days, there was no such thing as a review appearing two or three days after the event. You had to meet your deadline so that the review would appear on the very next day–that was the rule.

I marveled at how critics could sit and type reviews of plays, operas, ballets, or concerts within such a short time. But there they sat, Kerr, Thomson, Terry, and the others, all typing away as fast as possible and shouting, "Copy," once a page was filled. They handed it to the copy boys who came running for the pages to rush them to the copy editor who rushed them to the typesetter.

I was terrified to write my Montoya review. I kept looking at the large clock on the wall across the room, watching the minutes tick by. I started typing–and my mind went blank. I wanted to say so much, yet couldn't bring a single word to the page. I had no problem typing–I was a whiz at typing–but I had problems articulating what I wanted to say. It was a nightmare. My throat went dry. I felt dizzy.

"You having problems?" said a voice.

I looked up. It was Bill Flanagan, the young composer and my fellow stringer, who had been doing music reviewing for the *Trib* for some time. He had stopped writing his own review to come over to my desk.

"I'm definitely stuck," I said, "on this Carlos Montoya review. It's my first and I seem unable to write it."

"OK. Let me help you," said Flanagan.

And help me he did, by asking what I had heard, what I thought about it, and what the particulars of the program were. I told him, and he said, "Write all that down. Don't panic. You still have time. Each sentence will guide you to the next sentence. Just calmly tell the story of the concert you heard." He waited until I started typing, and then went back to finish his own review.

Miraculously, the words started coming. They weren't very good words, but the review got written. I praised Montoya. I praised the concert. I even let on that the guitar was not my all-time favorite instrument and that a whole evening of classical guitar music was a bit much. At the bottom of my review I typed the initials J.G., and it was the start of a huge and very long love affair between the *Herald Tribune* and I. It was also the beginning of my very close friendship with William Flanagan, whose kindness in helping a very stressed-out fellow in the throes of high anxiety was something I would never forget.

When I opened the *Tribune* on the following morning and found my Montoya review printed in its entirety on the entertainment pages, I was overcome with pride. I couldn't believe it! And there, at the bottom of my review were my initials–still! That night, Jane and I celebrated the birth of J.G., the music critic, and I vowed I'd move heaven and earth to get myself hired by the *Trib* as a permanent member of its illustrious staff. It would take a while for that to actually happen, but before it did, another event of even greater moment and import would take place: I would become a father! Oh, happiness! Oh, joy! And of course, it was time to move yet again!

Chapter 25

Being a music stringer for the *Tribune* was, for me, a truly fabulous thing. For one thing, it placed me in touch with one of the truly great American newspapers. For another, those initials, J.G. at the bottom of my music reviews, were beginning to actually mean something.

The "power of the press" is amazing. Suddenly, even though I was not on the *Tribune* staff, I became a known quantity in the New York music world. As I had been told by my new friend, Bill Flanagan, people would soon enough know who this J.G. was—and it was true. Press releases soon began arriving at the *Trib* addressed to John Gruen and phone calls too, which I could not take, because I did not have a desk or a telephone.

Still, it was fantastic being called by Jay Harrison, the *Trib*'s music editor, and assigned more and more concerts each week, and it was grand appearing with fellow critics from the *Times*, the *Daily News*, the *Mirror*, the *New York Post*, and the *Journal American*, among other publications, at Carnegie Hall or the Metropolitan Opera or The Town Hall, sitting in the best aisle seats, chatting and smoking during intermission, and hearing marvelous, middling, or mediocre music-making offered by marvelous, middling or mediocre artists.

And for me it was always a thrill and a panic to rush back to the *Tribune* building to write up whatever concert, opera, or recital I had just heard. In time, my panic abated. I began to be more relaxed and wrote the best reviews I could, both stylistically and in matters of content. I began to hang around after most of us critics and stringers were done for the night, and go with some of them for a nightcap downstairs at Bleaks, the *Trib*'s much-loved watering place.

Among the group was the *Trib*'s chief movie critic, Judith Crist, who at the time, also happened to be the arts editor of the Sunday entertainment section. You answered to Judy Crist—she was your boss—and she watched you like a hawk. Indeed, Judy was a formidable woman, tough of language, raucous of humor, bellicose if crossed, but a brilliant journalist and a caustic yet highly sensitive film critic, whose movie reviews could

make or break any given film. There was also Dave Paley, the department's associate arts editor, who saved us all from grammatical blunders
or unfortunate turns of phrase.

The fierce Judy Crist and the gentle Dave Paley became close friends and
colleagues of mine, and I knew that they both closely watched my reviews.
When Judy Crist once mentioned that my review of The Metropolitan
Opera's production of Debussy's *Pélleas et Mélisande* was elegantly crafted,
I somehow felt anointed and tried my best to continue writing as elegantly
as possible. This, alas, led to some rather flowery over-writing, which both
Judy and Dave were quick to nip in the bud. Generally, however, I sensed
that they both approved of my efforts to write intelligently and with a modi-
cum of originality.

My life as a stringer lasted approximately one year. It was finally
unbearable not to have a permanent position at the paper, and I begged
and hounded Judith Crist for a full-time job. Again and again, Judy echoed
Virgil Thomson's refrain of, "Someone's got to drop dead before a job
becomes available."

And then it happened.

No one dropped dead, but someone retired. That someone was Carlyle
Burroughs, the chief art critic at the paper. His hugely ambitious associate, Emily Genauer, replaced him and she was on the lookout for a bright
young assistant to be her associate art critic. Judy Crist called me and asked
if the job interested me. She had looked up my bio and saw I had a master's degree in art history. I qualified but only if Emily Genauer approved
of me.

I instantly jumped at the chance.

As for Genauer, I had noticed how rapaciously she bent over her
typewriter at the *Trib*. She was one of those highly articulate women, for
whom the expression "ball breaker" was invented. Aggressive, opinionated, competitive, bossy, humorless, and thoroughly irritating, she had a
certain Rosalind Russell snap, without the wit or the charm. She wore her
insistently black hair immaculately swept up, always with her signature red-
framed glasses planted firmly on her nose.

It was clear Genauer had waited years for her moment of glory. Now
that she had it, nothing would stop her from wielding her power or to make
her presence felt. I knew at once Genauer would never be my friend. She
reeked of suspicion. But I played up to her vanity and did everything to
allay her fears about being too smart or competitive. Upon formally meet-

ing her, I complimented her on her many "totally brilliant" articles and reviews and shamelessly told her how I simply "devoured" every word she had written the moment it appeared in print. She had, of course, carefully scrutinized my curriculum vitae.

"You know, John, we cannot have an art critic of the *Herald Tribune* writing about his artist wife," she said, sternly.

I quickly assured her it would never occur to me to write about Jane Wilson, her art, her talent, or her person. Finally, after endless questioning over a period of two or three days, I landed the job. My title was associate art critic and I would henceforth be allowed to use my full name as a byline, receive a small but decent salary, and reap all the benefits of a full-fledged staff member of the *New York Herald Tribune*.

The job entailed writing weekly art reviews, art-related articles, and assisting Genauer in whatever she dreamed up. The downside, apart from daily contact with Genauer, was that I was not allowed to choose the art shows I wanted to write about. Genauer had first dibs on all exhibitions, large or small. Still, she couldn't do them all, so I managed to get some of the important shows along with the dregs. But I wanted more independence and very much missed doing my music reviews I had done as a stringer. I decided to speak to Judy Crist about doing music reviews as well as art reviews.

"You'd be working night and day," she warned. "And all on one salary! You'd be running around to the galleries and museums during the day, write your art reviews, then go to the concerts at night, and write your music reviews afterwards. That's a heavy load. Is that what you really want?"

"It's what I really want," I told her. "I want to do both."

Thus it was that I became a full-fledged critic of music and art, the first critic on a major newspaper in the 1960s to assume both these jobs and disciplines. From my point of view, it was a major coup. No one else on the *Trib*'s cultural staff was doing that kind of double duty. I was the only one–and I was ready. For one thing, it partly freed me from the clutches of the self-important and increasingly jealous Emily Genauer. For another, the *Tribune* higher-ups would notice what an industrious fellow I was, and that might lead to God knows what.

But most of all, despite the hard work and long hours, I felt unbelievably privileged to be in the very midst of New York's cultural life. And, yes, I was ready for the power and the glory. I had always dreamed of some sort of stardom, and here it was, staring me in the face. It wasn't the movies, but I was definitely, decidedly, and absolutely ready for my close-up. Besides, I now had something truly precious to work for, and that was the beautiful, brand new living creature that had recently entered my life…my gorgeous little daughter, Julia.

When we were married, in 1948, Jane and I had decided there would be no babies for the next ten years. We were in our twenties and our twenties would be ours to do with as we pleased. Much of that decade was spent trying to find ourselves as artists and, certainly, as human beings. All of the 1950s were spent in New York, working, playing, moving, struggling, making friends, losing friends, going to parties, going to analysts, making contacts, being bad, being good, experimenting, feeling happy, feeling unhappy, reeling around, fooling around, going everywhere, going crazy, loving each other, resenting each other…I guess it was called living.

But the minute we hit our thirties, it seemed time to calm down and make a baby. As it turned out, a baby was instantly on the way, but a few weeks into her pregnancy, Jane suffered a miscarriage. It was a sad, confounding loss. We soon tried again, and this time, all went well.

On September 2, 1958, at 11:50 p.m., Julia Gruen was born at New York Infirmary on 15th Street and Second Avenue. A few days later, we brought our baby home in a beautifully woven basket we had purchased in a little shop of household goods on Bleecker Street. The minute we entered the apartment, I placed the basket on our dining room table, went to the record player, and put on a recording of Lotte Lehmann singing Schumann's *Frauenliebe und-leben*, with Bruno Walter accompanying at the piano. As the ten-inch LP began spinning and Lehmann began singing, I placed the basket on the floor right next to the speakers so that our Julia might be inundated by the sounds of Schumann's poignantly touching song cycle—so that music would instantly penetrate her tiny being.

How amazing it was to have a child in the house! How amazing to look at her—to look at her tiny body, her tiny, star-like hands, her perfectly configured little face and features, her blue, blue eyes; everything was so wondrously in place—so precise and finely composed!

As the 1960s were upon us, a lot of happiness was mine. Always and forever, there was Jane, my great love. There now was Julia, adorable and adored by us both—the most joyous part of us; the very center of our lives. And there was my new job, a meaningful, fulfilling, all-consuming job that kept me hopping and bouncing and hurtling into art and music on a daily basis. And yes! There was our brand new apartment at 317 East Tenth Street, facing historic Tompkins Square, in Alphabet City.

It was all quite marvelous and wonderful, but as every silver lining has a dark cloud, the only sour note was my father. On the night of Julia's birth, I telephoned him with the happy news. Upon learning we had a beautiful, healthy baby girl, all he could find to say was, "Well, the next time around, you'll have a beautiful baby boy!"

Chapter 26

The only word to describe our 1960s was "tumultuous." Here the words should really be spilling and spinning and reeling and crashing into each other, with events and feelings and experiences scattering, exploding, and ricocheting all over the place. What a decade! What a heap of living we were doing!

Our new home was in a predominantly Ukrainian/Polish neighborhood. Tompkins Square Park was the scene and haven of the young disenfranchised, freedom-seeking, peace-loving, free-love arbiters known as Flower Children. These impoverished, pot-smoking, long-haired, ill-kept, drum-beating hippies (as they became known), brought a colorful and festive atmosphere into the park. To the old-time residents, the Ukrainian, Polish, and Jewish immigrants, the Square had long been a European park, the center of their social life. Now it was becoming a noisy, chaotic, yet unthreatening place, where the young and the sexy improvised their lives. The old headscarf-wearing women and bearded men didn't know what had hit them. And so, for some ten years, they coexisted with the hippies as well as with the young mothers who, with their very young children, clustered around the park's sandboxes and the wading pool.

Jane found inspiration in every season of the year to paint the striking configuration of the Square, its trees, its statues, its fences and walks. (Some of those paintings now reside in the collection of the Hirshhorn Museum and Sculpture Garden in Washington, D.C. and in the collection of the Morgan Chase bank.)

Our brownstone, well kept and five stories high, housed several old-time residents on various floors. On the top floor lived an artist, with his wife and young son, an artist who would one day achieve great fame and wealth: the Colombian-born painter and sculptor Fernando Botero. Even in those early years, when we were all so young and making our way, Fernando was obsessed with the weirdly inflated figures, which would eventually become his unique and hugely successful signature style. A quiet young man, with fiery eyes yet gentle manners, Botero did not really fit the hot, Latin, macho cliché. He and his small family kept mostly to themselves, and we never quite got to know the Boteros.

But a Latin of an entirely different stripe and temperament would very soon enter our lives—a quite adorable and frenetic young Cuban artist named Waldo Díaz-Balart. Waldo not only became a close friend, but, to our greatest surprise, became our landlord! He bought the brownstone on Tenth Street and promptly moved in. The wealthy Balart family was a recent arrival from Cuba, having been close to the pre-Castro regime. Waldo, whose sister had married and later divorced Fidel Castro, elected to pursue art, producing works in the industrial hard-edge abstract mode. But these were not canvases. They were baked enamel constructions on heavy-weight steel, with the emphasis on "heavy." Waldo had flair, and his hybrid works, intended as wall pieces, had a kind of festive harlequinade energy.

Our new Cuban landlord worked hard at being an artist, but what he did best was give exhilarating dancing parties. His irrepressible passion for Cuban dancing turned his parties into veritable indoor festivals of street dancing, where everyone, single or in pairs, simply got up and did their own versions of the merengue, the cha-cha, the tango, and especially, the rumba. Waldo's energy, his broad, infectious smile, his boundless charm, his sexiness, good nature and his mastery of Cuban dancing made him the landlord from paradise.

Jane and I had long been dancing fools, and, as children of the big-band era, had very often partaken of those exciting dancing nights at the Café Rouge in the Hotel Pennsylvania, and other New York venues, where Glenn Miller, Tommy Dorsey, Jimmy Dorsey, Artie Shaw, Duke Ellington, Cab Calloway, Count Basie, and all the rest held forth, the epitome of 40s and 50s glamour and sophistication.

Waldo seemed to like women, one in particular, the British Charlotte Davy, who worked at Sotheby's. Charlotte had charm, vivaciousness, intelligence, and beauty to spare—and she suited his temperament perfectly. But it didn't take. Later came a sensitive Latin stunner named Brigida. Waldo even married this one. But alas, this one didn't take either.

Amongst the ladies Waldo took up with, there also appeared a few young men, most notably Louis Waldon, an absolute dead ringer for Steve McQueen. Waldo, beaming and beside himself with happiness, suddenly introduced us to Louis, and promptly installed him in the basement apartment of our brownstone, just beneath our floor-through, where he stayed for several years.

Louis was trying to be an actor. A Modesto, California native, he spoke an English that betrayed a certain resistance to in-depth education. But considering that a clamoring sexiness oozed from every pore of his body, this was probably a notable plus. Sexual ambivalence seemed to be his calling card, and in a day when gyms did not as yet produce pecs and abs of mass seduction, a shirtless, shorts-clad Louis Waldon, with his blue, blue eyes, sandy hair, pouty mouth, wicked smile, sturdy legs, and twangy voice, decidedly fit the bill of every girl's rough-and-ready boy-toy and every gay man's fantasy come true.

It was no wonder that Andy Warhol, Pop Art's *monstre sacrée*, under-ground filmmaker extraordinaire, and inventor of the "Superstar," took Louis Waldo under his lurid wing. One look at Louis and Andy knew exactly what to do with him. He instantly cast him in *The Nude Restaurant*, followed in quick succession by *Lonesome Cowboys, San Diego Surf, Flesh*, and *Blue Movie*. In all these films–conscious studies in banality and today considered cinematic breakthroughs–Louis placed his sexually charged persona in the service of scripts that were essentially hymns to boredom. Still, barriers were broken in *Blue Movie*, initially titled *Fuck*, in which Waldon and the beautiful Warhol superstar, Viva, engage in honest-to-goodness intercourse. As Andy explained to the arresting officers who closed down the film, "If I can show a man eating a mushroom, why can't I show a man fucking? It's part of life, isn't it? It's what people do–eat mushrooms and fuck!"

As Louis and Waldo were more or less inseparable, it stood to reason that Warhol would also find Waldo Díaz-Balart if not equally, at least partially delectable. With his lilting Cuban accent, tall stature, and sweet smile, Waldo would star in Andy's homage to Cuba: *The Life of Juanita Castro*. It would be Waldo's sole participation in Warhol's feverishly languid film oeuvre.

Thus it was that living on East Tenth Street proved colorful, fun, and ultimately productive. In time, I observed how the East Village was begin-ning to evolve into a neighborhood of widespread creative ferment. It was not only about Flower Children, dropouts, hippies, and runaways. It was also about cheap downtown rents attracting young artists of every stylistic persuasion, actors, playwrights, dancers, choreographers, musicians, compos-ers, writers, poets, even journalists (founding *The East Village Other*), who, intellectually inspired by impassioned drug-taking gurus such as Timothy Leary, John Cage, William Burroughs, Allen Ginsberg, and Jack Kerouac, unleashed an avalanche of newly-minted, often deadly-dull, but sometimes totally thrilling works that transformed an entire neighborhood, let alone an entire decade and beyond, into a free-floating laboratory of explosive experimentation.

I observed it all, mingled with its practitioners, saw, savored, or detested the results, and was a constant presence at East Village art openings, plays, concerts, poetry readings, and dance recitals. I was soaking it all up. Most importantly, I was taking notes, and as a *Tribune* writer, took the news of what was happening in the East Village to our Sunday magazine editor, Clay Felker, who said, "Write me an article about it. Make it long, make it exciting. We'll call it *The New Bohemia.*" The article was long and exciting and amazingly popular, and it formed the basis of my very first book, called, unsurprisingly, *The New Bohemia.*

As for my home life, there was Jane, there was Julia. Living above us was our Cuban bombshell, Waldo. Living below us was Louis, our basement sexpot superstar. Louis eventually came on to me. It was his mission in life to flirt outrageously with man, woman, or beast. At every opportunity, he'd stand entirely too close to me. He'd knock at our door at odd hours. He'd stand there in his underwear wanting to borrow a cup of sugar. Louis' wicked blue eyes far too often fixed on mine. He would step closer to me. Could he come in for a minute? Was Jane at home? She wasn't? Where was Julia? At school? Well, in that case, how about a drink? Just the two of us.

Did Louis succeed in seducing me?

Well, what can I say?

He probably did.

Chapter 27

Jane, in the meantime, painted Tompkins Square, Avenue B, a number of portraits of our Julia, some self-portraits, some still lifes. She had found a little studio just around the corner from us on Avenue B, boasting a pot-bellied stove and a private entrance. At that time, the early 1960s, we mingled with lots of artists, going to openings of Willem de Kooning, Franz Kline, Jackson Pollock, Jasper Johns, Robert Rauschenberg, Robert Motherwell, plus all of the artists showing at the Tibor de Nagy Gallery.

Jane Freilicher, who showed there, became our very special friend. I loved the fact that our group included the "two Janes," both painters, both terrifically talented, both the same age, yet both very different from each other. My Jane, as always, was "the quiet one," while Jane Freilicher was the chatterbox—opinionated, a delightful "kvetch," something of an injustice collector and always irresistibly witty. Brooklyn-born, bred, and educated (at Brooklyn College), Jane Freilicher became the darling of all the young poets clustering around John Myers and the de Nagy Gallery.

Actually, it was through knowing Jane Freilicher that we met them all—the aloof and distant John Ashbery, the ethereal yet electric Frank O'Hara, the anxious, overly-sensitive James Schuyler, the entirely too loud and raucous Kenneth Koch, the hysterically funny Arnold Weinstein. Indeed, Jane Freilicher and Joseph Hazan, the "older man" in her life, whom she would eventually marry, brought us into contact with many of the poets, writers, and artists who would, in very short order, form the fairly large nucleus of our group.

When, in 1960, John Myers invited Jane Wilson to join the Tibor de Nagy Gallery, it not only solidified our friendship with Jane and Joe, but brought my Jane into a professional milieu that would place her among young artists of increasingly distinctive reputation. By now, Jane Wilson had begun to produce landscapes of particular sweep and radiance, large, middle-sized, or small vistas in which color, composition, and a certain unique play of light combined to form canvases of compelling resonance.

As it turned out, Jane Freilicher was also producing beautifully wrought landscapes in which oil paint magically assumed the transparency, fluency, and moistness of watercolor. These were evocative works that spoke of "place," and the "place" turned out to be the south shore of Long Island, specifically, Water Mill, New York, a picturesque little hamlet situated between Southampton and Bridgehampton.

Jane and Joe had been coming to Water Mill since the mid-50s, renting an unpretentious yet wonderfully located two-story house on Flying Point Road facing Mecox Bay and at walking distance from the ocean. Like so many New York artists, Jane Freilicher found the south shore of Long Island conducive to both work and play. It was in 1957, not long after we became friends, that Jane and Joe began inviting us to come out to their house in Water Mill during the summer months. Indeed, they couldn't have been more hospitable or generous.

Joe, a darkly moody, handsome man of Sephardic extraction, had his own firm in New York's garment center, earning good money and enjoying a somewhat rarefied life surrounded by Jane's many artist and poet friends. We learned that as a young man, he once was the roommate of Tennessee Williams, although it was quickly added that Joe was as straight as an arrow. Joe loved to dance, with a particular penchant for Hindu dancing and Greek folk dancing, which we all participated in when the mood struck us–and Joe was our hugely energetic leader.

Life in the Hamptons was far more peaceable in the 1950s and 1960s than it has since become. Traffic was more manageable and the terminally chic aspect of the Hamptons, with its influx of the young, the beautiful, the wealthy, and the celebrated, had not yet come to the glittering fore. While the Fords, the Vanderbilts, and the DuPonts still regally summered and entertained in their fabulous "cottages" and oceanside estates, the Hamptons basically remained a cluster of small towns and villages, where ordinary people led more or less ordinary lives, and where artists could still afford to move into modest homes at modest prices.

By now, there are endless books, articles, tracts, even movies, charting the importance of the South Fork and North Fork of Long Island as unique visual and spiritual havens for artists of every conceivable style and stripe. From Thomas Moran to Charles S. Reinhart to William Merritt Chase, the South Fork, with its vast skies, open fields, and salty ocean breezes have, since the nineteenth century, been a magnet to painters and sculptors, as well as poets (think of Walt Whitman, born and bred on Long Island), all of whom have considered this small strip of land their inspiration and place of self-fulfillment.

Jane, Joe, their green parrot, Chuck, my Jane and I, and our Julia, made the trek to Water Mill in Joe's Volkswagen Beetle on the as yet unfinished Long Island Expressway almost every weekend. Once in the clapboard house on Flying Point Road, the two Janes set up their easels in the spare downstairs bedroom and worked on their canvases, continuing where they left off the previous weekend. What also continued was our social life.

The phone calls began and the get-togethers began. There was Larry Rivers, who had already purchased a house in Southampton and was living there with his two young sons and his mother-in-law, Berdie Burger. (He had recently divorced Berdie's daughter, his first wife, Augusta).

Larry, who was once madly in love with Jane Freilicher and even attempted suicide by slitting his wrists when she ultimately rejected him, was always ready for a party, for drinks, for sexy, outrageous banter, for fun, fun, fun! But Larry also had his serious side, plunging into long, convoluted conversations about art, life, death, people. He had an opinion on just about everything and everyone, and he was an irreverent, exciting presence.

Then, most importantly, came Fairfield Porter and his wife, Anne. Fairfield was our mentor, our guru, our peculiar and quite neurotic aesthetic leader. Older by some ten years than the rest of us, he had as early as 1940 settled with Anne (a very fine poet herself) and their five children in a grand old decrepit Southampton house on South Main Street. Relatively well off, Fairfield and his family shuttled between the Federal house in Southampton and a family-owned island off the coast of Maine.

The poet Kenneth Koch and his wife, Janice, had also rented a small house in Water Mill not far from Jane and Joe, and all the poets came out from the city and converged there. John Ashbery (after living in Paris for several years) was deemed the most promising of all our young poet friends. Indeed, John Ashbery and Jane Freilicher had become very close friends after she illustrated his first book of poems published in 1953 by the Tibor de Nagy Gallery. Ashbery, a striking-looking young man, always struck me as something of a cool cucumber–rather circumspect, not terribly open, not terribly warm. He and Jane loved exchanging bon mots, and their repartee was suffused with arcane metaphors and witty barbs that only they seemed to understand.

As for John's poetry, in the years to come, he would receive an avalanche of distinguished awards, including the Pulitzer Prize and the MacArthur "genius" award.

For all that, his poetry has always seemed to me to be distant and impenetrable. It was too self-consciously dense for my taste, too obscure, too wordy, too riddled with verbal enigmas. There was no real color (as in Wallace Stevens) and no real depth (again, as in Stevens, to whom Ashbery is continuously and, to my mind, erroneously compared).

Then there was Frank O'Hara, who frequently visited the Hamptons, and usually stayed with Larry Rivers, with whom he had had a quite lengthy and passionate affair. Frank, with his blue Irish eyes, his broken nose, his short and wiry stature, his wit and his whiny voice, was totally unique and truly made of poetry. I liked him enormously and loved his work. Frank's poems were the way he lived his life, and pretty much the way all of us lived ours.

Unlike Ashbery's, his was a vernacular voice, never simplistic, never pretentious, never dense. Frank wrote about the things that touched his heart–about loss, about love, about the ache and wonder of things–and he could as easily write about Lana Turner and Billie Holliday and James Dean as about Rachmaninoff or a beautiful boy briefly glimpsed on a busy New York street.

Frank, like John Ashbery, also adored Jane Freilicher, though not with the same obsessive intensity. Frank doled out his adoration to such tough and ambitious painters as Grace Hartigan and Joan Mitchell or the writer Patsy Southgate and to her then lover, the painter Mike Goldberg, each of whom looked to Frank as an intimate, as a father-confessor and/or feisty, fun-filled drinking companion.

It was no secret that Frank drank (we all did to various degrees) and together with his one-time lover and long-time roommate, the writer and pretty boy, Joe La Sueur, he led a fairly messy life. But Frank, despite his drinking and carousing and intense amours, held a steady job at the Museum of Modern Art, graduating from MoMA's Information Desk into a respected curator, ultimately becoming a force in the art and museum worlds. And, always, Frank made time for love–hopeless love such as with the unthinkably handsome young poet Bill Berkson, and mad love such as for the Canadian ballet dancer Vincent Warren. And there were many others, about whom Frank wrote poetry. Frank wrote his poems on the fly, on the job, during lunch, during parties, or during long hours in the

Jane Wilson and four-month-old daughter Julia, New York City, December 1958

John Gruen holding nine-month-old Julia, Water Mill, NY, 1959; photograph by Jane Wilson

Louis Waldon and Waldo Díaz-Balart, New York City, 1964

Jeannette and Richard Seaver, Water Mill, NY, 1964

Robert Rauschenberg, Flying Point Beach, Water Mill, NY, 1959

Pianists Robert Fizdale and Arthur Gold, Water Mill, NY, 1964

Jasper Johns, Flying Point Beach, Water Mill, NY, 1959

Frank O'Hara, Southampton, NY, 1961

Marisol (Escobar), Clarice Price Rivers, and Jane Wilson, Water Mill, NY, 1962

Willem de Kooning, Water Mill, NY, 1961

Willem de Kooning, Jane Wilson, and Julia, Water Mill, NY, 1961

"Young in the Hamptons," Water Mill, NY, 1961
(*Back row, from left to right*: Robert Rauschenberg, Maxine Groffsky with parasol, Fairfield Porter, Larry Rivers, and Morton Feldman
Front row, from left to right: René Bouché, Jane Freilicher, Jane Wilson holding Julia, Arthur Gold, Katie Porter, Naomi Newman, Anne Porter, Robert Fizdale, Lizzie Porter)

Julia's third birthday party, Water Mill, NY, 1961
(*Back row, from left to right:* Lisa de Kooning (little blond child), Frank Perry and his wife Eleanor Perry, John Myers, Anne Porter, Fairfield Porter, Angelo Torricini, Arthur Gold, Jane Wilson, Kenward Elmslie, Paul Brach, Jerry Porter (behind Brach), Nancy Ward, Katherine Porter, friend of Jerry Porter; *Second row, from left to right:* Joe Hazan, Clarice Price Rivers, Kenneth Koch, Larry Rivers; *Seated on couch:* Miriam Schapiro (Brach), Robert Fizdale, Jane Freilicher, Joan Ward, John Kacere, Sylvia Maizell; *Kneeling, from back to front:* Alvin Novak, Willem de Kooning, Jim Tommaney; *Front row, from left to right:* Stephen Rivers, Bill Berkson, Frank O'Hara, Herbert Machiz

John Gruen, Jane Wilson, and daughter Julia, New York City, 1960s; photograph by Hella Hammid

silence of the night. And because Frank died much too young, at only 40, run over and killed by a beach buggy on Fire Island, he became a legend. (Read Brad Gooch's fine biography of Frank, *City Poet: The Life and Times of Frank O'Hara*–it's all there and it's all true!)

Another poet in our group, James Schuyler, was without question as gifted as he was emotionally frail. His poetry was touched by elegance and an insouciant charm. He and John Ashbery collaborated on a witty novel called *A Nest of Ninnies*, which we all devoured when it was published in 1969. Jimmy became obsessively attached to Fairfield Porter. As Anne Porter once put it, "Jimmy came to dinner and stayed for six years!" Indeed, the Porters took the psychologically fragile young poet into their home, where he became part of the family, writing his poems, helping the Porter children with their homework, tending the garden, and generally making himself useful.

In time, Fairfield and Jimmy developed a sexually charged mentor/pupil relationship, producing chaos and grave psychological turmoil in them both. There are terrific Porter portraits of Jimmy Schuyler, and others of John Ashbery, Frank O'Hara (one in the nude), and, of course, of every member of his family. And there is a particularly fine painting of Jane Freilicher. What endeared Fairfield to me most, however, was his admiration of Jane Wilson's work and the fact that he painted not one, but two fairly large portraits of her. The first was painted in our 18th Street apartment in New York, the other in his Southampton studio. Both show Jane looking radiantly alert, yet rendered in Porter's no-nonsense, un-idealized, direct style.

Fairfield was such a strange man! He'd suddenly appear at our house or at Jane's studio, would sit for five minutes, look at what Jane was painting, then get up and leave as abruptly as he had come. It was his mode of keeping himself informed of what everyone was up to. In his awkward way, Fairfield kept up with his friends–and with what everyone was doing and thinking. He was not an outgoing person, and his words were few, but as Justin Spring's terrific book (*Fairfield Porter: A Life in Art*), makes amply clear, here was a man with an enormously complex inner life and a rich, awe-inspiring intelligence.

It was in 1960 that my Jane and I did the maddest, most terrifying, most wonderful thing in our entire life: we bought a house in Water Mill, a beautiful, shingled, two-storied carriage house, 100 years old, newly renovated, standing on one acre of beautiful lawn, surrounded by vast potato fields under a great big open sky. Most exciting of all was the upstairs, boasting a huge studio and a skylight, ready to receive Jane, who would become a bona-fide Long Island painter, along with becoming, to my hugely prejudiced mind, one of America's most gifted and beloved landscape artists.

Chapter 28

The duo pianists, Arthur Gold and Robert Fizdale, were also Water Mill residents, with a house not far from ours. They were a most sophisticated pair—fabulous musicians, fabulous cooks, and fabulous snobs.

"The Boys," as everyone called them were very grand indeed. They had already been soloists with the New York Philharmonic, under Leonard Bernstein, and were among the music world's most sought-after young duo pianists. It was little wonder they looked upon us all a bit from "on high."

They were, of course, utterly charming, handsome, well spoken, always carefully groomed—two young artists living their lives in the soigné, aristocratic European mold. They spoke fluent French, and loved nothing better than being surrounded by the crème-de-la-crème of musical, artistic and literary society. Most of all they loved the very rich—and the very social. So deft were they at cultivating high society that they were in constant demand for dinner parties where their wit and intelligence would be on glittering display.

Anyone who knew Arthur and Bobby well would tell you that Arthur was the "mean one" and Bobby was the "nice one." Of course, when it suited him, mean Arthur could play the complete charmer too. Basically, however, he was the fusspot, the complainer, the crank, the overly critical one. He could be stubborn and mean-spirited. Bobby, on the other hand, covered it all up by being the soft-spoken ameliorator, the "understanding" one, the sweet and endearing one, who, with a wink and a smile, made everything calm and elegant again.

Gold and Fizdale were wonderful hosts, giving superb luncheons and dinner parties for all kinds of important people, doing all the shopping and cooking themselves. What is more, they made distinguished names for themselves by commissioning important American and European composers to write works especially for them, which would then be premiered in New York and all over the world. As often as not, it was Gold and Fizdale's rich friends who supplied the funds to pay for these commissions, the wealthy soprano, Alice Esty, being, as noted earlier, among them.

Thus, commissions and subsequent publication of two-piano works by Virgil Thomson, John Cage, Aaron Copland, Alexei Haieff, Vittorio Rieti, Arthur Honegger, Francis Poulenc, Darius Milhaud, among others, enriched and widened the repertoire of the genre not only for themselves but for duo-pianists the world-over.

It could be said that Bobby and Arthur were quite fond of us, although Arthur, ever the crabby nay-sayer, thought we were making a huge mistake in buying our Water Mill house (no explanation offered and none requested). Although we were never famous enough nor rich enough to be on their "A list," "The Boys" considered us "valuable" in that Jane, quite apart from her great looks (in their minds always a dinner-party plus) was a significantly talented painter, and I, of course, was writing music criticism for the *Tribune*, which could be useful.

So we formed quite a pleasant friendship, but of the "B list" variety. We knew this, because Arthur Gold would call and say, "We're having Stravinksy, Balanchine, and Jerome Robbins for dinner tonight, will you both come for leftovers tomorrow night?" Of course, we'd accept instantly, knowing that the food, though a day old, would still be exquisite and the gossip scintillating, especially when talk turned to the previous evening with Stravinsky, Balanchine, and Jerome Robbins!

Gold and Fizdale had their separate amours, and there were lovers or ex-lovers wafting in and out of their lives in New York and Water Mill. The most endearing and enduring of these was the trim, diminutive, and talented Angelo Torricini, an interior decorator born on the isle of Martinique. Angelo was Arthur's friend, but he was really very much a part of the Gold and Fizdale household, making himself indispensable by helping to run and be a part of their heady social and professional life. Quiet, thoughtful, private, hugely observant and sensitive, and utterly without guile or malice, Angelo brought a note of serenity and grace into the rather quixotic life of his benefactors.

I always felt that Angelo was treated a bit shabbily by "The Boys." How amazing and marvelous then that quiet, sweet-natured, unobtrusive Angelo Torricini would years later meet an enormously wealthy older woman, whom he subsequently married and who, upon her death, would leave him her many, many millions! How deliciously ironic that Angelo emerged as just the sort of person Bobby and Arthur would go to any length to meet and cultivate.

If Gold and Fizdale led a charmed life, if they were admired and praised as artists and sought out for their charm, intelligence, and worldliness, they did not, alas, find favor with Julia Gruen, our otherwise peaceable two-year-old. This antipathy, singular in its depth, manifested itself by the onset of fierce and unabating howls from our Julia each and every time Gold and Fizdale made their appearance either in our home or at the beach or wherever.

Julia came around, after several long months. We repeatedly admonished her to stop howling and finally she did. We kept telling her what wonderful fellows Bobby and Arthur were, and how much they adored her. We even made up a little chant for her to learn, which went, "Gold and Fizdale, duo-pianists, Gold and Fizdale, duo-pianists" which, when Julia finally learned to say it, came out as, "Dold and Fizdale, two old pianists"!

I often suggested to Bobby and Arthur that they perform some of their new commissions for us on their two concert grands when we visited them. But Arthur instantly said, "No, we don't perform in the living room." Clearly they thought of themselves as artists who did not stoop to making music in the living room. Only once did Bobby relent, when he invited Jane to sing a Schumann song–and it was a lovely, beautiful moment hearing her sing with Bobby at the piano.

Bobby and Arthur were great and intimate friends of Jerome Robbins, who, in 1949, became an associate artistic director at the invitation of George Balanchine, creator (with Lincoln Kirstein) and choreographic genius of the New York City Ballet. Robbins' fame as New York's preeminent choreographer and director of Broadway musicals had already been sealed with such mega-hits as *Gypsy*, *Fiddler on the Roof*, and, most notably, *West Side Story*. He was, without question, the reigning choreographer of the American musical theater, and when we met him in the late 50s, was about to become the boy wonder of classical ballet.

Robbins had built his career as a dancer with American Ballet Theater, and in 1944 created his first ballet, *Fancy Free*, for ABT to a brilliant jazzy/blues-y score by his young friend, Leonard Bernstein. The work, which premiered at the Metropolitan Opera in New York, electrified the audience, and Robbins, together with 25-year-old Bernstein (and the young set designer, Oliver Smith), savored unprecedented success. The ballet, about three sailors on leave in New York, was as sexy as it was poignant, as filled with sassy humor as it was genuinely touching. All this was choreographed without once abandoning the strict precepts and discipline of classical dance. With one stroke, Robbins invented the vernacular, streetwise ballet without ever violating ballet's status as high art. While the steps were always balletic and pure, they had an easy, familiar, swinging inventiveness that audiences could easily identify with.

With *Fancy Free*, both Robbins and Bernstein launched their individual and separate careers. Who would have thought that Bernstein would soon emerge as the hugely beloved director of the New York Philharmonic, the youngest in its history and the first American? And who would have guessed that Robbins, so gifted, so brilliant, would, during the 1950s, turn out to be the much-hated man who named names to the House Un-American Activities Committee, led by Senator Joe McCarthy?

Chapter 29

I did not like Jerry Robbins and he did not like me. I had read Victor Navasky's book *Naming Names*, about people who ruined the lives of friends and acquaintances by giving the Un-American Activities committee the names of suspected Communist sympathizers. Robbins, a former member of the Communist party himself, was tapped by the Committee to cooperate with its witch-hunt. To save his own skin and career, Robbins named names. I and countless others found this treacherous in the extreme, and would despise him for it.

It amused me no end to learn that, years later, actor Zero Mostel, who had himself been blacklisted and did not work for ten years, had genuine contempt for Robbins despite the fact that he accepted Robbins' offer to star in *Fiddler on the Roof*, which Robbins directed and choreographed, when the show opened in 1964.

"I don't have to eat with him, do I?" Mostel asked his producers. When Mostel and Robbins met for their first rehearsal, Mostel called out to him: "Hi-ya, loose lips!" referring to the World War II slogan, "Loose Lips Sink Ships." Mostel categorically refused to shake his hand. *Fiddler* was a smash hit, running for over ten years. Mostel received rave reviews; Robbins got richer and richer, and became the god of Broadway. And still Mostel wouldn't shake his hand.

Robbins named names and ruined lives (read the Navasky book and weep!), but when it all blew over in the 60s, he behaved as though nothing had happened, and as the years passed, much of Broadway, the classical and modern dance world as well as the theater-going public, treated Robbins as one of America's greatest and most cherished artists. If in the dead of night he remembered his snitching and ratting, if he broke into a cold sweat, if he gnashed his teeth and beat his breast, his demeanor in the light of day appeared to be calm, cool, and collected.

At all times he evinced a certain neurotic edginess. Always one of those tense, furtive, paranoid types, Robbins' personality was as complex as it was unfathomable. Totally career-driven and a perfectionist in the dance studio, he could also become undone by a monumental sense of insecurity which, in turn, produced a veritable monster. Endless dancers I have talked to told me how they had been reduced to tears or driven into a frenzy of anger and frustration by Robbins' sadistic treatment of them. Hurling insults at even the most professional artist, Robbins, when detecting the smallest flaw or annoyed by what he deemed laziness or inattentiveness, was a master of the cutting remark, the humiliating put-down, the scathing look. And he thought nothing of dismissing dancers from his ballets on the spot. I have always thought that every performance of a Robbins ballet contained within it the seeds of fear—fear on the part of the dancers still in the throes of Robbins' deliberate cruelty and seething fury.

Was Jerome Robbins really as awful as I describe him? The answer is a resounding Yes. But of course, he had his pleasant, even endearing side. In fact, when we first met him, through Gold and Fizdale, he couldn't have been more solicitous toward us. At the time, during the early 60s, Robbins was in the midst of a serious romance. A closeted gay man, he began a relationship with a young woman by the name of Christine Conrad. Chris, who at the time was New York City's Film Commissioner, was an exceptional combination of sensitivity and endearing practicality. A lovely, clear-eyed, highly intelligent woman, she spoke her mind, but seemed always mindful of the feelings and well-being of others. She struck us as the perfect companion for a difficult man and, indeed, the two seemed surprisingly happy.

When Jerry invited Jane and me to spend a weekend with him and Christine at his house in Snedens Landing, New York, we accepted with pleasure. But I soon sensed that Jerry really liked Jane best and was quite resentful of me. Though polite, he didn't really cotton up to me. I noted his reluctance to participate in my banter about this or that event or person. He did not respond to my "boy reporter" love of the instant "interview," wherein I was given to asking far too many questions. I think in the back of his mind was the terrifying possibility that I might broach the subject of the McCarthy blacklistings and his part in them. I could have, but I didn't.

Still, that weekend proved exceedingly pleasant. We took long walks in the woods. We had long drinks on the enclosed terrace facing a magnificent view of the Hudson. On the following evening, while Chris was preparing dinner, I played some Chopin mazurkas. Jerry, who was just then working on his big Chopin piano music work for the New York City Ballet, namely, *Dances at a Gathering*, asked me to repeat one of the mazurkas, wondering about the tempi. He was using it as one of the *Dances*, but thought it went much faster than I was playing it. I pointed out Chopin's own tempo markings, which are much, much slower. Later, at the ballet's premiere, I noted he had slowed down his choreography to match the music of the mazurka. The weekend ended very happily with Jerry and Chris announcing that they would be getting married in a matter of months. At this news, we all embraced and I proposed a heartfelt toast to the happy couple—and the champagne began to flow.

We had another memorable encounter with Jerry Robbins. This was at Gold and Fizdale's in Water Mill. Jerry had rented a house not far from "The Boys," and it was Bobby's charming idea that our daughter, then aged nine (and now very much taken with "the two old pianists"), be in charge of making a dinner for Jerry that she would prepare all by herself, with the occasional "assistance" of Bobby and Arthur. Julia had of late become quite enamored of cooking. On the morning of the dinner, the three went shopping, and Julia chose a butterflied leg of lamb as her main dish, with haricots verts and baby potatoes. She chose the salad, the bread, and the cheese. It had already been decided that Julia would make the dessert herself, a lemon soufflé. The feast would include champagne before dinner, with other fine French wines during dinner. The guests included Jerry, Chris Conrad, Eugenia Delarova, the former Russian character dancer (a Water Mill neighbor once married to the great choreographer, Léonide Massine), her current husband, Henri Doll, Angelo Torricini, and ourselves. Nine-year-old Julia's dinner proved a triumph, particularly the lemon soufflé, which, in its gloriously risen perfection, couldn't have been more delicious. Jerry Robbins just beamed.

After dinner, Jerry, clearly delighted and in an inspired mood, got up and instructed us all to follow him out onto the lawn—it was still fairly light out—and we all gathered on the grass. Jerry now did the most wonderful thing. He began choreographing a dance on us, asking us to imitate what he was doing, telling some of us to move this way and some of us to move that way, and we all did his bidding. Julia was given a little solo variation—just a turn here and there, and some small, quite witty steps—then we all formed a circle and Jerry took Jane's hand and Chris' hand and led them in a slow pavane, while the rest of us were told to sway slowly in various directions.

This dance, done without music, as the light was fading over Mecox Bay and a huge moon hovered in the sky, was one of the most beautiful of our early Water Mill memories. Indeed, I'm certain it was this magical episode that prompted Jerry to later on create his enigmatic if rather tedious ballet *Watermill* for the New York City Ballet.

At the end of that particular summer, when everyone was back in New York, Jerry called Jane, who was holding some art classes in her studio, and asked if she would be willing to give him some drawing lessons. Jerry had long loved Jane's work and had attended some of her openings. Through Felicia Bernstein, he had heard that Jane was also a terrific teacher of painting and drawing. There was just one proviso: the lesson would have to be entirely private. No one else was to be present. Jane agreed, and for some six weeks, Jerry religiously appeared at Jane's studio, then located on Lexington Avenue and 87th Street, and diligently did drawing after drawing under Jane's observant eye and careful instruction.

"The talent was instantly apparent," recalled Jane. "Jerry was incredibly focused, incredibly concentrated, and the work was really quite personal and quite felt, especially when he drew what he saw out the studio window. The buildings across the street were being demolished, and he captured some of that frenzied, jagged, and noisy activity."

When the fall and winter and spring passed, and another summer was happily upon us, Bobby and Arthur often brought Jerry to our carriage house on Cobb Road for drinks or a party. Each time, Jerry would wax ecstatic over the beauty and charm of our place. He just couldn't say enough wonderful things about it.

By this time, Jerry and Chris Conrad had broken off their engagement and abandoned their marriage plans. Chris, devastated, quit her New York film job and departed for California, where she embarked on a screenwriting career. Jerry was now romantically involved with a young photographer named Jesse Gerstein, and it was now Jerry and Jesse, a handsome, wiry boy, who appeared at our house. One day I received a call from Jerry asking if we would rent him our Water Mill house for the following summer. He said he and Jesse loved our house so much, they simply had to spend a summer there.

We agreed and, when the time came, Jane set about to prepare the place for Jerry and Jesse, doing the usual heavy-duty cleaning, emptying closets, purchasing extra dishes, and doing all that needed to be done to receive summer tenants in the Hamptons. Jerry and Jesse eagerly moved into our house. Bright and early on the following morning, Jerry called me in New York.

"John, we're in your house, but I can't stay here."

"What's wrong, Jerry?"

"There's no place to sit! There are no tea towels! The place is filthy! I couldn't sleep. I'm not happy here," he said in a nasty growl.

"But Jerry, you kept saying how much you loved the house! You were crazy about it! What has happened?"

"I can't explain it, but I'm just very uncomfortable here. I've got to get out of here. Jesse will stay. Don't worry, you won't have to return the money."

We were, to say the very least, totally dumbfounded. What had come over Jerry? We called Bobby and Arthur. If they had an answer, they weren't talking. We called Eugenia Delarova, by now one of Jerry's closest friends. She thought he was having a nervous breakdown. I finally called his secretary in New York, who informed me that Jerry was, indeed, in a bad state. His father had recently died (we knew nothing of this), he had lost his house in Snedens Landing, and he was experiencing a huge amount of anxiety and inner turmoil.

As it turned out, Jerry did indeed move out of our house in Water Mill and left for Europe. Young Jesse stayed behind. When I talked with him, he said Jerry was in a terrifically anxious state but that he, Jesse, just loved the house and planned to stay the entire summer! We were not to worry about a thing. He'd take good care of everything.

We never knew if Jerry ever returned to our house or not. All we knew was that after this episode, our relationship definitely cooled. And it would cool even further when, several years later, I became a fairly visible critic and writer on dance. With every passing year, just about everyone thought Jerry Robbins had achieved the pinnacle of ballet artistry and that every ballet he choreographed was a work of unadulterated genius. Jerry simply could do no wrong. Everyone, including most dance critics, thought so. But I didn't think so, and I said so in public, in private, and in print.

Jerry was furious.

Chapter 30

During his lifetime, Jerome Robbins' fame was immense. Before his death in 1998, honors were heaped upon him and his work on Broadway, for American Ballet Theatre and the New York City Ballet, as well as for his own small company, Ballets U.S.A., brought him endless praise and accolades from a worldwide public.

For me, his best work was for Broadway, most notably *Gypsy* and *West Side Story*. In *West Side*, his energy was boundless and his choreographic ingenuity brought forth a balletic masterpiece. Abetted by Leonard Bernstein's inspired score, the work shone and bristled with originality even as it told a moving *Romeo and Juliet* tale of unabashed sentimentality albeit predictable.

As for his classical ballets, done primarily for the New York City Ballet, of some 50 works, there are perhaps six of lasting value: *Fancy Free, The Cage, Afternoon of a Faun, The Concert, Dances at a Gathering,* and *Les Noces.* The rest are well-made and infused with Robbins' special brand of crack-the-whip discipline that invariably elicited a certain awe on the part of dance audiences. But clunkers were rampant, and from very early on, too: *Interplay, Facsimile,* and *Age of Anxiety,* to mention three quite early works. Ballets such as *Watermill, The Dybbuk Variations, In G Major, Glass Pieces, I'm Old Fashioned, Antique Epigraphs, Opus 19: The Dreamer,* and *The Four Seasons* were, in my estimation, duds. Lots of people just adored his *Goldberg Variations* set to Bach. To me it was entirely too long, too self-indulgent (Robbins used all of Bach's repeats just to torture the dancers, I always thought), and hugely pretentious.

When, in one of my reviews, I dared suggest that, having run out of steam, Robbins went downtown, to the Judson Church, the experimental hotbed of contemporary dance, to steal ideas from such modern dancers and choreographers as Laura Dean, Robert Dunn, Lucinda Childs, placing some of their quite inventive movements and ideas into late ballets such as *Glass Pieces* and *Antique Epigraphs,* among others. Word got back to me that Jerry would never speak to me again. And he never did.

It didn't matter. I had always felt an enduring suspicion and anger toward him about his naming names. When friendship was possible during our early Water Mill days, he put a damper on it by never really allowing me to talk to him freely, to develop some sort of meaningful relationship. As I said earlier, he never really trusted me. And he was probably right.

When we first met Jerry, I was not yet a dance critic and writer. I was still a *Tribune* critic of music and art and an interviewer of composers, conductors, concert artists, painters, and sculptors. I mostly instigated these interviews, with the blessing of my editors. Most critics of my generation, writing during the 60s and 70s, held to an unwritten law that said one shouldn't become friends of the artists you wrote about. I thought that was a stupid idea. I wanted to be friends with the people I wrote about, not all of them, of course, but certainly with those who interested me–the geniuses, for example, and all those artists and performers, whose proximity would enrich my life, Jane's life, and Julia's life.

In a way, my editors at the *Trib* welcomed this notion, because it meant that interviews I conducted with hugely celebrated figures in the arts, would yield ever more personal results. In short, I could get ever more private or secret things out of them and present these revelations to a huge reading public. One such editor, Clay Felker, who ran the *Trib*'s Sunday magazine, called *New York*, encouraged me to get as close to my subjects as possible, mainly, of course, to get as much dirt on them as possible.

Felker was an interesting figure. Young, handsome in an all-American, expensive-prep-school sort of way, energetic and journalistically savvy, he singlehandedly changed the face of feature newspaper writing by encouraging his reporters to turn their pieces into bristling flights of fancy that would soon be dubbed "the new journalism." *Trib* writers such as Tom Wolfe and Jimmy Breslin were its chief practitioners, producing essays, interviews, and reportage that in flamboyance of language and stylistic daring turned a common newspaper piece into an altogether novel reading experience. Indeed, it was Felker who turned these and other relatively anonymous reporters into highly visible stars of the newspaper world.

Jane and I met Clay way before he came to work on the *Trib*. At the time, he was dating Dorothy Seiberling, an arts editor at *Life* magazine, who became a big fan of Jane's work. They didn't seem to us to be an ideal couple. Dorothy was clearly the more articulate and cultured of the two. Clay was restless, insecure, and superficial. Then, when he joined the *Tribune*, we got to know Clay even better. (We were very much around when he later courted and eventually married the actress Pamela Tiffin).

I was never one of the journalists Clay Felker groomed for "new journalism" stardom (I had to do that on my own). But I believe he saw me as a potential source for good reporting, good criticism, and good interviews. Still, we had very different personalities, and were never really comfortable with each other. Years later, when the *Trib* folded and he founded *New York* magazine, and when he asked me to be its chief art critic–which lasted for some five years–he would show his true stripes and our so-called friendship would come to an abrupt end.

In the meantime, back at the *Trib*, I slaved for the overbearing Emily Genauer and wrote music reviews under the rather disinterested eye of chief music critic Paul Henry Lang. Genauer invariably grabbed the choice art exhibitions for review, and Paul Henry Lang did the same for music, which, as chief critics, was, of course, their privilege. Occasionally, Lang would have to make a choice between reviewing a brand new production of an opera or, say, the New York Philharmonic, both of which might fall on the same night. When this happened, I would get lucky and he would ask me to review the concert he chose not to review.

It was just on one such occasion that I first reviewed the New York Philharmonic under the baton of Leonard Bernstein. With my first vision of Bernstein on the Philharmonic podium, I knew this was a person I definitely wanted to get to know and get to know intimately.

Chapter 31

I had, of course, followed Bernstein's career from its inception and had even heard him conduct various concerts at New York's City Center prior to his appointment to the Philharmonic. Indeed, there wasn't a time I wasn't intrigued by Bernstein, America's most prodigious and charismatic musical wunderkind.

Unlike his friend, Jerome Robbins, Leonard Bernstein was warm, open, gregarious, talkative, and loving. Of course, he had an ego the size of the Hollywood Bowl, but the man had character and a scary intelligence. When he cared, he cared hard. When he looked at you with his lynx eyes, he really looked at you and made you quake a bit. Of course, like Jerry, Lenny was tortured. But his turmoils seemed big compared to Jerry's which seemed small and pinched. That was because Lenny, in terms of character, was the bigger man, and Jerry was the smaller man.

To have watched Bernstein conduct an orchestra was to have seen an artist in the throes of ecstasy. Critics, as well as much of the public, found Lenny's podium pyrotechnics seriously off-putting, particularly during his early years. He gyrated, he swooped, he jumped, he lurched. This wasn't conducting, said the critics—it was showing off, it was egomania made visible, it was, in a word, awful.

Again and again, Lenny was shocked and startled as he read how his podium comportment obscured the music at hand.

"But I feel every last shred of the music!" he'd exclaim. "I'm completely lost in the music, and completely unaware of my actions or movements while I conduct. All I strive for, all I want to be, is at one with the orchestra— at one with the music."

It literally took years for the critics and audiences to come to terms with Lenny's podium image, of the young conductor jabbing the air and moving like a demented acrobat. But when, in his later years, Lenny did his Mahler symphonies, when he probed the Mahler soul and opened the vast mystical realms of Mahler's orchestral riches, those very same critics and that very same audience, now grown older and wiser, finally understood that

Bernstein, gyrations and all, was a genius conductor whose great humanism found and unlocked the secrets of Mahler's own tortured or ecstatic humanity. And so it was with almost every other composer Bernstein tackled.

As I began to know him, I found Lenny to be not only a great musician and humanist, but a man deeply drawn to all facets of the world he lived in. He genuinely thrived on all the phenomena of this world. Every blade of grass seemed to interest him. Indeed, the miracles of botany were but one of his intellectual obsessions. He loved the minutiae of geology and the wonders of astronomy. Most of all, he loved words (oh, the fiercely competitive word games he inflicted on family and friends!), and, as the son of a Rabbinical scholar, he loved and worshipped the mystical, the spiritual, the metaphysical, most notably the Kabbalah. As a Jew, he was enamored of all religions and often spent hours pondering the mysteries of Catholicism, Buddhism, and Islam.

His wife, Felicia Montealegre, born in Chile and raised a Catholic, had no objections when Lenny inculcated their three children, Jamie, Alexander, and Nina, in the history and rites of Judaism. But Lenny also loved for his children to explore and study the precepts of Catholicism, and discussions were fairly frequent in the Bernstein household on all matters spiritual and mystical. It must have been 1965 when I conducted my earliest interview with Leonard Bernstein. It was for the *Tribune*. At the time, the Bernstein family lived in an elegant pre-World War II building at 895 Park Avenue at 79th Street. The apartment, sumptuously decorated, boasted many rooms and a splendid wraparound terrace on one of the upper floors. In that first interview, the family's live-in nanny, Julia, showed me into the living room, with its two concert grand pianos, offered me a drink, and said that Mr. Bernstein would join me shortly.

When the maestro appeared, bells did not go off, but there was no question that an electric something had filled the room. And the electricity communicated itself by way of a presence that seemed veritably to change the room's temperature. He came in talking, he sat down talking, he lit a cigarette talking and, finally (still talking), asked me what month I was born in.

"September," I said. "September 12. I'm a Virgo."

"Ah, a Virgo! And so am I! Born August 25. We're astrological twins."

Thus began our interview, which centered on his career, on his conducting, on his critics, and on anything else he felt inclined to talk about. Bernstein was responsive, cordial, engaging, opinionated, focused, and quite flirtatious. Indeed, there was that about Lenny, that if someone appealed to him physically, he was moved to make his feelings known, not in any overt way, but by the momentary, lingering glance or perhaps the quick touch of his hand on yours.

In those days I was a pleasant-looking man—tall, very slim, well spoken, and quick with a smile and an amusing retort. I too had my flirtatious ways, but they were mostly kept in check and resorted to only when flirting would either get me what I wanted or seemed the fun and sexy thing to do. Although I was already in my early thirties and not the slip of a boy most older gay men favored, Lenny, only eight years older, seemed to find me attractive enough, and I was flattered.

Lenny liked what I wrote about him in the *Tribune.* He thought mine was a decent, even sensitive, journalistic portrait of a man caught in the vortex of an astonishing musical career that saw him veering from composing to conducting, all the while grappling with the demands of marriage, fatherhood, the strong pulls of a divided sexual nature, and the ego-fulfilling demands of unprecedented international fame.

That first article of mine would lead to many others, and would open a chapter in my life and in the life of Jane and Julia that would change at least the surface character of our young, struggling existence. It is said that fame, fortune, talent, and genius don't rub off. But I am here to tell you that in a way it does. Knowing the Bernsteins, being in their orbit, experiencing their closeness, having access to their friendship, their feelings, their generosity, and, above all, having close-up views of Lenny's enthralling musical genius, brought us into contact with a family that gave us a transporting vision of bien-être and the inspiring trappings of American success. Simultaneously, we were placed in touch with individuals who gave the words complexity and ambivalence a whole new meaning. Within the façade of glittering fame and all-that-money-can-buy freedom, there lurked the double specters of private despair and personal frustration.

Still, to have known Lenny and Felicia and their three children, while they were still so young, so beautiful, so active and healthy, was to have known total happiness.

Chapter 32

What was it about the Bernsteins that produced such transporting frissons? Much of it was their glamour and fame. When we first met him, Lenny was not only the music director of the New York Philharmonic, but was also the composer of *West Side Story, Candide, Wonderful Town,* and *On the Town.* He had already written symphonies, chamber works, art songs, and the film score for Elia Kazan's *On the Waterfront,* starring Marlon Brando. What is more, his highly touted *Young People's Concerts,* seen weekly on television, made him an enormously popular and beloved TV icon throughout the country.

Indeed, during the late 50s and 60s, walking down the street with Leonard Bernstein was like walking down the street with Marilyn Monroe. People recognized him, called him "Lenny," stopped and talked to him– all of which he tolerated and happily responded to. During all those years Lenny was at the very height of his celebrity; darkly handsome, in his late forties, unbelievably energetic, and hugely charismatic.

And Felicia was simply exquisite. Small-boned, trim, always elegantly coiffed and dressed, she offered the image of aristocratic finesse and polish. In a way, she was Lenny's exact opposite. Although a native of Chile, she was definitely not your stereotypical smoldering Latin bombshell, nor did she evince any vestige of the hot Latin temperament. Although Spanish was spoken in the household (all the children learned it), and although she could on occasion flare into peppery bursts of anger or gleeful raucous laughter, Felicia's basic style was that of a cool Park Avenue society matron, happily married to a world-famous conductor. More often than not, she displayed a charming yet insistent sense of entitlement, and she played her "I'm Mrs. Leonard Bernstein" card with unnerving regularity and confidence.

An actress of spirited talent (she successfully performed in many of the early "live" television dramas) and an early piano student of Claudio Arrau, Felicia Montealegre, as she was known professionally, brought genuine class into Bernstein's life and household–class in the sense that Lenny, with his rash verbal outbursts, his ego-driven needs and appetites, his frequent thoughtlessness, and his propensity to put his foot in his mouth, required the steadying hand of someone with tact, patience, humor, and endurance, all of which Felicia possessed to a remarkable degree.

The Bernstein children, too, were a lesson in outward bien-être. They were bright, attractive, well brought-up and unusually charming and entertaining. When we met them, Jamie, the eldest girl, was 15, Alexander, 12, and Nina, five. Vivacious, witty, scarily articulate and very pretty, Jamie was the apple of her father's eye. He adored her, as he did Alexander, a very sweet and poignant boy, just then going through some difficult growing pains and pre-adolescent discomforts. As for little Nina, she was utterly endearing. One evening, when opening the apartment door to Charlie Chaplin and his wife, Oona O'Neill, who had come to dinner, Nina looked up beaming and said, "Oh, I just knew somebody elegant was coming!" Another time, after pounding the piano for some minutes, she abruptly closed the piano lid, turned around and announced, "I haven't touched the piano in years!" At five, Nina was the irrepressible clown of the family.

It was after several subsequent interviews with Lenny—two more for the *Tribune* and one for *Vogue*—that Jane and I were formally invited to our first dinner party at the Bernstein home. We joined Lauren Bacall, Adolph Green, his wife Phyllis Newman, Betty Comden, her husband Steven Kyle, and Michael Wager for a superb dinner, lovingly prepared by the family cook. With the Bernstein children off in the farthest reaches of the apartment, the grown-ups, feeling quite mellow after several cocktails in the library, sat on dark purple velvet-covered banquettes and chairs in a mirrored dining room that proved at once intimate and luxurious.

There we sat with the fabulous Bernsteins; Lenny holding forth while everyone ate their food off the most ornately beautiful china with the most elegantly wrought silverware and drinking wine from the most aristocratically designed Baccarat glasses. I looked at them all in my haze of alcohol and cigarette smoke, and what did I see?

I saw and just hated the way Adolph Green ate his food, chewing visibly, and picking bits of food from other people's plates, though his wife Phyllis was mercifully droll and witty. Betty Comden, beautiful in her Garbo-esque way, laughed and smiled and chatted; Steven, her husband, was as mute as a rock—never uttered a single word all evening long, but just sat there with an empty grin on his face. The sometime actor and frequent pest, Michael Wager, nicknamed "Mendy," was, as I would note year after year, too loud, too annoyingly opinionated, too irritatingly and hysterically pleased with himself. As for Lauren Bacall, that was another story altogether. Simply put, she was a dream!

All of her friends called her Betty, her real first name, and she was glamour personified. Given my passion for movie stars, I couldn't wait to become her intimate friend, something that, alas, never really happened, but probably could have. Still, I made it a point that very evening to secure from her the promise of an interview in the very near future. Bacall was beautiful, elegant, intelligent, funny, sarcastic, outspoken, and very sexy! The quietest dinner guest of all, except for the comatose Steven Kyle, Betty Comden's peculiar husband, was my own wife, the much-admired and endlessly stared-at Jane Wilson. When we got home that night, she told me she was quite awed by it all, and that she felt uncomfortable in the midst of all that New York glitter. Of course, it pained me that Jane felt so constrained, so unable to participate in the flow of conversation and so intimidated by the evening. But that was Jane—and it would ever be thus.

Yet, as we saw the Bernsteins more and more, and as Jane continued to have more and more exhibitions, Felicia developed a strong and lasting admiration and affection for Jane Wilson and considered her to be not only a valuable friend, but also someone who might nurture and develop her own progressively intense interest in painting.

Indeed, it was Felicia Bernstein who, some years later, persuaded Jane to begin holding private painting classes in her studio, which would then become Felicia's disciplined framework for study. Not only did Felicia begin working with Jane on a weekly basis for some three years, but she brought a number of her friends into the group to study with Jane as well.

What is more, both Bernsteins, sometimes alone and sometimes together, would either buy or commission works by Jane, which eventually filled their New York apartment and their house in Fairfield, Connecticut.

There is no question that throughout the 1960s and 70s Jane and I enjoyed a unique and quite thrilling friendship with the Bernsteins. It would be a friendship that had its highs and lows, its fair weather and its doldrums and, for me personally, far too much emotional turmoil.

Chapter 33

In time we met Bernstein's own family–his parents, whom we saw only occasionally, and his younger siblings, Shirley and Burton, whom we saw a great deal of. This was a family of enormous complexity, made all the more complex by Lenny's extraordinary talent and superstardom.

Of them all, Shirley, Lenny's sister and the middle sibling, was the most interesting and tragic. From all Lenny would later tell me, it was clear that from the very first, her attachment to him was all-consuming. As Lenny's fame increased, he allowed her entry into his life, both private and professional, and Shirley eventually emerged as Lenny's surrogate, his omniscient spokesperson.

This would, of course, all come to an end when Bernstein not only acquired a private secretary (the ultra-devoted Helen Coates, his early piano teacher), but, far more emotionally wrenching for Shirley, an honest-to-goodness wife, who would now replace Shirley on so many levels. Indeed, when Felicia came into Lenny's life, it decidedly spelled the end of Shirley's role as official consort to the master.

What so touched me about Shirley Bernstein was her unrelenting passion for her brother, a passion that, through thick and thin and all manner of personal agonies, still kept her totally devoted to him. While jealousy and pain might have flared when Felicia came into the picture, Shirley swallowed her pride and ego, and found ways to keep herself as busy as possible, while also trying to be the best of all possible sisters-in-law, and with the birth of the three children, the best of all possible aunts.

For a while, Shirley tried acting, then moved into the field of agenting, handling a number of important playwrights. Later, she became a television producer with some rather alarming consequences. She had various short-term and long-term affairs, but the one thing she did not do was marry, and that, as everyone knew, was because her heart belonged to Lenny.

Burton Bernstein, whom everyone called Burtie, was the youngest son and, like all the Bernsteins, was highly intelligent and articulate. When we first met him, he was a staff writer for *The New Yorker*, and his stories and pieces were possessed of panache and feeling, especially one or two dealing with the Bernstein family and his famous brother.

At the time, Burtie was married to an interesting Dutch woman, Ellen, and they had two children. I loved Burtie because he was shamelessly though lovingly disrespectful of his older brother, always ready to poke fun at him, chastise him for one thing or another, or puncture the huge balloon that was Lenny's insatiable ego.

And some of his jibes truly hit their mark, such as the time when he asked Lenny, then at the height of his fame, why he didn't surround himself with people other than his old standbys, Adolph Green and Mendy Wager, and other such lifelong yet predictable friends. He kept asking Lenny, who was, after all, a world-famous figure, why he didn't develop close friendships with people equal to his own stature and renown.

Indeed, Lenny, who moved in circles that included world leaders, diplomats, politicians, scientists, intellectuals, and the greatest artists, writers, poets, and musicians of their generation, could as easily have formed lifelong friendships with any number of these. Yet, for whatever reason, Bernstein consistently preferred the company of Adolph Green, admittedly hugely musical and amusing; Mendy Wager, also musical and amusing but dull, who was really Felicia's friend (or "girlfriend," as she once confided to me); and other such familiar and predictable types–types whom Lenny could schmooze with and whom he could dominate and, yes, often look down on and make fun of.

I myself was in danger of becoming one of those predictable, "homey" types for Bernstein. But, luckily, there was Jane, who was not a schmoozer nor a kibitzer; nor, in fact, was I. Because I was quick and quite entertaining, I was often seen by both Lenny and Felicia as something of a buffoon, which of course I resented but had more or less brought upon myself. More to the point, however, and what really "saved" me, was that I was a member of the press, and Lenny knew very well that being on the right side of the press was both politic and eminently advantageous, especially with a member of the press who, if truth be told, quite worshipped him.

I would drop just about anything to do Lenny's bidding or simply be with him. Indeed, while I would never compromise my opinions or feelings when I was writing about him, the moment Lenny called, I instantly made myself available to him. When Felicia called with a dinner invitation–even at the last minute–and even if we had already eaten, we'd instantly call Julia's sitter, quickly get into our fineries, dash over to Park Avenue, and happily consume a second meal.

If it was a spontaneous "Let's go to the movies!" I'd immediately arrange for tickets so Lenny and Felicia wouldn't have to stand on line. In return, we were treated most royally. There were unexpected gifts from Felicia always, affectionate hugs from Lenny, and lots and lots of invitations to accompany one or the other to a host of events.

And of course, there were all those fantastic Bernstein-led New York Philharmonic concerts to which we were invited again and again, sitting either in the Bernstein stage right box with Felicia and assorted guests at Lincoln Center's Avery Fisher Hall, or in the best orchestra seats. To attend these concerts, often on a weekly basis, was to know blessed soul fulfillment.

In the concert hall, there was always that wonderful moment when the lights went down, and the concertmaster entered and took his bow, when the oboe sounded its "A" and the Philharmonic tuned up. Then came the hush, and Maestro Bernstein slowly entered to long applause. He'd climb the podium, unfailingly look up to Felicia and the rest of us, then turn his full attention to the music at hand.

After each concert, we'd be invited backstage to the green room, which was an event all its own. A select few, including Jane and me, were instantly admitted and served drinks while Lenny, usually in a sweat, and with the help of his dresser, changed into street clothes. Lines formed waiting to greet the maestro. These visitors might include long lost acquaintances, honored guests, adoring fans, and a string of handsome young men, all eager to be remembered, hugged, re-hugged, or kissed by the fabulously famous conductor.

For Felicia, the green room ritual usually proved an ordeal. Her job seemed to be to prod Lenny into speeding up his hellos and goodbyes, his hugs and his kisses, so that they might go to supper at that night's chosen restaurant, or return home with friends where supper might be waiting, or simply call it a night. But the greeting and talking, the kissing and hugging seemed endless. Often, Felicia, smoking one cigarette after another and gritting her teeth, would eventually gather her equally impatient entourage, get into her waiting car, and head for the appointed restaurant or home. Sometimes, Lenny never knew she had departed, which did not please him in the least. At such times, he might just wander into the night on his own or accept an invitation to go have a drink with one or two or three of the young fellows who had stuck around–just in case.

Chapter 34

Our friendship with the Bernsteins caused considerable havoc with our other friendships–notably with Jane Freilicher and Joe Hazan, Arnold Weinstein and Naomi Newman, and many others with whom we had formed close relationships. Everyone assumed that we would now be including them whenever Lenny and Felicia came to our house, whether for drinks, dinner, or a party.

For the most part, this did not happen. Resentments began building. Reproaches came our way. "I heard you and Jane had the Bernsteins over. I guess we're not good enough to be invited." "I heard the Bernsteins came to your house for dinner. How come you never invite us with them?"

It was true enough. We didn't invite some of our friends because, frankly, they would not really have interested the Bernsteins. Lenny would find dour Joe Hazan both tedious and ponderous, and he would probably draw a blank at Jane Freilicher's arcane bon mots and witticisms. Would the Bernsteins really respond to Naomi Newman's admittedly funny yenta-like humor or Arnold Weinstein's peculiar brand of irony? Maybe so, but I doubt it.

What it all boiled down to was that I felt we could not offer the Bernsteins what they were offering us, namely, people of enormous accomplishment and a star-studded milieu. Moreover, I knew from direct observation that Felicia absolutely loathed the idea of Lenny being put on display to people who could then go home and be able to say, "Guess who we had dinner with last night!"

A few years into our friendship with the Bernsteins we finally knew enough celebrated people ourselves to make our socializing with them more equitable. But at the beginning of our friendship with them, being with the Bernsteins meant excluding our "everyday" friends, both in New York and in Water Mill. Actually, Lenny and Felicia were quite happy to see us all on our own, especially when they visited us in Water Mill, which offered privacy and would for the first time bring them into contact with the Hamptons as a place of particular beauty. They already knew Gold and Fizdale and, of course, there was their old friend Jerry Robbins, who, by then, had a place in Water Mill. We'd all get together at our carriage house on Cobb Road for drinks and dinner or spend evenings at Bobby and Arthur's for great conversation, laughter, gossip, and superb food.

Of course, our other Water Mill friends–the great uninvited–Jane Freilicher, Joe Hazan, Kenneth and Janice Koch, and all the rest thought we had become the biggest snobs in the world–and they were probably right. Indeed, I strongly suspected that the rift that eventually occurred between the Hazans and ourselves was because we did not include them in my world of the stars (something I know Jane Freilicher coveted if only to make light or fun of), a world that came my way by dint of my job at the *Herald Tribune* and which I shamelessly sought out, and did not necessarily want to share with the world at large.

Still, it wasn't as though we stopped seeing our peers. On the contrary, we kept on seeing them again and again. It was just that we didn't see them when the Bernsteins were around. Indeed, for many years, we had become part of their set. They had not become part of our set–a quite large one back in the 60s and 70s–and there's proof, because I took countless photographs of all the young artists and poets and writers and musicians and composers with whom we associated, and who came to visit us in Water Mill or attended our parties in New York. Some 35 years later, these portraits and group shots would appear in my photographic memoir, *The Sixties: Young in the Hamptons*, published in 2006.

Among all those friends and acquaintances there appeared people with whom I formed very close attachments indeed. Yes, we loved the Bernsteins a lot, but they lived in a world apart…and they were older. The handsomest of our group was, without question, Alvin Novak, then a piano student of Kyriena Ziloti, whose father had been a pupil of Franz Liszt and a cousin of Rachmaninoff. Alvin had talent, but a concert career would elude him. His forte, it turned out, was teaching, and throughout the years he held various important posts in the piano departments of distinguished New York and Long Island music schools. He became a most sensitive and accomplished accompanist of the art song and lieder repertoire, performing brilliantly with the young, up-and-coming singers of the day.

Quite apart from his film star looks, Alvin was hugely intelligent and a true wit. At the time we met, he lived with the young painter John Button, an adorable, totally endearing, and quite wicked young man, whose potent sexual charms aroused many in our group, most notably Jimmy Schuyler, our poet friend, who went positively ga-ga over John, and said so in so many poems and a flock of recently published love letters.

But Alvin and John Button, whose remarkable interiors, landscapes and cityscapes will one day emerge as singular American artworks, would eventually part. And John died, much too young, of a heart attack in 1982.

Another close friend of the 60s and 70s was the gifted conductor Richard Dufallo. Of Czech descent, Richard had a great sense of humor, a great smile, tons of charm and talent to burn. We met him through the composer/conductor Lukas Foss, when Foss was director of the Buffalo Philharmonic. Richard was the orchestra's associate conductor. He would later become an assistant conductor to Leonard Bernstein of the New York Philharmonic.

Richard Dufallo made his home in New York and I found him quite irresistible. For one thing, he was amazingly sexy. For another he had an uncanny talent for being able to decipher the most complex, abstruse, difficult, and mind-boggling modern music scores imaginable. From Boulez to Xenakis, from Cage to Feldman, from Stockhausen to Takemitsu to Nono, Richard would premiere some of these scores with what seemed the greatest, most magical of ease. As a result, he came to be a specialist in fiercely contemporary music and was much in demand for his amazingly clear and lucid conductorial skills.

I think Richard loved me because I had worked at the *Tribune* and was now writing for *The New York Times*. Too, I was a great friend of Leonard Bernstein. When I did a piece about Richard for the *Times*, he loved me even more. All this loving, which I truly loved, encouraged, and took advantage of, took place even as Richard began wooing a beautiful young woman by the name of Zaidee Parkinson, a fine musician, a pianist of almost hysterical dedication. Zaidee was society. Her mother, Elizabeth Bliss Parkinson, was president of the Museum of Modern Art for years, and wielded considerable power among New York's haute monde. Zaidee's uncle, Anthony Bliss, was general manager of the Metropolitan Opera. Zaidee was gorgeous, with a million-dollar smile, a great face with dark, luminous eyes, and a sensual body. My Jane, totally mesmerized by Zaidee's electric beauty, would draw her again and again.

Zaidee and Richard seemed madly in love, and this mad love was amply fueled by the generous flow of liquor and frequent bouts of screaming fests. Theirs was one of those rip-roaring romances destined for a rip-roaringly unhappy marriage. (Richard had already been married and divorced, and had a daughter named Rene.) Soon, with Zaidee, there would be two sons, Basil and Cornelius.

We attended Zaidee and Richard's wedding. It was very grand. We saw them in New York, we saw them in the Hamptons, we saw them in Europe. We saw them constantly. And Richard conducted here and there. And Zaidee performed here and there. And Richard and I would see each other privately—very privately—and he would complain bitterly about Zaidee. And, it seemed, the drinking never stopped. Finally, Zaidee would call us at four in the morning demanding to know if Richard was in bed with us. And so it went. Soon there were ugly confrontations and Zaidee's jealousy and suspicions went out of control.

We stopped seeing the Dufallos. It was not a good thing for any of us. Some years later, they divorced. I believe the drinking stopped as well. I heard their two sons were immensely talented and that the eldest, Basil, became a much-respected classical scholar and the youngest, Cornelius, became a greatly gifted violinist and composer.

Richard, as he began to age, conducted mostly in Holland and had a busy and distinguished career leading such illustrious orchestras as the Royal Concertgebouw Orchestra and the Rotterdam Philharmonic, as well as the Berlin Philharmonic and the London Symphony Orchestra.

When he died of cancer some years ago, much time had elapsed. Richard remarried. He had fallen in love with yet another beautiful and gifted pianist, Pamela Mia Paul. When Richard Dufallo died, we attended his New York memorial. Zaidee was there. We hadn't seen her in years. She had become quite matronly though still radiant in her way. One of her boys spoke movingly about his father. There was a videotape of Richard conducting Mahler, and he was heard speaking. It was all too much. I was quite shaken. The young, passionate Richard Dufallo will always be a good memory for me; he was really very loving. I loved his talent, his great sense of fun, his special intensity…that wildness during our most intimate moments.

And then there was Jimmy—the brilliant young pianist, James Tocco.

Clearly, it was my time for falling in love with male musicians. We met Jimmy and his wife Gilan through mutual friends. Gilan was an Iranian beauty with dark, smoldering eyes and a dazzling smile. She too was a pianist, but had given it all up to devote herself to Jimmy's career, which was burgeoning. What a handsome, charming, sophisticated couple! We adored them immediately and quickly formed a close friendship.

Again, my role as journalist and my personal proximity to several major figures in the music world considerably enlivened our time together, and it did not take long before I felt that Jimmy should indeed meet Leonard Bernstein and, hopefully, excite the maestro enough so that he might engage James Tocco as a future soloist with the New York Philharmonic.

Jimmy had all the qualifications. He was young, good-looking, and immensely gifted. Boasting a repertoire of more than 50 concertos at his fingertips and a dazzling technique to match. Detroit-born, James Tocco won numerous prestigious European and American piano competitions and prizes and studied principally with the great Chilean pianist, Claudio Arrau. He soon emerged as a much-in-demand young concert soloist, performing with orchestras such as the Berlin Philharmonic, the London Symphony, The Chicago Symphony and the Los Angeles Philharmonic.

For whatever reason, Bernstein never engaged Jimmy to perform with the New York Philharmonic, although the two became quite friendly and got along famously whenever we all got together. On one memorable occasion, Jimmy and Lenny read through the two-piano version of Stravinsky's *The Rite of Spring* on the Bernsteins' two concert grands–an orgiastic musical entertainment enjoyed by a roomful of friends.

Because Jimmy's concertizing frequently took him abroad, the Toccos decided to spend part of each year in Europe and kept an apartment in Vienna. When I traveled to Vienna to interview the great Italian pianist Arturo Benedetti Michelangeli for the *Times*, I stayed with Jimmy and Gilan. And I took our 16-year-old Julia with me. The aging Michelangeli, notorious for repeatedly canceling appearances, had been engaged by the Vienna Philharmonic to perform Tchaikovsky's *Piano Concerto No. 1*. When the announcement was made that Michelangeli had once again cancelled (luckily, I had interviewed him before the cancellation), Jimmy was enlisted to take his place on a day's notice. He gave an unforgettable, standing-ovation performance of the Tchaikovsky warhorse. To my joy, I was able to include Jimmy's triumph in my Michelangeli article.

As our friendship with the Toccos intensified, and as Jane and I spent more and more time with them, it became clear to me that Jimmy was not a happy man. Although he concertized widely and with considerable success, and while he and Gilan seemed to have quite a loving relationship, Jimmy showed strong hints of frustration, dissatisfaction, and restlessness.

I instantly recognized the symptoms and saw in him some of my own inner turmoil.

It was, of course, the same old story.

Jimmy knew he was gay and needed desperately to express his feelings. He and I had many long talks about it. And with those talks, he touched my heart. He opened himself up to me again and again, and it was very moving, especially when he would also, on occasion, go sit at our Steinway and play some gorgeously articulated Handel or some heart-wrenching Chopin.

Because he seemed so vulnerable and because he played so beautifully, and because he was really such a sweet and serious young man who began to act so affectionately toward me, I could not help but respond…and I suppose you could call what happened next a sudden and unexpected and thoroughly bad case of fumbling gay love. Still, it was thrilling…and also quite scary.

Did Jane and Gilan suspect? I really don't know. For my part, I was genuinely shocked at the weight, strength, and violence of my feelings for another man. It was all most distressing, because frankly I never had any hankering whatever of setting up house with another man much less of ever giving up the life I had with Jane and Julia. Indeed, the idea of embarking on an exclusively gay life never entered my mind. It would have totally destroyed my equilibrium and sense of well-being.

What all this meant, I barely understood. It probably meant I was a totally selfish, self-centered, and a thoroughly untrustworthy human being—a kind of sexual betrayer, a faux homosexual who sees a sweet, talented, madly attractive gay guy and says, "Hey, I love my wife, but, oh, you kid!" All in all, my so-called gay life never really felt right, and on the various occasions I gave in to it, I always emerged more or less depressed and unhappy.

But Jimmy wanted the gay life, and he bravely made the break. He and Gilan separated and later divorced. What pained Jimmy most was that the break took place after he and Gilan had become parents of a baby girl, Rhoya, whom he adored.

After his separation from Gilan, Jimmy and I saw each other only sporadically. But on one memorable occasion, we both found ourselves in Germany, and we arranged to meet in Baden-Baden, where Jimmy was engaged to play the Szymanowski *Piano Concerto*. I joined him there and heard a thrilling performance of a little-known work by a brilliant Polish composer who also happened to be gay.

Jimmy and I spent two days together in Baden-Baden. They turned out to be as intense as they were emotionally tumultuous. Finally, they turned into a kind of sad, very loving, very poignant farewell, for Jimmy had resolved to leave America and move to Lübeck, Germany, where he was offered a piano professorship at the Lübeck Conservatory, and from where he would continue to travel, teach, and concertize the world over.

Chapter 35

Before there was Jimmy, there were other emotional and professional turmoils. For one, my exhilarating life as a critic of music and art at the *New York Herald Tribune* came to an abrupt end.

Actually, the demise of the paper was a slow and torturous process. We writers and reporters all knew that the *Trib* was not operating on a sound financial basis. What is more, there were frequent threats of major strikes, some of which came about and crippled operations for weeks on end. In a desperate move that many thought foolhardy, the powers that be, principally the *Trib*'s owner John Hay Whitney, decided in late 1966 to merge the *Trib* with two other local city papers, the *New York Journal American* and the *New York World-Telegram and Sun.* Thus, for almost a year, our beloved *Trib* became known as the *New York World Journal Tribune.*

Although quite a few *Tribune* writers and editors were laid off, I was retained not only as an arts reporter and critic for the new *World Journal Tribune,* but because I made a very strong pitch for it, as a weekly columnist writing a column called "The Pop Scene." Emily Genauer was also retained and remained my immediate superior. When she heard that I was given my own column, she blew all her gaskets. She thought I was not qualified to have a column of my own and produced a holy yammer about it to the paper's new bosses. It was pure, unadulterated jealousy, and her fury knew no bounds.

But my editors had always understood that Genauer, ever strident and aggressive and, alas, hugely conservative in her taste as an art critic, couldn't hold a candle to my ambitious forays into New York's outrageous avant-garde of the 60s, and they gave me my column, which the paper thought would, in some small way, enhance circulation.

Thus it was that "The Pop Scene," my weekly column, with my picture and name often prominently displayed on the sides of the paper's delivery trucks, boosted not only my ego but my standing at the paper. I was on top of the world! I was famous!

And it all came crashing down when, one fine morning, riding to work in a taxi, I heard on the cab's radio that on that very day, the *World Journal Tribune* would cease publication and would be no more. When I walked into the City Room you could cut the gloom with a knife. Most of the employees stood around disconsolately clutching their "Dear John" letters. When I got to my desk, there it was, waiting for me. I picked it up and began reading these ominous words: "It is with a real sense of personal regret that I must tell you that the *World Journal Tribune* is permanently ceasing publication with today's issue. Your employment must terminate at this time." It was signed Matt Meyer, President. The year was 1967.

I instantly called Jane and gave her the news. She was devastated. We both were devastated. I was out of a job!

There was some severance pay to tide us over. I had worked for the *Tribune*, and briefly for the *World Journal Tribune*, for some seven years. The loss of this job proved a genuine blow. Suddenly, after years of journalistic visibility, I was back to square one–it was horrible and frightening. But some weeks later, the phone rang and it was A.M. Rosenthal, one of the top brass at the *Times*. He asked me to come in. He said he had enjoyed my writing at the *Trib*. I was thrilled. A job at the *Times*! It was the pinnacle. And, to my immense joy and relief, Abe Rosenthal offered me a job.

"We'd like to offer you a two-year stint in our office in Los Angeles," he said. "You'd be covering entertainment–movies and Hollywood news." My heart sank. I said, "But isn't there something for me right here in New York?" He said no, there was not.

I was crushed. The reason my heart sank was simple. I can't drive a car. I had, in fact, failed my New York driving test four times! I knew that L.A. meant driving everywhere, and I simply couldn't do it, nor, considering my monumental lack of vehicular coordination, would I want to do it. When I told Jane about the offer, she too was less than enthusiastic, but for other reasons.

Jane was just establishing herself as an artist in New York, where the real creative action was. She was showing at Tibor de Nagy Gallery, she was beginning to be noticed, the Museum of Modern Art had already purchased a large landscape. At the time, California was an artistic wasteland–there was no thriving artistic community. Outside of less than a handful of artists, including Richard Diebenkorn, Elmer Bischoff, and David Park, California was a painter's desert. Jane didn't want to live in California and have to start her career all over again, not with New York, the new art capital of the world, paying attention.

The *Times* next offered me a reporter's job in Hawaii, and I was flattered by their persistence. "Tell your wife the sunsets in Honolulu are spectacular!" said Abe Rosenthal. Once again, I politely declined. But I begged Rosenthal to let me do some freelance writing right here in New York, and he said he'd see what he could do. On the very next day I received a call from Seymour Peck, then editor of the *Times'* Sunday "Arts & Leisure" section. We met, and he said he'd liked my various *Tribune* interviews and would I be interested in writing interviews for his section. I agreed instantly.

Thus began my nearly 25-year association with *The New York Times*. While I was not officially on the staff, I wrote for the paper on a very steady basis and became closely identified with the most prestigious newspaper in the country, if not the world. This new association with the *Times* found me even more visible in New York's cultural world as I began interviewing celebrated actors, musicians, composers, conductors, choreographers, ballet stars, modern dancers, film stars, and a seemingly endless array of the talented and the famous. My new editor, Seymour Peck, couldn't be more generous or helpful. A man of extraordinary energy, intelligence, and vision, he could also be a strict and spiky taskmaster, invariably finding ways to ask you to improve your stories so they would have greater relevance or punch. It was a challenge writing for Sy Peck, but if you dug deep into your subjects and carefully polished your articles, he'd call on you to write for his section again and again.

Of course, this stroke of good luck brought with it the freelance writer's lot: a limited income and the constant fear of not being called, of your services and talent not being in demand, of your having to constantly dream up ideas to submit to a busy editor. In short, there was no weekly paycheck, and with a family to support this was a scary state of affairs. Yes, I got lots and lots of work from the *Times*, but the pay was really minimal and you just never knew from assignment to assignment if the phone would ring as often as it had before. I was a nervous wreck for most of those early months and years of writing for the *Times*, but I didn't dare complain or rock the boat, and I loved being known as a *Times* writer.

Then, one evening, in the spring of 1967, the phone rang. I picked it up, and it was my friend, Leonard Bernstein.

"Viking Press has asked me to do a book in time for my 50th birthday," he said. "How would you like to write it?"

"Oh yes, absolutely!" said I, stunned and elated.

"Good!" said Lenny. "We'll do it in Italy this summer during my vacation!"

And so it happened that in early July of 1967, Jane, Julia, and I, as well as our long-haired dachshund, Sophie, flew to Rome, rented a car, and drove to the resort town of Porto Ercole where we had rented a house. It was not far from where the Bernstein family would stay in a luxurious villa in the small town of Ansedonia, one of the Italian Riviera's chic-est, most exclusive and private summer playgrounds. The two summer months with the Bernsteins proved both fabulous and very, very complicated.

The result was my book, *The Private World of Leonard Bernstein*, published by Viking Press in 1968. This was not a full-scale biography but more of an in-depth birthday memoir, in which Lenny and his family, as well as his sister, Shirley, his brother, Burton, and a handful of friends participated by way of some wonderfully candid interviews. And it was where Lenny himself expressed himself on any subject he wanted, including some very personal thoughts on his life, his career, his politics, his marriage, his children, and his close friendships with, among others, Aaron Copland. Too, he spoke of his insanely difficult relationship with conductor Artur Rodzinsky, his immediate predecessor at the New York Philharmonic, and had much to say about his rival Herbert von Karajan and his beloved mentor Serge Koussevitzky.

To this day, *The Private World of Leonard Bernstein* is the only book in which Bernstein expresses his innermost feelings in his own words. In addition, the book was enhanced by the many superb photographs taken by the photographer Ken Heyman, who captured every phase and aspect of the maestro and his world.

Needless to say, working on a book about Lenny with Lenny himself proved a major highlight of my writing career. But oh, the heartache! Our Italian summer with the Bernsteins came after we had known each other for quite a few years and had become very close. Felicia happily attended painting classes at Jane's New York studio, where she studied hard and produced some really fine work. I continued to follow Lenny's career, continued writing about him in the *Times*, in *Vogue*, and elsewhere, and there were endless social occasions during which Jane and I and large numbers of the Bernsteins' friends gathered for all sorts of get-togethers and festive occasions.

For example, almost all Christmases for some ten years were spent with them at their wonderfully cozy house in Fairfield, Connecticut. Indeed, Christmases at the Bernsteins, were always the high point of our holiday season. So our friendship was strong and secure, and, for the most part, hugely fulfilling and a great deal of fun.

Of course, I had always known of Lenny's homosexual inclinations. I dare say everyone had always known about them. Certainly the music writer, Joan Peyser, knew about them and quite shamelessly capitalized on them when she wrote *Bernstein: A Biography* (1987), a book exposing Lenny's every last gay encounter and relationship. Although the biography *Bernstein* (1994) remains the best of Lenny's biographies to date, its author, Humphrey Burton, also charted, more or less fully, Lenny's gay life. But neither of these authors had Lenny himself to work with and be in constant touch with. Most happily, and at his request, I had Lenny all to myself for *The Private World of Leonard Bernstein.*

I knew Lenny found me sufficiently attractive to give me the frequent fervent embrace or the long-held, often passionate kiss on the lips. But then Lenny embraced and kissed all the nice-looking young men who so often clustered around him. And not only that, he embraced and kissed practically all the artists and soloists who performed with him throughout his conducting career. There is no question but that no Bernstein curtain call was ever complete without the Bernstein bear hug or the Bernstein kiss.

In Italy, Jane, Julia, and I found ourselves in close proximity to Lenny, Felicia, and their three children. Our Julia, then eight years old, practically lived at the Bernstein villa, having found a special friend in Nina Bernstein and become a happy participant in all the swimming games, excursions, and playtimes of the Bernstein children.

As for Jane, she and Felicia would paint and make trips to Rome and elsewhere to visit museums as well as visit the nearby sites. As it turned out, Lenny's brother Burton, his wife Ellen, and their children also came to Ansedonia for the summer, sharing a villa with Don and Luisa Stewart. As the Bernsteins did very little socializing in Ansedonia, we were all one happy family, content to be in each other's company, except for the occasional times when we all were invited to go sailing on an acquaintance's yacht.

Lenny had arrived in Ansedonia immediately after an emotionally wrought ten days spent in Israel after the 1967 Six-Day War, where he had conducted the Israel Philharmonic in a victory concert on Mount Scopus in Jerusalem. It would take him a certain amount of time to begin relaxing enough to embark on our book project. Indeed, he had just completed a long Philharmonic season in New York and had accepted an invitation from the Vienna Opera to conduct a new production of *Der Rosenkavalier.* He had, moreover, resolved to instruct his son Alexander on his upcoming bar mitzvah. Last but not least, he would have to deal with me and the book project.

What was worse, out of the blue, Lenny announced to me he was an insomniac and that we would be taping most of the book during the nights he couldn't sleep. I usually slept like a log, and I needed my sleep! How was this going to work? I was nervous enough at the prospect of writing the book. Having to tape Lenny in the dead of night filled me with even greater apprehension. He, on the other hand, thought nothing of it. "You'll get used to it—you'll see," said Lenny. "It'll be nice and quiet."

Chapter 36

Imagine weeks of starry Italian nights. There are hushed nighttime breezes and nighttime sounds. The cicadas, so relentlessly chirpy and loud during the day, have finally gone mute. Lenny and I are on the villa's spacious veranda overlooking the sea, he, stretched out on a white wicker chaise, I, seated in a large wicker easy chair, my tape recorder on a small table between us. There are drinks—Scotch and soda for Lenny, Scotch and water for me. Each time we lift our glasses for a sip, the ice makes a loud tinkling sound in this silence. Of course, we are both smoking incessantly. I have taken my newly prescribed stay-awake pills. It is late, but we are both alert. The audiotape is going....

"I just don't know how much I can reveal myself," Lenny finally says. "Take a man like Picasso. Picasso lives absolutely openly. He lives in a bikini in the south of France; his morality is absolutely free. I myself have a much more bourgeois background. After all, I'm the son of a rather puritanical Mosaic-oriented Talmudic scholar. And as free as I have been, especially in my youthful years, I have never been able to escape from that strong puritan morality which comes to me both by way of my Talmudic father and the New England I grew up in, which make a very puritanical combination indeed."

Lenny pauses...then: "Although you may spend your youth fighting your environmental morality, protesting it, and showing what a rebel you are, it stays with you, even through some abortive attempts at psychoanalysis. I still have this bourgeois streak, and I will always have it. It's reinforced by my need to protect people I love. So, as I said, there's a limit to how much I can reveal myself."

But reveal himself he did. Not to the public. But to me. It was agreed I would be discreet. It was agreed Lenny could go off on tangents, could touch on myriad subjects, some clearly for the book, some definitely not for the book. It was up to me to know the difference. Lenny didn't want to stop the tape recorder and say, "This is off the record." He didn't want to interrupt the flow of his thoughts, his ideas, his musings. He needed to be free to express himself fully and honestly. He trusted me to protect him.

It all began very slowly.

During those Italian nights of ours, there was much on his mind. Next year would be the last year he would be conducting the New York Philharmonic–he was resigning after the 1969 season after ten years of being its most volatile and charismatic music director. He would become Conductor Laureate for Life, but it was wrenching for him to think of leaving the orchestra he so loved and nurtured for all those years.

He talked of his need to compose more and more. "I have hardly scratched the surface."

Perhaps with his resignation from the Philharmonic, the composing would begin to take precedence. Already, he was looking forward to his commission from the newly built Kennedy Center in Washington, D.C., for the opening of which he would write his highly iconoclastic and controversial *Mass.*

But, generally, throughout the first two weeks or so of our talks, I found Bernstein to be more or less depressed, restless, ill at ease. As he put it, "Right now, I'm kind of living from day to day. I feel of no importance at all. So it's very hard to talk about myself as though I mattered.

"I really can't reflect back. All I can do is reflect on the moments as they go by and try to extrapolate from these moments what the rest of my life must really be like, when I'm too busy to observe it.

"For example, as you probably noted, I find it very difficult to rest–and I'm in a period of rest. I find it hard to sleep at night or nap during the day. So far this vacation has not turned out the way I foresaw it: a kind of Eden-like calm and bliss, in which one will lie in the sun or sit in the shade or float in the water and all these thoughts will come to you, all these ideas, musical inspirations, and whatnot that will be bubbling up. Instead, everything gets more and more gray and opaque and vague."

Indeed, it was hard to prod Lenny out of his gloom, and when I tried to cheer him up or make him laugh, he did not really respond. I knew, of course, that although he agreed to do this book, he was also resisting it. That was mainly because he was genuinely reluctant to face his demons. He kept referring to the book he was just then reading, Marguerite Yourcenar's *Memoirs of Hadrian.*

"There's a passage I'd like to read to you–just listen:

'As to self-observation, I make a rule of it, if only to come to terms with that individual with whom I must live up to my last day. But an intimacy of nearly 60 years' standing leaves still many chances for error. When I seek deep within me for knowledge of myself, what I find is obscure, internal, unformulated, and as secret as any complicity.'

"That's exactly what I wanted to tell you the other night when you said, 'Dig deep into yourself and tell me'–and this is what I find: obscure, unformulated, and secret. It's very hard to find out what goes on inside."

But Bernstein knew we had to go on with it. He knew he could not renege on our project, and as time went on, and as he relaxed and his mood improved and as his body bronzed and as he swam for hours and participated in the everyday activities of his family, his attention to our book grew more pronounced and the ensuing weeks saw us both falling into our ritual nighttime taping sessions with ever greater ease–even enthusiasm.

And there was more. As we proceeded, and as Lenny gave me ever greater access to his feelings about so many people and about so many subjects and events, and about so many emotions, especially his guilt-ridden love of men, I found myself becoming more and more attached to and enamored of Lenny's mind and soul. A kind of love emerged–not necessarily the love that dares not speak its name (although, to be sure, there was that too), but a kind of fervent intimacy that is the result of a shared and very singular experience. As it turned out, *The Private World of Leonard Bernstein* was really a very loving and revealing book, a picture of Lenny as he really was up until then, a complex, brilliant man who, quite simply, made the world a better place by the force and genius of his extraordinary talent. And so when, during some of those Italian nights, Lenny felt inclined to be affectionate and sometimes more than affectionate; when, during a particularly poignant session of recollection he needed to pause and physically reach out to me, to hold me or be held, to kiss me or be kissed, it would happen–easily, silently, often passionately.

As my head reeled at this quasi-romantic turn of events and my own familiar guilts began stirring within me, another drama was unfolding. I became acutely aware that Jamie, Lenny's beguiling 16-year-old daughter, was developing a very strong and visible crush on me. At every turn, I felt the young heat of it as Jamie would look at me with all manner of longing. I do not exaggerate. At one point she handed me a small scroll upon which she had written me an impassioned love poem. It was all enormously touching and, in a way, quite painful to us both, because I knew I could not respond–it would have been utterly wrong. As this was happening, I said and did nothing to encourage the sweetly smitten Jamie.

What is more, and at the risk of sounding like an irresistible, death-to-men-and-women gigolo-intruder, I will add that Felicia Bernstein also manifested a certain penchant for me, probably out of ennui, for, truth to tell, there were many days in lovely Ansedonia when people went quite out of their minds with boredom. During dinner or drinks or at the pool-side, Felicia would give me certain looks, and there were, now and then, spontaneous hugs and little kisses. It was all quite innocent, really, and Felicia seemed merely ready for some heavy flirting with a fairly attractive in-house friend.

To clear the air of these bouts of heavy breathing, Felicia one day decided we should all take a trip—a trip without children. I had long suggested to both Lenny and Felicia that we visit Sardegna for its great beauty and ruggedness. Jane, as it turned out, was just then in Florence on one of her long museum jaunts, and so did not join us. It was the three of us and, on the very next day, off we drove in Lenny's just-acquired and splendiferous Maserati to Civitavecchia, where a boat would take us to Alghero and, finally, to the Hotel Porto Conte, where we had reserved rooms. The idea was to cross the island of Sardegna and explore the Emerald Coast. Then, after two or three days, we'd return to Ansedonia.

It was on the boat form Civitavecchia to Alghero (an overnight trip) that Lenny again jolted my feelings by expressing his happiness at our being together. Again, it was the middle of the night. Again, Lenny couldn't sleep and Felicia had long retired to her cabin. Alone, on deck with Lenny, I looked at his quite beautiful leonine head silhouetted against the sky, and felt a surge of excitement. As the rather decrepit old boat slowly drifted across the silent sea toward Sardegna, we moved very close to each other, and suddenly Lenny held me very tight and, once again, kissed me. The moment was breathtaking.

The next morning we landed, and those few days were unbelievably glorious because of the weather and Lenny's spirits. Never again would I see Lenny as happy as he was in Sardegna. There was a moment in an open field that will always stay in my mind and heart, and we both talked about it weeks later.

"I loved our madcap trip to Sardegna," Lenny said. "It was marvelous fun, stopping that time in the mountains. I was really as happy as I've ever been. It was so peaceful! The air was something I will never forget. And picking raspberries and not feeling rushed. And it was a beautiful time of day. And those white, white sheep in the distance and the sound of their bells…and the pure, pure air. God, it was beautiful!" When we got back to Ansedonia, the children all squealed with joy. Jane had returned from Florence and I was so happy to see her! And my little Julia was so loving and sweet, I couldn't stop hugging her. And Lenny and Felicia seemed exhilarated by our trip.

My middle-of-the-night tapings with Lenny finally came to an end by late August 1967, and our Italian summer with the Bernsteins was coming to a close. The experience was, to say the very least, unique. Lenny, despite his monumental ego, his moodiness, his several outbursts of bad temper, his capacity for hurting people, and his relentless need for always and forever being the center of attention, nevertheless brought me the singular reward of being in closest and most personal contact with one of the genuine gods of music.

Chapter 37

Upon our return to New York, we all settled back into our individual lives, and there was much to do. I now had the Bernstein book to write and, thoroughly recharged by my Italian experience with Lenny, I found that my energies were bubbling over, so much so that I went out of my way to invent new projects for myself–new projects that would keep me busy for years to come. Also upon my return, my former *Tribune* editor, Clay Felker, offered me the position of chief art critic at his newly created *New York* magazine, born of the old Sunday weekly insert he edited while at the *Trib.*

For her part, Jane returned to teaching art history at Brooklyn's Pratt Institute. It was a post that would spearhead a whole series of other important yet time-consuming teaching positions, including drawing and painting courses at the Parsons School of Design, the Cooper Union, and ultimately Columbia University, where Jane taught from 1976 to 1988. At Columbia, Jane became one of the department's most beloved teachers. In 1986 she was named the acting chair of the art department, a highly demanding position she held for two years before retiring from teaching altogether. Although Jane never stopped painting, and had had several major exhibitions during her teaching career, it was time for her at long last to make painting her priority.

But there was more. Ever since our friend, Jane Freilicher, took our four-year-old Julia to see Balanchine's *The Nutcracker* at the New York City Ballet, the idea of becoming a ballet dancer intrigued Julia no end. Of course, she had no idea what this would entail, but I myself thought that having our little girl take ballet lessons after school might be a wonderful thing. Nothing could be done while she was still so little, but in 1966, just before we went to Italy, when Julia turned eight, I arranged for her to audition for entry into The School of American Ballet, the official school of the New York City Ballet.

Julia had all the physical attributes of a potential classical dancer, and, even as a child, embodied Balanchine's aesthetic ideal–the small head, the long neck, the long, elegant legs, arms, and hands, and a poignantly beautiful face. It was thought by some of the teachers that her feet were a bit too tapered, which might eventually impede her pointe work. But she was accepted into the school and, in the following year, was cast as one of the "mice" in that year's perennial glorious Christmas production of Balanchine's *Nutcracker*.

For the next seven years, Julia studied diligently at SAB, while also maintaining her studies at Hunter College Elementary and eventually graduating from Hunter College High School in 1975. It never occurred to me that all this grueling work at both school and ballet was turning Julia into something of an introverted bundle of unhappiness. I, the ever psychologically sensitive interviewer of hugely creative and complicated people, didn't see that my own daughter was clearly suffering from all manner of insecurities and fears. At 14, 15, 16, admittedly "difficult" years for anyone, Julia seemed to me to be on the surface generally well adjusted, happy enough with both her schoolwork and ballet classes, and having a fairly good time with her ballet friends. Little did I know that she was suffering– and for good reason.

Of course, I wasn't blind to the fact (although I tried hard to be) that Julia, even as she was developing into a stunning-looking teenager, was also growing taller and taller–something that was anathema to the so-called "perfect" ballerina body or look. Her growing taller wasn't in the least bit bizarre; she just grew into one of those ravishingly tall and willowy American beauties, normal enough for a girl with tall parents.

But at five feet nine inches, the ballet stage was not the appropriate place for a classical dancer, no matter how lovely looking or well-trained. Even by Balanchine's standards–and he loved tall dancers–being that tall would not do, especially if you add the three or four inches in height when you get up on pointe.

And so, it came to pass that the School of American Ballet announced to Julia that despite her many years of training and all her dedication, she would not be entering the New York City Ballet. And Julia was crushed. And so was I–for me and for her. On that very "bad news" afternoon, I took my girl to the New York Philharmonic for a terrific Bernstein concert. Afterwards, we went backstage. I had earlier alerted Lenny about Julia's sad news, and in the green room, afterwards, Lenny took special pains to comfort her, and there were many little Bernstein kisses.

That same evening I took Julia to a Russian restaurant near Lincoln Center. Who should be there but George Balanchine dining with Karen von Aroldingen, one of his favorite ballerinas. Everyone at SAB knew that Balanchine had always liked Julia, and had kept his eye on her throughout the years. But he too realized she had grown too tall. On that evening, at the restaurant, he came up to Julia and told her how she must not grieve about what had happened.

"You will always have the ballet inside you," he told her. "It will always be with you, and you will always love it, and you will never regret having studied it." With that, like Bernstein a few hours earlier, Balanchine covered Julia with little kisses.

Giving me one of her great smiles, Julia later remarked, "Today, I received the spittle of the gods!"

It was all incredibly wrenching. All those years of study seemed for nothing. Lots of people suggested to Julia that she try going to ballet class elsewhere, and she did. She won a scholarship at the American Ballet Theatre School, where she studied for a year. People also suggested she move into the modern dance field, where being tall could be an asset. But Julia was too immersed in the classical technique to suddenly shift gears and embrace an aesthetic she did not particularly respond to.

Finally, the whole situation became too much and, at age 17, Julia abandoned dance altogether.

Good things happened to Julia during the following years. As for the bad things, we were, for our sins, barely aware of them, but they turned out to be scary and could have led to tragedy. Yet, for whatever reasons, none of Julia's very real troubles diminished her basic strength, her intelligence, her common sense, and her innate good nature. Still, there was considerable turmoil, pain, and unhappiness in a young life that seemed to have been predicated entirely too much on "pleasing father" and on the fulfillment of impossible expectations.

The fact is, Julia was, from earliest childhood, exposed to parents of a certain relentless ambition and to people of formidable accomplishment. It was no wonder that intimidation, insecurity, and frustration would govern much of her inner life, and would lead to rebelliousness. Be that as it may, quitting the ballet did not, happily, sour Julia's love of the dance. Indeed, she would remain close to many of her ballet friends and, as it turned out, would turn me into an avid, hopelessly obsessive balletomane.

I will say it here and now: it was Julia, with her own great emotional and instinctive knowledge of classical dance, who gave me the great gift of seeing and looking at dance in a uniquely discerning and passionate way. It was Julia, who with her subtle and nuanced understanding of the Balanchine aesthetic and technique, gave me insight into the many wonders of the New York City Ballet, its dancers, and its magnificent Balanchine repertoire.

I had long been an enormous fan of Balanchine, having begun my ballet-going days in 1948, when the New York City Ballet began its life at New York's City Center. But I would never have experienced the real depth or real beauty of what I was seeing had I not, 20 years later, encountered the same company and the same ballets filtered through the eyes of my young daughter, who had for seven long years been so personally involved in Balanchine's art and aesthetic.

Moreover, because I was for many years permitted to sit in on Julia's ballet classes (and other classes as well), I was able to absorb the very underpinnings of Balanchine's technique, which, while based on the most traditional classical discipline, subtly veered in matters of speed, clarity, and musical response.

It is an amazing fact that Julia and I share, in the most meaningful way, a life in dance that would extend into her adult life, and would encompass our seeing performances together given by almost every major ballet company in the western world. What is more, in her early years, during and after her time at SAB, Julia was herself frequently hired as a supernumerary in major productions of such visiting companies as London's Royal Ballet, the Stuttgart Ballet, The Royal Danish Ballet, The National Ballet of Canada, The Paris Opera Ballet, and New York's American Ballet Theatre. In whatever costumes, in whatever ballets, in whatever non-dancing roles, it was a joy to see our Julia moving or standing so beautifully on the professional stage.

Ultimately, though, Julia moved on with her life. A brief but intense stint as an 18-year-old fashion model in New York, Paris, and Milan (with some ravishing photographs of her taken by Richard Avedon), proved unsatisfying. Julia returned home and enrolled at Columbia University, where she majored in English literature and attended classes for some three years.

Then, wanting to work and earn a living, she answered a *New York Times* ad and landed a job with the Charles Cowles Gallery. She later moved on to yet another one, the Tony Shafrazi Gallery in SoHo, and in 1984, one of Shafrazi's most popular, talented and controversial young artists, Keith Haring, hired Julia to be his personal assistant.

It would be an association that dramatically and excitingly changed Julia's young life.

Chapter 38

When *The Private World of Leonard Bernstein* was published in 1968, Viking Press threw me a very swank party at a very swank East Side restaurant, the Running Footman. Tom Guinzburg, Viking's President and CEO, and his vivacious wife Rusty, couldn't have been more generous and I couldn't have been more pleased and elated. The book, with its transparent acetate jacket revealing a large close-up Ken Heyman photograph of Lenny's handsome face, had about it the sweet smell of success.

Lenny, Felicia, their family and many of their friends attended and my special favorite, Lauren Bacall, arrived dispensing her aura of total gorgeousness and glamour upon the festive proceedings.

Everyone had a great deal of fun and a great deal to drink and there was food and laughter, and there were times when Lenny and I exchanged glances and held those glances for just that moment longer. And, more than once, Lenny would tell me how pleased he was with what I had written. It was all quite fabulous and glorious and enthralling.

But did the euphoria last?

My Bernstein book received many favorable reviews throughout the country, including a fairly positive one from the *Times*, for which I was still writing on a regular basis. There were interviews, TV and radio appearances. Lenny participated in some of them. Sales of the book were very brisk indeed. It seemed as though every bar mitzvah boy was given a copy of the book with the admonition: "You see! You too can grow up to become a Leonard Bernstein."

Then, one Sunday morning, a week or so after the review had come out in the *Times*' Book Review section, there appeared a letter from the conductor Artur Rodzinski's son, Richard, strongly berating Bernstein for what he had said about his late father in my book, namely that Rodzinski, Lenny's predecessor at the New York Philharmonic, had tried to kill him—in fact, tried to strangle him—in a fit of jealousy over Lenny's incredible success following his Philharmonic debut.

Indeed, Lenny had given me a vivid and harrowing account of the events immediately following Lenny's sudden and momentous debut in 1943, when the Philharmonic's guest conductor, Bruno Walter, fell ill, and Lenny, then the Philharmonic's assistant conductor, stepped in at almost a moment's notice. Not only did the 25-year-old Bernstein conduct the orchestra with consummate passion and fire, but the debut coincided with the Philharmonic's national broadcast of that very concert–and not only did all of America hear Lenny make a phenomenal conducting debut, but every major music critic throughout the country, upon hearing him on the air, hailed the young American conductor as the country's next new musical genius.

In very colorful language, Lenny had related to me how Rodzinski, the Philharmonic's regular conductor, became so enraged and so livid with jealousy over Lenny's wild success that he became deranged enough to want to kill him.

To my complete astonishment, Richard Rodzinski's letter in the *Times* elicited a response from Bernstein that just about floored me. Lenny responded with a letter of his own, telling the younger Rodzinski that he had never said what appeared in my book–that he was never shown the Rodzinski portion of the book and implied that it was, in so many words, a total fabrication. In his published letter, Lenny said that he had never told me the story…and how he fully understood young Rodzinski's dismay, and what a wonderful and meaningful association he had had with Richard's late father and mentor, Artur Rodzinski!

I couldn't believe it! I mean, if I didn't have the tapes of Lenny recounting those melodramatic Rodzinski events, his assertion wouldn't be laughable. But what really hurt was that Lenny did not call me to say he was writing a response to Richard Rodzinski's letter.

I telephoned Lenny at once.

"How could you have written this letter?" I asked him point blank. "You know you told me every last word about Rodzinski that's in the book. Why would you lie about that? Why would you make me out to be a liar, as though I had invented the whole thing?"

"Well, John," Lenny replied, "you must be pretty naïve to think that I'm going to let Rodzinski's son think of me as his father's vengeful accuser–of saying he tried to kill me."

"But isn't that what actually happened?"

"That may be so," said Lenny, "but it's not what I want his son to believe."

Jane Wilson exhibition opening at Tibor De Nagy Gallery, New York City, April 1966
(*From left to right*: Bill Berkson, D.D. Ryan, Jane Wilson, Charles Addams)

Jane Wilson and John Gruen photographed for *Harper's Bazaar*, New York City, May 1965; photograph by Diane Arbus

Jane Wilson and Diane Arbus, New York City, 1965

"The Family" (John Gruen, Jane Wilson, and Julia), New York City, 1970; oil on canvas 58 x 60 inches; by Alice Neel, courtesy of the estate of Alice Neel

The Bernstein family: Nina, Jamie, Leonard, Alexander, and Felicia, New York City, 1968

Leonard and Felicia Bernstein weekending at the Gruens', Water Mill, NY, 1968

John Gruen and Leonard Bernstein, Ansedonia, Italy, 1967; photograph by Jane Wilson

Jane Wilson, Julia Gruen, and Leonard Bernstein, Flying Point Beach, Water Mill, NY, August, 1968

Fiftieth birthday party for Leonard Bernstein at the Gruens', Water Mill, NY, 1968
(*left:* Israel Citkowitz; *right:* Betty Comden)

Lauren Bacall, New York City, 1967

Jane Wilson, Betty Comden, Charles Chaplin, Oona O'Neill Chaplin, and John Gruen, Porto Ercole, Italy, 1967; photograph by Stephen Kyle

Richard Dufallo and Zaidee Parkinson, Water Mill, NY, August 1969

James Tocco, New York City, 1971

Rudolf Nureyev and Erik Bruhn vacationing, Greek Islands, 1964

Rudolf Nureyev visits Erik Bruhn backstage at New York City Ballet, New York City, 1963

I could tell Lenny couldn't wait to get off the phone.

Bernstein and I didn't speak for many, many weeks. When we did, the Rodzinski matter never came up again, and my feelings for Lenny cooled and diminished.

What did not diminish was the personal success I enjoyed with the publication of the Bernstein book. Jane and I had already had a remarkably active and very exhilarating social life during the 1960s. I mean, we really threw ourselves into the stream of all the glitter New York had to offer–from the latest discos to the newest clubs, from every major museum and gallery opening to every posh party–there we were! We did not have a lot of money, but it looked as though we had, because we entertained quite frequently if not lavishly. Indeed, our parties became quite famous.

What is more, there came a moment when we were known as one of New York's most glamorous couples, and were duly written about in *Vogue*, *Harper's Bazaar*, and elsewhere, and were photographed by the likes of Diane Arbus (our photo can be seen in Aperture's *Diane Arbus: Magazine Work*), Francesco Scavullo, and many others, and our names appeared in the various gossip columns of the day. Andy Warhol asked Jane to appear in his film *Thirteen Most Beautiful Women in the World*, and commissioned her to paint his portrait, which is now at the Whitney Museum of American Art. The great portrait painter Alice Neel asked us to pose for a large and very powerful family portrait of Jane, Julia, and me. It was all quite head-spinning.

My byline in the *Times*, *Vogue*, and elsewhere, and Jane's growing reputation as an artist kept us in the limelight. But with the publication of Lenny's book, things really took off and we were suddenly everywhere. Not that we just lived to be seen or lived to commingle with the worlds of music, art, movies, fashion and theater–which we did–or to go on meeting ever more celebrated people within those worlds–which we also did.

What we were mostly doing, along with all the social frou-frou and all the glitz, was working very, very hard–I at my writing, Jane at her teaching and painting. How we did it all, I'll never know. What I do know is that we were not heavy drinkers. We did not join the amphetamine/quaalude/marijuana/cocaine crowd. We simply did not dissipate. Self-preservation and our Julia kept us sane and safe.

Jane and I had by now been married for some 20 years. It was a fairly long journey for two people who had started out in Iowa as pretty virginal and innocent. Our marriage had its problems–but it was stable and, for the most part, quite amazing. Jane and I had much in common—we enjoyed many of the same things and of course, there was Julia, our great love.

For me, being with Jane and going out with Jane was always something of a thrill. From the very first, she was so quietly different! Later, in New York, people of all sexes kept falling in love with Jane—they found her mysterious and enigmatic and desirable. And she was genuinely glamorous in the best sense of the word, never ostentatious, never loud, never crude. She may have been inordinately quiet at social gatherings, but when she spoke, people listened, perhaps at the very shock of her saying anything. What people didn't know about Jane was that she was a terrific speaker when she taught or lectured, with a clear and rigorous mind and a wit that truly sparkled. It was, admittedly, a very strange thing, this difference between Jane's social silences and her public utterances—but that was Jane.

Furthermore, there was nothing silent or boring about Jane when it came to raising our daughter. She may not have been the most available, overprotective, and ever-present mother in the world, but she definitely wasn't silent. The care and goodness she lavished on Julia, the knowledge and good sense she imbued in her, were clearly and wisely administered.

There were times, earlier on, when Jane was close to leaving me. I could be pretty impossible and worse, I wasn't around all that much, what with working night and day during my *Tribune* years. And, of course, I had my private penchants, and I acted upon them when so compelled. Jane may not have known about them, but she probably sensed them.

The fact is, I was not a confessor. The thought of running to Jane after a stupid peccadillo and telling her all about it was totally out of the question for me. I didn't believe in confessing. It was an abhorrent waste of time and energy. I simply didn't believe in making Jane miserable, of hurting her or myself. What good would it do? Would it clear the air? No. Would it make things better? Not really. So I kept things to myself and hoped for the best.

And the best was on my side, because Jane loved me enough not to leave me. And I knew I would never leave Jane. Besides, as the 60s drew to a close, I got so incredibly busy that the thought of outside involvements made me shudder, unless, of course, the world were suddenly to stop and my prince were suddenly to come along.

Chapter 39

I look back on my 1960s with many emotional quivers and semi-quavers. I was still quite European in outlook and often reflected on my great good luck at having survived the horrors of World War II, a topic often touched upon when Jane and I made our visits to my parents, still living in Washington Heights.

My father, though by now fairly Americanized and fairly successful in his diamond dealing business, never stopped reminiscing about and pining for the "good old days" in Berlin and Milan, when, surrounded by his crown prince, Leo, and his other sons, Martin and Carlo, he led a life of European graciousness and gregariousness. Now, though safe from the tyrannies of dictatorships, he still longed for the familiarity and hominess of the old countries, where, whether as jeweler or travel writer, he rode the crest of popularity and success.

What my father had never stopped being, however, was insufferably critical and maddeningly obtuse and frustrated–frustrated at having struggled to bring his three sons to America out of war-torn Europe, only to see them disperse to other parts of the U.S., away from him and my mother; frustrated with me, who, though living just a subway ride away, barely acknowledged his existence, seldom came to see him and rarely telephoned.

My three brothers, though grateful for having had their lives saved through my father's indefatigable efforts, could not abide him or his constant criticisms, complaints, and demands. As soon as they could, each left New York to build a life of his own, a life that, from my point of view, was a sad reflection of what can happen when education is aborted and when persecution and war reduce individuals to content themselves with less than their real worth or abilities.

As it turned out, my eldest brother, Leo, met and married a singularly unpleasant Viennese woman, Bertha, whose fear of germs was only equal to her disdain for both Jane and me. They moved to Washington, D.C., where Leo embarked on a career selling D.C. souvenirs. Brother Tino, he who did not attend our wedding in Oskaloosa, Iowa, because one of his front teeth was missing, changed his name to Martin Vellere, permanently moved to Des Moines, Iowa, married a woman named Vivien, raised a stepson and, to the end of his days, was a shoe salesman in a local shoe shop. Brother Carlo also married a good, down-to-earth woman named Anne, had an adorable son, Stevie, moved to Los Angeles, and went into the knitting business, selling yarn and knitting needles. My brothers rarely visited each other or visited New York. There was little correspondence and no one ever really understood nor cared what Jane or I or Julia were doing with our lives—so much for brotherly love.

In any case, life went from intensity to intensity, as I worked fast and furious in the pursuit and discovery of as many creative worlds as possible.

It suddenly occurred to me that most of my writing to date, especially for the *Times*, hinged on interviewing other people. I missed writing for myself, doing some creative work that I could call my very own. Always enamored of the theater, and attending as many plays and experimental workshops as possible, I thought I should start writing some plays of my own, perhaps some gutsy one-acts. Of course, I would want to see them staged as quickly and as often as possible. After all, wasn't the theater in my blood? Wasn't my experience, back in the 50s, as the theater and film worlds' most fabulously gifted and wildly popular zither king sufficient entry into avant-garde theater at its loftiest or zaniest?

And so I sat down and wrote four one-act plays in quick succession and, believe it or not, they were produced and staged almost immediately. I showed these fledgling works to our friend Gaby Rodgers, who to my great shock positively adored them. We had known Gaby and her husband, Jerry Leiber, for a number of years. And they, like our friends the Duffalos, were volatile and combative, but we loved them and their two little boys, Oliver and Jed. Back in 1955, Gaby, a totally bewitching German-born actress, had starred with Ralph Meeker in Robert Aldrich's crime thriller, *Kiss Me Deadly*, based on Mickey Spillane's novel. The film has become one of the screen's great cult favorites, and Gaby's name is, to this day, linked with this small noir masterpiece. But Gaby also had quite a long and distinguished Broadway career, starring in such plays as *Mr. Johnson* by Joyce Cary and *The Hidden River*, opposite Robert Preston.

The explosive and hugely talented Jerry Leiber was the lyricist of the well-known pop songwriting team of Leiber and Stoller. Their vast output included many of Elvis Presley's greatest hits ("Hound Dog," "Treat Me Nice," "Loving You," "Trouble," "Steadfast, Loyal & True"), as well as some of Peggy Lee's most haunting songs. It was in the Leibers' living room one evening, that we first heard Jerry sing us Leiber and Stoller's latest song, "Is That All There Is?, which Miss Lee would turn into a smash ballad a few months later.

But back to my one-act plays of the late 1960s. Gaby Rodgers was just then embarking on a career as stage director and was, in fact, in the grip of the Polish avant-garde actor and director Jerzy Grotowski, whose company, then performing in New York, was all the rage. I believe Gaby had fallen in love with Grotowski and was utterly mesmerized by his methodology and technique, in which actors reacted both physically and psychologically to the most minute stage actions and brought their bodies and minds and voices violently to bear upon the subject of any given production.

We all went to see Grotowski, and what we saw was a company of athletic semi-nude actors bathed in lurid blue and red lights, writhing on the floor, howling in pain, entwined in each other's arms and legs and crawling all over the stage in agonized chaos as though caught in the direst, most horrific circles of Dante's *Inferno*. It was the latest in an acting technique that made Antonin Artaud's *Theater of Cruelty* seem like Noel Coward at his most soigné. But Gaby fell hard for Grotowski and even traveled to Poland to witness the company on its home turf.

I showed Gaby three of my one-act plays. They were titled *Soap Opera*, *The Treatment*, and *Never Tell Isobel*. These were somewhat acerbic light comedies, dealing mainly with marriage, the passage of time, and what growing old can do to you. Gaby read them, Jerry read them, and they both loved them. Gaby agreed to direct them and Jerry said he'd finance them. Gaby brought my plays to Ellen Stewart, the tireless, dedicated, and entirely magical founder of that off-off Broadway theatrical mecca known as Café La Mama, today still going strong and located on East 4th Street in the East Village. Ellen Stewart also loved my plays, and agreed to have them staged at La Mama. The year was 1969.

The first two plays, *Soap Opera* and *The Treatment*, were presented under the title *Fatal Beauty*, and Gaby had rounded up a lovely cast. She invited Jack Smith, the notorious filmmaker of *Flaming Creatures*, to design the inventive and fabulous sets. The plays, well attended, received a week's performances but garnered only a few passable reviews.

But it was with Gaby's direction of *Never Tell Isobel*, with a cast of 11, where the influence of Jerzy Grotowski reared its terrifying head. When I attended rehearsals of my more or less stylized drawing room comedy of manners dealing with couples grappling with the bonds of marriage, I found a rehearsal room that resembled bedlam. Gaby had elected to put the actors through the Grotowski meat grinder, having them scream at the top of their voices, grapple with each other on the floor, pull on a long heavy rope and tie it around each other in an agonized effort to act out the heavy chains of marriage. This turmoil went on for several days.

"It's to shake them up for the play, when we get around to actually rehearsing it," said Gaby in her bright, accented, tough-girl voice.

Those poor actors! They never complained, because this was serious avant-garde theater!! They were doing it all for art, and Gaby was their visionary director and mentrix.

Never Tell Isobel opened on January 22, 1969 at Café La Mama and ran through February 2. The reviews were pretty awful, especially Jerry Tallmer's in *The Village Voice*, who felt I had quite a lot to learn about playwriting. Still, the play found itself published in the 1981 edition of *The Best Short Plays of 1981*, a much-respected annual anthology that also featured plays by, among others, David Mamet, Murray Schisgal, Brian Friel, Christopher Durang, and Israel Horovitz, selected and edited by Stanley Richards.

I had one more brief and quite thrilling foray into playwriting. I wrote another longish one-act play called *Smut and the Baritone*, and submitted it to the playwriting unit of The Actors Studio, the prestigious New York acting conservatory headed by Lee Strasberg.

The play was accepted for a workshop production, and I was allowed to direct it. When we staged this comedy, dealing, I think quite amusingly, with pornography and marriage, Strasberg critiqued it and found it to be well structured, witty, finely acted by a cast of two, and well directed. He made wonderful comments on the "daring" subject matter, and praised my "chutzpah" at having had the guts to deal with it. I was in seventh heaven. But, alas, that was the end of my career at the Actors Studio. Strasberg died shortly after my play was seen, and, for whatever reason, I was not readmitted into the "new" playwriting unit.

I went on to write at least six more one-act plays, and collected them in an unpublished volume I titled *Nine One-Act Plays* by John Gruen. I sent them all to Gaby, but Gaby, who is still a dear friend, seemed to have lost interest in my playwriting genius and, despite some half-hearted efforts on my part to send my plays around to producers and directors, they have languished unproduced in my bookcase for over 35 years. (To my great amazement and utter joy, the brilliant director and actress Barbara Vann, who runs a small New York theatrical company named The Medicine Show, asked to see my ancient plays, and produced three of them in the winter of 2006. They included *Never Tell Isobel*, *Flowers*, and *Just The Two Of Us*, a farce about aging, marriage and depression, given a hilarious, wonderfully felt performance by Ms. Vann and Morton Banks.)

Chapter 40

I could never warm up to Clay Felker, my editor at both the *New York Herald Tribune* and at *New York* magazine. I always felt Clay had something missing—a heart, perhaps—and this, despite the fact that he hired me as the new magazine's chief art critic, a post I held for some five years. Felker had also been more or less responsible for the publication of my first book, *The New Bohemia*, the result of the article he had commissioned at the *Trib* back in 1965.

Talk about ingratitude! But the fact remained that this extremely personable, all-American, yuppie-type man, this Missouri-born journalistic visionary (for he was truly that), always seemed to me to be uncomfortable in his own skin—at least as a young man—and he made people around him, people like me, feel awkward and insecure.

I'm sure the reptilian Tom Wolfe never felt that way, nor the beer-guzzling Jimmy Breslin, two of Felker's protégés, who were brought to *New York* magazine from the *Tribune* and turned by Felker into the new journalism's superstars.

I couldn't turn out pieces like Wolfe's or Breslin's if you put a knife to my throat. It simply wasn't my style or inclination. But what a stink and scandal some of those early *New York* magazine articles created! I especially recall Wolfe's incendiary 1970s "Radical Chic" piece, viciously aimed at Leonard Bernstein's fundraiser for the Black Panthers. Actually, it was Felicia Bernstein, who had arranged and organized the whole thing. I know, because she told me so, and she invited Jane and me to come to the event in their New York apartment. The idea was to raise money for bail needed to free some of the jailed Panthers.

It was a very well-attended evening. Lenny spoke and Tom Wolfe, the uninvited guest, was brought by the greatly talented writer Barbara Goldsmith. The day Wolfe's article appeared in *New York*, a wildly incensed Lenny called me up and said, "If you want to remain my friend, you'll quit your job at *New York* magazine immediately, because anyone who works for that miserable publication is no friend of mine."

Felicia too admonished me, practically accusing me of having written the "Radical Chic" article myself. "You can't have it both ways, John!" she told me in a seething voice.

I told the Bernsteins that I'd be happy to quit working at *New York* if they'd start paying me my weekly salary. This, of course, they were not prepared to do. But the Bernsteins needn't have worried, because in time, my tenure at *New York* came to a miserable end.

There I was, quite happily doing my job as art critic of *New York*, reviewing all the major museum exhibitions, writing up endless gallery shows and writing the occasional art interview, when, after nearly five years, Clay called me into his office and demanded to know why I wasn't writing art columns dealing more with what went on in the back rooms of museums and art galleries. He felt very strongly that the art world itself needed to be explored and exposed, not individual artists and their sundry merits. He thought that some really good art-world dirt would surface if only I went looking for it.

"Look, John," said Felker, "I know you and Jane go to lots and lots of dinner parties. Why don't you just take along your tape recorder, put it in your lap, under your napkin, and start asking people some pungent questions. I bet you'll get some really interesting answers! Reviewing art is all very well, but you ought to go out there and do some real investigative reporting." When I refused this sneaky and totally unethical approach to investigative reporting, Felker turned very cool indeed.

In the meantime, word had come back to me that a hugely ambitious art writer by the name of Barbara Rose was dogging my steps. I also heard she was allegedly nibbling at Clay Felker's earlobes and vice versa. The upshot was that Felker called me up one day in early 1975 and announced that Barbara Rose would be replacing me as *New York* magazine's art critic. I gathered that, unlike me, Ms. Rose would shovel as much art dirt as possible into her new and revamped art column.

Did I cry over the loss of this job? No. In a sense, I was relieved. In those years, I had more writing assignments than I could possibly handle. Aside from my continuing biweekly or monthly articles for the *Times*, I had been writing a monthly column on the avant-garde for *Vogue*. I had also been invited to be a contributing editor to both *ARTnews* (where the brilliant Don Goddard was my favorite editor) and *Architectural Digest*, an association that kept me writing, traveling, and earning good money for some ten years.

Moreover, by the mid-70s, my passion for the dance really began to obsess me as much because of Julia's studies at the School of American Ballet as of my increasingly crazed love of this magical art. Needing desperately to do something about it immediately, I went to my friend, Tom Guinzburg, who presided over Viking Press, and practically begged him to let me follow up my success of *The Private World of Leonard Bernstein* with a book I wanted to call *The Private World of Ballet.* He was less than enthusiastic. But, splendid fellow that he was and is, he finally gave me the big nod, and I was ready to learn even more about the dance than I already knew.

My plan for *The Private World of Ballet* was to go directly to all major dancers and choreographers and ballet company directors in New York and in Europe and ask them to talk to me as candidly as possible about their lives, their loves, their careers.

What emerged was a very informative compendium, possibly the first of its kind, on the inner workings of the ballet world, and on the dedicated, demanding, and at times excruciatingly painful life of the ballet dancer.

I befriended over 100 dancers and choreographers, most of them connected with America's and Europe's major ballet companies. In conjunction with researching and writing the book, I attended hundreds upon hundreds of ballet performances, endless rehearsals, workshops and ballet classes, and saw as much of the greatest classical dancing done by the greatest classical dancers any one person could possibly see in one lifetime. It was also my unbelievable good fortune that the 60s, 70s, and early 80s proved to be the twentieth century's golden age of ballet, for it boasted a confluence of dancers the likes of which had not been seen in a century.

Too, we still had the presence of legendary early dancers, now turned teachers, who at ballet schools across the country were handing down their art to the next generation. Ballerinas such as Alexandra Danilova, Alicia Markova, Felia Doubrovska, Muriel Stuart and danseurs like Frederic Franklin, Anton Dolin, Igor Youskevitch, and Leon Danielian, among many others, not only imparted their glamour, glory, and knowledge to veritable armies of eager young ballet students, but made certain that the best of their charges would ignite the ballet stage as they themselves had done in years past.

This was also the time of the great Soviet defections, the first of which occurred in Paris in 1961, when Rudolf Nureyev, at age 23, sought asylum in the West. This was followed by Natalia Makarova's "leap to freedom" in London in 1970 and, in 1974, the defection to Canada of Mikhail

Baryshnikov. These superbly trained dancers emerged from a tradition harking back to the great ballet pedagogues of Czarist Russia, but were now frustrated by a Soviet regime and a repressive ballet management that would not allow them to properly spread their wings.

Indeed, these very great artists were eager to dance in the works of the West's great choreographers, Balanchine, Tudor, Ashton, and so many others, and anxious to join the ranks of the West's luminous ballet stars–artists such as Erik Bruhn, Margot Fonteyn, Anthony Dowell, Antoinette Sibley, Lynn Seymour, Carla Fracci, Maria Tallchief, Cynthia Gregory, Gelsey Kirkland, Suzanne Farrell, Edward Villella, Fernando Bujones, Marcia Haydée and Peter Martins, to name only a few of the greatest dancers of their time.

I was enamored of them all, and with the imminent publication of *The Private World of Ballet*, I plunged headlong into the dance world, convinced that as *A Chorus Line* would have it, "Everything is beautiful at the ballet."

Actually, a lot of it was. But some was not, especially when it came to those dreadful, jealous, mean-spirited, physically unattractive, utterly pretentious dance writers and critics of the New York press! What a bunch of leaden, earthbound know-it-all snobs this faction of the ballet world turned out to be! With a very few exceptions, I just loathed them all.

Chapter 41

In the late 1950s Jane and I met Edwin Denby, who was my all-time favorite dance writer and critic. Edwin, who became a friend, was decidedly not a part of the crew of creepy dance writers of my generation. Indeed, he had stopped writing dance criticism for quite some time. Edwin was also a poet, and one of the most cultured and civilized and gentlest people we had ever met.

His dance reviews, essays and articles, written for various publications during the 30s, 40s, and 50s, were lessons in clarity and sophistication. He could describe dance and dancers in ways that were as compelling as they were lucid and exact. I never had his talent, but Edwin Denby became my role model as a dance writer. When I told Edwin that I was going to enter the dance world, he said, "Oh, my! I wish you luck. Believe me, you'll need it." He didn't go on to say what a closed and insular and nasty world it really was, nor how hard it was for an "outsider" like myself to fit into it.

The very first intimation of what Denby had been warning me about came when Clive Barnes, then the chief dance critic of *The New York Times*, spat in my face after he had deeply objected to an article I had written for the paper. This charming episode, with Barnes' wife Trisha at his side, and Jane standing beside me, occurred during intermission at a New York City Ballet performance.

The article in question dealt with the City Ballet and some of its leading dancers, whom, I suggested, seemed imprisoned by their brilliant Balanchine repertoire, and were thus deprived of dancing in major classics such as Giselle or the full-length *Swan Lake* and *The Sleeping Beauty*. I went on to say that this was because, at the time, George Balanchine did not wish to have these full-length classics performed by his company and did not want his dancers dancing in them.

I wrote how really interesting it might be to see a glowing City Ballet ballerina such as Allegra Kent or Patricia McBride assuming the role of Giselle or Jacques d'Amboise or Edward Villella dancing the role of Albrecht. Clive Barnes hissed at me, saying I was a complete ignoramus for making such a suggestion, given the fact that Balanchine and the New York City Ballet were setting out to educate the world on a whole other premise of what classical dancing was all about.

Barnes had a point. But so did I, even if it was a point tinged with a beginner's naiveté. But did he really have to spit at me? I thought it was shocking, let alone disgusting. But it gave me vivid insight into the malicious depth to which some dance critics could sink. Nothing so dramatic ever happened to me again, but there was no question that the dance critics and writers of my day were worse than the most avidly obsessed balletomanes. While posing as the world's most objective and nonpartisan professionals, they actually had their own very clearly defined agendas, which they would trot out in print at the slightest provocation. And, aside from all that, what an ugly-looking collection of people most of them were!

I always thought that dance critics of a particularly alarming homeliness, especially the female critics, were drawn to the ballet, not only because everything was beautiful at the ballet, but because there was the vicarious pleasure of being part of a world that boasted some of the most ravishing-looking people imaginable, each producing breathtaking beauty by the minute. And what was ballet itself if not an idealized dream of perfection?

And so, I saw these people, with their bad bodies, bad faces, bad skin, bad legs, and bad hair, sitting in their good seats facing the ballet stage, eagerly devouring the perfect physical splendors of all that passed before them. There were one or two exceptions: the divine Joan Acocella, now writing for *The New Yorker*, had always seemed to me an unusually fascinating person, and her dance writing was at once fresh, informed, original, and exciting. This was undoubtedly because Acocella, unlike the others, had not specialized solely in dance writing, but was a masterful essayist in other creative fields as well. I also much liked Jennifer Dunning, who still writes most sensitively for the *Times.* More recently, the *Times'* Alastair Macaulay is a wonderfully candid dance writer and critic, and his opinions have flair, sweep, and a dollop of surprising cruelty.

But, one might ask, why was I so drawn to the ballet? Didn't I have an agenda as well?

I have talked about my daughter, Julia, to account for my great new passion. But in fact, I truly and genuinely loved the dance. For me, watching superb performances of a classic ballet, a work by Balanchine, a dance by Martha Graham or, simply a splendid tap dancer could give me goose bumps. I was transported by the body in motion and mesmerized by the combination of movement, music, décor, lighting–the whole creative ambiance that could result in an unforgettable evening of dance.

And I was furthermore well aware of the ironies of ballet, the perfection of line in bodies bending or turning or leaping in ways that looked natural but were dangerously unnatural in their means of execution. To me, it was astonishing that ballet training, with its 500-year-old tradition of shaping musculature in a way that would transform a dancer's body into an instrument of aesthetic pliability, could produce artists of such singular emotional expressiveness and amazing technical purity.

Yes, I too had an agenda. By endlessly going to see them dance and endlessly writing about them, I wanted to befriend all my favorite dancers, from the very great to the no-so-great yet still special. As with the musicians I befriended, and like a true fan, I wanted to be part of their world, their lives, their aura, their artistry. In short, I definitely wanted and needed dancers in my life. Especially the male dancer, who to me represented a certain kind of noble and poignant workhorse as well as a charming, attentive cavalier.

The male ballet dancer always seemed to be the exhilarating backbone of the stage. His mission and mandate was to lovingly "present" his ballerina–to guide her, lift her, promenade or embrace her, and then, alternatively, present himself as an entity of individual fire, conquering space by his runs and leaps and jumps and turns. To the monumental annoyance and fury of my fellow dance writers, two such artists became central to my life in dance: the Danish-born virtuoso Erik Bruhn, and the Russian firebrand Rudolf Nureyev. The first, I wrote a book about. The second, I quite lost my head over.

In the meantime, to further legitimize my dance credentials and credibility, I needed to become associated with America's most visible dance publication, namely, *Dance Magazine.* To that end, I telephoned its editor-in-chief William Como, who, recognizing my name through my many *Times* interviews, promptly invited me to lunch. We met at a midtown restaurant. Como, bejeweled in chains, bracelets, and rings, arrived with his managing editor Richard Philp. I told them both of my forthcoming ballet book and of my passion for the dance. I offered my services to *Dance Magazine.* These were promptly accepted, and, within a week or two, I was on the masthead and writing interviews. Later, I began a monthly column dealing with dance on television.

My steady but bumpy association with the magazine lasted some 20 years. Bill Como did a mostly good job editing the magazine, but, in truth, I could not abide his egomaniacal personality, his endless hissy fits, his shirts open to the waist in summer, his floor-length fur coats and fur hats in winter, his effete mannerisms, his kowtowing to foreign and domestic dance company directors, accepting their free airline tickets and hotel expenses in exchange for overly complimentary articles about their companies and dancers in his magazines.

The much put-upon Richard Philp, whom I quite liked at first, would eventually become editor-in-chief (Como died of AIDS in the 90s), and he too turned into something of an insufferable and quite weird egomaniac. Still, this connection, its yearly *Dance Magazine* Award, its slick color covers and photography, and my frequent exposure in its pages, served me well and I profited from the magazine's wide circulation in the dance world.

Then, even as I was sailing full speed ahead into my dance writing career, and even as I was beginning to court and befriend all the dancers I wanted to meet and know, already having dinner with some of them and inviting them to our house for parties, another one of those fateful telephone calls (the kind I got from Leonard Bernstein back in 1967) came my way. This time, it was a call from Gian Carlo Menotti, the then hugely popular and eminent Italian composer, famous for his uniquely theatrical operas, including his perennial Christmas favorite *Amahl and the Night Visitors*, and renowned as the charismatic founder of the Spoleto Festival of Two Worlds, which he had founded in Italy in 1958. Menotti said he'd read and loved my Bernstein book, and asked if I would be interested in writing his biography. He added that I would do our tapings at his home not far from Edinburgh, Scotland, in his palatial Palladian palazzo, "Yester House," which he had recently purchased in East Lothian at the foot of the Lammermoor hills. Were I amenable to the project, he would also want me to visit him in Spoleto, Italy, the ravishing hilly town near Rome, where, during July, the Spoleto Festival would be in full swing.

I told Menotti I'd have to think about it.

I did think about it, and within a few days and with joy in my heart, I called him back and accepted the project. I had even rounded up a publisher: the Macmillan Publishing Company, one of the best. We met for drinks at his small, elegant New York pied-a-terre in the East 60s off Madison Avenue and drank a toast to each other. Although Menotti spoke perfect English, we conversed at length in Italian, the language of my childhood.

I was now able to tell him how very moved I was by his opera, *The Consul*, with its story echoing my own experiences in war-torn Europe, when my parents had to flee Germany and Italy. Their efforts were met with the same sort of bureaucratic red tape his heroine, Magda Sorel, so heartbreakingly encountered in *The Consul*. And I told him how I had subsequently met the star of his opera, Patricia Neway, and how she became a champion of my songs, performing them back in the late 50s and early 60s. And I told Menotti of my great admiration for his work in general: *The Medium* and *The Telephone*, his marvelous opera *The Saint of Bleecker Street*, and the music of his ballets, *Sebastian*, *Errand into the Maze*, and *The Unicorn, the Gorgon and the Manticore*.

Menotti couldn't have been more pleased. He loved my enthusiasm for his work and felt he had made the right choice in selecting me as his biographer.

I looked at Menotti. He was really quite handsome, with a sweet, inquisitive look about him, a big beak of a nose, and a wicked twinkle in his eyes.

"I'll give you a list of all the people you must talk to," he said, referring to the seminal people in his life. "And, oh yes!" he added. "You must meet Chip!"

"Chip?" I asked.

"Yes. Chip is the boy I adore."

As July was soon upon us, I made ready to fly to Rome. I would then take the train to Spoleto for our first meetings. (Jane and Julia would stay behind.) I'd be back in my beloved Italy. It would be glorious and Menotti and his world would be fascinating to discover and plunge into. And, of course, I couldn't wait to meet Chip.

Menotti! So hugely famous! Two Pulitzer Prizes! What a great and glamorous subject. I was literally chomping at the bit!

Another book! Another homosexual!

Chapter 42

When Gian Carlo Menotti invited me to Spoleto, I knew my work would entail a complex round of events—operas, concerts, plays, ballets, art exhibitions. In addition, I would also be interviewing Menotti as well as a large number of people long associated with him and the festival. The schedule was daunting and I felt a certain panic at the thought of getting it all done within two or three weeks.

Then the idea struck me: why not take Andrew Mark Wentink with me? Andy Wentink had been my assistant on *The Private World of Ballet*, and he proved invaluable. It fell to Andy to transcribe my tapes and help me research a world I was not as yet entirely familiar with. Andy proved a treasure.

So off we went to Italy. And we found that Menotti was the Prince of Spoleto. He lived in the very grand Palazzo Campello on the central plaza of the little town. He was constantly surrounded by friends, acolytes, hangers-on, the festival staff (mostly bright young men, each one handsomer than the next), and, of course, all the fabulous artists—singers, actors, instrumentalists, dancers, conductors, poets, and playwrights—whom Menotti had invited to participate in his festival

There were many women around Menotti as well; some titled, some rich, and all, for the most part, either Italian or American. Each was jealous of the other, and each was madly in love with their darling, adorable Gian Carlo. He was their genius. He was their inspiration.

Some, like the fascinating American heiress, Alice Tully, gave pots of money; some, like the tireless, generous, and deeply committed Priscilla Morgan, lent their distinguished pedigrees and connections; others gave of their time, and still others acted as hostesses or tour guides. All worshipped him. And I could tell all too soon how very much Menotti thrived on their rapacious attention, and how he liked nothing better than to orchestrate envy and rivalry between them.

Like the brilliant stage director that he was, Menotti turned each festival season into a drama where all manner of crises and "disasters" were the order of the day, and where hurt feelings, bruised egos, slammed doors, sobs and tears had to be countenanced until the maestro came along with a magical solution—or not.

There was no question that Menotti was the sole arbiter of all the festival's private and public doings—the last word on how it should all be played out. And, in his charmingly devious way, Menotti himself was almost always the cause of much of the festival's ongoing chaos. Yet, at the end of the day, Menotti took care of everything: the play's leading lady was appeased and comforted, the opera's prima donna dried her tears and made up with the tenor, poets were retrieved from their sulks, the prima ballerina, though rudely dropped by her danseur noble, would still manage to dance with him that night.

It was during my very first private meeting with Menotti at his palazzo that I finally met his beloved Chip. It was a memorable moment. As Menotti and I were deep in taped conversation, a huge ruckus was heard near the palazzo's entrance below. In a moment, we heard the screams of the housekeeper: "Maestro, maestro! Venite presto!!" ("Come quickly!")

Menotti rushed downstairs, then came back up, holding a dazed Chip around the waist. Chip's face was bruised and bloodied and he was limping. It seemed he had been on his motorcycle and ran into something. He had clearly been drinking. Menotti brought him to their bedroom and washed him off very tenderly.

I saw Chip, seated on the bed, looking both angry and sheepish. He seemed to be in his late twenties. He eyed me suspiciously but said nothing. Though the room was in shadow, I could see what a handsome fellow Chip was, with blue, blue eyes and chiseled features. Still, just then, he was pretty much the worse for wear, and soon he lay back to sleep it all off.

"This is not how I wanted you to meet Chip," said Menotti, as he led me back into the palazzo's elegant salon.

"Poor Chip!" said Menotti. "He's Irish you know. He has a wild Irish temperament and he has a streak of madness in him. When I met him he bore the scars of an unhappy childhood."

Menotti recounted how he had met Chip several years earlier in Spoleto. He was a young ice skater turned actor and had a small part in a Tennessee Williams play. At the time, Chip suffered from frightening headaches and was also given to heavy drinking. He was moody, with fits of uncontrollable anger and bouts of serious depression. The composer fell in love with the very troubled young man and resolved to take him under his wing.

"I saw how sick the boy was. I took him to many famous specialists and each one gave me a different answer. Then, a wise doctor told me that all Chip really needed was affection, understanding, and a home. And that is when I thought of legally adopting Chip. Francis Phalen became Francis Menotti in 1974. Chip is now my son."

When, some days later, Menotti personally introduced me to Chip, I instantly sensed his resentment. He had, of course, been told I was writing Menotti's biography, and at first he categorically refused to be a part of the project. He refused to give me an interview and generally avoided me. It was only after Menotti pleaded with him again and again that Chip consented to a very brief taping session, which, as it turned out, centered mostly on how Menotti was being taken advantage of by the people around him. Still, there was no question but that Francis "Chip" Menotti quite doted on his adoptive father.

While Chip claimed his job was to organize Gian Carlo's life, in truth, he seemed really not up to the task. On the contrary, he caused endless chaos and antagonism whenever and wherever he stepped in to take charge of Menotti's activities. Throughout my stay in Spoleto, almost everyone I taped felt that Chip was an alienating presence–a negative, destructive force that was harming the composer at every turn. People disliked him, disliked his meddling and his boorish and sullen ways.

When in 1977, Menotti founded the American version of the Spoleto Festival in Charleston, South Carolina, Chip again played an active role in its operation. But, as in Italy, his presence created negative feelings all around. As late as December 2004, when neither Menotti nor Chip were any longer connected with the festival, Charleston's paper, *The Post and Courier*, ran a lengthy story centering on the festival's past problems. Menotti, because of "overt hostility," anger, and endless complications, had resigned from the festival in 1993, and Chip was clearly at the center of the controversy.

"Chip Menotti annoyed critics, politicians, patrons, and people in general during his time here," wrote reporter Daniel Conover. "While festival founder Gian Carlo Menotti was a popular guest, the city generally treated Chip like a gold-digging spouse out to seize the family business."

Menotti himself often entered the fray when things heated up for Chip. *The Post and Courier* reported that Charlestonians had finally grown weary of the Menottis' threats and tantrums. "The bottom line was Chip."

In a way, it was all very touching. The naughty child was hated and accused by everyone, yet forgiven again and again by his adoring father. The mischievous, badly educated, primitive, stubborn, meddling, and often violent son was nurtured, supported, defended, and loved by the famous composer, a gay man, who had always wanted a son to spoil and adore. Indeed, I witnessed firsthand how Menotti's adoration of Chip never wavered, how his voice softened whenever he spoke of him, how his eyes lit up, reflecting sheer happiness at the very thought of Chip.

I never really knew nor inquired whether Menotti and Chip had ever been lovers. I simply assumed they had been, given Menotti's past penchant for "broken," neurotic young men, like Nikiforos Naneris and Kinch Horan, to mention two long-lasting affairs in Menotti's past. And, of course, there was the young conductor, Thomas Schippers, so complex and talented, whom the composer had literally groomed for stardom, but who eventually broke Menotti's heart when he abandoned him to marry the fabulously wealthy Nonie Phipps.

And of course there was Menotti's very first love, the love of his life, composer Samuel Barber, whom he met at The Curtis Institute of Music in Philadelphia when both were teenage music students. Barber would emerge as one of America's premier composers who, like Chip, strongly objected to my writing Menotti's biography. Jane and I came to know Barber and admired him enormously. But he had a spiky, difficult personality, especially in his later years, and could make life very difficult for those around him.

If my intensely difficult work in Spoleto proved chaotic and nerve-wracking, and if Chip consistently made me feel unwelcome and unwanted, the next phase of my Menotti project proved surprisingly calm and, for the most part, intensely pleasurable. This was my visit to Menotti in Scotland at his magnificent home, Yester House. The word "luxurious" was clearly invented for Yester House and Gian Carlo Menotti, the laird of the manor, was at his most transformed, aristocratic and elegant within its sumptuous walls. If he was mostly frantic in Spoleto, here, in East Lothian, he was a man seemingly at peace with himself. Here I witnessed the private Menotti, the Italian who did not relish the Mediterranean sun and heat, but loved instead the moody Scottish rains and winds; the man who preferred solitary walks on the moors to convivial get-togethers in sunny Italian piazzas. I was drawn into the web of Menotti's other self, a self I would deeply respond to and feel a profound affection for. Not even Chip, with his sour demeanor, could spoil the beauty of my Scottish days with Gian Carlo Menotti. I felt I was living in one of his masterfully staged grand operas.

Chapter 43

Menotti had arranged for Yester House to be fully illuminated upon my arrival. It was a magical sight, the darkness all around and the stunning Palladian structure lit from within and without, like a star glittering in a moody, ebony sky. It was an operatic vision, really, a kind of Scottish setting for *Der Rosenkavalier*.

At the porte cochère, two young houseboys in indeterminate uniforms of heavy green cloth with red satin trim, stood ready to take my luggage. (Menotti had imported them from Ceylon). Menotti, with a tall gentleman, approached. This was Menotti's butler. I was introduced. He bowed, then quickly retired within. Menotti himself showed me to my room, the Red Bedroom. It was just before dinner and he announced that we would dress for dinner, and that, indeed, we would always dress for dinner.

Our schedule would remain more or less the same for the three weeks that I lived at Yester House. Each morning, breakfast would be brought to my room by one of the Ceylonese boys. At 11 a.m. I would meet Menotti in the library for another cup of coffee and discuss the day's schedule. I'd then have two hours to myself until lunch at 1:30 p.m., which would be served in one of the smaller dining rooms. Chip might or might not be present.

At 3 p.m. Menotti and I would meet in his study for at least three hours of taping, after which I would retire to my room, rest, bathe, and dress for dinner. We would convene in the large sitting room for drinks, where a crackling fire in the ornate fireplace enlivened the elegantly furnished room. Chip, without greeting, would appear, silently pour himself a drink, and sit by the fire.

Dinner was served promptly at 8:30 p.m. in the main dining room at a table seating 12. Menotti, immaculately dressed in a dark blue velvet smoking jacket and black bowtie, was the image of aristocratic refinement. Chip was also beautifully turned out in formal jacket and tie. I was the least formally dressed, but presentable enough. Food, generous and exquisitely prepared, was served by the two houseboys, now wearing different formal attire: black uniforms with crested silver buttons and small silver emblems at the collars. The boys, in their silent choreography, wore white gloves as they served each of us in turn, starting with the Maestro, then me, then Chip. Meanwhile, the butler silently poured superb vintage wines.

Chip must either have been given strict instructions to behave well toward me or was himself spellbound by the aristocratic calm and graciousness of Yester House. He stayed clear of me during the daytime hours, and never interfered with my taping sessions.

Menotti, for his part, luxuriated happily amidst the splendors of his home, the many beautifully appointed rooms, the grand, curving staircase, the huge, stunning ballroom with its vast, vaulted ceiling. He gazed at the old master portraits, the Raeburn, Constable, van Dyck and others, hanging here and there throughout the house. He was truly the master of all he surveyed.

After many of our dinners, Menotti would ask me to take long walks with him along the moors. He'd put on a long, woolen, hooded cape and carry a walking stick. I too was lent a cape and walking stick, and the two of us would stride silently side by side, like two figures out of tales by Edgar Allan Poe or Edward Gorey.

During my three weeks at Yester, Menotti was completing a chamber work, his *Fantasia for Cello and Orchestra*. He read books and newspapers, wrote long letters and occasionally spoke on the telephone, and with marked eagerness, gave fully of his time to me. I was never less than conscious of his charmingly bewildered looks, as though he had forever misplaced something–his better judgment, perhaps. Now just 63 years old, he had the look of a man in his 40s. Trim and obviously in very good health, he radiated a sense of physical well-being.

But what surprised me most about Gian Carlo Menotti was his strange emotional distance. He exuded a certain aloofness, a kind of chilly reticence and restraint that was almost shocking. For an Italian, he proved singularly undemonstrative, with never a hug or an embrace or a spontaneous gesture of affection.

No, I was not seeking physical attention or contact. In fact, there was not an ounce of physical attraction between us. Indeed, after my Bernstein episodes, I was more than happy to be doing a book free of the turmoils of emotional entanglement. I welcomed Menotti's detachment almost as much as I relished Chip's many absences during my visit at Yester House.

Amazingly, however, Menotti was never cool or distant, unemotional or aloof when it came to recounting his life to me. Only as a physical presence away from our sessions did he evince the restraint I spoke of. He was not precisely cold, but there was no immediate warmth either, just a kind of free-floating noncommittal friendliness that did not elicit a warm or enthusiastic response. Still, Menotti's famous charm was all-pervasive, especially when he regaled us with stories over lunch or dinner, recalling the foibles of friends and acquaintances or, indeed, when he told me the story of his life.

Our taping sessions were held in Menotti's study, which despite two huge, ornate fireplaces at either end, was the sparest room at Yester House: a piano, a desk, a bookcase, two chairs. We sat there facing one another. Sometimes the room was flooded in sunlight. Mostly, however, we looked out on a fogged-over landscape under a moody, moist, gray sky. When it rained and the winds howled, which was often, and the logs in the fireplaces were burning and flickering, the room turned into an oasis of intimacy. It was at those times that Menotti, responding to the elements without and the charged quietude within, would reflect upon his long-lost friendships, his long-lost loves, even his long-lost career, which by 1977 was sadly fading.

His closest relationships were achingly recalled. When he spoke of Samuel Barber, his oldest, most deeply loved friend, his voice almost broke:

"I suffer terrible guilts over Sam—just awful guilts. I've let Sam down so many times! I've disappointed him so much! I've made him suffer so! I've been re-reading the letters he wrote me when we were young students at the Curtis Institute—they're so touching, so nostalgic. To read them again was quite unbearable."

But Menotti did not linger on his guilts nor on Sam Barber. Again and again, he returned to the present, to his great love of Chip and of his retirement to Yester House.

"I would never have bought Yester House if it were not for Chip. I know it's ironic that after announcing so often to my friends that I would soon retire in a cave and lead a hermit's life or become some sort of a hospital nurse to expiate my sense of guilt, I should instead end my days in as splendid a retreat as Yester House. My buying it was really Chip's choice, his wish, and my last desperate effort to make someone happy. Perhaps it is too extravagant an homage to another human being. But I've come to the conclusion that if you're able in your life to make at least one person happy, you have achieved a great deal.

"Besides, I've chosen to live here, in Scotland, so that I could be completely cut off from my past. It was a desire to find a place where I could hide. I feel it is now time to take stock of my past. It is time for reflection. Both in America and in Italy I know too many people, and I have too many ties. Solitude is almost impossible there. You could put it this way: Italy created me, America nourished me, and Scotland will bury me."

When my book was finished and *Menotti: A Biography* was published in 1978, receiving some warm reviews, the composer was not entirely thrilled. He felt the book did not have sufficient breadth or scope to encompass his life—especially his creative life. When the time came to publicize the biography, and my publisher solicited help from Menotti to appear with me on television or lend his thoughts to magazine interviews, he declined.

But he was not sufficiently disappointed to prevent the book from being published in Italy. Indeed, he himself arranged for an Italian edition without consulting either me, my publisher, or my agent. What is more, I never received payment for the Italian edition. When I confronted Menotti about this, he said that instead of complaining, I should be pleased to have all of Italy reading my book. Considering the small sales the book garnered in America, its great success in Italy seemed an unlikely prospect.

But this rather astonishing act of Italian chutzpah aside, there is no question that my Menotti experience totally enriched my life. I loved the fact that Gian Carlo was Italian (he had never become an American citizen), that we could speak Italian together, that he had created the Spoleto Festival of Two Worlds, that I was part of his life for many, many months, that he gave me access to his most private, most intimate thoughts, that I met many illustrious musicians, poets, actors, artists, composers, some of whom became good friends, and that I had access to Menotti's entire musical oeuvre.

By the time I came to write his book, many people had told me how deeply old-fashioned Menotti's music seemed to be—how maudlin, how sentimental, how out of step with the times. But they were wrong. Yes, Menotti's music was sentimental and utterly accessible, but I came to love it because, more than anything else, it was honest—it was clear and filled with sincerity. And it was beautifully crafted, for Menotti was an inventive orchestrator and a superb melodist. As for his operas and large vocal output, he understood the human voice as few did before or after.

It is true that Samuel Barber, with whom Menotti shared many years of his life, became the more distinguished, more respected composer. But Menotti, for all his musical predictability and theatricality, had the virtue of writing music that was never pretentious, never heavy-handed. It was music that sprang from the heart, destined to touch the heart, nothing more, nothing less.

After the publication of my book, Menotti and I saw very little of each other. But strange and wondrous things began filtering down the musical grapevine as the years progressed. One day I learned that Menotti had introduced Chip to the daughter of Margaretta (Happy) Rockefeller, the wife of Nelson Rockefeller, New York's former governor. I heard that Chip had married the girl. I heard that Menotti was eager to become a nonno, a grandfather, and very soon, Chip and his wife produced two children, and Menotti's dream of dandling grandchildren on his knees became a happy reality. It was all marvelously improbable, but very true.

And Menotti, having made a pact with the devil, decided never to grow old. Recent photographs, taken when he was in his 90s, found him looking healthy and vigorous, with a full head of hair and eyes still reflecting humor, irony and mischief.

Still, fate ultimately did catch up with the ever-buoyant composer. On February 1st, 2007, the world learned that Gian Carlo Menotti, at age 95, had peacefully died at Princess Grace Hospital in Monaco with Chip, his beloved son, at his side.

Almost 30 years have passed since the publication of my Menotti biography. As I leaf through its opening pages, I can still hear Gian Carlo's voice telling me the stories of his childhood in his native Cadegliano, of his flamboyant, drama-prone mother, of his stern, taciturn father, of his five older brothers and sisters. These stories, like so many others he related, now read like fanciful Italian fairy tales or like distant dreams.

And that is how I think back on my own oddly elusive friendship with Menotti. It was like a fairy tale, like a dream, as if it had all been a tremulous mirage.

Chapter 44

Soon after my Menotti experience, I plunged back into the realities of the dance world and the art world, and all the other cultural worlds that kept me hopping morning, noon, and night.

Mostly, it was the dance world that occupied my body and soul—my body, because I literally ran from one dance event to the next, viscerally experiencing every dancer's movement, both physical and metaphysical. I attended ballet and modern dance performances offered by every major and minor company appearing in New York, simply because I wanted to. I sat in on workshops and ballet classes of every description, and I was deeply nourished by an art form that, at its best, literally set my heart and mind soaring.

With the 1975 publication of my book, *The Private World of Ballet*, and with my dance articles appearing regularly in the *Times, Dance Magazine*, and elsewhere, I was one of the most visible dance writers on the scene—and one of the most snubbed, scorned, and mocked by my fellow dance critics.

When, for the next ten years, I conducted a weekly radio broadcast, *The Sound of Dance*, over station WNCN, in which I interviewed practically everyone in the dance world, more bile and envy came hurtling my way. When I presented sold-out lecture-interviews with dancers and choreographers at the Metropolitan Museum of Art, my reputation as a substantive dance figure in New York may have risen with the public, but my name among my colleagues was still mud and, for the most part, I was thoroughly disdained. To them, I was a pretentious intruder who, in their eyes, had neither the background nor the knowledge they themselves so brilliantly possessed. I know they hated my guts and my success. Their "hellos" were pinched and false. And there were those who never said "hello" at all. But this did not prevent me from fervently pursuing one of my dance world goals: to befriend the dancers I really loved.

The greatest male dancer of my time was Erik Bruhn, but the most exciting male dancer of any time was Rudolf Nureyev. They were both right on the top of my "must-get-to-know-at-all-costs" list. Bruhn was

Apollo. Nureyev was Dionysus. Bruhn, fair and blue-eyed, personified balletic perfection. Nureyev, dark and wild-eyed, was balletic fire and brimstone. Together, they were like Janus, the Roman god of beginnings and endings, represented with a double-faced head, each looking in opposite directions. And, indeed, Bruhn would soon look back. Nureyev would soon soar forward.

Bruhn was 33 when he met Nureyev. He was the cool Scandinavian— very much the royal Dane. He was Prince Hamlet. Nureyev was 23, the smoldering Tartar. He was the young prince in every Russian fairy tale. Each held the ballet stage by the magnetism of their physical beauty and the supreme individuality of their artistry.

Before Nureyev defected from the Soviet Union in 1961, he had seen a film of Bruhn dancing. He resolved then and there to study with Bruhn, to seek him out and learn everything he could from him. Some of his Russian colleagues told Nureyev that Bruhn's dancing was like ice. "It may be like ice," he replied, "but it's ice that burns."

Soon after he defected, Nureyev traveled to Copenhagen; it was there that the two began their affair and formed a lifelong friendship. And it was in the classrooms of the Royal Danish Ballet School that Nureyev began to immerse himself in the traditions of Bruhn's own early training, in the traditions of the great nineteenth century Danish choreographer and pedagogue, August Bournonville, he of the swiftly skimming technique, of the long mime passages, of a style that required lightness, speed, musicality, economy, endless wit and charm. All this Bruhn imparted to an eager Nureyev by way of example and instruction.

When I myself first saw Erik Bruhn dance in the late 50s he was the reigning male dancer of his day. There simply was no one else. His performances were lessons in refinement and studies in characterization. What in ballet is known as purity of line—the body's perfect symmetry—was one of Bruhn's most salient attributes. But this dancer, for all his aristocratic demeanor, could also blaze across the stage and transform himself into a dazzling instrument of passion.

In all his classic roles, whether in *La Sylphide, Swan Lake, The Sleeping Beauty, The Nutcracker,* or *Giselle,* he combined classicism with virtuosity, and he did this with an ease that was as natural as it was astonishing. Then again, in roles such as Don José in Roland Petit's *Carmen* or as Jean in Birgit Cullberg's *Miss Julie,* he would bring down the house with his pyrotechnics and dramatic intensity.

But if Bruhn was the acknowledged master of male classical dancing, his quiet personality and his Nordic reserve did not permit him to capitalize on it nor to rigorously celebrate it. In short, he did not have the ego to continually place himself or his art on a pedestal.

It would take Rudolf Nureyev to catapult male classical dancing to heights not reached since the days of Nijinsky. And it would be Nureyev himself who, by the singular force of his talent and ambition, would within a brief time eclipse Erik Bruhn to become the most famous, most sought-after, most celebrated, and most controversial male ballet dancer of the twentieth century.

When I first met Erik Bruhn, he was still reigning supreme. I went to see him in *Giselle* at American Ballet Theater. In those days, his frequent partner was the glorious Italian ballerina, Carla Fracci, whose ethereal beauty echoed the nineteenth century precepts of the Romantic ballerina, all gossamer lightness and transcendent tenderness. The Bruhn/Fracci partnership, equally eloquent in Bournonville's *La Sylphide*, among other classics, had its apogee in *Giselle*, for each dancer brought a particularly poignant depth to their roles, and because for sheer physical beauty, the two offered an achingly poignant image of romantic love.

That night, after seeing *Giselle*, I was positively smitten by Bruhn and Fracci. I went backstage and introduced myself to them both. Bruhn couldn't have been more cordial. He accepted my compliments and was surprised that a working journalist would come backstage to greet him. Our talk went so well that when I asked if he might be free to join me for a drink, he readily accepted.

I also went to see Carla Fracci in her dressing room. We established an instant rapport, made stronger by my chattering away in fluent Italian. Indeed, for the next 30 years Carla Fracci and her producer/director husband, Beppe Menegatti, would become close friends. One summer, while Jane was off traveling in France, Julia and I accepted their kind invitation to spend time in their magnificent apartment in Venice–a memorable event for us both.

It was no secret that Erik Bruhn loved his Scotch. And he would often get into his cups and embark on marvelously acute, funny, or moving stories relating to his past, to life in Denmark, to his fellow dancers, to his love affairs. I was his eager audience, drinking in the life stories of a ballet genius.

During the early 1960s, even as Nureyev had come on the scene, Bruhn continued to astonish the world with his extraordinary dancing. But as the 1970s approached, he would dance less and less. And it was at this point that I proposed writing his biography. The marvelous stories I had heard were, of course, the initial inspiration. But I also knew no book about Erik Bruhn existed. I felt it was important there be one, and I wanted to be the one to write it.

At first, he seemed reluctant. He felt people would not be interested in his story and that it would be a terrible waste of time. Finally, however, I persuaded him to fully lend himself to the project and in 1979 *Erik Bruhn: Danseur Noble* was published by Viking Press.

Although Erik Bruhn was gay, women were madly attracted to him, two in particular: the ballerinas Sonia Arova and Maria Tallchief, both frequent ballet partners and both made to suffer the agonies of hell while involved with the Danish god of dance. But Bruhn's involvement with men could also be tortuous; there was a string of them both inside and outside the ballet world. Still, Bruhn's involvement with Nureyev—whom he always affectionately called "Rudik"—would be the all-consuming passion of his life, a life-altering relationship that, with its strong ironic overtones, would find Bruhn in love with the very man who, in matters of worldwide fame and charisma, would ultimately depose and eclipse him.

Chapter 45

By the time I was ready to embark on my splendid new adventure with Erik Bruhn, interviewing him in New York, traveling with him to Vienna and Copenhagen for long taping sessions, absorbing his aura and personality, seeing him dance, and interviewing all those who mattered in his life, there were events in my own life that were unfolding as well.

For one thing, after vowing never to leave the East Village, Jane and I felt compelled to move to the dreaded, bourgeois Upper West Side. Our years on East Tenth Street, so rich in atmosphere and so much fun to begin with, turned into something of a nightmare, due mostly to the rise of a dangerous drug scene being played out practically at our doorsteps. By 1968, Tompkins Square, across the street from us, once the playground of flower children and benign hippies, turned into a haven for drug dealers and users. We feared for ourselves and for our Julia, who, by the time she reached ten, was at an age when she could run a few errands on her own. Street life between Avenue A and B was getting hairy—it was unsafe and unsavory. Too, we had lived on East Tenth Street for well over ten years, and it was certainly time to move yet again.

Jane found us a truly great apartment on the Upper West Side in a charming, six-story building built in 1905. Yes, it was "Uptown," where the "old folks" lived, and yes, it felt mighty conservative and old-fashioned, but there was Riverside Park just down the street, and the Hudson River just below it. Broadway was also just a block away, and was bustling with people and rampant with shops, and there was Zabar's, the legendary food emporium with its tempting goodies and delicacies. It was also around the corner from the School of American Ballet, Julia's ballet school, which had been a very long commute from East Tenth Street.

Our large new apartment had very high ceilings and beautiful wood paneling and two fireplaces (which, alas, didn't work) and big windows, and the rent was incredibly reasonable. Actually, it turned out to be an absolutely smashing turn-of-the-century space, which we decided to decorate in our usual shabby-cheap art nouveau/art deco style. The greatest bow to this period look was to cover the living room and dining room walls with extravagantly luxurious Williams Morris and Mackintosh wallpapers, which Jane put up and which she had found in a small import shop on Lexington Avenue.

We hung chandeliers, bought secondhand chaise lounges and divans, armchairs and tchotchkes to go with our décor. This was, after all, our largest apartment to date, and we needed to fill it up. We felt younger than springtime in this gorgeously old-world place, which, we secretly felt, was really meant for people in their seventies and eighties. Little did we know that we ourselves would get to be in our seventies and eighties in that old-fashioned place!

But when we first moved in, nearly 40 years ago, I was in the throes of my writing career and in the midst of my life in dance and my life in art. I was also well-known as a journalist to instigate all manner of lecture programs, such as the ones I held at the New School for Social Research in the Village. I mentioned my weekly radio broadcasts, *The Sound of Dance*, a ten-year stint. But from 1972 to 1974, my New School lecture programs brought me considerable attention if not notoriety.

It was my idea to hold live interviews with wildly disparate people in the arts, to be held in the school's handsome auditorium. I felt the public would be interested in meeting a wide variety of artists, not just people working within one discipline. I thus rounded up the greatest musicians, singers, dancers, choreographers, and movie stars I could find. For a mere pittance, almost all of them agreed to be my guest, and they formed quite a roster of stellar personalities.

In the fall of 1973, on eight separate evenings, came Pierre Boulez, Isaac Stern, Schuyler Chapin, Louise Nevelson, Bette Davis, Tom O'Horgan, George Balanchine, and Lena Horne. In the following years my guests were Marilyn Horne, Larry Rivers, Roberta Flack, Alexandra Danilova, George Plimpton, and Ginger Rogers. And then I decided to give the entire series over to renowned pianists. I would interview them for the first half hour, then they would perform on the piano for the last half hour or so. Called "Piano Talk," the series boasted the pianists William Masselos, Jorge Bolet, Lorin Hollander, Byron Janis, Eugene Istomin, and Christoph Eschenbach.

These evenings at The New School, almost all of them sold out, proved smashing to audiences and guests alike. For my part, I felt deeply rewarded just talking to people I had loved and admired for years. Indeed, a whole book could be written on the subject of these very personal interviews, for some, like those with Bette Davis, Ginger Rogers, George Balanchine,

Alexandra Danilova, George Plimpton, Lena Horne, and Louise Nevelson proved truly memorable.

Jane's representation by the Tibor de Nagy Gallery had come to an end in 1966. In 1968 she decided to accept an invitation to join James Graham & Sons, a distinguished art gallery founded in 1857 and located on Madison Avenue and 78th Street. The gallery did not have the panache or exuberance of the Tibor de Nagy, and it did not have a John Myers to keep one hopping or drive crazy. The Graham was very sedate indeed, and its reputation as an early dealer of American paintings, the Hudson River School, the Ashcan School, the Eight, and the Stieglitz Arts Group, was solid and impressive. Situated in a handsome beaux arts building, the gallery boasted three floors, the last of which was devoted to contemporary art, where Jane Wilson would be showing until 1975.

The move for Jane was auspicious, for not only did the Graham Gallery give her the impetus to produce radiant new landscapes, but it led her to more fully concentrate on still life painting, a genre she had been exploring for some time in her private teaching and in her painting classes.

The Graham Gallery couldn't be more solicitous. Robert Graham and his son Robin, the owners, proved both welcoming and supportive. The contemporary wing's director, Terry Davis, loved Jane and her work from the very beginning and has remained a loyal friend to this day. As for Jane, she was more than happy to be associated with a gallery that also exhibited such notable American artists as Edwin Dickinson, Alice Neel and Lennart Anderson, among others. Best of all, she loved the Graham Gallery's understated air of distinction, its longstanding tradition of showing the best of early and late American figurative art.

It was at the Graham that Jane emerged as a superb still life painter. These works, with their compositionally Cubist allusions, their subdued color, their hint of Orientalism, suggested an avalanche of the imported riches found in Dutch still life. When I asked Jane to recall that period of her work, she told me that she considered still life as landscape on a table. Jane said she wanted to investigate the spirit of Dutch still life without the meticulous realism that many contemporary painters mistake for magic. What she wanted to do was to create a still life space that was not literal yet was unmistakably convincing.

Time seemed to fly for our small family. It was the mid 70s. Jane was teaching and painting and had a brand new gallery. I was my usual frantic self and would very soon be tackling my Bruhn book. As for our Julia, she was presently a Hunter High School student and was continuing her dance training at the School of American Ballet, growing more beautiful and taller by the minute.

And, of course, when day was done, Jane and I would attend endless dance performances, concerts, lots of parties, and lead a generally hectic and exciting social life. We made wonderful friends during that period, like the marvelous British actress Leueen MacGrath, three of whose five husbands we met in New York: the playwright George S. Kaufman, the tire heir Steven Goodyear, and the young, budding poet Steve Quinto (ironically, husband number five!). There was the gifted pianist Shirley Gabis, an early friend of Leonard Bernstein, who later married the distinguished American composer, George Perle. There was the beautiful and totally enchanting English Moira Hodgson, an early colleague at the *Herald Tribune*, who became a famous restaurant columnist for *The New York Observer* and whose husband Michael Shulan launched the visionary photo exhibition *Here Is New York*, documenting the Twin Tower disaster of 9/11. Another dear friend was the actress Ruth Ford, a legendary figure in the film, theater, art, and fashion circles in the mid-twentieth century. Ruth and her husband, the film star Zachary Scott, were as kind as they were glamorous. Their friendship meant a great deal to us. We also formed a warm friendship with Julie Whitaker and her husband, Michael Burke. Julie, a delicate, tender beauty of enormous charm, teaches at New York's prestigious Nightingale School, but we love her best for having named a mountain in her native Utah after the great French composer, Olivier Messiaen. Mount Messiaen is a tribute to the genius of the composer's music and to the iconoclastic vision of Julie Whitaker. Michael Burke, son of Kenneth Burke, astronomer, poet, writer, and greatly gifted sculptor, is a man of many parts. His sculpture is as imaginative and original as it is beautifully crafted.

We also saw a great deal of the painter James Rosenquist and his young wife, the greatly talented painter and writer, Mimi Thompson. The legendary drama teacher Stella Adler became a close friend, as did her beautiful daughter Ellen and her brilliant if remote husband, David Oppenheim. There was the gifted Trude Rittman, orchestrator and arranger for Rodgers and Hammerstein, Lerner and Loewe, and many other Broadway giants. And there was the Pulitzer Prize-winning composer and wicked diarist, Ned Rorem, whose outrageous good looks and many gay love affairs turned him into an American musical, literary, and sexual legend.

As we had done in the past, and because our new apartment was large enough, we took in a ballet student to live with us to keep Julia company when we were out on the town. The perfect student came into our lives in the early 1970s, and she proved a dream. Her name was Lisa Rinehart, a stunning 15-year-old, an all-American blue-eyed beauty with perfect skin and a perfect dancer's body, intelligent, hailing from Washington, D.C. and, as we soon learned, an extremely talented ballet student. Lisa took up residence in one of our bedrooms and proceeded to be a model companion for Julia and an altogether charming and adorable presence in our household. Within a year she would be the youngest member of the corps de ballet of American Ballet Theatre.

How extraordinary that both Lisa Rinehart and I would soon become deeply involved with two of the world's greatest dancers: I with Erik Bruhn, Lisa with Mikhail Baryshnikov.

Chapter 46

After Rudolf Nureyev's spectacular leap to freedom in 1961, the 1970s saw two more startling Soviet defections. There was the Leningrad-born Kirov ballerina, Natalia Makarova, who, in 1970, defected while the Kirov was performing in London. And there was the Latvian, Riga-born Kirov star, Mikhail Baryshnikov, reputed to be a new god of the dance, who defected in 1974 in Toronto. Both artists sang the same sad song: not enough freedom in the Soviet Union; not enough roles to satisfy them; no possibility to dance in works by Western choreographers; infrequent performances. In short, like their fellow Kirov dancer, Rudolf Nureyev, their hunger for vast new opportunities and their rage over Soviet repression were at the root of their search for artistic freedom. Of course, the lure of American money and personal superstardom were part of the potential equasion.

Makarova, whom I befriended soon after she defected and just before she joined American Ballet theatre, was that rare talent: an exquisitely delicate and dramatic dancer with a steely, immaculate technique. Her appearances in *Swan Lake, The Sleeping Beauty, Coppélia,* and especially *Giselle,* proved singular in their evocation of poetic depth and consummate musicality.

When the two Soviet defectors Makarova and Baryshnikov first performed together in 1974 in ABT's production of *Giselle* at the Metropolitan Opera (they were reputed to have become lovers at the time), New York's ballet world witnessed two artists of supreme accomplishment in roles seemingly made for them. A decade or so earlier, it was Erik Bruhn and Carla Fracci who offered perhaps the quintessential *Giselle.* Now it was Baryshnikov and Makarova, and soon it would be Baryshnikov and Gelsey Kirkland, the young American ballerina, whom Baryshnikov invited to become his partner at ABT, luring her away from the New York City Ballet, where she had been dancing leading Balanchine roles. As it turned out, he also stole her heart, and the Misha/Gelsey relationship would prove as passionate as it was stormy.

As may be gathered, Baryshnikov was something of a devilish young rabbit when it came to his love life and few would argue that his boyish allure, angelic appearance, and immense artistry proved irresistible to a large contingent of the generally lonely and solitary female dancers–especially those in the corps de ballet. But soon Baryshnikov's attraction to nubile young dancers would hit home.

It all happened in 1977, while I began my involvement with Erik Bruhn and was starting work on our book. At the time, Bruhn was curtailing his performances. At 49, he felt ready, if not to rest on his laurels, then at least to impart his vast knowledge and artistry to the next generation of male dancers. He would teach and he would do the occasional performance of character roles, such as the old magician Dr. Coppelius in *Coppelia* or as Madge, the witch in *La Sylphide.*

As it happened, in the summer of 1977, American Ballet Theatre was preparing for its European tour and Lucia Chase, the company's founder and director, asked Bruhn if he would consider performing in Jose Limon's stark modern dance masterpiece, *The Moor's Pavane*, assuming the role of the Moor. Though challenging, the role would not require classical technique or any pyrotechnics. It would be more of a daringly complex acting role. Bruhn accepted the challenge, and suggested to me that I accompany him and the company on two stops of its tour: Vienna and Copenhagen. In that way, he felt, we could not only begin our work together, but I would also be able to immerse myself in Bruhn's birthplace–Copenhagen–and interview his old teachers at the Royal Opera House and speak with all his Danish friends.

I happily accepted Bruhn's invitation, and also made the decision to take along Julia, whose friendship with the handsome young Danish New York City Ballet dancer, Ulrik Trojaborg, made it possible for us both to stay with Ulrik's parents, who lived a short bicycle ride away from Bruhn's own house in the Copenhagen suburb of Gentofte.

Ulrik's parents, Ruth and Dr. Werner (Troja) Trojaborg, whom we had befriended in New York, couldn't be kinder or more hospitable. They even provided me with an instant translator for my Bruhn project–their beautiful English-speaking daughter, Nanna, who proved of invaluable help during my stay in Denmark, sitting in on my interviews and solving all my Danish language problems.

When American Ballet Theatre presented *The Moor's Pavane* at the Tivoli Theatre, a sold-out house awaited the appearance of Erik Bruhn. He had not appeared on a Danish ballet stage in some seven years. As the curtain rose on the famous frozen circular tableaux comprised of Bruhn as the Moor, Cynthia Gregory as Desdemona, Ivan Nagy as Iago, and Sallie

Wilson as Emilia, a roar went up. Upon the work's conclusion, Bruhn took his solo bow. It was complete pandemonium. Bruhn had re-conquered the Danish ballet stage.

That evening, Bruhn threw a big company party at his house in Genthofte. It was one of the best, most high-spirited parties I ever attended. Everyone, from Director Lucia Chase to the wardrobe mistress, from the principal dancers to the corps de ballet, seemed exhilarated by Bruhn's phenomenal success, and Bruhn himself seemed as happy as I had ever seen him.

Of course, the champagne and liquor flowed, and there was lots and lots of food (dancers are always ravenous), and as the night wore on, people relaxed, forming groups here and there in Erik's huge living room. I was off in some corner, probably talking to Julia or Erik, when I noticed our beautiful young tenant, Lisa Rinehart, now a gifted young corps member of ABT, sitting on the floor across the room. Practically on top of her was Misha Baryshnikov. I observed them for some minutes, and soon became aware that Misha had begun whispering sweet nothings in Lisa's ear. It was a touching scene, which became ever more affectionate, ever more ardent.

I began to wonder if I shouldn't break it up. Lisa was, after all, in my care–that is, though touring with the company, she still lived with us in New York, and having the trust of her parents, I felt protective about her. More importantly she was 16 years old, and Misha did have a wicked reputation. I felt like a real priss, but I did march up to break it up. Misha gave me a sheepish look. He was not amused, but he did move away, while Lisa just smiled. It is, of course, no secret that some years later, long after Lisa had moved out of our apartment, she and Misha became constant companions. But that would not happen until after Baryshnikov had met and wooed the lovely actress Jessica Lange, with whom he fathered his first child, Alexandra.

As it happened, Misha once brought Jessica Lange to our apartment. She had just made the first misbegotten remake of *King Kong* and was most unhappy about it. In talking with her, I realized what a sensitive and intelligent young woman this was and I had a feeling she would go far if she had the strength to buck up and wait out the Hollywood grind, which, of course, she did.

Lisa Rinehart, whenever we encountered her, seemed very much in love with Misha Baryshnikov. She told us so. She seemed never to waver in her love, and no matter what one read in the gossip columns about Misha's various and sundry amours, Lisa's steadfast loyalty eventually paid off.

Today, the two seem like an old married couple. (Whether an actual wedding ever took place, we don't know, but I somehow doubt it). Still, there are three more Baryshnikov children! Our adorable Lisa gave birth to Peter, Sofia, and Anna. And the eldest, Misha and Jessica Lange's Alexandra, has done the improbable: made Baryshnikov a grandfather!

Lisa Rinehart danced with American Ballet Theatre for several years, rising to the rank of soloist. When, in 1980, Baryshnikov was made artistic director of ABT, remaining in that post for nine years, Lisa, ever more firmly involved with him, chose to leave the company. She resumed her interrupted academic schooling, tried her hand at choreography, but finally gave her time to Misha and, eventually, their three children. Lisa has never failed to send us Christmas and New Year's greetings since she came to live with us at the tender age of 15. She and Misha and their beautiful brood live in Palisades, New York. Misha, now in his sixties, has built himself an arts center in New York. He still performs, though, these days, rather cautiously.

He and I have never really warmed to each other. He has never cared for journalists, and I have consistently found him to be cool and distant. Still, Baryshnikov remains one of the world's superstars. In his prime, he simply took your breath away.

Jane and I recently ran into Lisa in Manhattan, near Jane's New York studio. She looked radiantly beautiful and, as Misha's companion and the mother of three young children, seemed to find life a constant source of amazement, amusement, bewilderment and joy.

It would seem that those words Misha Baryshnikov had whispered in Lisa's ear that night so long ago at Erik Bruhn's party in Copenhagen must have been very potent indeed!

Chapter 47

Erik Bruhn: What a strange and melancholic man he was!

He once told me he felt invisible. He told me that not only could he not see himself, but felt that others could not see him either. He said he felt he didn't exist. It was a palpable thing, his invisibility. And this from a man who was seen by thousands as he danced upon ballet stages the world over. Yet, what he told me rang oddly true. He had a circumference of silence around him—a mysterious something that somehow veiled him, placing him into some distant otherworldliness. Too, when Erik spoke, the sound of his voice was low and hypnotic. It was a deep, resonant growl that seemed to come from elsewhere, yet his words were clear and clearly articulated.

And there was his look. Erik was of average height (magically magnified on stage) with a face that in its classic proportion offered compelling reason to pronounce him unthinkably handsome. His deep-set, blue-gray eyes could mock or turn cold or be intensely attentive or be impossibly flirtatious. He had a great, all-encompassing smile and a surprisingly loud, raucous laugh that made heads turn. Mostly, however, he produced a stillness—in himself and in others. It may have been his Danish reserve or his Northern temperament, but it was a stillness that would come upon him suddenly, like an unexpected snowfall.

Sometimes, sitting and talking with Erik in his house just outside Copenhagen, there would be long, long pauses. These came when he would ponder questions I posed to him—about his childhood, his family, a particular relationship. He would think it through, then, after a long sip of Scotch (there was always Scotch), he'd answer as fully and honestly as his reserve would allow. Again and again, he'd come back to Rudolf Nureyev—to Rudik—the single human being Bruhn would relentlessly obsess over.

"That first time, back in 1961, right here in Copenhagen, at the Hotel Angleterre, it's where I first laid eyes on Rudik," Bruhn remembered. "Maria Tallchief brought him to me from Paris soon after he defected, because he wanted to meet me, because he wanted to work with me, to learn everything he could from me. He was so young! Just 23. He could barely speak English. Maria said he had almost no money. I looked at him, in his sweater and slacks–I saw how attractive he was. He had a certain style, a certain look. It was not a natural elegance, but somehow it all worked."

Bruhn told me that then and there he invited Nureyev to stay with him.

"I lived with my mother at the time, but I could tell Rudik needed a place to stay. And so, I took him home with me. Maria was furious. She wanted Rudik to stay with her. But Rudik accepted my offer. I saw him smiling. He seemed pleased. When we got to my place, I showed him his room, which happened to have a trapdoor in it. My mother was not there at the time. When she came home, I said, 'I'd like you to meet Rudolf Nureyev.' They shook hands through the trapdoor. It was oddly symbolic. These two people had a violent reaction to each other. It was like lightning. Mother was a Scorpio and Rudik was a Pisces. You can imagine! She just never got to like him. It never worked. It was a chemical thing."

And so it was that Erik Bruhn, then 33, and Rudolf Nureyev, at 23, began their long complex love affair and friendship.

"At first Rudik and I would take class at the Royal Danish Ballet, and he would be incredibly concentrated. People knew who he was but they didn't talk to him much. He seemed very strange to the Danes. To me, he seemed less strange. In class Rudik would always be in the first group and always in the middle–that is very Russian. I would stick to the second group and always stand in the back–that is very Danish.

"One day, Rudik said, 'Why don't the Danish people respect you more? You are such a great dancer and you are so respected in Russia.' I told him, 'What do you expect them to do, crawl on their hands and knees when they see me coming?' You see, in Russia they have a certain protocol about a dancer's rank and position, and Rudik wasn't used to seeing me being treated like everyone else."

I tried to picture the young Nureyev through Erik's eyes, and I too could see how attractive he must have been, with his Slavic beauty, youthful arrogance, and cocky self-assurance on display. But by this time, 1977, I had already become very well acquainted with Nureyev and had formed my own obsessions about him. Indeed we had formed our own complex relationship by the time I came to write Bruhn's book, and, as I regretfully told Bruhn, his beloved Rudik had categorically refused to be interviewed for the book.

"You may say that Erik Bruhn was a great influence in my development as a dancer," Nureyev told me, fixing me with a hard stare. "That is all you may say."

When I encountered such resistance from Samuel Barber and Chip Phelan during the writing of my Gian Carlo Menotti biography, Menotti himself strongly coerced the two most important people in his life to cooperate with me, and they ultimately did. But when I told Erik Bruhn that Nureyev would not cooperate on his book, he just shrugged, smiled and said, "That's Rudik for you! Jealous to the end!" Bruhn did not talk to Nureyev. He did not insist that Nureyev talk to me.

Still, almost to make up for it, Bruhn talked freely about Nureyev, unstintingly relating his passion for the stubborn, recalcitrant Tartar.

"When Rudik stayed with me in Copenhagen, rumors began to fly," Bruhn recounted. "People were wondering why he was living with me. Why we were together so much of the time. They saw us working together, laughing together, eating at restaurants together, discussing things, being affectionate with each other. People didn't quite know what was going on. Some people even said that Rudik had come out of Russia for the express purpose of 'killing me,' and how could I put up with that?

"I never believed that, of course. Only once did I use that against him and that was when we had a terrible argument. I got very mad and said, 'You just came to kill me!' When he heard that, Rudik got so upset he burst into tears. He said, 'How can you be so evil!' I know it was a vicious thing to say, but somehow I had to throw that at him, and I don't even remember why we were arguing.

"Anyway, during the first four years of our friendship there was a mutual inspiration. We even formed a small ballet group together, a four-some, and performed in Cannes and in Paris. We chose Sonia Arova and Rosella Hightower to be our partners, and we danced pas de deux and quartets, and it was wonderful being on the same stage with Rudik. And Rudik danced so beautifully, and he inspired my dancing as well. I know that Rudik would always say to everyone that I inspired him far more than he inspired me. But that was not so. I gained as much from him as I hope he gained from me."

What Nureyev gained from Erik Bruhn was class and refinement, if not as a person then certainly as a dancer. The animal magnetism that was the sine qua non of Nureyev's stage persona became somewhat tempered after dancing on the same stage with Bruhn or simply by watching Bruhn dance.

Too, the full-bodied propulsion of Nureyev's technique and the forceful drive of his interpretative powers, while always in singular evidence, would be further tamed and civilized when he formed his legendary partnership with Margot Fonteyn. Indeed, the lessons imparted to him by both Bruhn and Fonteyn transformed a brilliant primitive talent into a uniquely sophisticated yet always impassioned artist.

Indeed, to watch Nureyev perform with the rejuvenated Fonteyn in the Royal Ballet's production of MacMillan's *Romeo and Juliet* was, quite simply, to fall in love with him. As consort to the poignant Fonteyn as Juliet, Nureyev's Romeo, riding the crests of Prokofiev's magnificent score, was so ardent, so consumed, so totally heart-rending as to be utterly unforgettable.

By now, I had made it my business to write about Nureyev as often as I could—to have him on my radio program, to visit him backstage, to attend as many of his performances as possible. So enamored was I of his artistry and of his personal charisma, let alone his stunning good looks, that I did as much as I could to gain his attention and friendship. Again and again I invited him to our home for as many dinners and parties as he was able to attend. Invariably he'd arrive late, and always with an entourage. Jane didn't much care for that but she put a good face on it. Of course, I knew Julia worshipped him. As I said, we were all quite mad about the impossibly spoiled and madly attractive Rudolf Nureyev.

Because he was fiercely independent and because he traveled the world over, seeing him on a regular basis was not easy. Only when he came to New York as a guest artist with the Royal Ballet, the National Ballet of Canada, American Ballet Theatre, or with his own Nureyev and Friends, was there a chance to have any real time with him.

What made my life complicated was that I wanted to see a great deal of Rudolf Nureyev. And I did everything to be near him in an attempt to have a real relationship with him. In 1976, I obtained assignments from *The New York Times* and from *Vogue* to travel to London while he was there filming *Valentino*, Ken Russell's ill-fated movie about the world's greatest silent screen lover. I did this even as I was deeply involved in writing my book on Erik Bruhn.

Nureyev never seemed to mind my being around him. I think he really enjoyed my company, and, in one way or another, let me know it. And of course he was delighted to have articles written about him by someone who so clearly adored him.

I had to face it. The real problem for me was that even as Erik Bruhn kept telling me in so many different ways how madly in love he was with Rudolf Nureyev, I myself had fallen hard for him. This problem of mine was aggravated by the fact that I knew what a real bastard Nureyev could be—how badly he treated people, how selfish and self-centered he was, how uncaring and how cold-blooded. And yet, I also experienced his tender side, and knew that he was a great, great artist.

I always remembered his answer when I once asked Nureyev if a permanent relationship like marriage had ever been an option for him:

"For me, a permanent relationship like marriage would never work," he said in his clipped, Russian-tinged English. "It would never be an honest or sincere relationship. I would only think of myself. I would only think of my dancing—of my career. I would only think of being up there on the stage. Who has the guts to really share that? I don't think anybody does. And believe me, I don't want surf riders. I don't want anybody riding the surf from the waves I make."

Well, if truth be told, I did ride the surf from the waves Nureyev made, at least for a brief time in London, where he was busy making *Valentino*, a bad movie about the world's greatest lover, who was undoubtedly gay. Be that as it may, my book on Erik Bruhn proceeded. The Nureyev situation notwithstanding, I found working with Bruhn a total and unadulterated pleasure wherever we found ourselves, even though, to my shock, I experienced twinges of jealousy when Bruhn would tell me things like, "Rudik and I traveled a lot together. We saw each other constantly. For several years, we took vacations together. We had some of the best times sailing the Greek Islands. Rudik was so curious, so interested in everything. Those were wonderful years. The fact is, we were inseparable."

When Erik Bruhn told me this, he was referring back to the early 1960s, when he was still at the height of his career. As he put it, "There seemed to be no other dancer around. I could get any booking I wanted. My name alone was enough. This made me feel very isolated, and if it weren't for Rudik—his drive, his inspiration—I would have come to an absolute standstill. It was Rudik who kicked me into a new period. He boosted my career for another ten years. If it hadn't been for Rudik, I would have quit dancing long ago."

Finally my book, *Erik Bruhn: Danseur Noble*, got finished and was published (by Viking Press), and to my great delight, Bruhn was very pleased with it. Although the book that ultimately emerged was a fairly accurate and sometimes poignant account of Erik Bruhn's life and art, perhaps its most personal moments were those Bruhn devoted to his beloved Rudik. Indeed, its closing pages, bringing Bruhn to the year 1978, resonated with their still ongoing relationship: "Rudik will always be in my life. In thinking back on my friendship with Rudik, I would say that it has been intense, stormy, and at times very, very beautiful. I have probably done plenty of things to him that may have hurt and upset him. Well, he has done the same to me. And still we are very close. Rudik has enjoyed such incredible fame! I remember years ago telling him that I would never want to change places with him. I would never want to put up with the kind of things one had to put up with in order to maintain that kind of stardom. But Rudik told me that it was what he wanted, and that he was willing to pay the price for it.

"I suppose I am paying my own price for not having gone after all that fame. But then, I never wanted it. I don't think I could have survived that. Rudik enjoys being a public person. I don't. At any rate, my friendship with Rudik can never be lost. It will be there for all our lives. It will be there forever."

In 1983, Erik Bruhn accepted the position of artistic director of the National Ballet of Canada. At the time, he had formed a close relationship with the talented young dancer and choreographer Constantin Patsalas. Bruhn's Canadian venture proved both fulfilling and successful, and the company thrived under his visionary leadership. It came as a devastating shock to the entire dance world when, in 1986, Erik Bruhn, then only 58, died in Toronto of lung cancer.

Just days before, Rudolf Nureyev was at Erik's bedside. The two friends were meeting one last time. One can only conjecture what words might have passed between them. But of one thing I'm certain: Erik Bruhn, looking one last time into Nureyev's eyes, surely died a happy man.

Chapter 48

In 1976, Nicholas Kimber, my wonderful London friend, lent me his grand house on Thurloe Square when I came to London to observe and write about Nureyev's first attempt at movie acting.

Everyone was seriously nervous about the film's outcome, including director Ken Russell, who very soon realized that his star's English was heavily burdened by quite a pronounced Russian accent. Nureyev, portraying a great Italian heartthrob, came out sounding like a Soviet commissar. If this alone did not bode well, Nureyev's strong antipathy toward his costar, Michelle Phillips, caused even greater problems.

Phillips, late of the vocal pop group The Mamas and the Papas, was indeed an odd choice to play Valentino's wife, Natasha Rambova, who in real life was an American perfume heiress (of the Hudnut fortune), a fascinating, ultra-sophisticated dancer, actress, and set designer with a penchant for pretty women. Rambova brought considerable chaos into Valentino's short life. Nureyev considered Phillips ill-suited to the role.

"Rambova was a fabulous creature," he told me. "She was very flamboyant, very cunning, very intelligent. Phillips is hard and empty. She goes against my attempts at true emotion."

During one of their early scenes together, Nureyev became so incensed at Phillips' seeming lack of concentration and acting ability that he slapped her across the face in front of the entire cast and crew. As she stormed off screaming and cursing, Russell demanded that Nureyev apologize to her immediately, which Rudolf reluctantly did, and filming continued. I know all this because I kept a journal of my London adventures with Nureyev. If he was insecure about this project, he bravely soldiered on, finally working with a voice coach, Marcella Markham, to improve his English pronunciation and keeping his temper in check vis-à-vis Michelle Phillips.

Because each day's filming at Elstree Studios began at 7 a.m. and was finished at around 7 p.m., Nureyev's time to himself was limited. For the four months he would be shooting *Valentino*, he and his masseur and general factotum, Luigi, installed themselves in a large suite at London's fashionable Grosvenor House. If his days would be full, his nights would be free, and Nureyev alerted me to the fact that on most of his free nights, I would be his companion. "I'm a night person," he warned me, "so take plenty of vitamins."

Officially, my job was to report on Nureyev as Valentino, and, like my subject, I too religiously appeared on the set at Elstree at 7 a.m., standing or sitting in unobtrusive places, taking notes and observing the action.

One of the most exhilarating "takes" during filming was Nureyev doing a scene in which Valentino portrays Monsieur Beaucaire, one of his famous film roles. Wearing a white powdered wig, a beauty mark on his carefully powdered cheek, dressed in an eighteenth century black and silver doublet and pink vest, Nureyev looked positively stunning as he began a rigorous dueling scene atop a bridge. The grace, fluidity, and speed with which he negotiated his movements offered a thrilling glimpse of Nureyev the dancer. Indeed, it could be said that the only reason to see *Valentino* is to watch Nureyev move, because throughout the film, his movements are never less than noble and measured.

I spent three weeks in London, escorting Nureyev to events and performances he wished to see. Mostly, we drove everywhere in his Triumph TR7, a gift, he told me, from an Arab admirer.

"Tonight we'll hear some drumming," Rudolf announced one morning. "Pick me up this evening at 7:30 sharp. Don't be late!"

When I arrived at the Grosvenor, Luigi greeted me and said, "Rudolf is in a bad mood. Someone has sent him reviews of his Nureyev and Friends tour in America. They're all bad." But Rudolf did not mention the bad reviews as he appeared wearing a snakeskin suit and shiny black rain cap. "Let's go," he said. We jumped into his TR7 and, with Rudolf at the wheel, raced off the London's Collegiate Theatre.

The drumming turned out to be a performance by Ondekoza ("demon drums"), a company of 16 percussionists, dancers, musicians, and singers performing rituals from the countryside of Japan. Nureyev was mesmerized by the ear-splitting sounds and the visual beauty of it all. After the performance in the lobby, he was surrounded by fans. He signed autographs. He smiled. But as we drove back to the hotel for supper, I noticed a dark mood descending.

Back in his suite, Nureyev instantly turned on the television, leaving off the sound. The set flickered in the dining room as we sat down to eat.

Luigi served steak and spaghetti. I made a face. "It's unappetizing. I can't eat it." Nureyev had a few bites, then, shoving his plate away, said, "Let's not eat. Let's just drink." He filled our glasses with red wine. Luigi shrugged, took the dishes away and disappeared.

"So what's all the rage in New York?" Nureyev asked.

"Twyla Tharp," I answered.

"Why?"

"She's found a new way of moving."

"How? Show me."

I got up and began moving my torso and head in a bad Tharp imitation.

"It's horrible."

"It's horrible because I don't know how to do it."

Nureyev fell silent. He looked at the television screen. Some credits came on: *The Devil's Brigade* with William Holden and Cliff Robertson. Rudolf continued watching–with the sound off. I drank wine. Rudolf drank wine. Time passed. Rudolf became restless.

Suddenly he said, "When you write those articles about me, don't say I own a Triumph TR7."

"Why?"

"Because Moishe will buy one too."

Moishe was Nureyev's Yiddish version of Misha–Mikhail Baryshnikov, whom he considered his archrival and threat in the ballet world.

"I hear he's buying a house in Monte Carlo. I have a house in Monte Carlo. He's aping me," he added.

"I wouldn't worry about it," I told him.

More time passed. More wine was consumed.

We rose from the table. Rudolf walked to his bedroom. I followed him. He threw himself on the bed, saying, "You're a shit and a cunt and a bastard. All you journalists are. You're all trying to destroy me."

"Don't be ridiculous."

"You're all trying to crucify me–you are crucifying me! Read these reviews."

He took a sheaf of newspaper clippings from his night table and hurled them at me. I stood by the bed not moving, the clippings scattered on the bed and the floor.

"Oh, to hell with it." He said. "I'm sorry. Come here. Sit by me.

"Calm down," I said, sitting down on the bed.

"I have no one to calm down with. I am alone. I am always alone. Wherever I go, I'm an intruder."

Nureyev drew very close to me. He looked up at me. The room grew still. I looked at his face. There was anger in his eyes and a hint of desire.

"Don't go," he said. "You're a shit, but don't go. Stay."

I stayed.

Chapter 49

Toward the end of my second week in London, I threw a party for Nureyev in Nicholas Kimber's house, where I was living in super comfort. Nicholas had lent me the house, in part because he was an unbelievably generous fellow, and in part because he was a wildly devoted fan of Nureyev's. The thought that he might actually meet Rudolf through me threw him into fits of ecstasy.

It took a certain prodding on my part to persuade Rudolf to attend the party. "Parties bore me," he said. But he agreed to come, saying he'd stay for ten minutes. Of course, he stayed for hours, and as I had also invited members of the *Valentino* cast, including the utterly charming Leslie Caron (who, in the film, plays the tragedienne, Alla Nazimova), though not the out-of-favor Michelle Phillips, Nureyev felt obliged to stay put and be his charismatic self. Nicholas Kimber, in the meantime, was in all states of happiness, and having invited his own contingent of friends, most of them young, gay, and gorgeous, he instantly found favor with his idol, as Rudolf preened and glowed amidst a sea of male admirers. By the end of the night, fueled by vodka, the spiky, wary Nureyev had turned into a pussycat, and much later, his attentiveness toward me proved positively head-spinning.

However, during our next night's outing, Nureyev was back to being his suspicious and paranoid self. We had gone to see a Polish acting troupe, the Cricot Theatre Company, headed by Tadeusz Kantor, which was making its London debut in a converted TV studio. The company was presenting *The Dead Class*, an extremely lugubrious yet brilliantly performed piece in the tortured style of Poland's avant-garde playwright and director, Jerzy Grotowski.

After the performance, we were all invited to a reception given by the Polish ambassador and held in the theater's lobby. There, we ran into Kenneth Tynan, who was reviewing the play, and his wife, Kathleen. Rudolf engaged Tynan in a long conversation about the wonders of the production. Kathleen Tynan chimed in to say she thought it was all a bunch of rubbish.

At one point Rudolf eyed a handsome young bartender serving drinks. "Not bad!" he muttered under his breath. He sent me to inquire his name. "Find out if he's free later tonight–get his phone number." Rudolf wanted me to pimp for him. I refused. Then changed my mind. The bartender was not interested. "No dice, Rudolf," I told him. "It figures," he fumed.

Nureyev had been quietly consuming quite a bit of vodka. He became very lively, more and more talkative, discussing music, theater and literature with director Tadeusz Kantor. It was getting late. Rudolf had promised to have supper at the home of his close London friends the Goslings, Nigel and his wife, the former dancer Maude Lloyd, who had danced the first Caroline in Antony Tudor's great ballet, *Jardin aux Lilas.*

The Goslings were a writing team jointly known as Alexander Bland. They had known and championed Rudolf since his defection in 1961 and wrote many articles and several books about him. Whenever Nureyev was in London, they were almost masochistically at his disposal.

I prodded Rudolf away from the reception. I told him the Goslings were elderly and were waiting for us for supper–and it was getting awfully late. "OK! OK!" he said, and we both dashed to his TR7. On the way, Nureyev inserted a cassette into the stereo. I recognized it as a Beethoven sonata. Rudolf told me the pianist was Vladimir Ashkenazy.

"I love music more than anything else…this playing is quite virile. But Sviatoslav Richter is the greatest Beethoven interpreter in the world. He goes right into my heart, chest, spine–my whole being. Of course, there is Artur Schnabel. I have the complete Schnabel recordings of the Beethoven sonatas." Nureyev turned the volume way up. "Listen to this! I don't need anything else. Nothing compares!"

We arrived at Victoria Road. The Goslings appeared visibly exhausted. It was half past midnight. Still, they greeted us enthusiastically, and served a delicious supper of roast chicken and vegetables. Rudolf drank vodka with his meal. The conversation was lively and centered on the great Diaghilev ballerina Tamara Karsavina's 90th birthday, on the doings at the Royal Ballet, and on the progress of Rudy's role in *Valentino.*

Dinner over, we moved into the living room. Rudolf asked Gosling to turn on the TV–again, with the sound off. The small screen offered Boris Karloff in a horror film. Rudolf watched a while, then casually picked up a copy of Britain's premiere dance publication, *Dance & Dancers.* He leafed through it and as bad luck would have it, found a review of his seven-week marathon in London of Nureyev and Friends, which had taken place months earlier. The review seemed to be very bad. As he read it, I saw Nureyev becoming more and more agitated.

"The Jews are keeping me down," he suddenly said. "They're in control. The Jews are crucifying me."

"Why are you blaming the Jews?" I asked.

"The Jews are killing my career."

"Don't be absurd," I said. "You're being anti-Semitic, that's all."

"And you're the worst Jew of all," he instantly countered. "You've written bad, damaging things about me–and you're gong to do it again, I know it."

The Goslings tried to placate Nureyev. They told him to pay no attention to what critics say, that he was a unique, supremely gifted artist.

"The Jews don't seem to know that."

I felt disgusted and told the Goslings I was leaving.

"Sit down," Nureyev said sharply. Then, more quietly, "Don't go. In a bit I'll drive you home."

Ten minutes later we were back in Rudolf's car.

We were both silent for a long stretch of the drive. Then he said, "You've hurt my feelings by calling me anti-Semitic."

"That's exactly what you were being."

"You're labeling me."

"You have it in for the Jews."

"For the past 15 years, critics have tried to crush me–always, always! And you yourself have put words in people's mouths, like Makarova, who complained about me, and other people, who have said bad things about me. And you do this on purpose. You tell me you love me! But you don't love me at all. Of course, the press is controlled by the Jews–so I will never win."

I got angry. "You know, Rudolf, some of what the critics say about you is absolutely justified. You've been dancing too much, too often. There are times you look tired–the effort is showing. Too often, what you're doing doesn't look good."

"I want to die on stage," he said.

We reached my place in silence. It was very late. When he stopped the car, neither of us moved.

"Don't blame the Jews for things," I told him very quietly. "It's narrow-minded and could get you into big trouble. And it's beneath you."

It's alright," he said. "I will just go on. Anyway, my career is almost over, and I will overcome this also. You have all tried to annihilate me, but I survive."

I told Nureyev I couldn't bear getting out of the car on this bad note. I asked if he'd like to come in for a late-night vodka.

He shook his head, but took my hand and held it. He leaned over and kissed me on the cheek.

I got out of the car. He rolled down his window.

"Don't be my enemy, John."

And he drove off.

When I saw Rudolf again the next day at Elstree Studios, he greeted me as though nothing had happened and said, "Tonight we're going to the movies. Meet me at 7 p.m. at the Gate Cinema. Take the Notting Hill Gate tube. Don't be late. Be sure you eat something. The movie is Greek and it's four hours long. It's called *The Travelling Players.* After the movie we're going to a birthday party.

Amazingly, it was my birthday too–September 12!

"Whose birthday?" I asked.

"It's a Royal Ballet corps boy I'm crazy about," said Rudolf. I told him it was my birthday also.

"Today's your birthday? Well, well! We'll have a double celebration!"

The endless movie at the Gate Cinema was relentlessly dour. Rudolf fidgeted but insisted on sticking it out. "It's a masterpiece, but very boring," he said. "Let's go to the party." We got in his car, and when we arrived, I noted that Rudolf retrieved a large shopping bag from the back.

Geoffrey, the birthday boy, answered the door himself. He was very young, very blond, very handsome. We were in the elegant home of a balletomane doctor. The place was swarming with Royal Ballet corps dancers. In their midst Nureyev felt totally at ease–he was "family." Walking up to Geoffrey, he wished him a happy birthday. They hugged and Rudolf removed a book from his shopping bag–a coffee table book on Africa. Geoffrey registered delight. They stood and chatted for a long while. But Rudolf looked disconsolate.

He next walked over to where I was standing. He removed a package from the bag. "Happy birthday," he said rather glumly. I unwrapped the gift. It was a book, *A Servant of Many Masters: The Life and Times of Carlo Goldoni* by Timothy Holme. I opened it to the title page and found this inscription: "Anche per piccolo Goldonetto per ricordare per sempre" (Also for little Goldoni, something to remember forever). And the inscription went on: "Render unto God what is God's and to Caesar what is his." I thanked him profusely for his cryptic dedication and brushed a kiss on his lips.

"Geoffrey is not interested in coming home with me," Nureyev told me.

"Let it be, Rudolf."

"People I love don't love me back."

"Do you want to leave?"

"Yes. Let's go have a drink."

We drove to a small, dimly lit restaurant he knew in Soho. We sat in a booth. We ordered drinks—vodka for Rudolf, Scotch for me. Rudolf was quiet. He looked sad. "I will always be alone," he finally said. "It is my fate."

"Have you ever been psychoanalyzed?" I wondered.

"No. I really don't know anything about myself. Do you know about yourself? There are things not to be known and they should stay untouched. One should leave one's impulses to chance. It is better to do that rather than to calculate, prefabricate, analyze, and kill that something in us that we do not altogether understand."

I sensed Rudolf was in a mood to talk. I again broached the subject of his need to dance so incessantly.

"If I don't dance constantly, I crumble," he said. "Look, a dancer's life has a span of perhaps 20 or 25 years. In that time you have a good period at the beginning or in the middle or even at the end. This good period lasts, at best, five to seven years. I still feel I'm in a good period, and I really feel I have to dance nonstop. But, as you see, just now I have stopped. I've stopped for four months to make this movie. I will be resting my muscles. But, of course, I still give myself a class every day. I must stay in shape.

"Dancing for me is an absolute need. You see, being on stage is really very abnormal. There is something very artificial about it. Because I feel so alien on the stage, I have a need to be on it more and more and more. But once on it, I am lost. It's like a sacrifice—and I give of myself completely. The moment I'm on stage, things become multiplied and magnified. It's like having a nuclear reactor inside of me. There is a chain reaction and, suddenly, my whole body bursts into flames."

"And what about dancing with Margot?" I asked. "Does Fonteyn represent a need as well?"

"Absolutely. It's not just a need. It's an understanding. When there is no understanding and no trust between you and your ballerina, it doesn't matter how well you dance. It becomes like a two-headed eagle. You are doing one thing and your partner is doing another thing. When I dance with Margot it is one aim. There is one vision. It is painful arriving at that vision, but when we have found it, we go there together. There is no tearing us apart.

"But about my dancing so much…and all the bitching I get about it from people like you…I know I'm growing older. I know I'm clocking away my time on stage. I am aware that time is running out, and I must become selective and self-protective. But I have news for you. Dancing every night is not difficult for me. The more I dance, the better I dance."

Rudolf had been drinking steadily, and so had I. We were both sort of drunk.

"Now I have a question for you," he said. "Are you able to cry?"

"What a weird question," I said. "But yes, I can and I do, especially when I feel sorry for myself…and sometimes, dear Rudolf, when I watch you and Margot dance."

"Well, you're lucky. Unfortunately, I can't cry anymore. I used to be able to cry easily and it used to be so natural and believable. But it just doesn't work anymore. I've come to terms with my loneliness. Of course, I have friends–Margot, Erik Bruhn, Frederick Ashton, who were friends from the very beginning. But I don't see them as often as I'd like, because I fly around like crazy, dancing everywhere. I'm like a wandering angel or a wandering druid, and, as I told you, people like myself have difficulty with permanent relationships. People like myself take their pleasure where they can."

There was a long pause.

"Let's go home," I suddenly said.

"Yes, let's," said Rudolf.

Chapter 50

Valentino, Nureyev's first commercial film venture, was released in 1977, and moviegoers stayed away in droves. Reviews went from poor to dreadful. Ken Russell's direction was deemed mostly heavy-handed. Rudolf's acting was deemed more or less painful. People hoped to see him dance but all they got was a tango (with Anthony Dowell), a Russian accent, and lots of handsome posturing. Still, I thought the film had a certain allure, and Rudolf, at the height of his physical beauty, did cast a certain spell.

I wrote it all up for the *Times* and for *Vogue*, and considered my *Valentino* assignment a grandly fulfilling experience. Getting to know Nureyev, warts and all, was both thrilling and dismaying. I don't know if we parted as friends, given his dislike and suspicion of journalists and reviewers. But basically, my love and admiration for this amazing artist did not diminish, and the few intimacies we shared were memorable.

The night before I left London, I invited Rudolf to a farewell supper at the Savoy. It would be just the two of us. I formally thanked him for his cooperation and told him how much his friendship had meant to me. We ordered champagne. We toasted each other. When supper was over, and as we finally said our goodbyes, his warm embrace suggested his feelings toward me were not altogether uncaring.

At the Savoy, I extracted a promise from Rudolf: that he and Margot Fonteyn (should she be willing) would do a live interview with me at Town Hall in New York, when the two would be dancing with the Royal Ballet at the Metropolitan Opera the following season.

"Set it up with Margot, and I'll be happy to do it," he said.

And so, after my three weeks in London, I returned to my life in New York, to Jane and Julia, the New York dance world, the New York art world, and the New York music world–the worlds that were mine to explore and be totally consumed by.

From the middle of the 1970s to the middle of the 1980s, the dance world was my most immediate preoccupation. It was during those years that my passion for the New York City Ballet took root as I attended endless performances and as I delved deeply into its repertoire and its dancers. Again, my aim was to befriend those company dancers I admired greatly so that I might more fully understand the ways and workings of the company.

Most greedily, I wanted to befriend George Balanchine, to my mind the world's greatest living choreographer. The Balanchine ballets I had seen since 1948, when I was just finishing college, stayed with me like touchstones I needed to encounter again and again. At age 22, I didn't really understand Balanchine, but I knew enough to feel intriguingly confused by him. Like so many of his detractors, I too felt the work looked cold, mechanical, awkward—not beautiful, the way ballets were supposed to look. But with the years, all this changed, and like a flower opening in slow motion, the miracles of Balanchine's astonishing gifts were revealed to me. I came to savor the insouciance of his dancers' movements. I came to love the way their feet testily jabbed the floor, the way their taut, resilient bodies devoured space, the way they flicked their hands and thrust their hips and kicked their legs, all in response to Bach and Mozart and Tchaikovsky, to Fauré and Ravel and Stravinsky.

For me, to watch Balanchine ballets was to suddenly enter a paradise of physical and aesthetic wonders, where abstract movement and music combined to form a cool yet profoundly revealed humanity. Indeed, the structure of each of his works, from the greatest to the middling, invariably possessed both a clarity and a complexity that made palpably visible the human mind and heart at work.

Needless to say, I was hooked for life. And my daughter, Julia, was there even before I was. It was through Julia that I really began to meet the City Ballet dancers, who for more than ten years would be part of our daily lives. Still, it was Mr. B, whom we never saw socially, who remained the compelling enigma of my City Ballet years. My interviews with him, for the *Times, Vogue, Dance Magazine,* and in-person at The New School, were my attempts to fathom some of his secrets.

When I asked him to describe his earliest years as a choreographer for Diaghilev's Ballets Russes in Paris, Balanchine confessed to being both naïve and uninformed: "My first ballet for Diaghilev was *Le Chant du Rossignol,*" he said. "It was 1925. Little Alicia Markova danced in it. Matisse did the décor. Stravinsky, the music. But I didn't know anybody. I didn't know French. I didn't know any of the fabulous people who were around. I was absolutely stupid. I never read anything. Nothing. I could just see things. What I have, really, is that I see better than anybody else, and I hear better. God said to me, 'That's all you're going to have. It's not your business to think.' I said, 'Fine.' Anyway, then I met all these painters I never heard of: Utrillo, Rouault, Derain. There was Braque. Picasso was around. I didn't know who anybody was. And I met Ravel, and he wrote the opera *L'Enfant et les Sortileges.* I did the first production for Diaghilev. I did 12 ballets for him, including *Apollo* and *The Prodigal Son,* but then, in 1929, Diaghilev died, and everybody was desperate and looking around for other jobs—including me."

I asked Balanchine about his arrival in America in 1933 under the aegis of Lincoln Kirstein. (When asked how he felt setting foot on American soil, Balanchine answered, "I am happy to have arrived in a country that has produced so beautiful a woman as Ginger Rogers!") We spoke of his forming a ballet school before building a company. "But first a school," he had famously said.

"I am very conscious of the children who come to my school," Balanchine told me. "I like them to come early, and they appear in *The Nutcracker.* Then they grow. We know each other a long time. The girls who are with me now, I have known them since they were eight. So we know each other for about 12 years already. And they are intelligent, in spite of what people say. They may be stupid on this earth, but they are wise above the earth. This is a wonderful thing. They don't say anything, but they know, because it took a long time for them to learn. A dancer's body is a tool, and when I work with it, I make it for that particular person. Of course, woman is more flexible—she has a more ideal body for technique, for speed. Boys are made to jump or to lift a girl or to support a girl. But boys don't have speedy legs, because they are not built that way. I know how to teach. And I especially know how to teach a woman. Almost nobody knows. I think Petipa and I were the ones. Because it's very difficult to stage for a woman. You can just kill them or spoil them—it's very dangerous. Yet it is possible to choreograph for them without injuring them."

Balanchine shunned choreographing the so-called story ballet, preferring the challenge of the plotless, abstract ballet:

"It's not that I dislike the story ballet. It's that I don't like bad story ballets, lousy stories that have nothing to do with dancing. You see, ballet is not intellectual. It's visual. Ballet has to be seen. It's like a beautiful flower. What can you say about a beautiful flower? All you can say is that it's beautiful. So to make a story in dance is very difficult. Always you have to sit and read the story—but that's wrong. You have to look—to see. I mean, it's boring that you have to know that in a first entrance it's the father entering, then the son is entering, then his girlfriend, then the mother...and then her second cousin. No. Family relations are impossible to dance."

Venturing to a personal question, I reminded Balanchine how opposed he had always been to his ballerinas marrying. And yet, he himself was married to or lived with five of his dancers–Tamara Geva, Alexandra Danilova, Vera Zorina, Maria Tallchief, and Tanaquil LeClerq.

"Well...yes. But you see, when one of my ballet girls gets married, she's not she anymore. She's he. Because now she is Mrs. So-and-So, and it's over. For a female dancer marriage means the end of her individuality.

"I say dancers should have romances, love affairs, but not marriages. I have a few married dancers in my company. There's Allegra Kent, but she's an exception. She even has three children! Of course, she did not dance for six years, because each child takes away two years.

"But you asked about my wives. Yes, I was together with five wonderful dancers. But, you know, I have never left any of my wives. They have all left me. But then, you see, I am an Aquarius and an Aquarius is not sup-posed to be male at all. I am water and air–a spirit. These women I mar-ried, they were all muses. They married Apollo who inspired them to make something of themselves. And they did. They all became fabulous artists and fabulous people. And they learned a tremendous amount. Also, I may have made lots of mistakes. When you are young, you don't think. Now I feel I should not have married any of them. The point is I am a working man–a gardener. I was born that way. I am a servant. When I was married, I served. I served all my muses. I served like a spirit serves.

"The fact is, I am a cloud in pants."

Chapter 51

I have always thought that dancers were angels, because they seem to silently float above the earth, creating shapes and images and patterns that conjure feelings and emotions not of this world. (Think Giotto, Duccio, Fra Angelico.) I know that angels don't sweat. But they do stir the soul and send us messages. When dancers move, be it singly or in groups, in unison or contrapuntally; when they leap or run or, most poignantly, remain still, what we see are bodies transformed and transfixed by time and the impulses of music. Thus, dancers become heavenly bodies—they become angels and they arrive as messengers.

The message of dance is the dancers, and the message of the dancer is a vast and wondrous metaphysical miracle—a healing thing. When the dance is very compelling, when it is, say, Balanchine's *Divertimento No. 15* by Mozart, we are doubly healed and doubly blessed. The music is heavenly. The dance is angelic. Although I have seen many angels perform with almost all the major companies of the world, to me, the most angelic of them all are the ones who dance with the New York City Ballet. The reason is simple. They are fresher, newer, crisper, more innocent, lighter, less worldly, less knowing than all the rest.

When Mr. Balanchine, a Georgian, created the New York City Ballet, he knew he had come from an old, old country with an old, old and hallowed ballet tradition. Old Russia was in his blood, and even though he was the most forward-looking and visionary of artists, he understood the value of the established and the traditional.

He also understood that America was a young and vibrant country devoid of a tried and true ballet history. There were never any czarist ballet schools or companies in America. And so, when Mr. B said, "But first a school," he set about to fashion and foment a new way of moving. He did this not by abandoning the teachings of the old Maryinksy disciplines, but by superimposing upon them the primitive, blustery, fast-moving crosswinds of the New World.

As he put it, he could see better than anybody else and because his school was in the heart of New York City, he instantly took in and absorbed the dynamics of New York, its speed, its swiftness, its quickness, its alacrity, its sophistication, its cosmopolitan edge, its danger, and its elegance, and poured all these elements into the bodies of his dancers. He himself taught those first classes and forged a new, exhilarating classical technique that encompassed the city's energy, its strength, its speed.

Above all, he molded his dancers in ways that always included the allure of their very own individual selves, which is why a New York City Ballet dancer always emerges looking the same, yet thrillingly different. Balanchine gave his dancers a nuanced inner light that lent their movements the supple and resilient spring and sheen of the freshly minted.

Thus, whenever I went to the New York City Ballet I was enthralled, because when the lights dimmed and the curtain rose, and the music began, and all the dancers stood in place, their arms aloft and rising on pointe, the heavens parted and all those angels came flying my way.

The angels of my time, the 70s and 80s, had all been trained by Balanchine himself together with the small coterie of international teachers that comprised the faculty of the School of American Ballet. These dancers included Suzanne Farrell, Peter Martins, Allegra Kent, Jacques d'Amboise, Kyra Nichols, Ib Anderson, Merrill Ashley, Kay Mazzo, Patricia McBride, Edward Villella, Violette Verdy, Gelsey Kirkland, Robert La Fosse, Darci Kistler, Lourdes Lopez, Sean Lavery, and Helgi Tomasson, to mention just some of the principal dancers I saw again and again.

Certain of the dancers had a different look about them—a strangeness: Maria Calegari, Karen Von Aroldingen, Jean Pierre Bonnefoux, Nichol Hlinka, Adam Luders, Melissa Hayden, Ricky Weiss, John Clifford, Anthony Blum, and Sara Leland all seemed creatures apart, possessed of an awkward logic, yet unmistakably, Balanchine dancers.

But the dancers who became our friends during those years were those whom my daughter Julia had befriended during and shortly after she was a student at the School of American Ballet. This group was headed by Peter Martins and Heather Watts, who, at the time, were rising young stars of the New York City Ballet. Watts' back was slightly swayed, yet this often maligned, outspoken, and entirely charismatic ballerina offered performances at once individual and compelling. Today, married to the virtuoso Balanchine star Damian Woetzel, Heather Watts is currently enjoying her entirely deserved if surprising role as visiting adjunct lecturer (on dance) at Harvard University.

Peter Martins has long been the City Ballet's ballet master in chief, having assumed this post, at Balanchine's request, soon after Balanchine's death on April 30, 1983. The handsome Danish-born dancer, a product of the Royal Danish Ballet, brought a note of true aristocracy to the Balanchine aesthetic. From *Apollo* to *Vienna Waltzes*, from *Agon* to *Union Jack*, from Tchaikovsky's *Piano Concerto No. 2* to *Chaconne*, Martins' ballet performances were infused by technical refinement and interpretive sophistication. At City Ballet, he also became a choreographer of note, producing works that ranged from the mediocre to the marvelous. After a brief yet intense courtship, Martins married Darci Kistler, one of the company's most sublime ballerinas.

But when we knew Peter and Heather, the two were passionate, often sparring lovers. And to be in their company was to be privy to a truly intimate glimpse of the New York City Ballet in its ever-evolving life under Balanchine and Jerome Robbins.

Daughter Julia also brought a whole other group of City Ballet dancers into our lives. These were an energetic crew of corps boys, all of whom clearly adored Julia–John Bass, Peter Boal, Ulrik Trojaborg, Jock Soto and Bruce Padgett, among others. Of them all, the exceedingly handsome Danish-born Ulrik Trojaborg was Julia's special friend. Given their spectacular looks, their mutual interests, and the genuine affection they had for each other, the two seemed destined to make a young life together. Indeed, Julia and Ulrik were inseparable. Throughout the years, they even shared lofts and apartments together, and developed a relationship that included Jane and me, Ulrik's parents, and all of Ulrik's family and relatives in Denmark.

As it turned out, a romance between Julia and Ulrik did not materialize. Surface appearances and parental hopes notwithstanding, Julia had always known that Ulrik's amorous inclinations lay elsewhere, and that it was the very young Jock Soto who would one day become the love of Ulrik's life.

This may or may not have broken Julia's heart, but it certainly did not alter the course of her friendship with Ulrik, which remained strong and steadfast and would now include the increasingly impressive Jock Soto, who from the beginning showed signs of becoming one of City Ballet's most gifted dancers. Besides, Julia had by now also become deeply attached to the entirely charming and adorable John Bass, whose mischievous wit and sense of humor matched Julia's own.

And so, Julia's troupe of sweet corps boys, together with the entirely glamorous and feisty Peter Martins and Heather Watts, formed a small enclave of young dancers who would regularly appear at our parties, our dinners, and our cocktail gatherings, and whose presence among our artist and musician friends lent a certain soigné touch to our social life. It would all last some ten years, and would include yearly gatherings around our table for Thanksgiving, Christmas, birthdays, or whenever anyone felt the need to seriously "celebrate."

Chapter 52

Toward the end of the 1970s, Rudolf Nureyev briefly reentered my life or, to be honest about it, I reentered his. Having had considerable success with my live interviews in front of live audiences, notably at the New School for Social Research with various film stars and people in the arts, I wanted to present Rudolf Nureyev and Margot Fonteyn, the world's most famous and most glamorous ballet couple, in an interview to be held in New York's prestigious Town Hall.

They were then performing in New York with the Royal Ballet and, back in London, Rudolf had promised he'd appear with me if Fonteyn was also willing to sit for an interview. To my total joy, both agreed. A date was set and, together with a wonderful, hard-working young woman named Marilyn Egol, one of Town Hall's producers, I set about to make this event one of the most exciting and talked about in the city. And indeed, the moment word got out that Fonteyn and Nureyev would be appearing in person for their first live interview in New York City, the Town Hall box office was swamped. Within hours the evening was completely sold out.

I'm not exactly sure why or how this happened, but when I telephoned Rudolf on the morning of the evening's big event to say at what time Margot and I would be picking him up, he calmly announced that he would not be able to appear with me after all, that I should go ahead without him, that Margot would be enough of a drawing card.

I was speechless. Finally, all I could say was, "Rudolf, you can't do this to me." His answer was simple and to the point: "Yes, I can." And he hung up the phone.

I just stood there. I wasn't even angry—just in a state of total disbelief. But in a moment, my adrenalin started pumping. I instantly telephoned Margot Fonteyn. When I told her Rudolf had backed out of our evening, she was amazed. "Whatever has come over him?" she wondered. And she promised to call him immediately.

When Margot called me back, she said Rudolf was in one of his black moods. "He was muttering something about your *Valentino* articles," she said. "He sounded serious about canceling tonight."

Now I was furious. If Rudolf was so angry about what I had written about his film debut, he could easily have refused to appear with me, despite his London promise. Instead, he had agreed to appear, had accepted a $500 fee for his services, and had allowed the event to be publicized. By not appearing, he was not only breaking a contract, but was also being hugely discourteous to Margot and me, let alone disappointing the over 1,500 people who had purchased tickets to this gala event.

I called Rudolf again. Luigi, his masseur, answered.

"He doesn't want to talk to you."

I called Margot again.

"I'll see what I can do," she said.

"Margot, you know this isn't right."

"I know," she said.

I had no word from either Margot or Rudolf for the rest of the afternoon. I felt desperate and incredibly angry. At Town Hall, Marilyn Egol, was in a terrible state after I told her about the problem. People would want their money back. She had called earlier to say that barricades were being set up out on the street and that mounted police were gathering in front of the entrance in anticipation of an unruly crowd. Word had gotten out that Nureyev might be a no-show.

I had ordered a limousine to pick up my guests. When Margot got into the car, she said she had not heard from Rudolf, but told the driver to stop by his hotel anyway. When we got there, Margot told me to go into the lobby, get on the house phone, and tell Rudolf or Luigi that she, Margot, was waiting in the car downstairs, and would Rudolf please come down.

I did as she told me. When I was put through to Rudolf's suite, Luigi once again answered. I delivered the message: "Tell Rudolf that Margot is waiting downstairs in the car."

I hung up and stood in the hotel lobby–waiting. The minutes seemed like hours. No Rudolf. Then, an elevator door opened and out stepped Nureyev, dressed all in leather and looking great. When he saw me he said, "Well, here I am, you cunt. I'm doing this for Margot."

No one spoke throughout the ride to Town Hall, although I noticed Margot poking Rudolf in the ribs a couple of times, shaking her head, and giving him a wicked smile. For myself, the idea of conducting an interview with any kind of enthusiasm seemed utterly impossible. Having been put through the ringer by Rudolf the entire day, I couldn't see myself summoning up any kind of sparkle, spirit or spunk to make the evening either provocative or memorable.

In the end, however, it all worked out.

When Rudolf and Margot walked out on the stage together, a roar went up. People stood. People whistled. People hooted. Suddenly my energy and zest returned and I conducted one of the best interviews of my career. At the conclusion of the evening, all three of us held hands and bowed. The applause was deafening. It was a triumph.

But this episode, for all its ultimate glory, actually sickened me. That night I vowed never to speak to Rudolf again. I wanted no part of him, not his genius, not his friendship.

Looking back on my relationship with him, I knew full well I had no one but myself to blame. But then, as E.E. Cummings once so eloquently put it: "There is some shit I will not eat."

Chapter 53

My love affair with the New York City Ballet, which was hot and heavy throughout the 70s and 80s, did not prevent me from fulfilling my duties as an objective writer and critic reporting on the activities of other ballet troupes and their dancers performing in New York City—companies such as American Ballet Theatre, The Joffrey Ballet, the Feld Ballet, the Dance Theater of Harlem, the modern dance companies of Martha Graham, Merce Cunningham, Paul Taylor, Alvin Ailey, Lar Lubovitch, Alwin Nikolais, Morris Louis, Louis Falco, and Pilobolus, among others, as well as all the visiting ballet companies arriving from abroad.

The most spectacular ballet news of 1980 was Mikhail Baryshnikov's ascendance to the post of Artistic Director of American Ballet Theatre, a position held since 1940 by the doyenne of American classical dance, Lucia Chase. Baryshnikov held the post for nine years before resigning in 1989 in what seemed to have been a wild and woolly balletic huff.

The news of Baryshnikov's heading so grand a company as ABT was startling, because between 1978 and 1979, he had been a principal dancer with the New York City Ballet, where he seemed entirely content and happy and where his presence proved a financial if not an artistic boon to the company. Indeed, Balanchine's edict never to hire big-star dancers was temporarily suspended as Baryshnikov shone in such Balanchine master-pieces as *Prodigal Son* and *Apollo*. But he seemed, to these eyes, somewhat less than meticulous or confident in some of Mr. B's more astringently abstract works.

Then, off he went to ABT and a new chapter in ballet history unfolded.

I had always admired American Ballet Theatre. It had the substance and feel of an old-fashioned, somewhat shabby-chic European ballet com-pany, and its repertory was both conventional (they did all the classics) and quite diversified (from Antony Tudor to Eliot Feld to Glen Tetley to Twyla Tharp.) Basically, it was a touring company, and it believed in the star system. ABT invited all the Soviet defectors—Nureyev, Makarova,

Baryshnikov—as well as the latecomer Alexander Godunov, along with guest artists such as Erik Bruhn, Carla Fracci, Michael Denard, Paolo Bortoluzzi, and many others, to dance in its productions. At the same time, it nurtured its own company dancers, ballerinas, and danseurs such as Cynthia Gregory, Martine van Hamel, Eleanor D'Antuono, Marianna Tcherkassky, Royes Fernandez, Bruce Marks, Ted Kivett, Ivan Nagy, Fernando Bujones, and Patrick Bissell.

Under the guidance of Misha Baryshnikov, ABT attained a certain new prestige and effervescence. Aside from his own presence as a dancer—always a potent box office draw—Baryshnikov, along with his general factotum and ballet-freak extraordinaire, Charles France, engineered the resignation of various "older" dancers. What resulted was an influx of new, superbly trained young corps people, new star performers, commissions for exciting new choreography (by Mark Morris in particular), and, in general, a more streamlined company that gave ABT much needed éclat and renewed glamour.

I, in the meantime, kept writing, reviewing, interviewing, broadcasting, and traipsing from performance to performance, from company to company, from dance recital to dance recital, attending premieres of this, revivals of that and, in the midst of it all, beginning a brand new book, *The World's Great Ballets*, an elegant coffee table extravaganza commissioned by Paul Gottlieb, editor of Abrams, and published in 1981. I thought the project would be easy, writing up the more or less simple-minded plots of *Giselle, Coppélia, Swan Lake, The Sleeping Beauty*, and *The Nutcracker*. To a certain extent, it was easy, but as I got into it and, especially, as I needed to tell the plots of ballets that had no plots, such as Mr. Balanchine's abstract masterpieces or ballet by Tharp, Tetley, or Cunningham, things got considerably more complicated.

But help was on the way. Once again, I enlisted the very considerable talents of Andrew Mark Wentink, the entertaining, talkative, infuriating Andy, who guided me over any number of hurdles as I wended my way through 400 years of dance history in search of ballets and their histories for the book.

Andy and I stitched together a narrative for even the most abstruse works and, with the addition of ravishing color illustrations and a really stunning layout, *The World's Great Ballets* turned out to be quite a plush and valuable compendium of classical dance in all its various traditional and modern guises.

But while all this was going on, during the late 70s and early 80s, and just as Jane and I were hitting our early 50s, major dramas began to unfold in both our personal lives. Our parents all became ill and died within a few short years of each other. Suddenly, it was death and more death in quick succession.

My own parents lived into their eighties. Their long, complex lives, fraught with many miseries and disappointments, came to a close as my mother developed Alzheimer's disease, and as my father suffered through her various episodes of dementia. In those years, it wasn't called Alzheimer's. We all thought of it as senility or paranoia or just plain "going gaga."

The summer before my mother died, Jane and I brought her to Water Mill, to our country place, relieving my father of some of the relentless strain. My mother came willingly. That first afternoon, she sat quietly on our patio, some tea and biscuits at her side. The day was warm and sunny. She seemed calm and happy. I sat down near her with a book. Suddenly she looked up. "It's raining," she said. "Look! Your brother Tino is walking over there—in the rain. He's not dressed for the rain." And she started calling to him. "Tino! Tino! Come back into the house!" She rose and started walking toward him. "Tino! Come back! It's raining so hard! You'll get sick!"

That night we were awakened by the clatter of dishes in the kitchen. It must have been 4 a.m. When we got downstairs, there she stood, holding pots and pans. "It's time to fix dinner," my mother told us. "I must boil water for the potatoes. I must put the roast in the oven. The boys will be home soon. Father is coming. It's getting so late. I must hurry!" It was all we could do to lead her back to her room and to bed.

The next day she would not leave her room, and pounded on the walls and wept. When we tried to calm her, she did not know who we were. She did not know where she was. Dressed in a nightgown, she refused to put her clothes on. Jane very gently coaxed her into her summer dress. Later, sitting in the living room, she sipped some tea. Her hands were shaking. She looked very frightened. She refused to speak.

We brought my mother back to New York. The situation was becoming dire. My father did the best he could, but he himself was not well; a hernia operation had been scheduled for him. On the appointed day, we brought my father to Columbia Presbyterian Hospital. He would be operated early on the following morning and, we hoped, would be able to return home the next day. But there was no next day.

My father died on the operating table.

"The operation was a success, but his heart gave out," said the doctor, offering condolences, apologies, and saying all the right words to explain my father's sudden demise—old age, a weak heart, stress.

My three older brothers, Leo, Tino, and Carlo, all came for the funeral. My mother, who knew nothing of my father's death, was too ill and too out of it to attend. No tears were shed that chilly morning at a Jewish cemetery in New Jersey. It was a sad occasion, but for all the wrong reasons. I knew that none of us would miss our father. As his coffin was being lowered into the earth, I wished I were able to cry, I wished I could have loved my father more, I wished he could have loved me more. I wished I didn't feel so relieved, even strangely elated.

It was now decided that my mother should be placed in a home, which I set about finding. I found a somewhat woebegone facility just a few blocks from where we lived on the Upper West Side, and we thought this a boon because it enabled Jane and I to visit her whenever we wanted. We brought her up to our place and would even take her out for short walks in Riverside Park.

One day my brother Leo came to see her and was appalled at the condition of the home. He promptly arranged for our mother to be moved to a far more pleasant facility near where he and his wife lived in Washington, D.C.

As it turned out, my mother died within a matter of weeks.

She was very ill but still alive when Jane and I traveled to Washington to see her. All my brothers, together with their wives, stood around her bed as she lay dying. As if to hasten the moment, the last words she uttered were, "Schnell! Schnell!", the German word for "Quick! Quick!"

Thus it was that my parents died within a few months of each other. Then, two years later, it was Jane's parents' turn to die. Although they had long been divorced, Jane and her sister Ann still felt very close to both. Oddly enough, Jane's mother, like mine, died of Alzheimer's disease. And her father, like mine, died of a heart attack. And similarly, Jane's father had died before her mother. They died in Iowa, where Jane and Ann were born, and needless to say, the story of their lives was very different from the story of my own parents', though not so different in the quality and intensity of their mutual unhappiness.

Chapter 54

Life went on, however, and although my parents' passing in such quick succession left me reeling and feeling generally miserable, guilty, and upset enough to briefly revisit a psychoanalyst—the quite wonderful Mrs. Jeanette Hirsch—I kept busy enough to make the impact of their deaths recede with the passing months and years.

Of course, one never loses one's parents. They sit inside you like sentinels, like constant reminders of who you are and where you've come from. You can never really get rid of them. And the longer your parents lived, the longer it takes for them to recede from your consciousness. Even at this late date in my own life, my mother and father periodically make their presence felt—especially potent when each or both visit my dreams. And so, we proceeded with our lives.

In the late 70s, Jane changed galleries once more. This time she was heavily wooed by one Aladar Marberger, an intense, highly volatile young art dealer running New York's Fischbach Gallery on West 57th Street. Jane was eventually lured away from the staid and stable Graham Gallery, with promises of exhibitions and sales that would exceed those of the Graham, and with a gallery connection that would place her more fully and more visibly within the current flow of the growing art world.

From Jane's point of view, grateful as she was for the constant if somewhat complacent support of the Graham, she felt a need to shake herself up, to force herself to reexamine fundamentals. As successful as she was with her patterned still life paintings, seen to great advantage at the Graham, she was in need of some inner jolt.

Jane's life at the Fischbach Gallery delivered plenty of jolts. Her first show there was in 1978, and she would remain with the gallery for the next 20 years.

It was at the Fischbach that Jane gradually moved from still lifes, with their emphasis on indoor intimacy, back to the out of doors and the atmospherics of weather. She began painting her newly evolved and crystallized landscapes that would bring her continued critical acclaim as one of the country's leading landscape artists. Her work took on a radiance that was as stunningly articulated as it was compelling. Her color, built from layer upon layer of underpainting, assumed a richness, depth, and translucency that was singular in its understated lyricism.

Whether working in large, medium, or small scale, Jane's landscapes, seascapes, and skyscapes were almost always inspired by the air, light, and waters of Long Island, where we continued to summer every year. Indeed, although far from being a regionalist, Jane Wilson became known as a "Long Island painter," joining the great tradition of Long Island artists as stylistically disparate as William Merritt Chase, Fairfield Porter, and Willem de Kooning.

Our daughter Julia, in the meantime, began forging a life of her own. After graduating from high school, and after her years at the School of American Ballet, she did some modeling (Richard Avedon helped), then held various positions, including the editorship of a television publication, which broadened her writing and administrative skills. She also made the decision to enroll as a student at Columbia University, majoring in English literature, and some three years later went to work for the Charles Cowles Gallery, where her arts background, keen sense of aesthetics, and office skills were put to good use.

About a year later, she found a job that would literally change her life.

A *New York Times* classified ad advertised two positions with the Tony Shafrazi Gallery, an up-and-coming art venue in SoHo. One of these positions was as assistant to a Shafrazi Gallery artist who turned to be 24-year-old Keith Haring, the freewheeling, trailblazing, wildly ambitious, and unbelievably productive young firebrand who would become an indelible icon of the 1980s.

When Julia applied for the job, Haring was traveling abroad. Still, Tony Shafrazi, upon meeting Julia and hearing her qualifications, hired her on the spot. Haring had no idea that an assistant had been hired for him, and it was only after he returned from Europe that he met her.

Clearly, Shafrazi had made a wise choice. Julia had already been familiar with Haring's subway drawings and seemed very responsive to his work. She was conversant in French and Italian and had a smattering of German. She had an analytic mind. Her background in art history, her great love of music, both classical and popular, her knowledge of dance, her considerable writing skills, and her good looks (yes, this is her father speaking!) all helped land her the job. Besides all that, she had a terrific sense of humor and a charm and sophistication that counteracted Haring's somewhat awkward social façade and manner. Haring may not have known what and who he was getting, but what he got was choice.

Thus it was that Julia moved into Keith Haring's studio at 611 Broadway, where he and a young graffiti collaborator, LA II (Angel Ortiz), created an office space for her, decorating it from top to bottom with brilliant all-over patterns, an on-site work of blinding energy.

Julia recalled her first meeting with Keith Haring: "I liked him—just this guy in a studio. I really liked him a lot. Now, Keith never had a personal assistant before. He said, 'Am I supposed to ask you questions? Am I supposed to tell you what to do?' What really amused me no end was that his dealer, Tony Shafrazi, felt that I would have a maturing influence on this artist! Well, we were both exactly the same age, 24, and quite apart from my feelings about my being completely immature, I just couldn't see how I could be a maturing influence on him.

"Anyway, in 1984, I began working for Keith, doing everything from answering the phones to keeping the books to negotiating his contracts. I did it all and apparently did it well. Somehow I always knew that the most important thing I needed to do was to gain Keith's confidence. So I was always very honest and up-front with him. I also made it very clear to him that I had my own life, that I wasn't going to be just a little Haring-ette or a groupie. If he wants to invite me to a party, that's fabulous, but I'm not going to hang around smoking pot with him after work. And that was part of his trusting me. Because I was not after his fame, he understood that the glamour aspect of his life didn't interest me.

"Yet a lot of people would concur that once having met Keith—male or female, young or old—there always came a point where you did almost fall in love with him. It's crazy. I myself have fallen in love with plenty of gay men, and have suffered for it. But it wasn't like that with Keith—it wasn't about that. I mean, I wasn't attracted to him. It's just that there was this inexplicable something in him, an essence of goodness or trust or the essence in believing in someone and an innocence and generosity that just absolutely made you fall in love with him. Meeting Keith was meeting a person you would never meet again in your life—there would only be one!"

As Haring's career continued to expand, so did his personnel, and Julia came to run an office consisting of an accountant, a sales manager (for the many Haring products that began to emerge), and various assistants. As his international reputation increased, so did his trips to Europe and the Far East, many of them in the company of Julia serving as his front-ranking assistant on exhibitions, meetings, and publicity. There was no question that Haring relied on Julia more and more as she attended to the myriad details of his career–details that would free him to do his work and give him the time to paint and to play–the two things he enjoyed most in this world.

In time, Keith felt the need to move to a larger studio. Julia found him one at 676 Broadway, where the booming Haring "industry" would continue to flourish at its hectic and exhilarating pace. And close by, Haring's famous Pop Shop on Lafayette Street opened in 1986 to give him even further exposure and notoriety.

But true to her word, Julia also created a life of her very own.

At a Spring Gala held in 1985 by the New York City Ballet, she met a most dynamic and adorable man named R. Scott Asen, who promptly fell head-over-heels in love with her. A man of terrific appeal and almost as witty as Julia, he was a Harvard graduate, shorter than our willowy daughter, 15 years her senior, and dauntingly successful.

A venture capitalist, when they met, he was fast becoming a 1980s millionaire, while also spreading foot-tapping joy as a hugely talented down-and-dirty stride piano player. Indeed, when Scott came to our parties and sat down at our Steinway playing his raunchy renditions of classic jazz tunes, or when he sang those tunes in a lovely, lemony, off-the-cuff style, he instantly won every heart in the room.

Jane and I loved Scott Asen–and still do–and were sad when he and Julia, after four years of being together, split up. Happily, a love has remained between them, and the two continue to be close friends.

To speak of the 1980s is also to speak of the unspeakable. In fact, I don't really know how to talk about the great calamity of AIDS, except to say that it affected all of our lives in ways that were as unexpected as they were tragic. When, in 1981 and 1982 newspapers began publishing articles about a "gay cancer," none of us thought of it as a disease that would spread to epidemic proportions or as a disease unique to gay men.

As it turned out, the disease was not unique to gay men, but affected millions upon millions of straight men, women, children, and babies in various parts of the world, most notably Africa. But it was indeed a sexually transmitted disease and a high percentage of the victims seemed to be homosexual men.

This news spread like wildfire in New York and we, along with so many people working in the arts, became doubly concerned about our young gay friends, especially our young dancer friends, who were now burdened by the possibility of falling sick with an incurable illness. No medication seemed to effect a cure and the disease, with its frightening manifestations of skin lesions, devastating weight loss, and other debilitating symptoms, cut short the lives of endless, vibrant young men.

Suddenly, an atmosphere of fear and doom fell on the world of the young male dancer with news of one or another of them falling sick. At American Ballet Theatre alone, a whole crop of talented artists were stricken and died: Charles Ward, Clark Tippett, Peter Fonseca, Greg Osborne, David Cuevas. At the New York City Ballet, Tracy Bennett, Deni Lamont, Anthony Blum, and, most tragically for Julia and ourselves, John Bass, our sweet and loving corps-boy friend.

John, who died in 1985, was the first of our friends to bring the pain and suffering of AIDS close to home. It was misery to see this sunny, intelligent, beautiful boy deteriorating before our eyes. To the end, he tried to keep his spirits up, doing as much as he could to stay strong, being optimistic and witty and cheerful. We brought him out to Water Mill, where he had visited so many times before, and we tried not to show him our fear and our sadness.

When he died in his New York apartment, John was brought to Bellevue Hospital, and Jane and I were asked to identify his body.

There, in a darkened room, on a gurney, lay our sweet friend, John. It was unbearable.

Chapter 55

It would seem that the 1980s were a time for dying.

Nothing is more tragic than witnessing the death of the young. But, young or old, any death is marked by sorrow, and no one was more sorrowfully mourned than George Balanchine, when he died at age 79 on April 30, 1983, after a long illness.

Jane, Julia, and I attended Mr. B's funeral service, held at a Russian Orthodox Church on upper Madison Avenue, and stood for several hours holding a lit candle as a chorus of male voices lugubriously intoned the dirge-like Russian chants for the departed. During the service, we saw many familiar faces, from former wives to teachers to dancers to conductors to orchestra members to office workers to theater personnel.

Looking particularly forlorn was Balanchine's long-time personal assistant, the totally wonderful Barbara Horgan, much loved by the City Ballet, and most kind and helpful to me throughout my ballet-writing years.

But sad as it all was, the legacy of George Balanchine's work would continue to make this a better world. We would return to see *Serenade* or *Vienna Waltzes* or *Concerto Barocco* or *Liebeslieder Walzer* or *Symphony in Three Movements* and be revitalized. We would see *Apollo* or *Danses Concertantes* or *Western Symphony* or *Jewels* or *Stars and Stripes, The Nutcracker,* or *Who Cares?* and know that all was right with the world.

Thank God for Balanchine, because the 80s continued to be the decade of death.

As already noted, Erik Bruhn, one of the world's great dancers, died in Toronto of lung cancer in 1986 when he was only in his mid-fifties.

And then there was Keith Haring.

It could be said that Keith was almost destined to die when he did. Given the circumstances of the times and within the context of his ever increasing popularity and celebrity, let alone his seemingly insatiable hedonism, Keith, was, as he himself told me, the perfect candidate to contract AIDS. It still seems utterly bizarre and unlikely that in the mid-80s Keith Haring, the most sought-after young artist of the moment, should have wanted me, the least hip-hop type imaginable, to write his biography.

I was well aware that sex, drugs, and rock-n-roll were rampant in the 80s and I was cognizant of the fact that, as in the 60s, a huge underground was at work shaping a vast new avant-garde. The East Village, as in my time, was once again rife with new clubs, galleries, venues for music, videos, theater, film, plus the miracles of computerized art. Too, there emerged the truly daring and dazzling world of graffiti art, which Keith would respond to though never participate in. Still, he befriended and sometimes even collaborated with some of its gifted practitioners.

Indeed, Keith, with his boundless energy, his love of making art, his great generosity, and his absolute certainty that art belonged to every man, woman and child put on this earth, this totally endearing young artist, called me up one day and said, "How would you like to write my biography?"

Of course, I instantly thought my daughter Julia, who was by now firmly ensconced in Haring's world, put him up to it. But, in fact this was not the case.

"Look," said Haring on the phone, "you've written about every artist who ever inspired me, and you've known these people personally–Andy Warhol, Roy Lichtenstein, Larry Rivers, Robert Rauschenberg, Jasper Johns–name them! Now you've got to write about me!"

"Keith, how old are you?" I said.

"I'm 29," he replied.

"Isn't that awfully young for a biography? You've still got a heap of living to do!"

At this point, I had absolutely no idea Keith had already tested HIV positive. I had no inkling he was sick. I told Keith I'd have to think about writing a book about him. And, frankly, now well into my sixties, I just didn't know if I was up to exploring the heady, fast-paced, unpredictable world of Keith Haring.

Several months passed. Then, one day, Julia called with the news that Keith had contracted full-blown AIDS, and was in treatment and taking lots of medications. She thought I should go ahead with the book. And I agreed.

Keith and I met for lunch in a Mexican restaurant in Greenwich Village to discuss his biography. I told him I had read a really good book by George Plimpton and Jean Stein about Edie Sedgwick, one of Andy Warhol's superstars. The book, called *Edie*, traced her life and background by way of interviews with every person that had ever been close to her, forming a kind of biographical oral history.

I told Keith that although *Edie* was written after Sedgwick had died, the format was one I felt comfortable with, given Keith's youth and relatively recent arrival on the art scene. Moreover, having him around, and having his voice sprouting ideas and feelings about everything under the sun would be a very big plus and, I told him, a boon to future art historians.

In short, in addition to doing major interviews with Keith himself, I would also interview everyone who meant anything to him, from his parents and sisters to his friends, teachers, fellow artists, lovers, collectors, gallery dealers, and museum directors. And, of course, I would attempt to have everyone speak very candidly and honestly about him. I told Keith that I expected no less of him, that I would want him to go deeply into himself to talk as honestly as he could about his life, his art, his lovers, and, yes, his illness.

"When do we start?" Keith said.

Prentice Hall agreed to publish the book, which would eventually be called *Keith Haring: The Authorized Biography.*

Keith, true to his word, not only made time for the project, but provided me with a long list of people he felt should be interviewed for the book. He also made time for the two of us to get together for long taping sessions, some of which took place in New York City, others, in our summer house in Water Mill.

In addition, Keith also arranged for us both to travel to Europe so that I might interview his many European friends, collectors, and dealers. Upon our return we flew to Los Angeles, where Keith again introduced me to people he felt should be part of his book. And, wherever we found ourselves, Keith always made time for some one-to-one talks and tapings. Moreover, because I do not drive, Keith rented cars, both in Europe and in California, and drove me everywhere. To say that Keith was being helpful is to underestimate his genuine desire to make this book project happen–and quickly.

Not once did Keith interfere with my taping sessions with others–in fact, he would absent himself the moment introductions were made. He'd take off on some appointment or other, then would pick me up when my sessions were over.

It should be understood that well before I undertook the writing of his book, Jane and I had gotten to know Keith Haring simply as a friend. He visited our home, he came to our parties. Of course, his being Julia's boss was the entrée to our close relationship, although, as an art critic, his work had been familiar to me even before Julia went to work for him. Still, I know it was because of Julia that Keith so very often included us in the exciting whirl of his social life.

I mean, here we were, twice his age and not a little weary, and yet he would insist we attend the parties he hosted at the latest clubs around the city, or would invite us to such classy restaurants as Mr. Chow, where a party of 100 of Keith's closest friends would nonchalantly imbibe endless bottles of Cristal champagne and eat the most exotic and expensive Asian foods.

Attending any of Keith's New York art openings was yet another iconic 1980s experience. Thousands upon thousands of people would show up at the Shafrazi Gallery in SoHo, where the atmosphere soon turned red hot and where people strained to look at work that was as electric and dizzying as it was erotically charged.

And at the exhilarating center of it all, amidst his high-voltage paintings, stood Keith in his high-top sneakers, his T-shirt and Harold Lloyd glasses, his crooked grin, his wiry, abrupt gestures, signing posters of his show or talking animatedly to the various arbiters in the worlds of art, fashion, photography, music, movies, theater, dance; to collectors, to dealers; to everyone from Madonna to Andy Warhol and back. These were real Keith Haring events, real Keith Haring happenings—unique unto themselves as symbols of a tumultuous era where an excess of drugs, fame, talent, money, loud music, and illness collided to produce unbelievable highs and terrible lows.

All this, and more, I witnessed way before any mention of a Haring book. But then came the writing of it. And just as I had begun to assemble, transcribe, and edit the many dozens of tapes which would constitute my Haring biography, Keith's condition started to deteriorate. Near the end of January, 1990, Julia reported that Keith was unable to make it to the studio, that he had begun to develop respiratory problems, and that his immune system was in chaos.

On February 16, 1990, Keith Haring, age 31, died in his duplex apartment on New York's LaGuardia Place. The death-filled 80s had just ended, and there seemed little hope that the 90s would diminish the flow of AIDS victims.

Keith never saw or read his biography, which was duly published in 1991, came out as a Simon & Schuster paperback in 1992, and along with a British edition was translated into German, Dutch, Japanese, and Italian. It was serialized in various magazines, including *Vanity Fair*, and, I dare say, *Keith Haring: The Authorized Biography*, with its great cover photograph of the artist by William Coupon, proved a wonderful success. Would Keith have liked it? I'd like to think so. But then, one never knows. What is certain is that the book and Keith's own words in it truly stand as a testament to who he was, what he believed in and what he hoped to accomplish as an artist.

Keith's will instructed that Julia Gruen be made executive director and board member of the Keith Haring Foundation, as well as coexecutor of his estate, positions she holds to this day.

On Keith's 32nd birthday, May 4, 1990, Julia Gruen organized his memorial. It proved an extraordinary event.

Thousands filled the Cathedral Church of St. John the Divine. Mayor David Dinkins spoke, Jessye Norman sang, Heather Watts and Jock Soto of the New York City Ballet danced. Keith's family was there—his parents, Joan and Allen, his sisters, Kay, Karen, and Kristen, his closest friend, Kermit Oswald and his family. There were many speakers and performers. It was all incredibly moving. Keith Haring, an awkward, unprepossessing boy from Kutztown, Pennsylvania, had now moved into the realm of American popular culture—a beloved, visionary young artist, whose irrepressible sense of jubilance and justice produced an imagery that was as powerful, witty, and indelible as it was original.

Chapter 56

Enough of death!

Let's get back to me, my work as writer, critic, journalist, bon vivant, gadfly, busybody, father, husband, queer, neurotic workaholic. Let's just go back to my old self as handmaiden to the stars, reveler in reflected glory, and needy intimate of the super-famous.

Why was being with the stars so important to me?

As some have so delicately put it: "John Gruen is nothing but a star fucker." Some have said it was because I wanted desperately to be famous myself. To be a celebrity. To receive a star's attention and adulation. To get the best table in the best restaurant. To make as much money as they (actually, the pursuit of money was never a burning desire). To be placed within the realm of the publicly beloved and revered, to be admired and worshipped.

At the same time, I didn't really want any of that. I was smart enough to know there's always a price to be paid, always some awful suffering connected with it. The fact is, I was quite content in my role as intruder to the stars, the newspaper man possessed of a certain power, to whom the stars presented their most felicitous face. I did enjoy the frisson of being the one to get them to open up and tell me all their secrets—well, almost all their secrets.

And it was genuine joy to meet them all, from Bette Davis to Francis Bacon, from Lena Horne to Lucian Freud, from Vladimir Horowitz to Henry Fonda, from Maria Callas to Judy Garland, from Leopold Stokowski to Sir John Gielgud, from Angela Lansbury to Samuel Beckett, from Renata Tebaldi to Jean Louis Barrault, from Tennessee Williams to Lotte Lenya—and so many more. (Talk about name-dropping!)

All my editors trusted me to make good on getting all my subjects to open up and talk—to get them to reveal not only matters pertaining to their profession or craft but to their inner selves—some facet of their lives that would afford readers an unexpected glimpse into the "real" person they were reading about.

And that's what I gave them—again and again. And, I must say, some of the stories I gathered were pretty personal, some quite moving, others quite riveting.

Gian Carlo Menotti and his adopted son, Chip

Maria Callas, ca. 1970; photograph by Michael Ochs Archives/Getty Images

Judy Garland in her London hotel suite, ca. 1970; photograph by Keystone/Getty Images

John Gruen with Lena Horne (*bottom left*), John Gruen with Bette Davis (*bottom center*), New York City, 1972; photographs by Alix Jeffry

John Gruen with Joanne Woodward, New York City, 1980s

Samuel Beckett, New York City, 1964

Julia Gruen, John Gruen, Erik Bruhn, Lisa Rinehart, New York City, 1970s; photograph by Jane Wilson

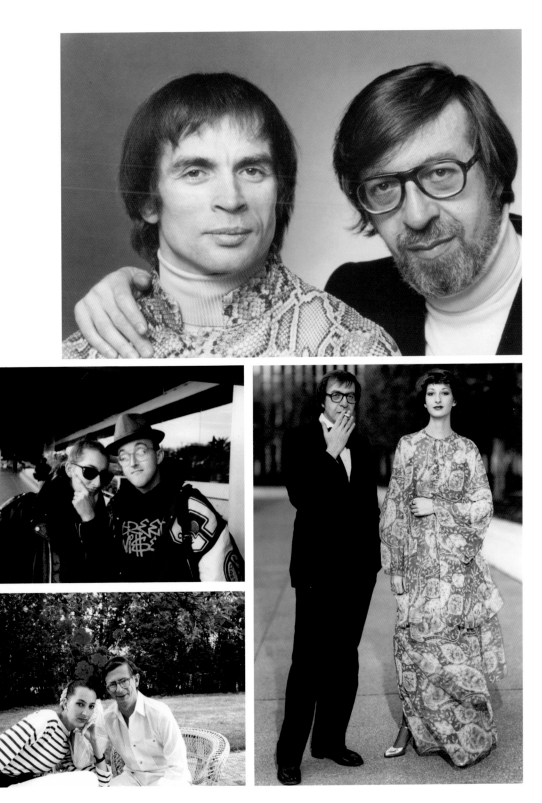

Rudolf Nureyev and John Gruen, New York City, 1975; photograph by Jack Mitchell

Julia Gruen and Keith Haring, Monte Carlo, 1989

Julia Gruen and Scott Asen, Water Mill, New York, 1988

John and Julia Gruen, New York City; photograph by Richard Avedon

Jane Wilson paintings
top left: "Descending Moon," 1991; *top right:* "Solstice," 1991; *bottom:* "Moon and Wheat," 1990; courtesy DC Moore Gallery, New York

Julia Gruen with Ulrik Trojaborg (*top left*) and with Jock Soto (*center left*), Water Mill, NY, 1994

Heather Watts and Jock Soto; photograph by Paul Kolnik, courtesy of New York City Ballet

Fortieth wedding anniversary gift for John Gruen and Jane Wilson, March 28, 1988. Forty babies, written dedication, and center drawing by Keith Haring. *Top:* Heather Watts; *center:* Scott Asen, Jock Soto, Ulrik Trojaborg, Nilas Martins; *bottom:* Bruce Padgett, Julia Gruen, Peter Martins; photograph by Steven Caras

Ulrik Trojaborg, Heather Watts, Chester held by Scott Asen, Water Mill, NY, 1991

Tiziano and Angela Terzani, Florence, Italy, 1998

Shirley and George Perle, New York City, 2001

Sidney Talisman, Jane Wilson, and Alvin Novak, Water Mill, NY, 2001

Margaret Logan and Charles Coulter, with their 1928 Chrysler Imperial,
Southampton, NY, 2002

Scott Murphree, Water Mill, NY, 2004

Lukas and Cornelia Foss, New York City, 2002

Julia Gruen with Chester, Water Mill, NY, November 1999

Jane Wilson and Julia Gruen on Jane's 81st Birthday, Water Mill, NY, April 29, 2005

John Gruen, Southampton, NY, 2002; photograph by Jane Wilson

Since newspaper and magazine interviews are and have always been tenuous diversions with the shortest possible lifespans (unless they end up in libraries, book collections or the internet), I thought I'd dig up some of my more memorable interviews, quote from them, and recall some of the circumstances surrounding them.

Maria Callas, for example.

It was 1971. She had not performed in an opera since 1965. Her career had come to a standstill, but she had accepted an invitation from the Juilliard School in New York to hold a series of master classes. She had also made her straight acting debut starring in Pier Paolo Pasolini's film *Medea*. The movie was set to open shortly in New York.

I reach Callas at the Plaza Hotel. A *New York Times* interview is arranged.

"Will you take me to dinner?" says the languorous, softly accented voice on the telephone. "We can dine in the Oak Room downstairs."

"But of course," I reply.

"Be sure you get a quiet table in the rear. Be sure a telephone is at the table. Shall we meet tomorrow? I'll be at the restaurant at eight."

I secure the table. I secure the telephone. I order a drink. I wait. Then she appears. Callas! La Divina! Tall, slim, solitary, her sleek, dark hair pulled back in a chignon, she stands in the darkened entrance of the elegant restaurant. She wears a green, red, and brown paisley floor-length dinner gown. The maître d' brings her to our table. I rise. I look into her eyes. I kiss her hand. We sit. I am enthralled.

At 47, Callas is gorgeous. Her face has extraordinary strength, with a wide, intelligent brow, aquiline nose, and large liquid eyes. We order drinks. She asks for a vermouth cassis. I order another bourbon sour. Callas asks to taste my drink. She finds it delicious and promptly steals my orange slice. She eats it with a smile. We talk of her master classes.

"I would like to pass on to the young ones what I myself have learned– what I've learned from the great conductors I've worked with, from my teachers, and especially from my own research, which has not stopped to this day. My aim was never to make a career. It was to serve music. And what I wish to accomplish with my young people is to draw their own individual abilities so that they will go out there and fight for music, so that they will carry on what I myself have fought for all my life."

For dinner, Callas orders roast beef "very, very rare" and some string beans. I casually compliment her on her slimness and broach the subject of her former weight, which in her early years was considerable. She throws me a certain glance, then smiles and says, "Yes, I have lost a great deal of weight–it's no secret. When I made my very first recordings, *Lucia, La Gioconda,* I was still heavy. When I recorded *Traviata* around 1953 I had already lost about 35 pounds. All my other Angel recordings–and there have been many–were done as you see me now, with all the weight lost. The fact is, I chose to lose weight and it certainly did not affect my voice. The fact is, when you portray a beautiful woman, you should not be fat. It's an injustice to the public. We owe them a total performance. Also a woman's vanity enters into it. Why should a woman be heavy, if she can be lighter?"

I ask Callas whether she has stopped singing, whether she has permanently retired from the stage, since she has not appeared in public for six years.

"I have not stopped singing," she replies quite forcefully. "I work on my old roles every day. I take a lesson every day. When I am ready I will return. But if I will not return, I will not make a tragedy of it. The trouble with returning to the stage is that the public always wants more and more and more. If you give of yourself 100 percent one time, they expect 200 percent the next time. And then 300 percent. When the public gives you triumph, it demands more and more, and I can't fight that. I find that terrifying."

Dinner over (without the plugged-in phone ringing or being used once), and after much talk about her unhappy childhood, her estranged parents and sister, and her difficult marriage to Giovanni Battista Meneghini, Callas invites me to her suite on the Plaza's 17th floor. She offers a glass of brandy. We sit in beautifully upholstered easy chairs, a coffee table between us.

"I would rather not talk about Onassis, and you are trying to make me talk about him," says Callas in a chiding voice. "I will only say that it was an experience. We both have very strong personalities. And he could be quite cruel. When he began his relationship with Mrs. Kennedy and began inviting her on his yacht, he forbade me to be on the yacht with her. He did not wish his mistress to meet the wife of a president. This was cruel.

"At any rate, all I can say is that when one person tries to change the other, then it's time to go. And that cuts a long story short. I cannot be changed and neither would I have liked to change him.

"As for my career, there were times when I was under very, very heavy attack. That's when you show yourself, when you find out whether you have self-control or not. I will tell you that I have hit bottom quite frequently, but I never show it. I consider it bad manners. Furthermore, I never attack.

People have said that Callas has her way of fighting. Well, my way of fighting is not fighting. Once somebody declares war on me, that's when I freeze completely. I do not show anything. It costs me a great deal, of course.

"I was given fame, and when I had it, I thought I could finally relax, and just continue to make good music. Well, I was wrong. You have to fight to keep alive. Naturally, I have a temperament, that's why I'm considered an artist. I have a mind of my own—I know what I have to do. And I don't like being told what to do, because I work harder than anybody.

"But look I have an offstage life as well. I am a very normal human being. I am healthy-minded. I have good judgment. When I'm offstage, I'm just like any other normal woman who goes shopping, goes to the movies and shames her friends, because she comments on a lot of things or screams with laughter or cries like an idiot. Yes, I have very few friends, but the ones I have are true to me. To tell you the truth, I do not like being called La Divina. I resent it. I am Maria Callas. And I am only a woman."

At that, Callas rises. "It is getting late," she said.

I also rise as she walks me to the door. Callas stops. I stand before her. She looks up at me and with great tenderness places her arms around me and kisses me on the lips. It is a lingering kiss—a magical kiss. She whispers, "Good night." I leave the room. I walk down the hall. I wait for the elevator.

I am still mesmerized by our farewell. I almost say it out loud: "Callas kissed me!"

Maria Callas, the most influential operatic soprano of the twentieth century, died in Paris in 1977. She was only 53.

Samuel Beckett, the 1969 Nobel Prize winner for literature, was a man deeply acquainted with nihilism and depression.

"The major sin is the sin of being born," he told me in a whisper. "Even before the fetus can draw breath it is in a state of barrenness and of pain. I have a clear memory of my own fetal existence. It was an existence where no voice, no possible movement could free me from the agony and darkness I was subjected to."

We are in the home of his American publisher, Barney Rosset, who, as publisher of Grove Press and my former boss, brought out Beckett's first U.S. publications.

Beckett does not want to talk to me, has no interest whatever in an interview for *Vogue*. But I assure him it will help the sale of his books in this country. He reluctantly relents.

As he speaks, Beckett's head is bowed. Slowly he lifts his face. His eyes meet mine. They are cold, dispassionate eyes, pale blue, set in a skeletal, lined, and craggy face.

In awarding Beckett the Nobel Prize, Karl Ragnar Gierow, secretary of the Swedish Academy, said: "The degradation of humanity is a recurrent theme in Beckett's writing, and to this extent his philosophy, simply accentuated by elements of the grotesque and of tragic farce, can be said to be a negativism that knows no haven. But Samuel Beckett has a love of mankind that grows in understanding as it plumbs further into the depths of abhorrence."

I ask Beckett to speak of his writing.

"I cannot do it," he answers. "It is impossible, because I am constantly working in the dark. It would be like an insect leaving his cocoon. I can only estimate my work from within. If my work has any meaning at all it is due more to ignorance, inability, and an intuitive despair than to any individual strength. I think that I have perhaps freed myself from certain formal concepts. Perhaps, like the composer Schoenberg or the painter Kandinsky, I have turned toward an abstract language. Unlike them, however, I have tried not to concretize the abstraction."

Beckett makes his home in Paris, but he was born in Ireland on April 13, 1906. He moved to Paris in the 1920s. His first two novels, *Murphy* and *Watt*, were written in English. His subsequent novels, *Molloy, Malone Dies, The Unnamable,* and *How It Is,* were written in French. In 1953, his play *Waiting for Godot* proved a vast international success. Other plays, *Krapp's Last Tape, Happy Days,* and *Play,* followed. All of Beckett's writing is steeped in desperation, but its content and style illuminates the human condition in ways that are humorous, poetic, and enigmatic. Above all, he views existence as agonizing and remorselessly futile.

Beckett wants the interview to end. He continues to stare at the floor. Suddenly he says, "Writing becomes not easier, but more difficult for me. Every word is like an unnecessary stain on silence and nothingness." He adds, "Democritus pointed the way: 'Naught is more than nothing.'"

Beckett hated his stay in New York. He disliked its tempo and its people. "People look unhappy here," he says. "Even young housewives with their heavy shopping bags carry about them a sense of despair. And I sense great hostility in the faces of the men. But, of course, that's inevitable. It is the weight of every man's fear and emptiness that produces this look. Somewhere he must know that self-perception is the most frightening of all human observations. He must know that when man faces himself, he is looking into the abyss."

Chapter 57

The sob queen of all time, Judy Garland, had come to town–to the Hotel St. Regis. I instantly alerted the *Times* and asked to do the interview. I was overjoyed and hastened to prostrate myself at her feet, because, needless to say, I was one of her most ardent fans.

Like every other self-respecting quasi-gay boy, I had fallen in love with Judy while still living in Italy, first as Mickey Rooney's pal and some-time heartthrob in all those Andy Hardy movies, and then, when I got to America, as Dorothy in *The Wizard of Oz.*

Throughout the years, I suffered through the various sagas of her very bumpy life, from her pill addictions to her turbulent marriages, from her fat periods to her thin periods to the drugs and the alcohol, from the total glory of some of her greatest movies (*Ziegfeld Girl, Meet Me in St. Louis, A Star Is Born*) to the ecstatic highs of her concert performances, all the way down to her sad, ignominious death on June 22, 1969. Judy Garland, broke, sick, homeless, dead at 47.

I desperately needed to come face to face with this 45-year-old monu-ment to suffering, this paragon of survival and showbiz glitz and glitter. And there she stood, thin as a rail, in a little black dress, standing amidst her chattering children, Liza, Lorna, Joey, and her future son-in-law, Peter Allen, in one of the messiest hotel rooms it had ever been my pleasure to lay eyes on.

Wherever you looked there was chaos: open suitcases on the bed, clothes spilling out of them, clothes strewn across chairs, thrown on sofas and on the floor, half-filled glasses everywhere, liquor bottles, newspa-pers, magazines, record albums, jars of makeup, bottles of pills, bottles of perfume, phone messages, bills, photographs–pure, unadulterated movie star chaos.

"Please make yourself comfortable," says Judy, all giggles and smiles, "if you can find a place to sit, that is. The children are just off. Now, let me order us some shrimp from room service–you like shrimp, don't you? And let's get some drinks too."

It's spring of 1967. Garland has come to New York to attend her daughter Liza's wedding to Peter Allen. She's also here to hold a press conference, arranged by Twentieth Century Fox, about her forthcoming role in *Valley of the Dolls,* Jacqueline Susann's epic tribute to Hollywood stardom at its most drug-drenched and sex-besotted.

When everyone has left, Judy clears a space on a large sofa, plunks herself down, and motions me to sit by her. The shrimp and a bottle of vodka arrive. At last, we are alone. But the phone rings. Judy answers it. It can't be good news. Judy sounds frantic, furious, and at the end, resigned. It's a long phone call. Finally, she hangs up.

"You don't want to know what I'm going through," she says, lighting a cigarette. "That phone call–they're taking my house in California; the banks are taking it. I don't really know what happened. Well, if worst comes to worst, I can always pitch a tent in front of the Beverly Hilton and Lorna can sing gospel hymns! That should see us through, somehow!

"In a way, I'm glad they're taking the house. It's too big, too impractical. Besides, the man who lived there before didn't love his wife. That sort of put a pall on it from the beginning. There are acres of gardens, and a swimming poll, and the place needs at least four servants and four gardeners to keep it in shape. I never really liked it. It looks like a Gloria Swanson reject. I say good riddance!"

Everything is spoken with an anxious laugh. And, along with frequent swigs from a large glass of vodka, she lights one cigarette after the other. Judy is clearly stressed out. But she shows no bitterness, no anger, just a terrible helplessness.

Judy Garland has not appeared in a film since *I Could Go On Singing,* made in England in 1962. It was not a success, although Garland fans, including me, would have it otherwise. But she has had all manner of unkind press and producers have found her increasingly undependable. When Twentieth Century Fox offered *Valley of the Dolls*, she accepted immediately.

"My slanderous press already has me walking off the set," says Judy. "The set hasn't even been built, but already they have me walking off it! It's this kind of ugly slander that keeps me out of work. What am I supposed to do about it? I really need to work. I'm happiest when working and when I work I give a lot, because my job is entertaining. I love acting, and I especially love singing for an audience. No matter how many people hurt me, when the orchestra starts playing–I just sing!"

Judy's eyes light up and her words, spoken with that poignantly familiar break in her voice, ignite countless images of Garland singing all her songs, responding to the cheering crowds, transporting those who have cherished her ever since "Over the Rainbow" made her name synonymous with heartbreak and bittersweet joys.

We touch on her legend. Garland gets up with a short laugh. She walks around the room, takes another swig of her drink, lights another cigarette. "If I'm such a legend, then why am I so lonely?

"If I'm such a legend, then why do I sit at home for hours staring at the damned telephone, hoping it's out of order, even calling the operator asking her if she's sure it's not out of order. Let me tell you, legends are all very well if you've got somebody around who loves you, some man who's not afraid to be in love with Judy Garland!"

I look at Judy. Her face is gaunt, her eyes enormous. Just now, she seems anxious and disconnected. Still, there's that electric something that makes one feel protective of her. She reels around a bit. Suddenly, she goes to the bed and picks up an LP record.

"Mercury pressed this in 1964, but never released it," she says. "That just about killed me. They said I sound lousy on it—that I'm not up to snuff. Now, just listen to this record and tell me if I sound lousy on it."

Judy puts the test pressing on the record player, and a song from Noel Coward's *Sail Away* starts it off. Judy comes on singing it in an upbeat tempo and her voice comes across fast, loud and clear. This is followed by "Something's Coming" from *West Side Story*, which Judy sings with that held-in, always charged intensity of hers.

As the song gathers momentum, Judy in the room begins singing along with Judy on the record, throwing up her arm, hunching her body, now raising herself on the balls of her feet and belting out the song, now stopping and laughing and saying, "Christ! That doesn't sound bad! That song works!"

The record spins along. Next comes "Just in Time." "Listen to the key changes in there, will you. Doesn't that just about kill you?" Judy sings along again, her voice warm and supple, always a bit trembly.

The foreclosure of her house forgotten, the slander forgotten, the loneliness forgotten, Judy sings with Judy on the unreleased record and nothing really seems to matter. She's up there giving a performance and she knows she's got everyone in the palm of her hand, because she's Judy Garland and there's nobody, but nobody, like her!

And so, on a more or less happy note, our interview ends. There is a glow around Judy. I can't resist embracing her. She's so frail! She's so vulnerable. She's so helpless. She's so—Judy Garland!

As it turned out, Judy, ever frantic, ever anxious, never did get to make *Valley of the Dolls*. Besieged by insecurities, her on-the-set behavior was described as "untenable," and no amount of love, admiration, and devotion could induce her producers to put up with Judy's demands, delays, and tantrums. So they dropped her and replaced her with Susan Hayward.

Chapter 58

The most enigmatic of my many subjects was the painter Lucian Freud, Sigmund's grandson.

I had been told that he detested interviews and that I'd have a very difficult time obtaining one. But obtain one I did in London, in September of 1977. I was on assignment for *ARTnews* magazine, and Freud's London art dealer, Anthony d'Offay, seemed to have persuaded Freud that an article in one of America's most popular art magazines would be beneficial to his career, which in 1977 was not yet the career it is today.

It is arranged that Freud and I meet at the d'Offay Gallery at 9 Dering Street. I arrive early. D'Offay is cordial but somewhat on edge. Freud might not show up at all. But then, a slim, somewhat unkempt figure enters the gallery. This is Lucian Freud. Wearing dark brown, baggy corduroy pants, a loose tweed jacket, and a dark wool scarf knotted around his neck, he has the rumpled look of someone who had gone without sleep for days. The face, covered with what appears to be three-day stubble, is extraordinary—a composite of the poetic features of Jean-Louis Barrault and Charles Baudelaire. The eyes, a watery blue-green, are restless and intelligent. D'Offay makes introductions.

Freud has brought with him a small painting wrapped in a sheet. He removes the sheet and hands the work to d'Offay. It is a portrait of an elderly woman. I ask who it is.

"It's my mother," Freud says. "I've done several portraits of her recently. She's nearly 80, and very abstracted. I pick her up in the mornings, and we have breakfast somewhere. Then we come up to my studio, and I paint her. It's strange. She used to be a very aggressive woman. She was like that all her life, and I saw very little of her—didn't want to see her—didn't like being with her. Then, when my father died, she tried to kill herself. She was saved by a rather nasty relative of ours, a woman who enjoyed tormenting me. Anyway, after that, my mother changed radically, and became very docile. I began to see her and, for the first time, paint her."

This personal revelation notwithstanding, Freud announces he cannot give me an interview. "Interviews mean nothing to me. I only do things that have some meaning for me."

I ask Freud if I might at least visit his studio.

"Very well, I'll drive you there. My car is just outside."

The car, as it turns out, is a magnificent Rolls-Royce, a Silver Cloud, a bit dusty for wear, but extremely elegant. We drive in silence for some 20 minutes, passing from neighborhood to neighborhood, until we reach a particularly desolate section of London. Freud refuses to divulge the exact location of his studio, and is relieved to note that the city and its unfamiliar sections were an enigma to me.

Finally, the Rolls stops in front of a row of rundown tenement houses facing an empty school playground. Getting out of the car, Freud leads the way to one of these houses, which I observe, bears no number, no name-plate, no bell. He unlocks the front door. We climb a short flight of stairs. The studio consists of two small rooms, each more or less identical in size, and each containing a single bed, an easel, a painting table, and one or two chairs. There are newspapers, magazines, and books strewn on the unmade beds, and both rooms bear a general mustiness and untidiness. Freud tells me that one of the rooms serves as his daytime studio, while the other is used exclusively for nighttime painting.

"I have daytime models and nighttime models," he explains. "The people who pose for me at night are encouraged to fall asleep, because I like painting the sleeping figure. I need very little sleep myself, and often paint long into the night."

In the daytime studio, the walls are splattered with multicolored dots of pigment. "It's a way of reminding me which colors I've used, before I mix the paints." Aside from the tiny splatters of paint, the walls are covered with innumerable scribbles, names, telephone numbers, addresses, and cryptic messages. Nervously, and almost too rapidly, Freud places several small canvases on the easel. Some of the paintings are finished, others are in progress. One work is a head of his mother. As in the painting he had brought to d'Offay, the expression of the old woman bears a feeling of terrifying withdrawal and inwardness. Another painting shows a portly, middle-aged man, sitting rigidly in a chair. "He's a businessman. I liked the way he looked, and asked him to pose. He sits very, very still." Two other small portraits, one of a young sad-eyed woman, the other of a tense young man, are painted with what might be termed obsessive realism.

As in all of Freud's work, a mysterious "otherness" makes itself felt, as if each subject is somehow hypnotized by the artists, as if Freud himself transfixes his sitters in ways that render them vulnerable to their own state of anxiety and fear. This relentless concern with the psychological can be understood in the light of Lucian Freud's own background and artistic development.

Born in December 1922, Freud lived in Berlin until 1933. His father was Ernst Freud, an architect, and a son of Sigmund Freud. The family was well-off and privileged. Summers were spent near Potsdam, on the estate of Freud's maternal grandparents. Leading a comfortable and cultivated bourgeois life, the family soon found itself in the grip of a political atmosphere that disrupted the pattern of its existence. From 1929, seven-year-old Lucian was exposed to schoolmates eagerly mimicking their elders in "games" of looting, lighting fires, and placing ominous symbols on the walls. He saw destructive and dangerous street gangs jeering at Jews, and fell victim to fears he had never encountered before. The effect of these notorious circumstances marked young Freud for life. He knew the enemy at firsthand, and his imagination was shocked into a lasting subversion and anger.

When, in 1933, the Freud family settled in London, the youngster, now aged ten, carried his confusion and anger to alien ground. Far from seeking acceptance in a new and welcoming country, he sought immediate independence, resisting the "safety" of a normal education. He was in and out of schools with regularity, preferring the color and chaos of the London street scene, through which he would roam, fixing his attention upon the faces he would much later celebrate in paint. At 17, he published his first drawing, a self-portrait, in Cyril Connolly's magazine *Horizon*. At 19, he stowed away abroad a merchant ship, and for five months was on convoy duty. Throughout, he would draw endlessly, and, upon leaving the Merchant Navy, resolved to work full-time as an artist.

In 1974, the Hayward Gallery in London gave Freud a retrospective exhibition. Here, one could chart the artist's development as an acutely receptive investigator of a relentlessly private vision. The exhibition made clear Freud's adherence to a style that is unique by virtue of its poetic and awkward logic. Nighttime nudes contain a sealed-in, claustrophobic intimacy that suggests a threatening and perverse languor. Several portraits of naked girls, done in the 60s, recall the work of Francis Bacon, minus the stark terror. And yet, the poses and general ambiance have that fearful "something" that gives Freud's oeuvre its intonation of emotional disarrangement and paralysis. Even the lush and steely still lifes have it.

Finally, however, it is the portraits, the faces of the people he knows, that mark Freud as an artist of uncommon strength and originality.

Freud once wrote, "My work is purely autobiographical. It's about myself and my surroundings. It is an attempt at a record. I work from the people that interest me, and that I care about. In rooms that I live in and know. I use the people to invent my pictures with, and I can work more freely when they are there."

Now, as Freud and I stand in his studio, he reiterates these sentiments. "I have to be close to these people. I have to understand them. I must know what they're feeling. It's the only way to get at the essence of their character."

Freud's words are interrupted by a sudden loud knock at the downstairs door. He runs down the stairs and returns with a telegram. "It's from one of my daughters," he tells me. "She says she's feeling blue and wants to see me. You see, she's just broken up with her husband. I must go to her."

But instead of making haste to see his daughter, Freud presently invites me to have a drink with him at a nearby pub. We return to the Rolls, and drive a short distance before stopping at yet another rundown section of London. We enter what appears to be a laborer's bar.

"I don't really have a neighborhood pub, but this is the one I like." The place is very large, and boasts a billiard table standing near a spacious rectangular bar. Workmen of all sorts seem to know Freud. There are greetings all around. We sit at the bar, and Freud enters into a brief conversation with a burly house builder. He chats amiably with the bartender, a husky man with friendly eyes. Freud orders absinthe. At the same time, he orders a drink for an old, stooped man sitting some distance from us. When the drink is placed before him, the old man looks up and feebly waves to Freud in silent thanks. Freud seems moderately relaxed as we sit drinking amidst the clicking of billiard balls.

In this atmosphere of congenial camaraderie, I venture to question Freud about his childhood, his family, his life.

"What kind of boy was I? Well, I had a very conventional childhood in Berlin. Then, around 1929, I became aware of being a Jew. Suddenly, one was an outsider, someone to be hunted down. I rebelled, of course, and became very resentful. I would disappear from home and let no one know where I was. I was very secretive and would drive my parents wild. Anyway, in 1932 we came to England. I have two brothers, one younger, one older. The eldest, Stephen, has become conventional to the point of eccentricity. He plays golf, and never does anything out of the ordinary. My younger brother, Clement, has become a very public figure.

"He's become a household word in London. He's a member of the House of Parliament. He lectures. He writes. He's a TV personality. He makes dog food commercials. Everybody knows who he is. I can't really tolerate him. He's become absurd. My mother says it's all my doing. But I don't see how. Anyway, I never see him.

"I've been married several times. Once to Jacob Epstein's daughter, another time to a titled girl, a Guinness heiress, Lady Caroline Blackwood. I hated the society part of all that. I have several children strewn about. But I only get the pleasure out of them. I take them out or go to see them. Basically, I am a loner. I do as I please. My day starts early. I like working in the mornings. Usually, I pick up my mother and see her or paint her. In the afternoon, I wander about. I like walking the streets. I call people from street phones. I see very few people, actually. I have rooms in various places. I don't have one permanent address—no house."

Freud speaks quickly and in staccato sentences. Though relatively at ease, an undercurrent of impatience makes itself felt. It is almost as though the very sound of his words grate on him or, more likely, that the allusion to his private life seems an irritant that renders him deeply uncomfortable. Still, the answers come, and with unusual candor.

"My family has never forgiven me for not attending my grandfather's funeral. But I found doing so would have been utterly meaningless to me. I don't carry the burden of being Sigmund Freud's grandson. It is not a weight on me. Of course, I remember him, and I knew him to be always very good, very kind, very modest. He had two children, Anna and my father, Ernst. Anna Freud has become a most eccentric and strange woman. Freud wanted her to lead a normal life, but she decided to dedicate her life entirely to him. She never married. After her father's death she became a world-famous lecturer and writer on Freud. But she also became a complete recluse, never going out, never seeing a play, a movie, an exhibition. I was told that as a child she had strange habits. For example, she would never put on a single garment unless it was first crushed and crumpled by her governess. As she grew older, she became a very harsh and formidable woman. I must say, I never really liked her. She could also be cruel. When my mother married my father, Anna told her that she would find Ernst nothing much, once she got to know him, things like that.

"Now, Anna has become an old woman. She looks very strange, all stooped over, like a hunchback. She has little use for me or my brothers. And I resent her. I remember when I went to art school here in London, she once expressed admiration for a portrait drawing I did. I must have been about 16. I decided to give her the portrait as a gift, but told her that she would have to have it framed, because I hadn't any money at the time. Well, she was unwilling to spend the money on the frame, and never took the drawings. That left its mark, of course. But my memories of my grandfather are very good. He was a gentle man, very full of love for us."

Freud pauses. Then, taking several more sips of absinthe, continues to reflect on his illustrious relative.

"My grandfather always knew that drugs would ultimately help to alleviate psychological problems. But he also knew that the human element would, at times, prevent drugs from being effective. Anyway, when he was still alive, he never realized that his writings and his books would one day be read the world over. When he drew up his will, he stated that if there should ever be any royalties from his writings, they would be divided between his three grandchildren. Well, you can imagine! The royalties became astronomical, and we, the three grandchildren, receive quite a large income. Naturally, his own children—my father and especially Anna—were furious. Anna felt it was a grave, grave injustice for the grandchildren to receive all that money, particularly since she feels that none of us care a hoot about Freud's writings.

"I must confess I've not read many of my grandfather's works. I read his *Studies on Hysteria*, which I liked very much, but I've not read much beyond that. I've never been psychoanalyzed myself. I'm very wary of it."

Turning to his life as an artist, Freud claims that he is as much of a loner among his fellow artists as with people in general. "If I have a best friend, it must be Francis—Francis Bacon. I've known him a very long time. We went to school together. Of course, he has a very different personality. He is very gregarious and can do things I could never do. He is a less private person. Back in the 50s I did what I think is a rather successful portrait of him. Actually, I don't see much of Bacon these days. You see, I don't see much of anyone. If I see anyone, it's the people I paint."

Freud finishes his absinthe. He rises, pays for the drinks, and makes brief farewells to his pub acquaintances. "I suppose I'd better go and see my daughter. She'll need some comforting. Come along—I'll drop you at your flat."

Back in the Rolls, Freud drives in silence. Indeed, the artist seems to have fallen into a long reverie that emphatically excludes the stranger next to him. At my door Freud stops the car. My departing "thank yous" draw no response. He merely stares at me, then drives away.

Chapter 59

And so it went. More and more interviews year after year after year.

When the 1980s hit, with their calamitous presence of AIDS, a new sense of seriousness and concern fell upon the New York arts community. My interviews now frequently included talk of death, of AIDS, of illness, of everyone's innate fragility. And it seemed as though with whomever I spoke evinced a newfound love and respect for the work they were involved with and for the miracle–and brevity–of life.

As it turned out, along with my ongoing magazine and newspaper work, two major new interviewing avenues opened up to me during the 1980s. The first brought me in close and hugely satisfying contact with a large radio-listening audience. I became part of the all-classical New York music station, WNCN, which gave me the opportunity to present a weekly, hour-long program I named *The Sound of Dance*. Its focus was on the city's many dance events, from which I invited company directors, choreographers, or dancers to come on the air to discuss their particular seasons, programs, or careers. The format also included recordings of music from the ballets or modern dance works being presented. It seemed a wonderful way of publicizing the city's dance events and, more importantly, bringing dancers and choreographers into the homes of thousands of listeners who seldom if ever had the chance to meet the idealized and seemingly mysterious people of the dance world.

I did this for ten years, until the station folded. I loved being a radio host. It was wonderful talking to Martha Graham, Merce Cunningham, Paul Taylor, Lar Lubovitch, Twyla Tharp, Mark Morris, George Balanchine, Frederick Ashton, Antony Tudor, and to the famous or fledgling dancers who, under my insistent prodding, revealed their private and professional lives week after week. And I loved working with the people at the station–the wonderful engineer, Charles Pitts, the splendidly intense music director, David Dubal, and his very engaging assistant, Margaret Mercer.

But I positively hated the man the station brought in to revitalize its programming, one Mario Mazza, a singularly unpleasant and oily individual, whose creepy personality made most everyone at the station cringe—especially me.

My other 80s interviewing venue was the Metropolitan Museum of Art, in whose Grace Rainey Rogers Auditorium I conducted live interviews with people in the arts—from choreographers to ballet dancers to jazz singers to film stars. I lectured at the Met for some ten years, and the person I dealt with there was Hilde Limondjian, a woman whose veneer of sweetness and light concealed a steely, arrogant toughness. To me, every word out of her mouth sounded insincere—and she seemed a paragon of honeyed hypocrisy.

Finally, we parted ways over, what else, money. The Met Museum was raking in thousands of dollars from almost all of my events, and I was paid a pittance. When I asked for an increase in pay, the sickeningly saccharine Ms. Limondjian refused—and I called it quits. But lecturing for years at the Met was a real feather in my cap—and, I dare say, a number of my evenings, notably "The Balanchine Ballerinas," "The Balanchine Men," "The Balanchine Wives," "Five Ladies of Jazz," and "Douglas Fairbanks, Jr.: His Life and Films" proved enormously popular.

As the 80s drew to a close, I had been working as a journalist, critic and lecturer for some 35 years—and I was reaching the ripe old age of 65. It was an age of a certain consequence, not yet entirely over the hill, but old enough to experience a certain ennui at the prospect of more years of the same. My beloved *Herald Tribune* had folded years ago and with that, my seven-year stint at that great paper had come to an end. My 25 years of freelance work at *The New York Times* was beginning to ebb, due in part to the untimely death in an automobile accident of Seymour Peck, my dynamic editor of the Arts & Leisure section. My writing for *ARTnews,* which had been frequent and steady, also diminished as a new, young editor sought new voices for its pages—especially his own. I did continue writing at a steadfast pace for *Architectural Digest* (the pay was fabulous) and for *Dance Magazine* (the pay was nil). In addition, there were the books. By 1990 there were 12 of them, including collections of art and dance interviews and a children's book, *Flowers & Fables.*

An earlier book, *The Party's Over Now,* charting my post-college New York life in the art world in the 1950s and 1960s, and long out of print, became something of a cause célèbre in the 1980s and 1990s because it was rediscovered to be an intensely personal record of the abstract expressionist painters then living, working, and drinking in New York and Long Island. The book, which was either hated or adored by the art world, brought me a certain notoriety, which I quite relished.

But in 1993, after experiencing a definite fatigue with all the writing I had been doing, wanting nothing more to do with editors, and having finally had my fill of the radiantly renowned and revered, namely, the stars, a sudden surge of renewed enthusiasm came over me.

A bookseller by the name of Glenn Horowitz called me one day, saying he had just finished reading *The Party's Over Now*, and was looking at the photographs I had taken of all the artists and poets who had come to visit us in Water Mill back in the late 50s and early 60s. Horowitz said he had just opened a bookshop and art gallery on Newtown Lane in East Hampton, and wondered if I still had the photographs included in the book. He said that if they were still available, he'd like to exhibit them in his new space.

This call proved entirely momentous.

I told Glenn that most of the photographs in the book were indeed available and nothing would please me more than having them exhibited at his bookstore and gallery.

Thus it was that on July 17, 1993, Glenn Horowitz Bookseller presented *Young in the Hamptons*, a photo exhibition featuring some 45 black and white portraits I had taken of the young Robert Rauschenberg, Jasper Johns, Larry Rivers, Willem De Kooning, Marisol, Grace Hartigan, Fairfield Porter, Frank O'Hara, John Ashbery, Kenneth Koch, and Jimmy Schuyler, among many others.

To my utter amazement, all kinds of wonderful things happened as a result of this very modest show. A dealer by the name of Bianca Lanza–an imposing and endearing dynamo–brought the entire exhibition to her gallery in Miami's South Beach. I went down for the opening, and, although nothing sold, it was marvelous having a show outside of New York. The next year, in 1994, a very posh New York dealer, Jason McCoy, held the same show in his Fuller Building gallery at 41 East 57th Street. This showing proved a turning point in my newfound career as a photographer.

A curator of the Whitney Museum of American Art, Adam Weinberg, appeared at the Jason McCoy Gallery, liked what he saw, and invited me to donate all of the photographs to the Museum's "Special Collection." Said Weinberg, "These photographs are historic! They belong in the Whitney!"

In return, he said he would arrange with the museum's director, David Ross, and its librarian, May Castleberry, to have me photograph artists who were in the Whitney collection. A new archive would be built compiled from my portraits. Of course, I was thrilled and delighted to undertake this new project. And so, the "John Jonas Gruen Whitney Project" was born. To date, the venture has yielded the Whitney an archive of well over 300 portraits of Whitney artists, New York gallerists, and other art personalities. (The project continues to this day with the support of my initial champion, Adam Weinberg, who, fabulously perceptive fellow that he was and is, has become the Whitney Museum's current director. All the photographs are available for viewing at the Whitney's library, which is currently headed by the museum's librarian, the brilliant and caring Ms. Carol Rusk.)

A word about the sudden addition to my given name, Jonas, as my middle name–John JONAS Gruen. As it happens, there is another John Gruen, a very fine photographer, working in New York City. Because I wanted to avoid confusion between us, I decided that all my photographic work would henceforth bear the name John Jonas Gruen, while my writing projects would continue to be signed John Gruen.

Thus it was that in the 1990s I embarked on what I expect will be my final career–that of professional photographer.

I was 67 when I received that exciting call from Glenn Horowitz to hold a photo show at his bookstore. The prospect of cutting down on my writing and becoming a full-fledged photographer was, to say the very least, very daunting. Of course, I had been taking photographs all along for some 40 years, never thinking of it as a way of earning a living. Too, I had worked at a distinguished photo agency, Rapho-Guillumette, and was inspired by the likes of Brassaï, Man Ray, Doisneau, et al, whom I met professionally. But to start all over again as a 67-year-old photographer? Would I really be able to make a living at it? Would I really be any good at it? Would I be accepted as a photographer?

The fact is, I did not look back. After all, photography had always been a passion, and so I plunged right in, shooting my way into photographic bliss and a life wherein images fixed and frozen in time would henceforth become my Senior Citizen obsession.

Chapter 60

Senior Citizen?

What a ridiculous description. To me, it evokes an army of decrepit old men and women slowly hobbling towards a giant portal marked EXIT.

Me, a Senior Citizen? Not possible!

Jane, a Senior Citizen? Not possible!

Julia, already in her mid-thirties? Not possible!

By our mid-sixties, Jane and I were as busy as ever. Alright, it wasn't a life of mad socializing or of party-giving or dinner-giving or of rushing to every other cultural event New York had to offer. No. We had already done all that. But we had our health and we labored at our usual pace and produced a great deal of work.

Jane, who held exhibitions every two years, decided to switch galleries one more time in 1999. Bridget Moore, the director of the DC Moore Gallery at 724 Fifth Avenue, one day suggested to Jane that if she ever thought of going with another gallery, DC Moore would be happy to welcome her.

Because her gallery's roster of artists included some of the day's major women artists–Janet Fish, Mary Frank, and Yvonne Jacquette, among others–and because the gallery had a very fine reputation, Jane gave Bridget Moore's suggestion some serious thought. Besides, her years at the Fischbach Gallery seemed to have run their course, especially with Neil Winkel dead of AIDS and its director increasingly oblivious to Jane's increasingly commanding landscapes.

Jane happily moved to DC Moore and, to this day, her relationship with Bridget Moore and her fine staff, including Edward DeLuca, Heidi Lange, Sandra Paci, Kate Pollack, and Mark Valenti has been both friendly and commercially viable.

For her part, Julia's work at the Keith Haring Foundation continued apace, with many new strides being made on behalf of Haring, whose name and reputation in Europe, Asia, and South America had increased with each successive year. In time, Julia enlisted Deitch Projects, headed by

Jeffrey Deitch, one of New York's most forward-looking and prestigious art galleries, to represent Haring worldwide, and she has spearheaded and personally supervised almost all of Haring's most important exhibitions, including a Whitney retrospective in 1997. Today, largely through Julia's efforts, Haring is considered a major American artist, whose prices at auction have soared and whose reputation worldwide has phenominally increased.

As a result, Julia herself has become a visible and quite charismatic figure in the international art world. She travels far and wide, presiding over the installations and openings of most of Haring's exhibitions and continues to be the spokesperson and authority on this unique American artist for whom she began working when both were a very tender 24.

For myself, the 90s found me genuinely focused on photography. Although the advent of digital cameras and their popularity had quickly swamped the field, I held fast to my trusty Nikon N50 and still take pictures the old-fashioned way—pictures that require the services of film, a photo lab, and a printer. Working solely in black and white, I explore various subjects that interest me and have by now amassed thousands of images that, for better or for worse, constitute quite substantial output.

Of course, I started much too late. As a well-known photography dealer recently put it to me, "John, you've arrived 70 years too late—the pictures you are now taking have all been taken!" He was, of course, referring to Walker Evans, Ansel Adams, Margaret Bourke White, Arnold Newman, and all the other great American and European photographers working a generation ago. He was right, but not right enough for me to give it all up or fall into some sort of psychological slump. I believe every photographer has a unique way of seeing the world, and I think that, even at their most familiar or banal, my images have a touch of individuality.

Do I make a living as a photographer? Of course not! If truth be known, I live mostly off our savings. And, as in our youth, Jane pays for most of our bills. But occasionally, a photograph of mine will sell, and I've been fortunate in having had some good exhibitions both in New York and in the Hamptons. And the show at Glenn Horowitz, *Young in the Hamptons*, became a book, published by the Italian firm Charta, and many of the portraits done for the Whitney are in another book, *Facing the Artist*, published by the distinguished German house of Prestel. So, my very late photographic career is yielding some rewards after all.

Years run fast when one grows older. It's really so strange what happens when time passes so quickly. One morning I woke up and I was 70! That felt strange indeed. And Jane was 72! That was even stranger.

We see our doctors. (My eyesight, my blood pressure, Jane's cholesterol, her cough.)

And the years keep on passing.

And suddenly, I'm 75.

And getting old often depresses me.

Where did the time go? What did I accomplish? What kind of life did I lead? What kind of person am I, really? Boring old man questions! But I should answer at least some of them.

As for the person I am, it's really quite simple. I'm a humanist with oodles of prejudices. I'm an aesthete. While almost every aspect of human existence or endeavor has some political component, I can't really call myself a political person. My convictions, beliefs, and tenets are totally ambiguous. My sentiments are liberal. And I hate injustice. I'm not a joiner. I have an elitist streak in me. I'm not exactly a snob, but I'm most comfortable with people of education and erudition and artistry. I love people who have great, interesting looks. I know I'm not a bigot, but I have almost no black friends nor friends or acquaintances of any other color. I'm not a fearful person, but I fear cultures I know very little about. Indeed, I have a primitive fear of the unknown. Even nature scares me—large bodies of water, mountains, vast open spaces.

Inside me resides a charming cynic and a whining old Jewish woman; a sophisticated man of the world and a trembly coward. I'm goodhearted but despise and fear beggars, the relentlessly needy, the homeless. At times, I will go to any lengths to be helpful and kind, but at the last moment I stop short of giving of myself. It's an unattractive, inward retreat that I barely understand.

I would give my life to my own—to Jane, to Julia. But to no one else. (Still, I'd probably make the grand gesture, the beau geste! Somewhere in me there lurks a daredevil. I would probably save anyone, given the right circumstances and audience!)

When the year 2000 came around, we were totally stunned. We had made it to the twenty-first century! And then, only one year later, as my 75th birthday loomed, the world as we knew it was suddenly changed.

Just one day before my birthday, on September 11, 2001, the twin towers in New York's financial center were destroyed by a terrorist attack. My birthday fell on the next day, September 12, and a gloomier day could not be imagined.

On that brilliant, crisp, sun-filled morning of September 11, the TV images were devastating. First one tower, then the next was hit by a plane and, as fire and billowing black smoke rose to the skies, and as hundreds of people ran from the site, and as the silhouette of thousands of people inside the two burning buildings were seen through windows, trapped and trying to escape (some ultimately throwing themselves out of the windows), I knew I was witness to a tragedy of unimaginable proportion.

Two days later I went to photograph what I could of the disaster. I walked through smoke-filled streets, through rubble, amidst chaos and destruction, seeing gas-masked policemen everywhere, and people walking as in a daze. It was all utterly unreal, and the pictures I took that day and in subsequent days have a haunted, surreal look.

America went to war in 2001.

A chill fell on my refugee, immigrant heart.

Chapter 61

Life (and death) went on.

Our friend, the painter Larry Rivers, died of cancer in 2002, and on August 22 of that year, a memorial service was held at Guild Hall, in East Hampton. Larry was 79, and we had known him for nearly 50 years.

The memorial service was very well attended. As I looked about me, I suddenly realized that almost everyone in the audience was more or less our age—in their mid- to late-seventies and over—and that we had known most of these people forever. As Jane and I sat in the darkened auditorium, I also realized that this was some kind of "end of the line" gathering. But it wasn't really all that depressing, because to his dying day, Larry was nothing if not energetic, still painting, still full of curiosity and still endlessly talkative. Indeed, this was a rather uplifting and even entertaining memorial. Still, we had all grown quite old together, and it was a shock.

John Ashbery was to have opened the ceremony. But he was late, and so Stevie Rivers, now a rehabilitation counselor, opened the proceedings. How like Larry he was! Same looks, same voice, same energy—an amazing resemblance. He told the audience what it was like growing up with his dad, a young single father, trying his best to do the right thing by his young sons. He recounted that one of the biggest pleasures in his life was arguing with his father—arguing about anything and everything under the sun, be it about politics or art or psychiatry or whatever…that his dad was the most verbal and opinionated man he had ever met, and he would miss those long, exhilarating, often contentious talks.

When John Ashbery finally arrived, he looked frail and had to be helped up on the stage. He was as stooped as Pope John Paul in his ailing years, and like the Pope, he peered out at the audience, and spoke in a constrained, somewhat tremulous voice. He related his early years of knowing Larry and Frank O'Hara, and all the young poets of our day, and he read an excerpt from an appreciation *The New York Times* had asked him to write about Rivers. John's words were nothing less than eloquent.

Next came Arnold Weinstein, the poet and playwright (he would die just a few years later), who had collaborated with Rivers on Rivers' auto-biography, *What Did I Do?* (and, with whom, ages ago, I collaborated on our musical *Undercover Lover*, for which I wrote the music). Arnold read an uproarious excerpt from Larry's autobiography and the audience roared.

Later, dour Jane Freilicher, who once had an intense affair with Larry Rivers, stepped up and read "To the Harbormaster," a poem by Frank O'Hara, which she said Larry himself had read at O'Hara's funeral some 40 years earlier. Jane read the poem in her typical flat, uninflected voice–she seemed unmoved by Frank's passionate words. Both Gwynne and Emma Rivers, his ravishing daughters by Clarice Rivers, spoke (Gwynne also sang), and it was all most touching.

The conclusion of the memorial had Larry's jazz band onstage, playing Larry's composition, "A Monk in the Country," and, as a finale, we heard a tape recording of the pop tune "Everything Happens to Me," with Larry singing the vocal in his inimitable raspy style. It was Larry's typical, ironic and very funny way of saying "goodbye" to all his many friends.

"Look," he seemed to be saying. "I'm dead! How ridiculous can it get! But then, everything happens to me!!"

All of us departed Guild Hall with broad smiles on our faces.

Chapter 62

Some 25 or 30 of us had been invited to a post-memorial out-of-door buffet luncheon at the Water Mill home of Clarice Rivers, who had, in fact, been long separated from Larry, but never divorced him and had never stopped caring for him.

All of Larry's children and grandchildren came, including his teen-aged son, Sam, whose mother, the painter Daria Dusheck, was also in attendance.

Sitting and picking at my lunch and drinking some white wine, I looked around me and felt as though my life were passing before me. Here, as at the memorial service, I saw all the friends with whom we had been young, except now they were sort of walking or sort of ambling or sort of limping or sort of sitting.

There, chatting with her son Tom, was Ellen Adler, daughter of Stella, still quite buoyant, who soon would join us and tell us again how Marlon Brando, "the love of her life," once asked her to marry him and how she turned him down. She'd tell us again that now he was old, ailing, and alarmingly overweight—a wreck of the once undisputed god of stage and screen. (Ellen's stories about Brando have been standard fare around all our dinner tables for well over 40 years).

I myself was sitting next to Sidney Lumet and his wife, Pidie. One of America's great filmmakers, Sidney, too, was aging. We had met Lumet when he was married to Gloria Vanderbilt, and saw him off and on when he was later married to Lena Horne's daughter, Gail, with whom he had two beautiful daughters.

Sidney and I talked about the recent demise of his TV series, *100 Centre Street*, and reminisced about his days of early television, when he directed shows on *Omnibus* and *Playhouse 90*, a time when TV productions were still performed "live," like actual plays.

We remembered Sidney's directing *The Dybbuk*, the great Jewish classic, for *Playhouse 90*, starring Carol Lawrence and Theodore Bikel, for which Sidney invited me to compose the music. And we remembered how the show's choreographer, Anna Sokolow, didn't think that my score sounded Jewish enough, how she insisted I add many more Jewish swoops and lilts–and especially more Jewish "soul."

"For Anna, nothing was ever Jewish enough," said Sidney, with a laugh.

Sitting some distance from us was Earl McGrath, from whom I cut myself off completely. It was sad that someone I liked so very much, and whose wife, Camilla, I thought was such a splendid person, should have treated our 40-year-old friendship so shoddily.

In the mid 90s, McGrath, an art dealer with a gallery on West 57th Street, offered me a show of my portraits of artists and poets. I couldn't have been happier, especially when Earl said I would now be a part of his regular roster of artists.

My show went quite well. There were numerous sales and even a commission or two. But then, two years later, when it came time for me to have another show, Earl got cold feet, and never alluded to my having a show with him again. I complained. I asked what was wrong. But Earl never mentioned a show again. I felt betrayed, and I haven't spoken to him since. People had continually warned me that there was a big element of the flake in Earl McGrath. This time I believed them.

At the next table sat Lukas and Cornelia Foss, he, the famous conductor, composer and pianist, she, the gifted painter. Lukas seemed to be ailing (some said with Parkinson's disease). We met the Fosses through Leonard and Felicia Bernstein, some 30 years ago. While Lukas has, of late, been called a genius composer, and an extraordinary conductor, I have always thought his greatest calling was that of concert pianist. To me, his later, highly atonal compositions seemed self-conscious versions of John Cage, Morton Feldman, Earle Brown. Still, I've always loved Lukas–a strange and marvelous man.

When we were all young, Lukas' wife, Cornelia, did something very shocking. She packed up their two small children and their cat, left Lukas, and went to Canada to live with the great Canadian pianist Glenn Gould, with whom she had fallen in love. They lived together for some four years. For us, it was a great, mysterious, and quite thrilling love story. But, in the end, Cornelia returned to her husband and to her painting life in New York. She never looked back.

Suddenly, who should arrive at the luncheon but Jane Holzer, known as Baby Jane Holzer back in the 60s. Baby Jane was one of Andy Warhol's major superstars, and here she now was, an elderly glamour girl, still sporting that long blond mane and flashing her dazzling smile. Jane, intelligent and mensch-y, was one of Larry Rivers' good friends. But during the Pop Art years, she was one of Warhol's most charismatic stars. She was amazing, because she did absolutely nothing to really merit superstardom. I mean, she appeared in several of Andy's weirdly compelling films, sitting around and looking totally ravishing. But few detected an ascending star in the cinematic firmament. Still, Jane had something! And amidst that wild, drug-infested, sex-besotted Warhol crowd, she was one of the nicest, most levelheaded, least pretentious people we had ever met.

And now, coming over to join our table were Jeannette and Dick Seaver, friends from long ago, whom we have always admired and loved. The Paris-born Jeannette was once a fabulously beautiful and very talented concert violinist, who could have had a great career (I once heard her perform Glazounov's violin concerto, and she was clearly an artist), but, finally, decided to gave it all up to become a truly great cook, an author of fabulous cookbooks, and to raise three adorable children. Dick Seaver is the brilliant editor and translator, who followed me as a staff member of Grove Press way back in the 1950s. We formed a warm and lasting friendship. Today, both Jeannette and Dick Seaver run their own publishing firm—Arcade Publishing—and they are as interesting, kind, and loving as ever.

And, finally, over in one corner, chatting with some friends, stood Maxine Groffsky, probably the best looking and most carefully groomed in that aging crowd. We met Maxine a lifetime ago, when she was waiting on tables in a Water Mill restaurant—The Five Spot—where we all hung out. One night, Larry Rivers made serious passes at this lovely red-headed young waitress. Maxine, amused by it all yet quite flirtatious herself, instantly made clear by word and deed that she was not your everyday waitress.

Later we learned that Maxine came from a very well-off New Jersey family, that she wanted to be on her own and meet people in the Hamptons, and, most tantalizingly, was the model for the love interest in Philip Roth's first novel, *Goodbye, Columbus*. We easily understood why. Maxine was a sexy, dreamy girl.

Before we knew it, Larry and Maxine were an item, and the relationship lasted a number of years. It was a romance both blustery and exciting and the two seemed destined for a very loving yet tempestuous life together. As it turned out, Larry discovered he was really crazy about Clarice Price, the very lively and capable young music teacher he had recently imported from Wales to come take care of his two small sons. And it was Clarice Price that Larry eventually married.

Maxine did not despair—at least not for very long. She went on to become deeply involved with the writer Harry Mathews, went to live in Paris, and, most happily, became the Paris editor of the illustrious *Paris Review*. (Today she is an Editor Emeritus of that splendid publication). In the more recent years, Maxine established herself as a distinguished literary agent—and, what is more, she is happily married.

But like so many other women, Maxine never really stopped caring for Larry Rivers. And she has never stopped taking extremely good care of herself. Even today, this radiant redhead is a lesson in what a quick and limpid mind as well as superb self-maintenance can accomplish.

Chapter 63

As I'm nearing my 80s, I don't really know how to end this book. I could devote a whole chapter to the 1993 production of *Radiant Baby*, based on my book, *Keith Haring: The Authorized Biography*. The musical had lyrics by Ira Gasman, a book by Stuart Ross, and music by Debra Barsha. The show, directed by the esteemed George C. Wolfe and presented by the Public Theater on Lafayette Street, caused me more heartache than I wish to remember. Suffice it to say that the musical, ten years in the making, caused some seriously bad feelings between my daughter, Julia, and me (as the highly protective director of the Keith Haring Foundation, she strenuously objected to the project). That was one thing. Even worse, although I was hired as the show's artistic consultant, Wolfe, whose work I had admired enormously throughout the years, paid absolutely not the slightest attention to any of my suggestions for improving a faltering show. In fact, he paid no attention to me at all. Although I sat in on rehearsals on a daily basis, it was as if I did not exist. (The invisibility of the old?) I couldn't believe how rude and offensive Wolfe was. Needless to say, it spoiled the entire venture for me.

With a weak, unimaginative book by Ross, and too many "thumping" ersatz disco-influenced songs by Barsha, the show and its script had some serious structural flaws, and failed to please most critics. *Radiant Baby* died after two months at the Public's Newman Theater. Still, the production, with a vast array of Haring images (Julia ultimately relented about supporting the musical), the show did make a certain compelling impression, and the actor playing Keith Haring, Daniel Reichard, was remarkably touching and true.

Another musical, *Undercover Lover*, this one with a book by Arnold Weinstein and Frank O'Hara and with about 20 songs that I had composed (all arranged by a very young William Bolcom), was given a full, if rather uneven production in 2005 by a small New York theater company called Medicine Show. Directed by the company's cofounder, Barbara Vann, as an homage to Weinstein (Vann knew both Arnold and Bill Bolcom, and had already produced several of their works), *Undercover Lover*, first seen in 1963 at Adelphi University in Garden City, Long Island, proved a very charming dud in its 2005 revival. It was far too long and far too weighed down by too many of Weinstein's leaden ironies.

Of course, I adored all the actors and all the singers performing my songs–and just regretted terribly that Arnold was too ill to attend. Indeed, Weinstein died of liver cancer that September, just a month before our opening.

While *Undercover Lover* was up and running, Arnold's agent Sam Cohn at ICM called to invite Jane and me to Arnold's memorial service, which would take place on Broadway, at the Walter Kerr Theater.

It was astonishing, infuriating, and totally shocking to me that during the memorial not one single speaker or performer mentioned the fact that one of Arnold's musicals–*Undercover Lover*–was just then being performed in a small theater in New York City. Not Bill Bolcom (who had, after all, arranged all the show's music, and who had even attended a performance on the previous night!), not Robert Brustein, not John Guare (who, instead of mentioning *Undercover Lover* dug up and quoted from a rather silly interview I had conducted with Arnold years earlier), not Sam Cohn, his agent, not Scott Griffin, his biographer, not a single soul told the packed theater that a real live Weinstein show was currently to be seen just a few blocks from the theater we were all sitting in. It was an omission that broke my heart as well as Barbara Vann's. It was a miserable, utterly inexcusable oversight on the part of the memorial's organizers. Surely, Arnold, just weeks after his death, deserved to have his currently running show talked about and publicized and made a fuss over, no matter how flawed it might have been. So much for the THEATER!

Chapter 64

My happiest times now are spent in our summer home in Water Mill. It's where Julia comes every weekend with her sweet dachshunds, Otis and Charlotte. I adore watching them play and romp and chase one another. And Water Mill is where the trees are. And the big sky. And the big ocean. It's where old friends and neighbors come to have dinner, beautifully prepared by Jane Wilson, my Fanciulla del Middle-West.

Alvin Novak and Sid Talisman come bearing wine; Marcella Free comes bearing lavish, home-grown roses. Margaret Logan and her fascinating husband, Charlie Coulter, come bearing vegetables and fruits from their effulgent garden. Julia's friend Tom Gallagher is a regular guest. The East Hampton Historical Society's director, the brilliant Richard Barons, and his wife, Rosanne, bring more wine, more flowers. My favorite Hamptons music and book reviewer, who writes for the Southampton Press, the gifted Fred Volkmer and his wife, Linda, arrive with heavenly dessert. It's all very festive and lively and fun.

Another great source of joy for me is keeping up with my Italian life—seeing my Italian friends in New York, Carlo and Manuela Filiaci (he's a distinguished psychiatrist, she's a gifted artist), and, before his recent death in Italy, the writer and journalist, Tiziano Terzani and his wife, Angela. Tiziano has become something of a legend in Italy, a visionary, vehemently anti-American political writer, whose books on Asia and personal commitment to Buddhist and Hindu mysticism brought him an impressive following. Both seven-year-old Julia and I met Tiziano in 1965 while returning to the States from Italy on the S.S. Leonardo Da Vinci. Tiziano, handsome in the extreme, was a very young, brash, Florentine intellectual, just married to the beautiful German-born Angela Staude. They were sailing to New York for graduate study in Asian languages at Columbia University and to observe American life.

Our friendship lasted well over 40 years, and while our political views diverged dramatically, and while possessed of a certain stubborn arrogance, self-deceiving egomania, and hard-headedness, Tiziano offered stimulating and provocative ideas on the state of the world and on his own spiritual journey.

And so it was that I was never too far from Italian things and people, and speaking the language with our Italian friends invariably rejuvenated me.

In December 2005, our Julia made me a splendid Italian gift: she invited me to accompany her on a trip to Venice, Vicenza, and Milan—one of our rare father-daughter trips—mainly to view a huge Keith Haring exhibition she had co-curated at La Triennale de Milan with the enterprising Italian director and curator Gianni Mercurio. The show, which also included superb video footage of Haring by Mercurio's gifted wife, Christina Clausen, proved an unprecedented success, with an endless stream of people flocking to see it.

Being with Julia in my late 70s in the country and city of my childhood was an emotionally fulfilling experience. (Julia would do the same for my 80th birthday, in 2006). The two of us walked for miles, visited museums, saw a number of Julia's Italian friends and professional acquaintances, and lunched or dined at some of the best restaurants Venice and Milan had to offer. Our time spent at Harry's Bar in Venice was particularly memorable, as we talked for hours and partook of the restaurant's world famous bellinis.

But, of course, returning to Jane, to New York and Water Mill, was coming home to where I belonged. And, unlike all those many years ago, when we were in the midst of every social or creative whirl, our days are now spent mostly with each other. Indeed, Jane and I have become veritable hermits—especially out in Water Mill.

Because I don't drive (I failed my test over and over again), Jane and Julia have been doing all the driving for years. But lately, because of her poor eyesight, Jane is not allowed to drive at night, and so it's a stay-at-home life in the Hamptons, which suits us fine.

We rise early. When it's very hot, we immerse ourselves in our pool. I don't swim, but love the "dead man's float," and as I float, I feel cool and suspended and weightless and calm. Basically, good things happen in Water Mill! Jane paints in her wonderfully spacious studio, a converted hay mow, or does watercolors. I photograph or write or read or play the piano. And, in recent years, I've had other rewards.

Just a few season ago, the splendid Penelope Wright, program director of the Rogers Memorial Library in Southampton, offered to devote an entire evening at the Library to my early songs, the ones I wrote in the 50s and 60s, hoping to conquer the art song world as a twenty-something composer. My favorite tenor, the young and gifted Scott Murphree, and the soprano Lara Nie were the singers for the occasion. Alvin Novak, my oldest friend, was at the piano. Many people came to hear my youthful offerings, and I was enormously touched by it all, because nearly 50 years had elapsed since I had heard those songs, and it was deeply moving to hear them sung again with such tenderness and artistry, especially the songs performed by the extraordinarily sensitive Scott Murphree.

And summers in Water Mill also afford me a return to music criticism, which evoked memories of my reviewing days at the old *Herald Tribune*. As it happens, during the summer, the Hamptons offer two music festivals: The Bard Music Festival of the Hamptons and the Bridgehampton Chamber Music Festival. A remarkable and loving friend, the writer Sheridan Sansegundo, who is the arts editor of the *East Hampton Star*, asked if I would review some of the Festival concerts for the paper. And so, for several weeks out of each summer, I've been sounding off in print to my heart's content, much to the glee or consternation of my newfound readers. And for all those good things–the revival of my songs, the music reviewing, and more–I have Alvin Novak to thank. It was he who opened those doors for me, and I love him for it.

Chapter 65

In the middle of the night, when I rise to answer nature's calls, and am half asleep, I become vaguely conscious of my heartbeat. It beats quite calmly, that old heart of mine. I return to bed. My sleeping Jane is warm by my side. And what do I think about as I struggle to re-enter sleep?

I think of Chester, Julia's wire-haired dachshund. He too had a heart that beat quite calmly. And it beat for 17 long years...until it beat no more.

Madame de Stael had it right when she wrote, "The more I know of men, the more I like dogs."

I found Chester for Julia in 1988. She and Scott Asen were living together then, and Julia wanted a wire-haired dachshund. I found him in a pet shop on New York's Upper West Side, not far from our apartment. I entered the store. A wheat-colored, wire-haired pup lay snoozing in a cage atop a smooth-haired cage mate. I approached. The wire-haired pup opened its eyes, saw me, bestirred himself, came to sit in front of me, and stared at me with a look of uncommon intensity. Right then and there, we were irresistibly drawn to each other.

I asked to hold him. When I did, the die was cast. This dog would be Julia's, but in a profoundly atavistic way, it would also be mine. Julia named him Chester. I named him Cesarino, and proceeded to speak Italian to him at every opportunity. Soon Cesarino, also known as Cesare, l'Imperatore di Sicilia, Sardegna, e tutta La Spezia (so dubbed by Jane), understood me perfectly, and we communicated in Italian for all the years to come. Of course, I didn't see Chester all the time. He was Julia's dog, and she adored him and was unbelievably good to him, as indeed was Scott.

But in the summers, Chester was a constant presence in Water Mill, and we watched him grow from tiny pup to little dog, to regular dog, and at every stage, he let us in on all his endearing young charms. He was a fabulous athlete, and, on Flying Point Beach, he ran, ran, ran with a speed that took everyone's breath away.

Cesarino was very musical. When Julia and I played four-hand piano together, he jumped on a nearby couch, stretched out, looked up at us, and listened. I believe Schubert was his favorite composer. But he also loved Dvorak.

A few years ago, Julia took Chester to Paris—for three months, no less! The two lived in a chic little apartment on the Ile Saint Louis. Their walks by the Seine, past Notre Dame, and near all those great-smelling Parisian food shops and restaurants filled Chester with a newfound sense of bien-être, sophistication and worldliness. Because of his Italian, the French being spoken all around him seemed quite familiar and decipherable. The French adore dogs, far more than they adore people, and Chester, with his unusual coloring, wiry texture, his sweet face and open friendliness, caused the French to endlessly pet and pamper him.

But then, we all spoiled him rotten. Back home, he was often fed good, home-cooked Jane Wilson food. At the dinner table, I loved feeding him morsels off my own fork. Chester very delicately removed the offerings, making a slight noise when his sharp little teeth touched the tines. When this happened, we all burst into gales of laughter, and Chester, smiling, wagged his tail and waited for more.

Mostly, however, I loved Cesarino because he and I had an understanding. And this understanding became deeper as we both grew old. Chester always knew what I was thinking (or so I thought), and the way he showed this was in the way he would stare at me. From his corner of the living room couch in Water Mill, he just stared and stared and stared at me. It was hypnotic. It was even a bit distressing, because his stare was so penetrating, just as it was when I found him. But as he stared, I felt he understood me in ways no one else understood me. And when I stared back at him, and he would not leave my gaze, he let me know we had an understanding...a magical understanding that was a great comfort to us both.

Cesarino's old age was not good. He grew blind and deaf and lame and, finally, became incontinent. Julia's care and attentiveness to her old Chester was incredibly moving. At the end, he could barely move, and we had to bring him to the vet. Julia, Jane, Tom Gallagher, Scott Asen, and I, his closest family, bade farewell to Cesarino. Although he could not see me, he looked up and stared at me briefly...just one more time. And it was unbearable.

Then, for the last time, Cesarino closed his eyes.

And this is the end of his story...and of mine.

Most likely, there will be other endings to come.

Acknowledgements

The emotional travails inherent in writing a memoir are many, and I owe a debt of gratitude to various individuals who have helped me to overcome the psychological stumbling blocks I so frequently encountered. First and foremost, I want to thank my wife, Jane Wilson, who gave me the freedom to navigate some of the more turbulent waters of our life together without complaint or objection. My great thanks also to our daughter, Julia Gruen, who read an early draft of this book, and greeted the disturbing and unexpected with kindness, understanding, and, good humor. Some parts of the memoir were dictated to assistants, who transcribed many audio tapes and helped with my research. Most thorough and helpful in this respect were Jason Mastropierro and Robert Gandini. I am deeply grateful to two friends, Anne Cole and Cynthia Navaretta, who edited early versions of the manuscript. When the publishing firm powerHouse Books agreed to bring out this memoir, I encountered a cultural enterprise that made clear the all-encompassing vision of its founder, Daniel Power. I wish to thank Daniel and his wife, Susanne, for their faith in my book. My special gratitude also goes to my editor at powerHouse, the sensitive Tami Mnoian; to the extraordinary Kiki Bauer, my gifted designer; and to the remarkable public relations magician, Sara Rosen.

John Gruen
New York, 2007

Index

Callas Kissed Me...Lenny Too!

A Critic's Memoir

© 2008 powerHouse Cultural Entertainment, Inc.
Text © 2008 John Jonas Gruen
Photographs © 2008 John Jonas Gruen, unless otherwise noted

Published in the United States by powerHouse Books,
a division of powerHouse Cultural Entertainment, Inc.
37 Main Street, Brooklyn, NY 11201-1021
telephone 212 604 9074, fax 212 366 5247
e-mail: callaskissedme@powerHouseBooks.com
website: www.powerHouseBooks.com

First edition, 2008

Library of Congress Cataloging-in-Publication Data

Gruen, John.
  Callas kissed me... Lenny too! : a critic's memoir / by John Gruen.
    p. cm.
  ISBN-13: 978-1-57687-424-0 (hardcover)
  1. Gruen, John. 2. Wilson, Jane, 1924- 3. Gruen, John--Marriage. 4. Art
critics--United States--Biography. 5. Portrait photographers--United
States--Biography. 6. Authors, American--Biography. 7. Women
painters--United States--Biography. 8. New York (N.Y.)--Biography. 9. New
York (N.Y.)--Intellectual life. 10. New York (N.Y.)--Social life and
customs. I. Title.
  CT275.G79135A3 2008
  709.2'2--dc22
                                    2007051456

Hardcover ISBN 978-1-57687-424-0

Printing and binding by Midas Printing, Inc., China

Book design by Kiki Bauer

Front cover: John Gruen, New York City, 1957; photograph by Jane Wilson
Back cover: John Gruen and Jane Wilson, New York City, 1964; photograph by
Francesco Scavullo for *Harper's Bazaar*, courtesy of the Francesco Scavullo Foundation
Page 3: The Gruen family in their Tompkins Square apartment, New York, 1961;
photograph by Ernest Sato

A complete catalog of powerHouse Books and Limited Editions is available upon request;
please call, write, or visit our website.

10 9 8 7 6 5 4 3 2 1

Printed and bound in China